# Grit Lit

# GRIT LIT

*A Rough South Reader*

*Edited by*
Brian Carpenter and Tom Franklin

The University of South Carolina Press

© 2012 University of South Carolina

Published by the University of South Carolina Press
Columbia, South Carolina 29208

www.sc.edu/uscpress

Manufactured in the United States of America

21 20 19 18 17 16 15 14 13 12    10 9 8 7 6 5 4 3 2 1

Library of Congress Cataloging-in-Publication data will be found at the end of this book.

This book was printed on a recycled paper with 30 percent
postconsumer waste content.

# Contents

# Preface

*What's Grit Lit?*

Tom Franklin

First off, it isn't grits, that white breakfast stuff that southerners eat, though perhaps that's part of it. It's not the quality Rooster Cogburn possesses in Charles
Portis's *True Grit* either, the grit that means you can take the reins in your teeth
and charge your horse headlong into gunfire, though perhaps that's another
part of it. And it's not the hundred-pound bags of sandblasting grit I loaded
onto trucks for four years in my early twenties at a plant in southern Alabama
(a setting I later used in my story "Grit"), though that's certainly part of it,
too—to be worked like a mule for wealthy plant owners in Detroit, underpaid,
sweating, breathing silica dust alongside men with ruined backs, men whose
fathers had worked at the same plant, men who never even considered college,
men who used racial epithets.

National Public Radio librarian Nancy Pearl says Grit Lit is "filled with
angry, deranged, and generally desperate characters who are fueled by alcohol
and sex."[1] Yes, they drink. They smoke—weed and pills and sometimes meth.
They're usually white, usually rednecks, Snopesian. Broke, divorced, violent—
they're not good country people. Writer Tony Earley divides southern literature
into two groups: those on the right side of the tracks, who sip mint juleps in
Miss Welty's yard, sweating politely under the magnolias in seersucker suits;
and those on the wrong side of the tracks, whose characters make shine, shoot
or stab one another on occasion, and cruise around in their pickups tossing
beer bottles along the side of the road while looking for armadillos to flatten.[2]

Grit Lit's something else, too, though. In a country where master of fine
arts programs exhale new writers like stale breath, the practitioners of Grit Lit
have more often than not come from the very landscape they describe; they've
fought their way up from the ground. William Gay worked for thirty years as
a carpenter, housepainter, and paperhanger before publishing *The Long Home*.
His hardscrabble life was his education, beginning as a sharecropper's son and

continuing through the navy, his way out. Larry Brown was a firefighter for twenty years. Harry Crews grew up stripping tobacco in Georgia. They bring an authenticity to the page that can't be invented. The difference between them and their characters is empathy; they're the generation between outright bigotry and progress, still reeling from their own enlightenment. They were the sensitive guy at the dogfight, the guy who shot the deer even though he'd rather be at home reading. It's the gang of writers who've lived the life and written about it with intelligence and honesty and aplomb and glee. And while some of us second- or third-generation Grit Litters did earn M.F.A.s, we feel vaguely guilty about it and know we're a level less pure than our older, grittier counterparts.

So what's Grit Lit? It's the dirty South seen without romanticism or the false nostalgia of *Gone with the Wind* fans. People who are interested in the South as it really is, not moonlight and magnolia but grit in your workboots, especially if it's a steeltoe with the leather so worn at the toe that the metal shows, the same peeling boot staggering out of a bar after screwing up things for the night. It's the walnut handles of the .38 in somebody's waistband outside the bar, the hawk-billed knife, the sawed-off shotgun, the razor of yore. The one-hitter, the empty pill bottle, the meth pipe. It's a man with little hope of salvation trying to salvage what he can, even if it's only beers from the side of the highway as log trucks rumble by, carrying off the forest one shivering load at a time. It's the audacity that brings this man to life on the page and makes you root for him. It's somebody up from the ground saying, "Hold on, I ain't dead yet." That's Grit Lit.

# Acknowledgments

Thanks go to the all of the authors and their agents and publishers for granting permission to reprint these stories; to Carol and Meghan McLaurin for permission to reprint excerpts from the works of Tim McLaurin; and a special thanks is owed to Jim Denton, Linda Haines Fogle, and the staff of the University of South Carolina Press for their editorial expertise and for making this book a reality.

*Tom Franklin would like to thank:*

Brian Carpenter, my coeditor on this book, who conceived the project and saw it through with class and grace. Thanks, too, go to Nat Sobel and Beth Ann Fennelly, for their usual (and unusual) patience.

*Brian Carpenter would like to thank:*

Mark Lucas, who first introduced me to southern literature and who still hosts a Grit Lit barbecue every year at Centre College in Danville, Kentucky;

Joseph Flora, for introducing me to the work of Harry Crews, Tim McLaurin, and Larry Brown and for being my mentor and friend for many years;

Fred Hobson and Michael McFee, for their invaluable advice and encouragement;

Gary Hawkins, for introducing me to the "Rough South" (and for allowing us to use that phrase in our subtitle);

Nat Sobel, for believing in this project and for introducing me to Tom Franklin;

Tom Franklin, without whose effort and good faith this book would not exist;

my parents, Bob and Wanda, for their love and support and steadfast faith in the family English major;

my children, Rowan, Sutton, and Cate, for their patience;

and, most of all, my wife, Michelle, the love of my life, who stood behind me every day of the eight years it took to put this book together. This one is for you, M.

**CREDITS**

*Memoirs*

"Preface: Deciding to Live," "River of Names," quotes from the Introduction, by Dorothy Allison Copyright 1988 Dorothy Allison from *Trash,* reprinted by permission of The Frances Goldin Literary Agency. From *On Fire: A Personal Account of Life and Death and Choices* © 1993 by Larry Brown. Reprinted by permission of Algonquin Books of Chapel Hill. All rights reserved. From *Keeper of the Moon: A Southern Boyhood* Copyright 1991 Tim McLaurin. Reprinted by the permission of Dunham Literary as agent for the author. Originally published by W. W. Norton & Company. "A Body in the River" from *Boy with Loaded Gun* © 2000 by Lewis Nordan. Reprinted by permission of Algonquin Books of Chapel Hill. All rights reserved.

*Stories*

"Ride, Fly, Penetrate, Loiter" from *Long, Last, Happy,* copyright 1985, 2010 by Barry Hannah. Used by permission of Grove/Atlantic, Inc. "Samaritans" from *Facing the Music* © 1988 by Larry Brown. Reprinted by permission of Algonquin Books of Chapel Hill. All rights reserved. "River of Names." Copyright 1988 Dorothy Allison from *Trash,* reprinted by permission of The Frances Goldin Literary Agency. "Pit" from *Town Smokes* © 1987 Pinckney Benedict. Originally published by Ontario Review Books. Reprinted by permission of the author. From *The Sharpshooter Blues* © 1995 by Lewis Nordan. Reprinted by permission of Algonquin Books of Chapel Hill. All rights reserved. "Your Daddy in Time" from *Winter Birds* © 1994 by Jim Grimsley. Reprinted by permission of Algonquin Books of Chapel Hill. All rights reserved. "Jacksonville" © 1998 by George Singleton. Originally published in *The Carolina Quarterly.* Reprinted by permission of the author. "Sleepy Gap" by Robert Morgan is reprinted from *The Balm of Gilead Tree: New and Selected Stories* by permission of Gnomon Press. "Where Will You Go When Your Skin Cannot Contain You?" © 2006 by William Gay. Originally published in *Tin House.* Reprinted by permission of the author. "Sorry Blood" from *Welding with Children* by Tim Gautreaux, copyright 1999 by the author and reprinted by permission of Picador c/o St. Martin's Press, LLC. "Redneck Boys" from *Given Ground* by Ann Pancake © University Press of New England, Lebanon, NH. Reprinted with permission pages 99–110. "The Coal Thief" from *The Name of the Nearest River: Stories.* Copyright 2010 by Alex Taylor. Reprinted with the permission of Sarabande Books, www. sarabandebooks.org.

*Quotes*

Quote by Harry Crews from "The Freedom to Act: An Interview with Harry Crews," by Rodney Elrod, *Getting Naked with Harry Crews: Interviews,* ed. Erik Bledsoe, UP of Florida, 1999: 182. Reprinted by permission of Rodney Elrod. Quotes by Dorothy Allison from "Introduction: Stubborn Girls and Mean Stories." Copyright 1988 Dorothy Allison from *Trash;* and from

"Lecture I: Mean Stories and Stubborn Girls," *The Tanner Lectures on Human Values* (delivered at Stanford University May 14th and 15th, 2001), reprinted by permission of The Frances Goldin Literary Agency. Quote by Dorothy Allison from "Dorothy Allison Talks about Working-Class Guilt, the Film Version of 'Bastard Out of Carolina' and Coming Out—As a Science-Fiction Fan," by Laura Miller, Salon.com, March 31, 1998. Reprinted by permission of Salon Media Group, Inc. Quote by Larry Brown from *Big Bad Love* © 1990 by Larry Brown. Reprinted by permission of Algonquin Books of Chapel Hill. All rights reserved. Quote by Larry Brown. Reprinted from Kay Bonetti, Greg Michalson, Speer Morgan, and Sam Stowers's *Conversations with American Novelists: The Best Interviews from The Missouri Review and the American Audio Prose Library* by permission of the University of Missouri Press. Copyright © 1997 by the Curators of the University of Missouri. Quote by Larry Brown from the documentary *The Rough South of Larry Brown,* directed by Gary Hawkins, as quoted in *Conversations with Larry Brown* (Jackson: University Press of Mississippi, 2007), 160. Reprinted by permission of Gary Hawkins. Quote by Tim McLaurin from *The River Less Run* (Asheboro, N.C., Down Home Press, 2000), 128. Reprinted by the permission of Dunham Literary as agent for the author. Quote by Tim McLaurin from "An Interview with Tim McLaurin," by Joe Mandel, *Pembroke Magazine* 36 (2004), 133. Reprinted by permission of Joe Mandel. Quote by Lewis Nordan from "Get Back to Where You Once Belonged: Down in Delta Land with Lewis Nordan," by James L. Dickerson, *BookPage* (February 2000). Reprinted by permission of *BookPage.* Quote by Lewis Nordan from "An Interview with Lewis Nordan," by Blake Maher, *The Southern Quarterly* 34.1 (1995): 118. Reprinted by permission of *The Southern Quarterly.* Quote by Barry Hannah from "Barry Hannah: Murder and Madness in Mississippi," by Ellen Kanner, *BookPage* (July 2001). Reprinted by permission of *BookPage.* Quote by Barry Hannah from "Writer Barry Hannah," by Terry Gross, *Fresh Air,* National Public Radio, July 31, 2001. Reprinted by permission of NPR. Quote from Dominic Luxford, "Breece is Back," *The Austin Chronicle,* July 6, 2002. Reprinted by permission of Dominic Luxford and *The Austin Chronicle.* Quote by Jim Grimsley, from "Jim Grimsley: Tales of Southern Courage," by Lisa Howorth, *Publishers Weekly* 245.46 (November 15, 1999). Reprinted by permission of *Publishers Weekly.* Quote by Dale Ray Phillips from "Old Times on the Haw: An Interview with Dale Ray Phillips," by George Hovis and Timothy Williams, *The Carolina Quarterly* 55.3 (Summer 2003). Reprinted by permission of George Hovis. Quote by Robert Morgan from "Robert Morgan: Interview," by Ron Hogan, Beatrice.com (2000). Reprinted by permission of Ron Hogan. Quote by William Gay from "Interview: William Gay," by Kenny Torrella, Middle Tennessee State University Tennessee Literary Project. Reprinted by permission of Randy Mackin. Quote by Daniel Woodrell from "Seeing Red: The Writer's Life and Life in Venus Holler, Courtesy of Daniel Woodrell," by Leonard Gill, *The Memphis Flyer* (Books, September 10, 1998). Reprinted by permission of Leonard Gill and *The Memphis Flyer.* Quote by Tim Gautreaux from "Tim Gautreaux," by Christopher Scanlan, *Creative Loafing Atlanta,* June 17, 2004. Reprinted by permission of *Creative Loafing Atlanta.* Quote by Ron Rash from "Ron Rash," by Robert Birnbaum, *The Morning News,* November 7, 2005. Reprinted by permission of *The Morning News* and Robert Birnbaum. Quote by E. E. Cummings from "Buffalo Bill's." Reprinted with the permission of Liveright Publishing Corporation. Quotes by Dorothy Allison, Will Allison, Rick Bragg, Ann Pancake, George Singleton, Lee Smith, Alex Taylor, and Brad Watson courtesy of the authors.

# Introduction

*Blood and Bone*

Brian Carpenter

*The miracle of the world, the miracle of a rebirth of the senses, the miracle of an accepting heart can only be paid for with blood and bone.*

Harry Crews

## LARGE AND STARTLING FIGURES

On the wall next to my desk hangs a photo of the novelist and former boxer, bartender, and carnival barker Harry Crews. This is not your typical author photo. Crews is leaning forward in a sleeveless T-shirt with his arms crossed. On his right shoulder is a death's head tattoo. It is hard to make out the legend underneath, but from reading Larry Brown's account of meeting Crews, I know that it is a line from E. E. Cummings:

> *How Do*
> *You Like*
> *Your Blue-*
> *Eyed Boy,*
> *Mr. Death?*[1]

His eyes are hidden behind a pair of dark wrap-around shades, but I am more intrigued by his boxer's nose, busted nine times, and the serious Mohawk

---

Epigraph from the introduction to *Classic Crews: A Harry Crews Reader* (New York: Poseidon Press, 1993), 15. Reprinted with the permission of Simon & Schuster, Inc., from *Classic Crews: A Harry Crews Reader by Harry Crews.* Copyright 1993 by Harry Crews. All rights reserved.

sticking out the top of his shaved head.[2] Put it all together and Crews looks more pit bull than literary lion. And this was after he had gone sober.

I mention this photo because it was my first introduction to Crews and to what has come to be known as the "Rough South." It intimidated the hell out of me then and does even now that I know more about the man behind the image. Crews was in his early fifties and more or less off the bottle when he adopted the "'do and the 'too," though even before then he had that look about him, what one reviewer described as the face of a "madman who eats roofing nails for breakfast."[3] The more I read about Crews and became accustomed to the sort of hyperbole usually reserved for descriptions of professional wrestlers, the more I came to realize that it was actually a fair description of a writer who had spent much of the late seventies and early eighties cultivating a reputation as the South's preeminent gonzo redneck. For more than a decade, Crews played the literary outlaw, exposing the readers of *Esquire* and *Playboy* to the hardscrabble underbelly of America via his vodka-fueled profiles of cockers, carnies, gator poachers, and weed-smoking hillbillies. What Pamplona did for Hemingway, the cockfights down in Jacksonville did for Crews. This never-say-no approach to participatory journalism took Crews ringside to a dogfight in rural Florida, where he promptly managed to get himself knocked out cold before the fight had even commenced; to Valdeez, Alaska, where he woke from a three-day drunk to discover a hinge tattooed on the crook of his arm; and to an obscure outpost in the mountains of North Carolina, where, whacked out on a country cocktail of vodka, acid, and homegrown weed, he found himself standing barefoot in the dark at the edge of a waterfall.[4]

Which is to say, when I look at this photo of Crews, I know I am looking at the "real deal," just as I also know that I am looking at a lifelong performance artist, someone who lived it, shaped it, and served it up like no one else in the history of southern literature.[5] But as anyone who has ever read a word of Crews can attest, if you want the true picture of the man, you need never have seen the photo at all. With Crews, as with the other writers in this book, the proof is not in the image, impressive though it may be, but in the words, the stories they tell, as much as in the lives they lead.

Take, for example, Crews's friend and fellow writer Tim McLaurin, the snake handler turned novelist, who made a habit of bringing along his prized rattler whenever he gave a reading. Like Crews, McLaurin, who once toured the South under the name "Wild Man Mac," knew how to draw a crowd.[6] Those fortunate enough to witness the spectacle of the burly, thick-shouldered ex-marine barehanding a canebrake rattler while calmly discussing the fundamentals of storytelling tend to agree that no one ever drove home the maxim "no conflict, no story" quite like McLaurin.[7] Essayist Hal Crowther recalled that after one such reading McLaurin "milked a rattlesnake and drank the venom, then bit off the snake's last rattle" because "he thought his readers felt cheated if he just read a story." Afterward, when Crowther invited the writer home to meet some friends, McLaurin offered to bring the snake. Crowther set him straight: "Tim," he told him, "they just want to meet you."[8]

My coeditor, Tom Franklin, and I have taken a similar approach in putting this book together. That is, while we are perfectly aware how alluring and provocative the Rough South image can be, we have tried to form a collection that will refocus the attention back where it belongs—on the writing itself rather than on the alleged exploits of the contributors. I say this with some hesitation because that image was partly what drew me to the Rough South in the first place. Talent is one thing, but no doubt what continues to impress many readers is the story behind that talent. The very idea that a son of a sharecropper such as Crews could by sheer force of will have raised himself from such humble beginnings—in his case, the "worst hookworm and rickets part of Georgia"—remains a tale to rival any of the author's own fictions and no doubt accounts for the continued popularity of what most consider to be his finest work, the devastatingly candid memoir *A Childhood: The Biography of a Place*.[9]

Indeed when we first conceived this anthology, we considered including only a few writers: Crews, McLaurin, Dorothy Allison, and Larry Brown—all children of the working class and, above all, survivors for whom writing became a way out, the "blood and bone" of a desperate "desire to live."[10] Yet we soon realized that such a biographical approach had its limitations and that by restricting ourselves only to those who had "walked the walk," so to speak, we would be neglecting the work of a good many others who had just as much to say on the subject, not to mention the two writers whom many consider to have had just as much influence on Rough South fiction as Crews, namely, Barry Hannah and Cormac McCarthy.[11] Which is why it is fair to say that this book is not so much about the Rough South itself as the response of the southern imagination to that place, a place that is arguably just as mythical in its own right, just as much a piece of "fictional geography," as Tara or Yoknapatawpha.[12]

## A ROUGH HISTORY

The question remains, of course, why publish a Rough South anthology at all, and why begin with so recent a figure as Harry Crews? After all, the Rough South has been an established part of the southern literary landscape since the

beginning, dating back to the early eighteenth century when the Virginia aris-
tocrat William Byrd saw fit to record his reservations about his less sophisticated
neighbors to the south. That tradition continued into the nineteenth century
with the rise of the southwestern tale, rippers and stretchers and knee-slappers
about horse swaps, bear hunts, and bare-knuckle brawls—the sort of tales
Samuel Clemens grew up hearing as a boy and would later perfect into art.
With the twentieth century came the phenomenon that was Erskine Caldwell's
*Tobacco Road,* which in turn spawned what Flannery O'Connor dubbed the
"School of Southern Degeneracy"—lurid, often erotically charged pulp fiction
depicting poor whites as leering "redclay satyrs" and lusty backcountry vixens.[13]

Why, then, not begin at the beginning, or at the very least with Twain or
Caldwell, or with William Faulkner for that matter, who first made his name
with an admittedly "horrific tale" of a bootlegger gone bad; with Vereen Bell's
acclaimed but sadly overlooked 1941 novel *Swamp Water;* with James Agee's
classic novelistic profile of depression-era Alabama sharecroppers, *Let Us Now
Praise Famous Men;* or with O'Connor, whose characters frequently obsess over
the distinctions between "trash" and "good country people"?[14]

For one, it is necessary to consider not only those who have written about
the Rough South but how they wrote about it and why. The blue-blood Byrd,
for example, was typical in his condescension toward poor whites when he described his Carolina neighbors as a primitive tribe of yahoos notable mainly for
their promiscuity and "disposition to Laziness."[15] We note, too, the great care
the authors of the old southwestern tales—most of them genteel men of learning, doctors, ministers, scholars—took to distinguish themselves from the class
of ruffians about whom they wrote. Even Faulkner, for all his early posturing
as a backwoods bohemian, felt the need to distance himself from the popularity
of *Sanctuary,* the infamous southern noir classic he later dismissed as a "cheap
idea . . . deliberately conceived to make money." It was Faulkner, of course,
who gave us that singular archetype of Rough South fiction, the unscrupulous,
indomitable Flem Snopes—the shiftless patriarch of Jefferson's most infamous
clan, whose rise and fall Faulkner chronicled in his tragicomic Snopes trilogy.
Yet tragic though Flem's tale may be, Faulkner never let us forget that a Snopes
is still a Snopes, "like colonies of rats or termites are just rats or termites," and
that the real tragedy is that a low-born scoundrel like Flem was ever allowed to
succeed at all.[16]

More typical was the approach taken by Faulkner's younger brother, John,
a novelist in his own right, who had no such qualms about exploiting the usual
redneck stereotypes, turning out such country kitsch as *Cabin Road* and *Uncle
Good's Girls* that sold thousands of copies alongside provocatively titled pulp

like *Cracker Girl* and *Backwoods Hussy*.[17] O'Connor satirized these Caldwell-inspired imitators in an early story called "The Crop" about an aspiring hack named Miss Willerton who sets out to write a story about poor whites. "Miss Willerton had never been intimately connected with sharecroppers," we are told, but "she had read a novel dealing with that kind of people" and judged them to be "as arty a subject as any." To her mind, at least, the form was well established: "There would have to be some quite violent, naturalistic scenes," she observes, "the sadistic sort of thing one reads of in connection with that class." O'Connor, of course, had no more contact with "that class" than did Caldwell, the preacher's son, but she knew enough to know that flesh and blood could never be reduced to simple formula and that any writer who hoped to capture the South as it really is would gain nothing by perpetuating the old stereotypes. Accordingly, when poor whites do turn up in O'Connor's fiction, in "Parker's Back" or "Good Country People," for instance, they tend to be in on the joke rather than the butt of it, though their insight into their own character remains somewhat limited. Though the mysteries of faith and revelation do enter into their lives, they are more often unwitting emissaries of enlightenment, mere "instruments of grace" rather than its recipients.[18]

### A HARSH BEAUTY

This brings us back to that "large and startling figure" (to quote O'Connor) that was Harry Crews.[19] It is worth noting that even Crews himself was initially reluctant to write about his Rough South past, and that as a young writer the very thought of being a tenant farmer's son made him so "ashamed," so "humiliated," he said, that he "could not bear to think of it, and worse to believe it." Yet after a series of false starts and artistic failures—all, he conceded, part of "an effort to pretend otherwise"—Crews finally set aside his "fear and loathing for what I was and who I was" and came to the "dead-solid conviction" that the only things worth writing about were all the "beautiful and dreadful and sorry circumstances that had made me the Grit I am and will always be. . . . Once I realized that," said Crews, "I was home free."[20]

Dorothy Allison experienced a similar epiphany when writing the semi-autobiographical tales that would form her first collection, which she intentionally titled *Trash,* she said, "to confront the term and claim it honorific." Said Allison, "I originally claimed the label 'trash' in self-defense. The phrase had been applied to me and to my family in crude and hateful ways. I took it on deliberately. . . . What it comes down to is that I use 'trash' to raise the issue of who the term glorifies as well as who it disdains." For both Crews and

Allison, the decision to write their own stories about their own people became a way not only to confront their troubled pasts but to reclaim and redefine a tradition that had often treated them and their kind with contempt. For Allison in particular it was an opportunity to "glorify the people I loved who were never celebrated" and to "take a little revenge" on those who had portrayed them "as if they were brain-damaged, or morally insufficient, or just damn stupid."[21]

Yet if their work can be seen as an act of defiance, it is also notable for its deep ambivalence and ruthless self-scrutiny—a consequence, no doubt, of growing up in a society where, as Crews explained, an unabashed curiosity in the human condition, "untempered by pity or compassion," was not merely a necessity but a "sanity-saving virtue."[22] If Crews's grotesque depictions of his fellow grits have on occasion invited the scorn of certain critics—including one who accused him of trying to "out-Caldwell Caldwell"—they also succeed in humanizing a people traditionally typecast as "indolent reprobates" or "hillbilly comics," said James H. Watkins, finding in their "apparent ugliness" a "harsh beauty."[23]

This is particularly true of Allison, who remains unflinching in her observations on her own people, who she says are not to be confused with the "good poor" of popular myth. Said Allison, "We were the bad poor. We were men who drank and couldn't keep a job; women, invariably pregnant before marriage, who quickly became worn, fat, and old from working too many hours and bearing too many children; and children with runny noses, watery eyes, and the wrong attitudes. . . . We were not noble, not grateful, not even hopeful. We knew ourselves despised." If such stark portraits convey the "shame and outrage, pride and stubbornness" that come with growing up poor and white in the South, they also restore a certain dignity to their subjects by letting us see them as they see themselves. As Allison explained, "My family's lives were not on television, not in books, not even comic books. There was a myth of the poor in this country, and it did not include us, no matter how hard I tried to squeeze us in." For Allison, as for Crews, the chance to tell these stories has been nothing less than a way to reclaim their own identities as children of the southern underclass, a heritage they claim today, according to Allison, "with a full appreciation of how often it has been disdained."[24]

## THE BOTTOM RAIL ON TOP

Take a good look at the success of Allison and Crews and you see more than the evolution of a stereotype. You see the continuing shift in southern literature away from the genteel, aristocratic-agrarian view of old to what critic Robert Gingher called a less privileged, "grit-poor" perspective from the "rough edges . . . of life."[25] Some call it, rather facetiously, the "White Trash Renaissance," as if it were some sort of conscious literary movement, though it is fair to say that most of the writers here do write with a heightened awareness of one another and of their Rough South roots.

There was a time, of course, when the southern writer felt compelled to establish his genteel credentials, as the poet Allen Tate did when he claimed to be a descendant of one of Virginia's first families (a lie, it turned out—Tate having been misled by his own mother, no less); or as William Faulkner did post-Nobel, pulling on a pair of cropped pants and a pink riding jacket to play the Virginia Gentleman for his publisher's publicity photo shoot.[26] Yet today many a southern writer finds himself in the peculiar position of having to defend his own Rough South pedigree, which in turn has resulted in what Hal Crowther has called a curious game of "dueling hardships," a "competition for the humblest origins—who ate the most squirrels and chitlins, used the rankest outhouse, or grew up with the most lint in his hair." Said Crowther, "Writers whose parents were solvent or—God help them—educated have been sent to the back of the bus."[27]

This explains why someone like William Gay got credit not just for being a great writer, or for coming up the hard way, or for sticking it out and finally getting his first book published when he was in his fifties, but for being the kind of writer who had won all of the acclaim and yet still preferred to live back home in Hohenwald, Tennessee (population 3,820).[28] The implication being that all those Pushcarts and O. Henrys and *Best American Short Stories* citations are all well and good, but in the end what really matters—by Grit Lit standards, at least—is not the week you spent at Bread Loaf or Sewanee but your hard-won tenure at the School of Hard Knocks. Survey the biographies on the backs of the books by most of the writers included here and you will invariably find, along with the awards won and degrees taken, the requisite blue-collar résumé. Not that you need know that Harry Crews tended bar or that Larry Brown hauled pulpwood, that William Gay painted houses or that Tom Franklin worked in a grit factory to know you are in the presence of a great writer, but when it comes to selling the Rough South, every proof of authenticity counts.

Little wonder, then, that most critics (and, admittedly, even the editors of this anthology) tend to emphasize the more sensational aspects of the Rough South image, which is why, despite all evidence to the contrary, the prototypical Rough South writer continues to be portrayed as some kind of literary barnburner or redneck savant—a Snopes with an M.F.A. If not quite true, it is nevertheless an image that publishers and publicists (not to mention the writers themselves) have done little to discourage. Whether deserved or not, there would seem to be more than enough anecdotal evidence, apocryphal or otherwise, to support such claims, be it the one about the time Larry Brown allegedly stomped on the table of a critic who had given him a bad review (not true) or the one about Barry Hannah bringing a pistol to class to demonstrate the six fundamental movements of the short story (true, more or less).[29] It is an image Grit Lit writers themselves frequently contend with and on occasion even poke fun at, as George Singleton did a few years back when he enclosed with his Christmas cards a photo of himself leaning against a pickup with a beer in one hand and a shotgun in the other.[30]

It should come as no surprise then to find that when critics do praise these writers, it tends to take the form of the backhanded compliment, as when *Kirkus* dubbed Brad Watson a first-rate "cracker realist" or when *Booklist* hailed Larry Brown as "the King of White Trash."[31] Much of this ambivalence no doubt derives from Grit Lit's reputation for authenticity both on the page and in real life—the expectation that we are in the presence of the "real deal," someone who has lived what he has written and has the scars to prove it, when, of course, the reality is much more complicated. A prime example being Larry Brown, the "real deal" if there ever was one, who found himself marketed throughout his career, noted Keith Perry, as any number of contradictory, "extraliterary" Larry Browns: "firefighter, ex-Marine, the sharecropper's son who flunked English, the next William Faulkner," but rarely just "Larry Brown, writer."[32]

Even the term "Grit Lit" itself has been transformed over the years from a "facetious shorthand" into a familiar and more readily marketable "brand," said Scott Romine, a commodity as deeply "embedded" in the South's ever-thriving "economy of cultural reproduction" as *Gone with the Wind* or Elvis.[33] Whether it is "hick chic" or "hick shock," the trend among not just southern writers but American writers in general, "when it comes to the kind of characters they choose to populate their fiction," claimed Robert Rebein, has been and will likely continue to be "downwardly mobile."[34] You could blame this on the market (hardly likely—Grit Lit is an "acquired taste," according to Romine, and a tough sell to most) or on some sort of "po' folks" nostalgia for the "bad old days," though it probably has just as much to do with that indescribable impulse Barry Hannah can only hint at in *Ray,* that peculiar "something," as Ray's wife tells him, "that wants to set yourself deliberately in peril and in trash."[35] So call it Grit Lit or "dirty realism," trailer-park Gothic or "country noir," when we talk about southern literature these days, the bottom rail is on top.

## BLOOD MOMENTS

The irony, of course, is that this Rough South revival comes at a time when the Rough South itself has begun losing ground to a new-and-improved South of condos and high-rises, megamalls and office parks. Yes, poverty and violence are still very much in evidence even in the Sun Belt but certainly not to the degree that they were in the days when Harry Crews was growing up on a dirt farm in Bacon County, Georgia, back when there was not enough money, claimed Crews, to "close up a dead man's eyes" and where the passage of time itself was often marked by the day a particular fight took place.[36] Yet if it is true, as Fred Hobson contended, that savagery in the South has "gone the way of the hoopskirt" and that prosperity has replaced violence as the "prevailing southern myth," it is also true that this violent legacy remains a formidable and lingering presence in the southern imagination.[37]

Violence is an ever-present threat in most of these stories—the inevitable consequence of what Chris Offutt called "point-blank living," a "hard-living, hard-playing" approach to life.[38] "Anything worth doing [was] worth overdoing," Harry Crews recalled of his father—and it was true too of the uncle who raised him—"he was drunk going in and coming out, and incredible in his violence, with the scars of a perfect set of somebody's teeth in his cheek under his left eye."[39] Tim McLaurin, who grew up on the wrong side of Fayetteville, North Carolina, considered himself lucky to have survived at all: "Here I am sitting today, alive and well at age 41, but I can name you ten friends, people I have known very well—who are dead today, either through car wrecks, or murder, or suicide—very graphic ends to their lives."[40] Crews attributed this pattern of self-destruction in part to a vicious cycle of poverty and isolation; as he recalled of his own people, "they were locked into social circumstances" that led to a "kind of raging frustration that found its outlet in rank violence."[41] Little surprise, then, that so many of Crews's novels end in bloodshed; in his world violence is often the cause and the solution—the only out. Yet even for a writer like Barry Hannah, who grew up in the relative comfort of a middle-class Mississippi neighborhood, violence remained an obsession. "It seems to be out of my nightmares," said Hannah, a self-described pacifist (and lifelong gun enthusiast), who nevertheless confessed to being a "student of violence because of what it does, because of how it quickens the character of those around it."[42] For Crews that was where the story was—those "blood moments" when you "find out who the hell you are, what you really are, what you really believe."[43] And that is where most of the characters here find themselves, at the ends and extremes of life, facing down death and the inescapable fact of their own mortality.

In his essay "The Violence That Finds Us," Crews, who claimed to have broken—or had broken for him—nearly every bone in his body, contended that it is not love, not faith, nor any of the old "verities and truths" that Faulkner famously invoked in his Nobel address, but violence, or the threat of it, that shapes us and makes us who we are. "I would maintain that it does not make us bad," said Crews, "it only makes us human."[44] It is a view likewise shared by Cormac McCarthy, who may be the one southern writer whose reputation for violence—at least on the page—exceeds that of Crews. "There's no such thing as life without bloodshed," claimed McCarthy, whose apocalyptic tales of souls in peril are known for having "more corpses than commas." Said McCarthy, "Death is the major issue in the world. For you, for me, for all of us. It just is. To not be able to talk about it is very odd."[45] On this point McCarthy's readers need not look far for evidence, having witnessed his characters suffer death or near death by all manner of bedlam and natural catastrophe: jackknife, buckshot, dynamite, train wreck, avalanche, stampede, lynch mob, irate mule, and flying floor buffer—all of it administered with a godlike wrath that rumbles through his novels like Old Testament thunder.

Yet if violence is destiny in the Rough South, it is likewise a means of moral reckoning. Look beyond all the macho posturing and you will find that McCarthy and the rest are not so much concerned with getting their licks in as they are with understanding the how and why, the cause and consequence of what Crews called the "need to bleed." Whether it is Crews's own motley horde of freaks and misfits or Larry Brown's heartsick, lust-driven loners, they invariably come off just as displaced, just as full of existential angst, as any of Walker Percy's uptight suburban trust-fund philosophers. The difference, of course, is in how they choose to respond to it. As Crews put it in "The Violence That Finds Us," "Are you plagued with a sourceless anxiety? Do you worry about the existence of God and whether or not there *is* order in the universe? Are you unhappy for no apparent reason? Do you obsess over the future of your children? If the answer to any of the above is yes, *then go and get your ass kicked.* . . . You will be purified and holy. . . . Nose-to-nose combat is better than a psychiatrist, is never as humiliating and is not nearly so expensive."[46] (Then again, you could just have a beer and read some Harry Crews.) Whether or not you agree with him, what Crews is suggesting here—that violence can be a particularly effective antidote to suburban malaise and existential doubt—goes a long way toward explaining the continuing appeal (and vicarious thrill) of Rough South fiction. It is the reason why Harry Monroe, the restless, gun-obsessed hipster in Barry Hannah's novel *Geronimo Rex,* skips class to stalk the hapless white supremacist Whitfield Peter; and why the melancholy Mr. Raney in Lewis Nordan's *The Sharpshooter Blues* advocates the therapeutic benefits of firing off a few rounds inside the house: "It relieved stress. It cemented relationships, strangers or partners in marriage. It helped most anybody, the least of these my brethren, as Preacher Roe might say. It cleared the air."[47] But beyond the irony, beyond the deadpan, what writers like Crews and Hannah and Nordan keep coming back to is one thing—blood and bone and what it costs us, the gut-level, bone-deep ache of it, the wounds worse for being so often self-inflicted.

Crews, in particular, seemed compelled to explain the complexities behind our more violent rituals, be it a bar fight between friends (a ritual "full of joy and love masquerading as anger") or the near-hysterical forms of bloodlust on display in the mob gathered for a dogfight."[48] "In practice," Flannery O'Connor said, "the southerner seldom underestimates his own capacity for evil."[49] Looking out over the crowd, Crews recognized the familiar characteristics of his own kind, a people "stubborn, wrongheaded, self-destructive," and realized he was staring directly into the dark heart of the national character: "Here was the faith that brought the black man from Africa, the faith that still kicks the shit out of American-born Mexicans in Texas, the faith of the officer saying in his laconic but believing voice, 'We had to destroy the village in order to save it.' It was so ugly it was beautiful. It was mine and I would no more deny it than I would deny my own blood. And disguise that faith how you will, it lives, breathes, and gets fatter every year in this great country of ours. Give us the world and this would be the paradigm we'd use to remake it."[50] The terrible paradox Crews saw here reminds us that what sustains us is not necessarily what is good for us, whether it is public policy or cultural myth. That this native bloodlust is not exclusively southern, or even exclusively American, would seem obvious enough. In *Keeper of the Moon,* Tim McLaurin recalled turning his telescope to the heavens as a boy and finding a world remarkably similar to his own: "Life was marked by chaos, and even in the seemingly ordered expanse of the sky, there might be sudden fire. Compared to the cold drag of eternity, to travel swift and in brilliance, to burn one last image against the sky, seemed comforting."[51] The stories we tell about ourselves matter more than we know, which is why even today, in a South where the majority of the population no doubt prefers the comparatively bloodless blood sports of SEC football and the WWE, the idea of a Rough South, a Savage South, a benighted South, continues to haunt the southern imagination like some kind of predatory myth. It is why the blinded brother in Tom Franklin's story "Poachers" holds fast to the outer dark and to the specter of violence that took his sight, why in the end the consolations of a harsh place remain for many a "strange and terrifying comfort."[52]

## READING THE ROUGH SOUTH

There is a story by Larry Brown called "92 Days" about a struggling Mississippi writer and sometime housepainter named Leon Barlow. One day Barlow receives a letter from an agent in New York, who tells him, "We are returning your novel not because it is not publishable, but because the market at this time is not amenable to novels about drunk pulpwood haulers and rednecks and deer hunting. Our comments relate more to its marketability than to its publishability, and even though this novel is hilarious in many places and extremely well-written with a good plot, real characters, refreshing dialogue, beautiful descriptions and no typographical or spelling errors, we do not feel confident that we could place it for you. We would, however, be delighted to read anything else you have written or will write in the future."[53] Barlow responds the only way he can: he drops the rejection on the pile with the rest of them and fires off a profanity-laced reply—then tears it up, has a beer and a smoke, and gets back to work. I always smile when I read that scene, and not only because of the truth of it. Brown, of course, was no stranger to rejection, having struggled for seven long years, through five unpublished novels and more than a hundred short stories, before finally publishing his first book. What makes me smile is the thought of him sitting there in that little room off the carport at his home in Yocona, Mississippi, writing this rejection to himself knowing that he had in fact found a reader out there somewhere, that he had finally gotten through. Since then the market for Rough South fiction has definitely grown more than "amenable," no doubt thanks to the success of Brown and others like him, to the point that when we sat down to put this book together the problem was not what to include but what to leave out. There was simply too much to choose from.

The surprising thing was that it had never been done before. Though the last three decades have seen the South anthologized more than ever, with numerous volumes devoted to Souths both Old and New, surreal and "Christ-haunted," covering every state, every region (from the Gulf to the Delta to Appalachia), every genre and subgenre (from nature writing to women's writing, from African American to Jewish American, from erotic to gothic to noir and even southern vampire mystery), there has yet to be a single volume devoted to stories written from the perspective of one of the most ubiquitous and yet most misunderstood characters in all of southern literature—the poor southern white.

It is not hard to imagine why. Aside from the obvious unfashionableness of publishing a book written largely by and about white southern males (hardly a promising avenue from a marketing point of view), there is the poor white's long-established reputation for being "primitive," "illiterate," and "culturally sterile," according to Wayne Flynt—the very antithesis of all things literary.[54] "It's hard to care about such people," said the critic Matt Wray, adding, "It's even harder to take them seriously."[55]

Yet over the last forty years that is precisely what Wray, Flynt, Lewis Killian, and others have done by exploring the history and psychology of poor southern whites. That this surge of interest in "Dixie's forgotten people," as Flynt called them, has coincided with the recent renaissance in Rough South literature is certainly no accident, nor should we underestimate the considerable influence of Cormac McCarthy, Dorothy Allison, and Harry Crews, whom Larry Brown called "my uncle in all ways but blood."[56]

Still, why a Rough South Renaissance, and why now? While it would be folly to try to draw a direct line between the social upheavals of the sixties and the emergence of this new generation of Grit Lit writers, it is hard to deny the impact of the civil rights movement on the white southern psyche and particularly on poor southern whites, who for generations had tended to define themselves in mostly negative terms, not for who they were but for who they were not, at a time when to be poor and white in the South was more a matter of being *not* black.[57] Only after the death of Jim Crow, when there was "no more segregation to defend and no more North to defy," said James C. Cobb, were poor southern whites finally able to "reconnect with their true identity." Where "redneck" had once been synonymous with the "aggressively ignorant, uncouth, and lawless," by the late 1970s, with a southerner in the White House (and his media-savvy brother on TV in a "Redneck Power" T-shirt), the redneck image now ranged from comic ( Jerry Clower) to cool (Burt Reynolds) to countercultural (Harry Crews), all of which, claimed Cobb, was enough to make even a proper southern gentleman "not only less disdainful but even downright envious."[58]

Needless to say, Grit Lit is not about redneck manifestos or white victim-hood or the identity politics of the "new minority"—something to make good ol' boys feel good about themselves. Nor is it about merely exchanging one set of clichés for another, trading moonlight and magnolia for moonshine and Marlboro, any more than it is about being able to navigate backcountry roads by moonlight with the bottle turned up and the steering wheel between your knees. If anything, it is about getting beyond the caricature and introducing a little compassion and complication into the conversation.

Granted, all those old familiar slurs—"cracker," "redneck," "white trash"—may indeed have gone mainstream—on movies, television, comedy albums, novelty caps, T-shirts, bumper stickers ("MY HEART BELONGS TO BUBBA")—in a way that other racial and ethnic slurs likely never will. But as for being "accept-able" among poor southern whites themselves, try testing that hypothesis at your local honky-tonk and see what happens. Even the more euphemistic "Grit Lit" and "Rough South" carry with them a certain stigma, what Dorothy Allison calls that "general uncomfortable angle" of being "low-class," which is why you still see writers who shy away from such labels altogether. "That's always going to be there," says Allison, "the self-conscious rejection of the redneck ethos. No one wants to be cast into the outer darkness of racism, violence, and inappropriate behavior—except those of us who have found a certain pride in our wayward tribe."[59]

That is one reason why this book's title is what it is and not something more willfully provocative like *White Trash: A Redneck Reader*—not that *Grit Lit: A Rough South Reader* is any less troublesome in its own way. Indeed there are probably more than a few folks out there who consider a Rough South reader to be a contradiction in terms, just as there are likely some who would say that "Grit Lit" and "Rough South" are too ambiguous, too likely to be taken at face value rather than for the euphemisms that they really are. As a literary term, "Grit Lit," which has been in currency at least since the mid-1980s, may not have always had the most complimentary associations, though it can most likely be traced back to the genre's godfather himself, Harry Crews, and the "Grits" column he wrote for *Esquire* back in the late 1970s—"grit" being Crews's own preferred alternative to the pejorative "cracker" or "redneck," not to mention a term more suggestive of the sort of resilience often portrayed in these stories.[60] Still, even "Grit Lit" casts a far wider net than this book attempts to cover, which is why the true emphasis properly belongs on the sub-title, drawn from filmmaker Gary Hawkins's documentary series of "Rough South" profiles of Crews, Tim McLaurin, and Larry Brown. Hawkins's own definition is somewhat ambiguous: "Rough South gets the thing whittled down to the working class," he says, "but even that is false. . . . The Rough South is no less complicated than the rest of the South."[61]

## "GRIT LIT" VS. "ROUGH SOUTH"

So what is the difference between "Grit Lit" and "Rough South"? As Dorothy Allison once joked, "If it has ten swear words and a pickup truck in a sentence, it's almost certainly 'Grit Lit.'"[62] While there is likely some truth to that, for the purposes of this book we have defined "Grit Lit" as typically blue collar or working class, mostly small town, sometimes rural, occasionally but not always violent, usually but not necessarily southern. (Indeed some of the best Grit Lit writers in America—Donald Ray Pollock of Ohio, Bonnie Jo Campbell of Michigan, Benjamin Percy of Oregon—are not even from the South.) Whereas "Rough South" we define as mostly poor, white, rural, and unquestionably violent—Grit Lit's wilder kin or Grit Lit with its back against the wall and somebody's going to get hurt.

Some might hear that and think it is all just toothless caricature and bare-foot local color—somewhere between Ernest T. Bass and the "squeal like a pig" scene from *Deliverance*—but read it and you see that the Rough South is not so much a fixed place as it is a point of departure. Realism and naturalism are the obvious starting points, but from there it is just as likely to head off into southern gothic (William Gay, Pinckney Benedict) or county noir (Daniel Woodrell), magic realism (Lewis Nordan), or the postmodern and "post-southern" (Barry Hannah), as well as that same old southwestern frontier (Tim Gautreaux, Cormac McCarthy) where it all began.

None of this—the poverty, the violence, the dark, earthy humor—necessarily makes Rough South lit any more authentically "southern" than the rest of contemporary southern literature, though it probably does make it appear more recognizably "southern" to most readers (especially to those not from the South), even if the South it portrays probably bears little resemblance to the South familiar to the folks who actually buy and read Grit Lit. Nor is it accurate to say that son-of-a-sharecropper Harry Crews was any more "southern" than son-of-a-lawyer Walker Percy was (though you can bet a number of folks might side with the boy from Bacon County). Maybe it is just that Rough South writers "*do southern*" (to borrow Noel Polk's phrase), or what most people tend to think of as "southern," better than most.[63]

That is why the Rough South as a genre is likely to be with us as long as people continue to believe in the existence of this place we call "the South." It is also why, even as the South continues to evolve from a largely backward, rural region into "the South of Interstate 12 and Highway 190," as Percy put it, Grit Lit is no more likely to disappear from the South than the Western has out West.[64]

So the Rough South may not be the "real" South any more than Cheever's Westchester or Roth's Newark is the true North. But damned if it is not just as real as Tara and as true as Yoknapatawpha. Like those places, the Rough South is just one of many Souths to contemplate. As bluegrass is to country, and rockabilly is to rock, Rough South is to Grit Lit. Think Grit Lit with a stronger accent.

## PLAIN WHITES, JIM CROW,
## AND THE "MINNIE PEARL PRIZE"

What else can we say about these Rough South tales?

For one, the famed southern sense of place is never more urgent than it is here. Whether the territory be the meth-scarred hills and hollows of Daniel Woodrell's Ozarks or the haunted gothic wilderness known as the "Harrikin" that lies at the edge of William Gay's own fictional postage stamp, Ackerman's Field, Tennessee, the message is clear: know the place you come from or it just might kill you.

Class is equally pressing here, the old resentments between high and low, plain white and poor white (seen most obviously in Tim Gautreaux's "Sorry Blood" and Larry Brown's "Samaritans"), though more often the struggles are "intraclass," as critic Erik Bledsoe pointed out, between those wanting to move up or out and those just trying to hold on to what they have.[65] If the writers here do not mourn the Lost Cause or the old South not forgotten, it is because it was never theirs to lose in the first place. (How do you lose what you never had?) Likewise, if they do mention "the War" at all, they are most likely referring to Saigon, not Shiloh, Baghdad, not Bull Run.

Race is a less contentious issue here than one might expect, reflecting perhaps the region's dramatic transformation from the apartheid state that was the Jim Crow South to the more integrated South of the post–civil rights era. This new sensitivity can readily be seen in Larry Brown's novel *Dirty Work,* about the friendship between two wounded Vietnam vets (one black, one white, both southern), Tom Franklin's *Crooked Letter, Crooked Letter,* and Lewis Nordan's haunting *Wolf Whistle,* which reimagines the most notorious hate crime in the history of Mississippi, the racially motivated murder of the black teenager Emmett Till, and the deep psychological wound left in its wake.

Few Grit Lit writers have been more forthcoming on the subject than Alabama native Rick Bragg, who in his memoir *All Over but the Shoutin'* recalled his own experiences in the segregated sixties as "a time of horrors": "I grew up in a house where the word *nigger* was as much a part of the vocabulary as 'hey' or 'pass the peas,'" said Bragg. "If I was rewriting my life, if I was using this story as a way to make my life slickly perfect," he said, "this is the part I would change. But it would be a lie. It is part of me, of who I was, and I guess who I am." For Bragg reconciliation came not with the "uneasy and imperfect peace" that followed the end of segregation but with the recognition that "hungry does not have a color," this after some black neighbors brought Bragg's family some food when his father had "run off," a gesture made even more remarkable by the fact that Bragg and his siblings had recently thrown rocks at one of their children. "I would like to say that we came together, after the little boy brought us that food," said Bragg, "but that would be a lie. But at least, we didn't throw no more rocks."66 Still others, such as Dorothy Allison, have sought to "[blur] the boundary" between the races, noted John Duvall, by exploring how class affects our understanding of what it means to be "white" or "black," as we see in Allison's novel *Bastard Out of Carolina,* where the poor white Ruth Ann "Bone" Boatwright comes to identify more closely with her black neighbors after her middle-class relatives dismiss her as "nigger trash."67

One thing readers will no doubt notice is that of all the stories collected here, only a few were written by women. To fans of Rough South fiction, this will not likely come as a surprise. As bookseller Candler Hunt has said of George Singleton's stories, "This is not your mother's southern fiction."68 Truth is, you would be hard pressed to find mama here at all. With the notable exception of Dorothy Allison and a few others, the Rough South genre remains by and large a boys club—Harry and Barry and Larry and their literary brethren—with a taste for violence and the hypermasculine. Why so few women have written or at least published (an important distinction) stories about those on the "wrong side of the kudzu," as Jill McCorkle observed, is not as obvious as it might seem.69 Recalling the tales he heard as a boy, Harry Crews noted that "it was always the women who scared me. The stories that women told and that men told were full of violence, sickness, and death. But it was the women whose stories were unrelieved by humor and filled with apocalyptic vision . . . as stark and cold as legend or myth."70 One need only read one of Allison's self-described "mean stories" like "River of Names," a horrifying accounting of lives lost, or Lee Smith's description of a hellfire preacher snuffing out a cigarette in his own cheek in *Saving Grace,* to know that theirs is far from grit "lite." As Smith once said, "We'll bring you a casserole, but we'll kill you, too."[71]

While Smith acknowledges that "a writer *does* have to write about what she knows" and that "women's spheres have traditionally been more domestic and relational as opposed to the out-of-door, more work and survival-oriented world of 'boy books,'" she believes that "this is changing" and points to writers Holly Goddard Jones and Jeanette Walls as examples.[72] Ann Pancake likewise cites the double standard applied to men and women when it comes to the Rough South, noting that it is probably easier for men to wear the "Grit Lit" label because men in the South—even those from more privileged backgrounds—have always been able to "dip in and out" of more manly "working-class activities" like hunting and hard drinking and still retain their status, whereas most women either cannot or simply do not want to do such things and would invite scorn if they did.[73] As Allison puts it, "Men can earn a certain repute for being rough. Women in the same territory get addressed as dykes or inheritors of the Minnie Pearl prize just for being their mama's girls."[74]

Yet as Allison and others have shown, the field is wide open for Rough South stories by and about women beyond the accustomed roles of vixen or victim. Nor are the Rough South stories written by men as "claustrophobically male-locked" as one might expect.[75] Robert Morgan, for instance, has proven particularly adept at writing from a woman's point of view, as have Larry Brown and Daniel Woodrell, whose complex portrait of Ree Dolly in *Winter's Bone* gives us, said Allison, not merely a heroine but a "genuine American folk hero."[76]

## OF MOONLIGHT MELONMOUNTERS
## AND MANURE THIEVES

No serious survey of the Rough South would be complete that failed to mention just how funny much of it is. Perhaps "funny" is not quite the word for the sort of humor one finds here. "Nauseatingly hilarious" is how Tim Gautreaux recalled the scene in Erskine Caldwell's "Saturday Afternoon," where the town butcher takes his rest "with a hunk of bloody roast under his head."[77] ("Strangers who went in to buy Tom's meat for the first time were always asking him what it was that had died between the walls," says Caldwell.)[78] The South may have changed since Caldwell's day, but that same morbid species of "unresurrected wit" (Gautreaux likened it to an "anesthetic" or "refreshments at an execution") is still much in evidence among the writers collected here, most of whom write with a wink and a nod to Faulkner's Snopeses and O'Connor's misfits and that old tall tale tradition wherein, said Gautreaux, folks are "always doing amusingly desperate, picturesque and depraved things."[79]

We also see a good bit of what William Gay called "survivor humor," which grows out of that "stoic quality" that gets people through the hard times. "I ran into it a lot growing up, listening to old guys' stories," said Gay. "They were fatalistic about getting perpetually screwed by life, and they survived on laughter."[80] We see this in Dorothy Allison's "River of Names" ("What's a South Carolina virgin?" "'At's a ten-year-old can run fast.") and in the deliciously wicked joke (the one about the "long pig") at the heart of "Kindred Spirits," Brad Watson's dark riff on revenge tales and old hunting yarns.[81] Not exactly the sort of thing you will hear from the Blue Collar Comedy Tour.

Rather than try to explain precisely why all of this is funny (always a losing proposition), we have assembled a short list of favorites chosen by some of the writers themselves. As Pinckney Benedict noted, "It seems to me like it's almost all humor, of the very darkest and most bitter sort."[82] There's the one about the preacher and piccolo player (too long and frankly too raunchy to go into here) in Larry Brown's *Dirty Work* and the "dangling thangling" (which is just as gloriously depraved as it sounds) in the O'Connor-inspired "A Roadside Resurrection."[83] There's the mystified farmer's encounter with the "manure thief" in William Gay's *The Long Home* and Albright's calamitous run-in with the crimper in *Provinces of Night*.[84] And the whiskey-soaked one-man wrecking crew that is Uncle Trash in Mark Richard's "Strays," who cheats his little nephews out of their last church-offering nickel then "stands in the sink and sings 'Gather My Farflung Thoughts Together.'"[85]

Sometimes it is just a line, like what Hard Candy tells the unfortunate rodent in Crews's *A Feast of Snakes* before she drops him into the rattler's cage: "Nobody's gone hurt you, little rat. We just gone let the snake kill you a little."[86] Or the half-wit grocery clerk Hydro's last words to the boy in the zoot suit ("We are plumb out of tortillas.") right before he blasts him into eternity in Nordan's *The Sharpshooter Blues*.[87]

Pretty much any page out of George Singleton would qualify (though you would do well to start with "This Itches, Y'all" or "Outlaw Head and Tail") as would the entirety of Crews's *Car* and Nordan's *Music of the Swamp* (especially the first paragraph of "How Bob Steele Broke My Father's Heart"). Add to that *Norwood* by Charles Portis, whom the *Believer* once described as "like Cormac McCarthy, but funny," which hardly seems fair to the man who gave us both the "moonlight melonmounter" in *Suttree* ("He's damn near screwed the whole patch," the farmer marvels) and the "idiot child" in *Child of God* who gnaws the legs off his little bird "playpretty" because "he wanted it to where it couldn't run off."[88]

If that last example seems especially grim (so wrong and yet so perversely right), we might do well to remember Roy Blount Jr.'s observation that the best humor almost always has about it a certain "tang of meanness," which may in turn act as a kind of "preservative—vinegar for pickling real fellow feeling and love of the world."[89] If nothing else, it tells us that this hardy old strain of Rough South humor, born of necessity and "nourished in adversity" (to borrow Lewis Killian's phrase), is alive and well and (thankfully) as mean and ornery as ever.[90]

## BEYOND THE ROUGH SOUTH

A final word about these so-called Rough South writers. However convenient such labels as "Grit Lit" or "Rough South" might be for critics and the editors of anthologies, they hardly begin to account for the diversity and range of work produced by the writers collected here, be it Barry Hannah, whose subjects ranged from Jeb Stuart to Jimi Hendrix to Jesus Christ; Jim Grimsley, a prolific playwright who has also published a trio of well-received science-fiction novels; Robert Morgan, the respected poet and author of a biography of Daniel Boone; or Larry Brown, some of whose stories—particularly "Boy and Dog" and "Julie: A Memory"—are as inventive and experimental in form and narrative as anything to be found in contemporary fiction.

Whatever you choose to call these writers, it is our hope that this book will lead to a greater appreciation of their work and of that rich and still evolving tradition that is the Rough South. As Rick Bragg recalled of his rough kin in *All Over but the Shoutin',* "Against my will, I grew fond of them. I would have liked to have known them better."[91] We hope this book will give many others the opportunity to do just that.

# MEMOIRS

# HARRY CREWS, *A Childhood:*
## *The Biography of a Place*

Born in 1935, Harry Crews grew up in Bacon County, Georgia. He spent his adolescence in Jacksonville, Florida, where he lived until he left at age seventeen to join the marines. Crews later returned home to study at the University of Florida but left after his second year to tour America on his Triumph motorcycle, during which time he worked as a bartender, carnival barker, and short-order cook. In 1958 he resumed his studies at UF and later graduated with a master's degree in English education. After writing four unpublished novels, Crews published his first book, *The Gospel Singer,* in 1968 and soon after accepted a job teaching writing at his alma mater. He went on to publish seven more novels over the next seven years, including *Naked in Garden Hills* (1969), *Car* (1972), *The Gypsy's Curse* (1974), and *A Feast of Snakes* (1976). In addition to writing a regular column for *Esquire* during the late 1970s, Crews also wrote stories and profiles for a number of magazines, including *Sport* and *Playboy,* many of which were collected in the books *Blood and Grits* (1979) and *Florida Frenzy* (1982). In 1978 he published his acclaimed memoir, *A Childhood: The Biography of a Place,* though it would be many years before the publication of his next novel, *All We Need of Hell* (1987). After that Crews published several more novels, including *The Knockout Artist* (1988), *Body* (1990), and *Celebration* (1998), and the novella *Where Does One Go When There's No Place to Go?* (1995). A collection of interviews, *Getting Naked with Harry Crews,* was published in 1999. He was also the subject of four documentaries, including the Emmy Award–winning *The Rough South of Harry Crews* (1991), and a film of his 1973 novel, *The Hawk Is Dying,* was released in 2006. Crews retired from the University of Florida in 1997 and continued work on a second volume of memoirs tentatively titled *Assault of Memory* until his death in 2012.

Crews's classic memoir *A Childhood: The Biography of a Place* is required reading for anyone seeking to understand the Rough South. "*A Childhood* is not about a forgotten America," writes Richard Sherrill, "it is about a part of America that has rarely, except in books like this, been properly discovered."[1] In this, the book's first chapter, Crews recalls the hard life and times of the sharecropper father he never knew.

> Everything about him—the way he stands, his every gesture—suggests a man of endless and exuberant energy, a man who believes in his bones that anything worth doing is worth overdoing. His is the gun that is always drawn; his is the head that is turned back under the whisky bottle. He has already had enough trouble and sickness and loss in his short life to have broken a lesser man, but there is more often than not a smile of almost maniacal joy.[2]

**FROM *A CHILDHOOD:***
***THE BIOGRAPHY OF A PLACE***

My first memory is of a time ten years before I was born, and the memory takes place where I have never been and involves my daddy whom I never knew. It was the middle of the night in the Everglades swamp in 1925, when my daddy woke his best friend Cecil out of a deep sleep in the bunkhouse just south of the floating dredge that was slowly chewing its way across the Florida Peninsula from Miami on the Atlantic to Naples on the Gulf of Mexico, opening a route and piling dirt for the highway that would come to be known as the Tamiami Trail. The night was dark as only a swamp can be dark and they could not see each other there in the bunkhouse. The rhythmic stroke of the dredge's engine came counterpoint to my daddy's shaky voice as he told Cecil what was wrong.

When Cecil finally did speak, he said: "I hope it was good, boy. I sho do."

"What was good?"

"That Indian. You got the clap."

But daddy had already known. He had thought of little else since it had become almost impossible for him to give water because of the fire that started in his stomach and felt like it burned through raw flesh every time he had to water off. He had thought from sunup to dark of the chickee where he had lain under the palm roof being eaten alive by swarming mosquitoes as he rode the flat-faced Seminole girl, whose name he never knew and who grunted like a sow and smelled like something shot in the woods.

He had not wanted her, but they had been in the swamp for three years. They worked around the clock, and if they weren't working or sleeping, their time was pretty much spent drinking or fighting or shooting gators. So since he could not have what he wanted, he tried to want what he could have, but it had been miserable, all of it because of the way she sounded and the way she smelled and the mosquitoes clotted about their faces thick as a veil and the heavy black flies that crawled over their legs.

"It weren't all that good," daddy said.

"No," said Cecil, "I don't reckon it's ever *that* good."

Gonorrhea was a serious hurt in the days before they had penicillin, and the hurt was compounded because daddy had resisted getting any treatment or even telling anybody until the pain finally forced him to do it.

"I don't know what I'm gone do."

"I do," Cecil said. "We gotta get out of the swamp and find you a doctor."

Cecil felt some obligation to help, not only because they had been friends since childhood but also because it was Cecil who had left Bacon County first to work on the trail and was later able to get his buddy a job working with him. It was all in the best tradition of "If you git work, write." And when Cecil wrote that there was steady work and good pay to be had in the Everglades, Ray had followed him down there.

He got on one of the gangs cutting right-of-way and in less than two years worked his way into the job of dredge operator. He was then not yet twenty and it was a sweet accomplishment for a boy who had no education, who was away from the farm for the first time in his life. But the clap soured the whole thing considerably.

Cecil was waiting for him when he came out of the doctor's office in the little town of Arcadia, Florida. It was the third doctor daddy had seen, and this one agreed with the other two. The word was final.

"He says I got to do it."

"Jesus," Cecil said.

"It's no other way."

"You gone do it?"

"I don't see no other way. Everyone I seen says I got to have one taken off. I guess I do if it ain't no other way."

"Jesus."

On the long drive back to the swamp in Cecil's Model T Ford in the shimmering heat of early summer, they didn't talk. Daddy did say one thing. "I won't ever have any children if they take it off. That's what the doctors said. All three of'm said it."

Cecil didn't say anything.

Did what I have set down here as memory actually happen? Did the two men say what I have recorded, think what I have said they thought? I do not know, nor do I any longer care. My knowledge of my daddy came entirely from the stories I have been told about him, stories told me by my mother, by my brother, who was old enough when he died to remember him first hand, by my other kin people, and by the men and women who knew him while he was alive.

It is demonstrably true that he went to work on the Tamiami Trail when he was seventeen and worked there until he was twenty-three. He did get the clap down there and he did lose a testicle because of it in the little town of Arcadia. He came back to Bacon County with money in his pocket and a gold watch inscribed on the back: "To Ray Crews, Pioneer Builder of the Tamiami Trail." Cecil got such a watch, as did several of the men who saw the job through from start to finish. Those are facts, but the rest of it came down to me through the mouths of more people than I could name. And I have lived with the stories of him for so long that they are as true as anything that ever actually happened to me. They are true because I think they are true. I, of course, had no alternative. It would have been impossible for me to think otherwise.

Jean-Paul Sartre in his autobiography *Words,* when writing about a man's tendency to smother his son, said his own father sired him and then had the decency to die. I've always thought that because my daddy died before I could ever know him, he became a more formidable memory, a greater influence, and a more palpable presence than he would ever have been had he lived. I'm not sure precisely what that says about me, but surely it must say more about me than it does about my daddy or his death. It also says a great deal about the people and the place I come from. Nothing is allowed to die in a society of story telling people. It is all—the good and the bad—carted up and brought along from one generation to the next. And everything that is brought along is colored and shaped by those who bring it.

If that is so, is what they bring with them true? I'm convinced that it is. Whatever violence may be done to the letter of their collective experience, the spirit of that experience remains intact and true. It is their notion of themselves, their understanding of who they are. And it was just for this reason that I started this book, because I have never been certain of who *I* am.

I have always slipped into and out of identities as easily as other people slip into and out of their clothes. Even my voice, its inflections and rhythms, does not seem entirely my own. On journalism assignments during which I've recorded extended interviews with politicians or film stars or truck drivers my own voice will inevitably become almost indistinguishable from the voice of the person with whom I'm talking by the third or fourth tape. Some natural mimic in me picks up whatever verbal tics or mannerisms it gets close to. That mimic in myself has never particularly pleased me, has in fact bothered me more than a little.

But whatever I am has its source back there in Bacon County, from which I left when I was seventeen years old to join the Marine Corps, and to which I never returned to live. I have always known, though, that part of me never left, could never leave, the place where I was born and, further, that what has been most significant in my life had all taken place by the time I was six years old. The search for those six years inevitably led me first to my daddy's early life and early death. Consequently, I have had to rely not only on my own memory but also on the memory of others for what follows here: the biography of a childhood which necessarily is the biography of a place, a way of life gone forever out of the world.

On a blowing March day in 1927, just before his twenty-third birthday, my daddy started back home with his friend Cecil in the Model T Ford. They had been down in the swamp for six years, though, and they were in no particular hurry. With a bottle of whiskey between them on the floorboard, it took nearly three weeks to make the 500 miles up the coast of Florida on U.S. Highway 1, a blacktop double-lane that followed the edge of the ocean up from Miami to Fort Pierce to Daytona and on to Jacksonville. From Jacksonville, they cut up toward the St. Marys River, which divides Florida from Georgia. The air went heavy with the smell of turpentine and pine trees as they drove on north through Folkston and Waycross and finally through Alma, a town of dirt streets, a cotton gin, a warehouse, two grocery stores, a seed and fertilizer store, and a doctor, who had—besides a cash register—some pens out back to hold his fees when they came in the form of chickens and goats and hogs.

In the car with him as they drove, there was a shoebox full of pictures of my daddy with five or six of his buddies, all of them holding whiskey bottles and pistols and rifles and coons and leashed alligators out there in the rugged dug-out sea of saw grass and mangrove swamp through which they had built the Tamiami Trail.

As I work, I have those pictures, yellowed now, still in a pasteboard shoebox where they have always been kept. For better than four decades, when the old shoebox wore out every year or so, the pictures have gone into a new shoebox. I once put them in a heavy leather album, the better to keep them, I thought. But after a week or so, I took them out again. The album seemed wrong. I did not like to look at them caught in the stiff, protected pages. I gave no thought to why I didn't like to see them there, but I believe now it was because a worn and vulnerable pasteboard box more accurately reflected my tenuous connection with him whom I never knew but whose presence has never left me, has always followed me just out of reach and hailing distance like some vague, half-realized shadow.

Looking at them, I think I see some of what my daddy was and some of what I have become. He was taller than I have ever grown, being as he was six feet two and weighing always about 170 pounds. Everything about him—the way he stands, his every gesture—suggests a man of endless and exuberant energy, a man who believes in his bones that anything worth doing is worth overdoing. His is the gun that is always drawn; his is the head that is turned back under the whiskey bottle. He has already had enough trouble and sickness and loss in his short life to have broken a lesser man, but there is more often than not a smile of almost maniacal joy, a smile stretched around a mouthful of teeth already loosened by pyorrhea, a disease which would take the two front teeth out of the top gum before he died shortly after my birth.

They made their way up the coast of Florida, stopping here and there, staying at one place in Jacksonville for nearly a week, drinking and being rowdy in the best way of young men who have been on a hard job and now have money in their pockets, always talking, rehashing again what they had done and where they had been and where they were going and what they hoped for themselves and their families, even though my daddy carried with him the sure and certain knowledge that he would never have any children.

"It ain't the worst thing that could happen," Cecil said. "You ain't but a partial gelding."

"That ain't real funny, Cecil."

"I reckon not. But it still ain't the worst thing."

They were on the St. Marys River in a rented rowboat, drifting, drinking, ignoring the bobbing corks at the ends of their lines, not caring whether they caught anything or not after six years in a swamp where fish had been as plentiful as mosquitoes.

Daddy said: "If it ain't the worst thing, it'll do till the worst thing comes along."

Cecil gave his slow drunken smile, a smile at once full of kidding and love. "The worst thing woulda been to let that old man and his boy eat you alive."

"They'd a had to by God do it."

"Oh, they'd a done it all right. They'd already et several before they started looking at how tender you was."

"I guess. Dying cain't be all that hard though. Without thinking about it at all, people drop dead right and left."

Cecil said: "It's one thing to drop dead. It's sumpin else to have your head pulled off."

These were not violent men, but their lives were full of violence. When daddy first went down to the Everglades, he started on a gang that cut the advance right-of-way and, consequently, was out of the main camp for days, at times for more than a week. When he almost got killed working out there on the gang, Cecil almost killed a man because of it. Daddy's foreman was an old man, grizzled, stinking always of chewing tobacco and sweat and whiskey, and known throughout the construction company as a man mean as a bee-stung dog. He didn't have to dislike you to hurt you, even cripple you. He just liked to hurt and cripple, and he had a son that was very much his daddy's boy.

Because my daddy was only seventeen when he went out there, the full fury of their peculiar humor fell upon him, so much so that once it almost cost him a leg in what was meant to look like an accident when a cable snapped. If it had only been some sort of initiation rite, it would have one day ended. But daddy was under a continual hazing that was meant to draw blood.

When he got back to camp, he found Cecil over by the mess wagon. When he'd finished eating, daddy said: "I'm scared, Cecil. That old man and his boy's gone kill me."

Cecil was still at his beans. "He ain't gone kill you."

"I think he means to."

Cecil put his plate down and said: "No, he ain't cause you and me's gone settle it right now."

Cecil was six feet seven inches tall and weighed between 250 and 275 pounds depending upon the season of the year.

"Cecil, that old man don't know how strong he is his own self."

"He's about to find out. You just keep his boy off me. I'll take care of the old man."

They found the old man and his boy on the dredge and the fight was as short as it was brutal. They locked up and went off the dredge into the mud, the old man on the bottom but with his hands locked on Cecil's throat. He would have killed him, too, if Cecil had not thought to provide himself with a ten-inch steel ringbolt in the back pocket of his overalls which he used to break the old man's skull. But even with his head cracked, it took two men to get his hands from around Cecil's throat.

The old man was taken out to a hospital in Miami and his boy, whom daddy had managed to mark superficially, a cut across his forehead and another down the length of his back, went with him and nothing more was heard of the matter. At least for the moment. But a little over two months later word came into the swamp that the old man and his boy were coming back.

"Me and Luther's comin back to settle. We gone take the biguns one by one and the littluns two by two."

Cecil sent word back on a piece of ruled tablet paper. "If you and that boy come out here for me and Ray, have your boxes built and ready. You gone need'm before you git out again."

For whatever reason, the old man and his boy did not come back into the swamp. The matter had been settled. Surely not to everybody's satisfaction, but settled nonetheless. They had done it themselves without recourse to law or courts. That was not unusual for them and their kind.

Up in Jeff Davis County, just about where I was born and raised, a woman's husband was killed and she—seven months pregnant—was the only witness to the killing. When the sheriff tried to get her to name the man who'd done it, she only pointed to her swelling stomach and said:

"He knows who did it, and when the time comes, he will settle it." And that was all she ever said.

In Bacon County, the sheriff was the man who tried to keep the peace, but if you had any real trouble, you did not go to him for help to make it right. You made it right yourself or else became known in the county as a man who was defenseless without the sheriff at his back. If that ever happened, you would be brutalized and savaged endlessly because of it. Men killed other men oftentimes not because there had been some offense that merited death, but simply because there had been an offense, any offense. As many men have been killed over bird dogs and fence lines in South Georgia as anything else.

Bacon County was that kind of place as they drove into it finally toward the middle of March in 1927. There were very few landowners. Most people farmed on shares or standing rent. Shares meant the owner would supply the land, fertilizer, seed, mules, harness, plows, and at harvest take half of everything that was made. On standing rent, you agreed to pay the landowner a certain sum of money for the use of the land. He took nothing but the money. Whether on shares or on standing rent, they were still tenant farmers and survival was a day-to-day crisis as real as rickets in the bones of their children or the worms that would sometimes rise out of their children's stomachs and nest in their throats so that they had to be pulled out by hand to keep the children from choking.

The county itself was still young then, having been formed in 1914 and named for Senator Augustus Octavius Bacon, who was born in Bryan County and lived out much of his life in the city of Macon. Bacon County is as flat as the map it's drawn on and covered with pine trees and blackjack oak and sand ridges and a few black gum and bay trees down in the bottomland near running creeks. Jeff Davis and Appling counties are to the north of it, Pierce and Coffee counties to the east, and the largest county in the state, Ware, joins its southern border.

There was a section of Bacon County famous all over Georgia for moonshining and bird dogs and violence of one kind or another. It was called Scuffletown, not because it was a town or even a crossroads with a store in it, but because as everybody said: "They always scuffling up there." Sometimes the scuffling was serious; sometimes not.

About a month before my daddy drove back into the county, Jay Scott opened his mouth once too often to a man named Junior "Bad Eye" Carter. He was called Bad Eye because he was putting up wire fence as a young man and the staple he was driving into the post glanced off the hammer and drove itself deep into his right eye. He rode a mule all the way to Alma, where the doctor pulled out the staple, but the eye was gone forever. Having only a left eye gave him an intense, even crazy stare. Talk was that he could conjure with that unblinking, staring left eye.

For a long time there had been bad blood between Bad Eye and Jay Scott over a misunderstanding about some hogs. Bad Eye was chopping wood for the stove when Jay walked up. The woodpile was just inside the wire fence that ran along the public road. Jay stopped in the road and for a long time just watched him. But finally, watching wasn't enough.

"Watch out, old man, a splinter don't fly up there and put out that other eye."

Bad Eye kept on chopping, the strokes of the ax regular as clock ticking. He never even looked up.

"Splinter in that other eye, we'd have to call you Bad *Face*."

Ruby, Bad Eye's wife, saw the whole thing from the water shelf on the back porch of the house where she was standing. Jay saw Ruby on the back porch and said, loud enough for her to hear: "Why don't you git your old woman out here? They tell me she does most of the ax work for you anyhow."

That was when Bad Eye looked up, a big vein standing in his forehead.

"You stand out there in a public road and talk all you want to. But don't come over the fence onto my land. Don't reckon you'd have the stomach for that, would you?"

Jay came across the ditch, put one foot in the wire and one hand on top of the fence post, getting ready to climb up and swing over. But he never did. That was as far as he got. Bad Eye, who had started chopping again, never missed a stroke, but drove the blade of the ax through Jay's wrist and two inches deep into the top of the post. Ruby said she bet you could hear him scream for five miles. Said she bet somebody thought they was slaughtering hogs, late in the year as it was.

Jay tied off his arm with his belt and then fainted in the ditch. When he woke up, Bad Eye was sitting on the woodpile with the bloody stump of a hand.

"This here hand belongs to me now, sumbitch. Found it on my land."

Jay fainted again. Two of Bad Eye Carter's kinsmen were killed in the fight to get the hand back. Jay wanted to give it a Christian burial. They never did get it back, but Bad Eye went fishing one day and didn't come back. They finally found him floating in Little Satilla River. His blue and wrinkled body had raised the fifty pounds of rusty plow points tied about his ankles.

It was this part of the county that my daddy and his people came from, back up in what's known as the Forks of the Hurricane, not far from Carter-town, which was not a town either but simply a section of the county where almost every farmer was named Carter. The Forks of the Hurricane was where two wide creeks rose in Big Hurricane Swamp and flowed out across the county, one creek called Little Hurricane and the other Big Hurricane. I was a grown man before I realized that the word we were saying was *hurricane* because it was universally pronounced harrikin.

So daddy came back to the home place, where his own daddy, Dan, and his mama, Lilly, lived with their family, a family which, like most families then, was big. His brothers and sisters were named Vera, D. W., Bertha, Leroy—who was crippled from birth—Melvin, Ora, Pascal, and Audrey.

Daddy's granddaddy had once been a slave owner and a large landholder, but his family, like most families in that time and place, had fallen on evil days. They still owned the land they lived on, but they had to constantly fight the perpetual mortgage held by the bank. There was a place to put your head down and usually enough to eat, but when daddy came home from the swamp, farmers were saying there wasn't enough cash money in the county to close up a dead man's eyes.

Daddy proceeded to do what so many young men have done before him, that is, if not to make a fool of himself, at least to behave so improvidently that he ran through what little money he'd been able to get together working in Florida. Cecil drove off to live in the mountains of North Georgia, so daddy bought himself a Model T Ford and he bought his mama a piano and he bought himself a white linen suit and a white wide-brimmed hat. I don't know how he could have managed it after the car and the piano, but he may have bought himself several of those white suits, judging from the number of pictures I have of him dressed in one. In the first flower of his manhood, he was a great poser for pictures, always with a young lady and sometimes with several young ladies.

I lift the lid off the shoebox now and reach in. The first picture I see is of him, his foot propped up on the running board of his Model T Ford, standing there with a young lady wearing her bonnet, the sun in their faces, smiling. And looking into his face is like looking into my own. His cheekbones are high and flat, and a heavy ridge of bone casts a perpetual shadow over his eyes. There is a joy and great confidence in the way he stands, his arm around the girl, a cock-of-the-walk tilt to his pelvis. And along with that photograph there are others: him sitting under a tree with another young lady, she short-haired and wearing a brimless little hat almost like a cap; him leaning against the front fender of the Model T, still in that immaculate white linen suit with yet another young lady; him standing between two girls in their Sunday frocks on the bank of a river, probably the Little Hurricane.

There is no doubt that in that time he was, as they say in Bacon County, fond of lying out with dry cattle. Maidens, or at least those young ladies who had never had a child, were called dry cattle after the fact that a cow does not give milk until after giving birth to a calf. An unflattering way to refer to women, God knows, but then those were unflattering times.

He was also bad to go to the bottle, as so many men have been in the family. He drank his whiskey and lay out with dry cattle and stayed in the woods at night running foxes and talking and laughing with his friends and was vain enough to have it recorded as often as he could with somebody's camera. It must have been a good time for him then, a time when he did not yet have a wife and children or the obligations that always come with them.

Because of the stories I've heard about him, his recklessness, his tendency to stay up all night and stay in the woods when he probably should have been doing something else, and his whiskey drinking, I have often wondered if in some way that he could not or would not have said, he felt his own early death just around the bend. He had been an extremely sickly child and Granddaddy Dan Crews had never thought that he would raise him to manhood. When daddy was three years old, he got rheumatic fever and from it developed what they called then a leaking heart. After he developed the trouble with his heart, apparently from the fever, his kidneys did not work the way they should and he would swell up from fluid retention and spent much of his childhood either sitting in a chair or half reclining on a bed.

The doctors in Baxley and Blackshear and even as far away as Waycross—about thirty-five miles—had been unable to help him. Granddaddy Dan in desperation mailed off for some pills he saw advertised in the almanac. Daddy's brother, Uncle Melvin, told me that when the medicine came, the pills were as big as a quarter, the size you might try on a horse. Granddaddy Dan took one look at them and decided he couldn't give them to his boy as little and sick as he was. So he put them on the crosspiece up over the door and forgot about them. But daddy, then only five years old, but already showing the hardheaded willfulness that would follow him through his short life, began to take the pills without anybody knowing about it. Whether it was the pills or the grace of God, the swelling began to go down and within a month he was able to get out in the field and hoe a little bit and in the coming weeks he gradually got better.

But he always had that murmur in his heart. Mama says she could hear it hissing and skipping when she lay with him at night, her head on his chest, and it was that hissing, skipping heart which eventually killed him. That and his predisposition to hurt himself. There seemed to be something in him then and later, a kind of demon, madness even, that drove him to work too hard, to carouse the same way, and always to be rowdier than was good for him.

Maybe it was his conviction that he would never have children that was hurting him, doing bad things in his head and making him behave as he did. He had to have thought of it often and it had to give him pain. Families were important then, and they were important not because the children were useful in the fields to break corn and hoe cotton and drop potato vines in wet weather or help with hog butchering and all the rest of it. No, they were important because a large family was the only thing a man could be sure of having. Nothing else was certain. If a man had no education or even if he did, the hope of putting money in the bank and keeping it there or owning a big piece of land free and clear, such hope was so remote that few men ever let themselves think about it. The timber in the county was of no consequence, and there was very little rich bottomland. Most of the soil was poor and leached out, and commercial fertilizer was dear as blood. But a man didn't need good land or stands of hardwood trees to have babies. All he needed was balls and the inclination.

And in that very fact, the importance of family, lies what I think of as the rotten spot at the center of my life or, said another way, the rotten spot at the center of what my life might have been if circumstances had been different. I come from people who believe the *home place* is as vital and necessary as the beating of your own heart. It is that single house where you were born, where you lived out your childhood, where you grew into young manhood. It is your anchor in the world, that place, along with the memory of your kinsmen at the long supper table every night and the knowledge that it would always exist, if nowhere but in memory.

Such a place is probably important to everybody everywhere, but in Bacon County—although nobody to my knowledge ever said it—the people understand that if you do not have a home place, very little will ever be yours, really *belong* to you in the world. Ever since I reached manhood, I have looked back upon that time when I was a boy and thought how marvelous beyond saying it must be to spend the first ten or fifteen years of your life in the same house—the *home* place—moving among the same furniture, seeing on the familiar walls the same pictures of blood kin. And more marvelous still, to be able to return to that place of your childhood and see it through the eyes of a man, with everything you see set against that long-ago, little boy's memory of how things used to be.

But because we were driven from pillar to post when I was a child, there is nowhere I can think of as the home place. Bacon County is my home place, and I've had to make do with it. If I think of where I come from, I think of the entire county. I think of all its people and its customs and all its loveliness and all its ugliness.

# DOROTHY ALLISON, "Deciding to Live"

Born in 1949, Dorothy Allison grew up in Greenville, South Carolina. She earned a bachelor's degree from Florida Presbyterian College and later studied anthropology at Florida State University before moving to New York where she wrote articles for *Poets and Writers* magazine and the *Village Voice* as well as numerous feminist publications. Allison's poetry collection, *The Women Who Hate Me,* was published in 1983 and was followed in 1988 by the story collection *Trash,* which won the Lambda Literary Award for fiction. Her highly acclaimed first novel, *Bastard Out of Carolina* (1992), was a *New York Times* best seller and a finalist for the National Book Award. Allison's other works include the essay collection *Skin: Talking about Sex, Class and Literature* (1994), the memoir *Two or Three Things I Know for Sure* (1995), and the novels *Cave-dweller* (1998) and the forthcoming *She Who.* In 2007 she was awarded the Robert Penn Warren Award for Fiction and elected to the Fellowship of Southern Writers. A frequent lecturer at colleges around the country, Allison lives with her family in northern California.

A self-described "Zen Baptist" and "working-class writer," Allison battled through years of poverty and abuse before she became "the one who got away, who got glasses from the Lions Club, a job from Lyndon Johnson's War on Poverty, and finally went away to college on scholarship." In "Deciding to Live," she vividly recalls her early struggles and the artistic awakening that led her to "get it down, to tell it again, to make sense of something—by God just once—to be real in the world, without lies or evasions or sweet-talking nonsense."[1]

I don't believe in fate, except some days. And I don't believe that fighting really hard and sacrificing necessarily makes a difference, but sometimes it does. I sometimes wonder how our family has survived at all. I feel that about working-class women and families, that some do everything and lose everything. And some don't. I just don't see enough of it in literature. I don't see enough honor paid.[2]

There was a day in my life when I decided to live.

After my childhood, after all that long terrible struggle to simply survive, to escape my stepfather, uncles, speeding Pontiacs, broken glass, and rotten floorboards, or that inevitable death by misadventure that claimed so many of my cousins; after watching so many die around me, I had not imagined that I would ever need to make such a choice. I had imagined the hunger for life in me insatiable, endless, and unshakable.

I became an escapee—one of the ones others talked about. I became the one who got away, who got glasses from the Lions Club, a job from Lyndon Johnson's War on Poverty, and finally went away to college on scholarship. There I met the people I always read about: girls whose fathers loved them—innocently; boys who drove cars they had not stolen; whole armies of the upper and middle classes I had not truly believed to be real; the children to whom I could not help but compare myself. I matched their innocence, their confidence, their capacity to trust, to love, to be generous against the bitterness, the rage, the pure and terrible hatred that consumed me. Like so many others who had gone before me, I began to dream longingly of my own death.

I began to court it. Cowardly, traditionally—that is, in the tradition of all those others like me, through drugs and drinking and stubbornly putting myself in the way of other people's violence. Even now, I cannot believe how it was that everything I survived became one more reason to want to die.

But one morning, I limped into my mama's kitchen and sat alone at her dining table. I was limping because I had pulled a muscle in my thigh and cracked two ribs in a fight with a woman I thought I loved. I remember that morning in all its details, the scratches on my wrists from my lover's fingernails, the look on Mama's face as she got ready to go to work—how she tried not to fuss over me, and the way I could not meet her eyes. It was in my mama's face that I saw myself, in my mama's silence, for she behaved as if I were only remotely the daughter she had loved and prayed for. She treated me as if I were in a way already dead, or about to die—as unreachable, as dangerous as one of my uncles on a three-day toot. *That* was so humiliating it broke my pride. My mouth opened to cry out, but I shut it stubbornly. It was in that moment I made my decision—not actually the decision to live, but the decision not to die on her. I shut my mouth on my grief and my rage, and began to pretend as if I would live, as if there were reason enough to fight my way out of the trap I had made for myself—though I had not yet figured out what that reason was.

I limped around tight-lipped through the months it took me to find a job in another city and disappear. I took a bus to the city and spoke to no one, signed the papers that made me a low-level government clerk, and wound up sitting in a motel room eating peanut butter sandwiches so I could use the per diem to buy respectable skirts and blouses—the kind of clothes I had not worn since high school. Every evening I would walk the ten blocks from the training classes to the motel, where I could draw the heavy drapes around me, open the windows, and sit wrapped around by the tent of those drapes. There I would huddle and smoke my hoarded grass.

Part of me knew what I was doing, knew the decision I was making. A much greater part of me could not yet face it. I was trying to make solid my decision to live, but I did not know if I could. I had to change my life, take baby steps into a future I did not trust, and I began by looking first to the ground on which I stood, how I had become the woman I was. By day I played at being what the people who were training me thought I was—a college graduate and a serious worker, a woman settling down to a practical career with the Social Security Administration. I imagined that if I played at it long enough, it might become true, but I felt like an actress in the role for which she was truly not suited. It took all my concentration not to laugh at inappropriate moments and to keep my mouth shut when I did not know what to say at all.

There was only one thing I could do that helped me through those weeks. Every evening I sat down with a yellow legal-size pad, writing out the story of my life. I wrote it all: everything I could remember, all the stories I had ever been told, the names, places, images—how blood had arched up the wall one terrible night that recurred persistently in my dreams—the dreams themselves, the people in the dreams. My stepfather, my uncles and cousins, my desperate aunts and their more desperate daughters.

I wrote out my memories of the women. My terror and lust for my own kind; the shouts and arguments; the long, slow glances and slower approaches; the way my hands always shook when I would finally touch the flesh I could barely admit I wanted, the way I could never ask for what I wanted, never accept if they offered. I twisted my fingers and chewed my lips over the subtle and deliberate lies I had told myself and them, the hidden stories of my life that lay in disguise behind the mocking stories I did tell—all the stories of my family, my childhood, and the relentless, deadening poverty and shame I had always tried to hide because I knew no one would believe what I could tell them about it.

Writing it all down was purging. Putting those stories on paper took them out of the nightmare realm and made me almost love myself for being able to finally face them. More subtly, it gave me a way to love the people I wrote about—even the ones I had fought with or hated. In that city where I knew no one, I had no money and nothing to fill the evenings except washing out my clothes, reading cheap paperbacks, and trying to understand how I had come to be in that place. I was not the kind of person who could imagine asking for help or talking about my personal business. Nor was I fool enough to think that could be done without risking what little I had gained. Still, though I knew the danger of revealing too much about my life, I did not imagine anyone reading my rambling, ranting stories. I was writing for myself, trying to shape my life outside my terrors and helplessness, to make it visible and real in a tangible way, in the way other people's seemed real—the lives I had read about in books. I had been a child who believed in books, but I had never found me or mine in print. My family was always made over into caricatures or flattened into saintlike stock characters. I never found my lovers in their strength and passion. Outside my mother's stubbornness and my own outraged arrogance, I had never found any reason to believe in myself. But I had the idea I could make it exist on those pages.

Days, I went to training sessions, memorized codes, section numbers, and memo formats. Nights, I wrote my stories. I would pull out scraps of paper at work to make notes about things I wanted to write about, though most of those scraps just wound up tucked in my yellow pad. What poured out of me could not be planned or controlled; it came up like water under pressure at its own pace, pushing my fear ahead of it. By the end of the month, I'd taken to sitting on the motel roof—no longer stoned, but still writing. By then I was also writing letters to all the women I really didn't expect to see again, explaining the things that writing my stories had made real to me. I did not intend to mail those letters, and never did. The letters themselves were stories—mostly lies—self-justifying, awkward, and desperate.

I finished that month, got assigned to a distant city, put away my yellow papers, and moved—making sure no one who knew me from before could find me. I threw myself into the women's community, fell in love every third day, and started trying to be serious about writing—poems and essays and the beginnings of stories. I even helped edit a feminist magazine. Throughout that time I *told* stories—mostly true stories about myself and my family and my lovers in a drawl that made them all funnier than they were. Though that was mostly a good time for me, I wrote nothing that struck me as worth the trouble of actually keeping. I did not tuck those new stories away with the yellow pads I had sealed up in a blanket box of my mother's. I told myself the yellow pages were as raw and unworked as I felt myself to be, and the funny stories I was telling people were better, were the work of someone who was going to be a "real" writer. It was three years before I pulled out those old yellow sheets and read them, and saw how thin and self-serving my funny stories had become.

The stuff on those yellow pads was bitter. I could not recognize myself in that bitter whiny hateful voice telling over all those horrible violent memories. They were, oddly, the same stories I'd been telling for years, but somehow drastically different. Telling them out loud, I'd made them ironic and playful. The characters became eccentric, fascinating—not the cold-eyed, mean, and nasty bastards they were on the yellow pages, the frightened dangerous women and the more dangerous and just as frightened men. I could not stand it, neither the words on the page nor what they told me about myself. My neck and teeth began to ache, and I was not at all sure I really wanted to live with this stuff inside me. But holding on to them, reading them over again, became a part of the process of survival, of deciding once more to live—and clinging to that decision. For me those stories were not distraction or entertainment; they were the stuff of my life, and they were necessary in ways I could barely understand.

Still I took those stories and wrote them again. I made some of them funny. I made some of them poems. I made the women beautiful, wounded but courageous, while the men disappeared into the background. I put hope in the children and passion in the landscape while my neck ached and tightened, and I wanted nothing so much as a glass of whiskey or a woman's anger to distract me. None of it was worth the pain it caused me. None of it made my people or me more understandable. None of it told the truth, and every lie I wrote proved to me I wasn't worth my mother's grief at what she thought was my wasted life, or my sister's cold fear of what I might tell other people about them.

I put it all away. I began to live my life as if nothing I did would survive the day in which I did it. I used my grief and hatred to wall off my childhood, my history, my sense of being part of anything greater than myself. I used women and liquor, constant righteous political work, and a series of grimly endured ordeals to convince myself that I had nothing to decide, that I needed nothing more than what other people considered important to sustain me. I worked on a feminist journal. I read political theory, history, psychology, and got a degree in anthropology as if that would quiet the roar in my own head. I watched other women love each other, war with each other, and take each other apart while never acknowledging the damage we all did to each other. I went through books and conferences, CR groups and study groups, organizing committees and pragmatic coalition fronts. I did things I did not understand for reasons I could not begin to explain just to be in motion, to be trying to do something, change something in a world I wanted desperately to make over but could not imagine for myself.

That was all part of deciding to live, though I didn't know it. Just as I did not know that what I needed had to come up from inside me, not be laid over the top of my head. The bitterness with which I had been born, that had been nurtured in me, could not be eased with a lover or a fight or any number of late-night meetings and clumsily written manifestos. It may never be eased. The decision to live when everything inside and out shouts death is not a matter of moments but years, and no one has ever told me how you know when it is accomplished.

But a night finally came when I woke up sweaty and angry and afraid I'd never go back to sleep again. All those stories were rising up my throat. Voices were echoing in my neck, laughter behind my ears, and I was terribly terribly afraid that I was finally as crazy as my kind was supposed to be. But the desire to live was desperate in my belly, and the stories I had hidden all those years were the blood and bone of it. To get it down, to tell it again, to make something—by God just once—to be real in the world, without lies or evasions or sweet-talking nonsense. I got up and wrote a story all the way through. It was one of the stories from the yellow pages, one of the ones I had rewritten, but it was different again. It wasn't truly me or my mama or my girlfriends, or really any of the people who'd been there, but it had the feel, the shit-kicking anger and grief of my life. It wasn't that whiny voice, but it had the drawl, and it had, too, the joy and pride I sometimes felt in me and mine. It was not biography and yet not lies, and it resonated to the pulse of my sisters' fear and my desperate shame, and it ended with all the questions and decisions still waiting—most of all the decision to live.

It was a rough beginning—my own shout of life against death, of shape and substance against silence and confusion. It was most of all my deep abiding desire to live fleshed and strengthened on the page, a way to tell the truth as a kind of magic not cheapened or distorted by a need to please any damn body at all. Without it, I cannot imagine my own life. Without it, I have no way to know who I am.

One time, twice, once in a while again, I get it right. Once in a while, I can make the world I know real on the page. I can make the women and men I love breathe out loud in an empty room, the dreams I dare not speak shape up in the smoky darkness of other people's imaginations. Writing these stories is the only way I know to make sure of my ongoing decision to live, to set moment to moment a small piece of stubbornness against an ocean of ignorance and obliteration.

I write stories. I write fiction. I put on the page a third look at what I've seen in life—the condensed and reinvented experience of a cross-eyed, working-class lesbian, addicted to violence, language, and hope, who has made the decision to live, is determined to live, on the page and on the street, for me and mine.

# LARRY BROWN, *On Fire: A Personal Account of Life and Death and Choices*

Larry Brown was born in 1951 in Oxford, Mississippi. His family moved to Memphis, Tennessee, when he was child before returning to Oxford, where his father worked as a farmer and his mother ran a small country store. After high school Brown served two years in the marines and later joined the Oxford Fire Department, where he worked for seventeen years. In 1980 he began writing in his spare time, producing several novels and stories before publishing his first collection, *Facing the Music,* in 1988. A year later Brown published his first novel, *Dirty Work* (1989), and in 1990 the story collection *Big Bad Love,* which was made into a film in 2001. Brown's next two novels, *Joe* (1991) and *Father and Son* (1996), both received the Southern Book Award for Fiction. His other works include the memoir *On Fire* (1993), the essay collection *Billy Ray's Farm* (2001), and the novels *Fay* (2000) and *The Rabbit Factory* (2003). In 2004 Brown died suddenly from heart failure and was laid to rest on his farm in Tula, Mississippi. His last novel, a work in progress titled *A Miracle of Catfish,* was published in 2007. Since then Brown's life and work have been the subject of a documentary, *The Rough South of Larry Brown* (2008); a book of critical essays, *Larry Brown and the Blue-Collar South* (2008); and the biography *Larry Brown: A Writer's Life* (2011).

Brown's memoir, *On Fire,* began "out of boredom," he said, during those long, sleepless nights at the Oxford firehouse when there was nothing to do but "get up and make some coffee and write down everything that had happened that day."[1] The passages included here are as haunting and true as anything he ever wrote.

What [being a firefighter] showed me was that poverty causes many of these terrible tragedies, because the people who are on the lower end of the economic scale are the ones who have the lousy housing, who live in the firetraps. Why? Because the wiring is bad, because somebody's been careless, somebody's put a penny in the fuse box and there's a wire under the rug, or the smoke detector doesn't have a battery in it, or their child has never been told not to play with matches and catches the curtains on fire, then catches their pajamas on fire. Of course, it can happen to anybody. Some fellow can go out and have a car wreck in his big Cadillac. But so many times you may go from the biggest mansion in the city of Oxford that morning down to the most squalid shack on the other side of town that evening. You can figure which one's going to be the worst. . . . All that stuff is what I write about—and the way it made me feel.[2]

**FROM *ON FIRE: A PERSONAL ACCOUNT***
**OF *LIFE AND DEATH AND CHOICES***

The year is 1975. I have been a firefighter for less than two years, and I'm in a 1974 red-and-white LTD, speeding down through the Mississippi Delta to light a Christmas Tree this summer night. There are about six other off-duty firefighters in the car with me, and it's ten o'clock in the morning, and we're all drinking beer. Actually some of us are getting a little happy. We've stopped at a beer store in Batesville and we're having a wonderful time, heading off into adventure.

We come down out of the hills and flatten out into the Delta where there are few trees and thousands of acres of cotton growing. The heat lies in ripples over the land but we have the air conditioner going full blast. I feel myself getting a little woozy and I know it's going to be a long day.

The bad thing about drinking beer on a trip to a fire school is that eventually you're going to have to start making pit stops. It's best to hold it for as long as you can, because once you start peeing, that's it. Before long you'll be stopping all the time.

The first one we make is behind a cotton pen on a long deserted stretch of road with few houses. The Highway Patrol would frown on our actions if they happened to come by, so we all try to hide behind the little building. It's still a long way to Greenwood, but there are plenty of beer stores between here and there. Just how many, we don't know yet, but we'll find out. We hope to arrive in Greenwood around one, maybe two. We were supposed to arrive in Greenwood around twelve. But we don't have a whole lot of responsibility about us on a trip like this. The trunk is packed full of our turnout gear, our coats and boots and helmets and gloves. I've never been to a Christmas Tree before, and I'm a little nervous about it. We've been told that the temperature will reach 1,500 degrees.

We stop at a couple more beer stores. We go past the penitentiary, Parchman, see the high walls and the barbed-wire fences, and we shake our heads, glad we're not in there.

We notice that the price of beer goes up the deeper we get into the Delta. It's nearly twice what we pay for it in Oxford, but we don't complain. We can't stop now. But we're having to stop the car every twenty minutes because some of us have stronger bladders than others, and when the pain gets too bad, it doesn't matter where we are. We'll leap out behind trees, jump down in ditches, while the others sit in the car with the windows down and hoot and scream and throw beer cans. We're an accident looking for a place to happen.

We roll into Greenwood an hour late, all of us happy and find the classroom and walk in as all heads turn to view the latecomers. They all shake their heads. They all know we're those crazy fuckers from Oxford. The class has been underway for some time. The man is explaining the properties of Liquid Propane gas, LP, and it's no laughing matter. Three Vicksburg firefighters have recently been killed in an LP explosion, burned to death and beyond recognition, a fire truck destroyed. We look at slides of what was left of their turnouts. We're told that we don't want to see the slides of the men who had worn them. We sit all the way to the back of the room, and we don't take notes because none of us thought to bring notebook or pencil. The class goes on and on and we're hungry and still thirsty.

We're told to be back just before dark, and then they turn us loose on Greenwood. We decide to go looking for something to eat.

The place to eat turns out to be a bar that serves hamburgers and things. We all go in and order beer and food and stay there most of the afternoon. We figure it doesn't make any sense to sober up now, so we don't.

When dark arrives, we're in a parking lot with a new lime-green fire truck, maybe a Seagrave or a Mack, and about a hundred other firefighters from cities all across Mississippi. The State Fire Academy is teaching this course. A large LP gas truck is parked off to one side, and in the center of the parking lot there is a big framework of metal pipes that resembles the rough shape of a Christmas tree, with a base about fifteen or twenty feet in width. A line has been laid from the gas truck to the tree, and the Greenwood Fire Department's pumper has charged the hand lines. A flaming rag will be laid on an arm of the tree, and the gas in the truck will be turned on, and a ball of fire about twenty feet tall will erupt and intensify, and we will go up to the thing with only our hoses and turnouts for protection, and we will shut it down while holding the fire at bay.

One group of firefighters gets up to be first in line on the hoses, but we step up and tell them that we want to go first. We man the hoses and the Oxford firefighters pick the man who will have to crawl up and shut off the valve, who happens to be me.

The whole town has turned out to see this. The pumper is throttled up, adrenaline kicks in with a rush, the hoses are as hard as iron. Two groups of three men form on each side, and I hang back with the group on the left, my position the last one in the line. Some instructors from the academy stand with us. There is no joking or laughing now. One little fuckup and somebody will be burned badly. Everybody is ready. A firefighter in full turnout gear walks to the pipe framework, the Tree, and lays a rag on it that has been soaked in kerosene. He lights it with a cigarette lighter and runs out of the way. The rag lies there burning, one small point of light in the night, and the man at the gas truck opens the valve. Holes have been bored in all the pipes, and the gas rushes out in small blue flames, dancing in tiny blue spots only for a moment. He increases the volume and all the flames come together into one, and it starts to roar and change color. The blue-and-white fire comes out like water under pressure and it completely obscures the pipes. It towers over our heads and the awful heat touches us where we stand, fifty feet back from it. The two groups open the nozzles of the hoses in a fog pattern, and we start forward. The instructors tell us to keep our heads down, make sure our face shields are down. Our collars are pulled up and snapped tightly around our throats, and the gauntlets of our gloves are pulled up over the sleeves of our coats.

The two groups walk closely together, meshing the two fog streams so that there is an unbroken barrier of cool water between us and the fire. We get closer and the flames push forward over the fog streams. The instructors call, Steady, steady now. We go forward until we stand two feet from the living ball of fire. It is incredibly bright now, the flames reflected on the face shields of my companions. All of us are relying on each other. We have to trust each other not to run. The instructor makes us stand there, steady, until he sees that we are holding the fire at bay, and then he points to me. I drop to my knees and go forward, and I crawl between his spread boots. The parking lot is brighter now than day. There is a valve right in front of the instructor's boots, and I lie on the wet black bright asphalt and reach out with my gloved hand, the killing fire right above me, the terrible heat right over my neck. I turn the valve swiftly until it closes and the fire diminishes, drops, goes out. I get up, go back to my position at the end of the hose, and we back away, wet, steaming, droplets of water obscuring our vision behind the face shields. We did it right. At other times, at other Christmas Trees in the future, in other cities, it will not be done right, and once I will see my training officer badly burned because of the fear of a stranger, and take on a scar on his forearm the size of an elbow patch, something he will wear forever, but this time, this first time, we do it right.

Our gig done, we head for another bar.

We're still in Greenwood and we're still in a bar and there is a band from California playing. They have lots of horns and a pretty female lead singer and we're dancing in our uniforms with all the women in the bar. Some of the other firefighters have joined us until there are so many firefighters that we have taken over the bar with our happy debauchery and our loud jokes.

There is a woman in this bar with a set of breasts that are spectacular, that are not to be believed, that have attracted the eyes of every man in the bar. She dances so fine that I think she has to be a professional dancer. I go over and dance with her, but I'm no match for her. I don't know what I'm doing, I'm just flopping and jerking my body around on the dance floor, making a fool of myself. Her breasts are as big as my head, but she's not a big woman. She must be a go-go dancer. Before long she starts slinging me around like a rag doll. She seems stronger than me and I'm embarrassed. She finally slings me into a chair and oh how the boys do howl. I'm having a sinking spell. I don't feel very good and we're still a long way from home.

It's later still and we're drunker still, riding back up through the Delta, and the lights are on outside the prison camps, and they look smoky, and scary, and our driver gets on the car's PA system, which is hooked into the fire department radio, and announces through the outside speakers that WE WILL NOT PISS AT THIS TIME, 10-4, over and over, very loudly, loud enough to nearly wake the dead, in fact, and I hope nobody comes after us, that they won't lock us into the penitentiary for disturbing the peace.

We ride back up into North Mississippi and we're not so chipper now, some of us having sinking spells, some of us asleep. When we finally get back to Oxford, the fire station is dark and quiet, the men on duty asleep. I get in my car and go home, not to my home in my house trailer but to Preston's, my father-in-law's home, where MA is sleeping because I've been gone and she is pregnant with Billy Ray. I crawl into bed with her and she sleepily asks me how it was. I say it was okay, thinking about how I tried to dance with a go-goer, and I hold onto the round ball of her stomach, where Billy Ray sleeps and grows, and I wonder what he is, what he will be.

We go to a house in Oxford down on North Seventh Street, the same neighborhood where we burned down all the old decrepit houses years ago to clear the way for improvement and progress. FHA has built low-cost housing, small brick homes, tiny yards, an improvement over the past in some ways. This house is full of a number of drunk or doped-up folks, and there is a fire behind the stove, and it's Saturday night. There is a leak in the pipe that feeds the appliance, and we pull the stove away from the wall and shut off the valve. The fire goes out. Some of the paneling is scorched, but the fire hasn't spread. We look around. Holes are poked in many of the walls, sheetrock and paneling alike. There is ruined food on plates on the counters. Cabinet doors are torn off. I go outside with a spanner wrench to shut off the main valve to the house and a drunk guy approaches me, calling me a white something or other. I hold up the wrench and show it to him. He backs off and leaves me alone, goes off somewhere into the darkness of the yard. I shut off the valve and go back into the house. The lady of the house, knit slacks, a saggy sweater, a filthy knit toboggan on her head, is drunk and cussing, Who this muddafucka what muddafucka muddamuddafucka. The smoke alarm has been sounding the whole time and it won't quit. I go outside to the utility room where she says the breaker box is and push the door open maybe ten inches, and then it stops, jammed tight with ironing boards and boxes of empty bottles, trash, clothes, beer cans, lawn chairs, junk and more junk. I step back out into the carport and look down to see bloody footprints all over the concrete, the footprints of a child, all red and perfectly outlined with the grain of the toes like fingerprints. The smoke alarm is still going off. Some child somewhere in this house or neighborhood has cut a foot badly and is walking around with it bleeding. I go back into the house. The smoke alarm is a piercing, pulsating series of short shrieks that hurt the eardrums. A bunch of drunks are still in the living room arguing hotly. My partners look nervous. They think knives may be pulled, guns fired, rightly so. Cap'n Brown, let's get the fuck out of here, they say. The smoke alarm is still going off and it won't shut up. I walk back into the hall where it's mounted and yank the wires loose. The son of a bitch shuts up then. We go back through the living room and there are plenty of young punks who smirk in our direction. The storm door doesn't have any screen or any glass. We tell them to call the gas company Monday. I don't know how they'll cook until then. We go out across the yard and Engine 10 sits throbbing at the curb, the side mirrors on the cab vibrating in their rubber mounts. I swing up into the driver's seat, take the pump out of gear, let off the airbrake. My partners climb into the front seat and the jumpseats mounted behind the cab. We're glad to be getting the hell away from here, but I can't help but worry about the child with the bleeding foot.

I swing the pumper away from the curb and step down hard on the pedal and she downshifts and then shifts up and we gain speed. I take off my helmet and the wind feels good in my hair.

Later, when we get back to the station, we find out that somebody has left a piece of equipment at the house, but naturally nobody wants to go back and get it. I'm the captain, I have to go back and get it. I get into the van I drive sometimes and tell them I'll be back in a few minutes. If they have a call while I'm gone, somebody can drive the pumper and I can meet them there in the van.

The drunks are still in the yard and in the house, still arguing. I don't say anything to them, I just get out and go into the house and pick up the re-chargeable light that was left behind and head back out with it. Even the police don't like to come down here on Saturday night, and they have guns.

A house burns on North Seven Street one night when I'm off duty, taking a vacation day. Uncle Bunky and Poot Man go through the front door and a corpse is on the floor, his eyes red and his dead hand reaching for the doorknob and the life-giving air six feet away.

A man who lives in a nice house in a nice neighborhood in Oxford has the not-nice habit of getting drunk and then falling asleep in bed smoking a cigarette. In several instances several months apart, he catches the house on fire. Another shift goes over and puts the house out both times, and his insurance company rebuilds it both times.

And one night, a few months later, when Poot Man is on duty, they get a call to the same house. This time he's on fire in his bed. He dies, despite their efforts. One month later, Poot Man resigns, and nobody blames him. There are days when all of us are taken to our limits.

We're sitting in the day room of the fire station watching television one night, eating some things, drinking some coffee, talking, laughing. The fire phone rings and suddenly there is dead silence from us. Anderson, a new guy who is not from around here, picks up the fire phone and answers it, listens, smiles, then chuckles, then laughs, then hangs up the phone and continues to stare at the television.

Wally says, Well? Anderson just chuckles again. He never looks away from the television. He's really tickled by whatever he's just heard on the fire phone.

Some asshole on the phone, he says, still chuckling. Guy says, Ma name is Irvin Stepp and Ah live on Lizard Road and ma house is on far.

Chuckle.

Lizard Road. Like there's some place named that.

We sit frozen for a second. Anderson giggles again. Then the rest of us leap up and run and start getting our turnouts on and cranking the trucks because we know Irvin Stepp and where his house is on Lizard Road.

Most all the trouble I was ever in was caused by drinking, whether it was trouble with the law or fights or whatever, because whiskey twists my head and I need to stay away from it unless there's somebody around who can take care of me, but there's nothing more enjoyable to me than to get into my truck late on a summer evening and ride down the road for an hour or so, drinking a beer, looking out at the fields and the warm horizon where the sun has just gone down, listening to Otis Redding or ZZ Top or Leonard Cohen, and watching the road go by. I love the land I was born to and I never tire of seeing the seasons and the weather change over it, or the hawks that sit high in the trees, or the rabbits that bound across the road, or the coons that band together in spring when they're rutting, or later at night, the owls that swoop low across the ditches or fly down to light in the road in front of you with mice caught in their talons, owls that glare at you with a hateful look before gathering their prey and swooping back up into a black and rainy night on their huge beating wings.

Cookout. The whole department. Fishing, drinking beer, water skiing, or boat-riding anyway since it's only March, out at Sardis Lake north of town. We're going to cook a pig but first we have to kill the pig. Captain Louie and I, a lowly nozzleman, arrive at the pigpen for the execution at the designated time and look at the pig, who is pink and grunting in curiosity with his nose lifted as we stand outside the pen and study him. We've all been laying these plans for weeks. We're going to haul our boats and our campers and our camping equipment and tents and Coleman stoves and barbecue grills out to the lake along with our sleeping bags and spend the whole damn weekend out there, sleeping under the stars, having a good time. The people who are on duty today will come out as soon as their shifts are over. It's going to be really fine. But first we have to shoot this pig.

Louie hands me a loaded Ruger .22, a nice little semi-automatic pistol. It's heavy in my hand. The pig grunts and walks up to the wire of the pen. He seems friendly. If he were a dog he'd be wagging his tail.

This pig's not that big. He's probably what's commonly known as a shoat hog, a young boar that hasn't had his nuts cut out with a sharp knife yet.

All right, Brown, Louie says. Shoot the sumbitch right between the eyes. He's standing there drawing hard on a cigarette, one hand on his hip, ready to get this over with so we can dress the pig. We're in charge of getting the pig.

I point the pistol at the pig. He's looking all around, sniffing at the air. He thinks we've come to feed him something, maybe. I hold the sights right between his eyes—what if I shoot him in the eye?—but he weaves his head around and the gun waves around in my hand as I follow his head.

He's looking right at me, I say.

Hold your head still, you son of a bitch, Louie says. But the pig keeps moving around, grunting, oinking, making the noises pigs do.

I can't do it, man, I say, and I lower the pistol.

Gimme that damn gun, he says, and snatches the pistol away from me. In a blinding movement that doesn't seem to allow for the possibility of aiming, he slips the safety and pops the pig dead square between the eyes. The pig screams and keels over, all four legs stiff, quivering on the ground, dead as a hammer.

Captain Louie unloads the pistol and sticks it in his pocket and bends the wire of the pen down and straddles it, telling me to come on and help him, a little disgusted with me, I can tell.

You ever steam-cleaned a hog? Louie says, as he cranks up the steam cleaner at his father-in-law's combination wrecker yard/auto repair/used furniture store. You can buy fireworks here, too. The pig is lying across the tailgate of Louie's GMC pickup, a little blood running down his nose. Louie explains that it ought to work, hell, all you do when you scald one at home is pour scalding water on him and scrape the hair off with a knife. You know this steam is as hot as scalding water, he says. It makes sense to me.

Louie puts the steam to the hog and I pick up a knife and start scraping the hog, and sure enough, the hair starts coming off, softened by the steam. We'll have this sumbitch slick as a baby's ass in no time, he says. People stand watching us at our work.

Later in the night, lots of people have gone to sleep. MA is asleep. Most of the wives are asleep. Actually there are very few people up. Rob gets up once in a while to get another Lite.

Hillbilly and I squat beside the fire, looking at each other and looking at the pig.

Later, much later, maybe around two or three in the morning, Rob and Hillbilly and I are the only ones still up. Everybody else has crawled into their nice warm vans and campers and cars and trucks and gone to sleep. Rob stands up, drains his last Lite, and says, Throw the sumbitch in the lake or burn him up, I'm going to sleep. He disappears into the night and Hillbilly and I look at each other.

For the rest of the night, freezing on one side and burning on the other. Hillbilly and I turn the pig and put the sauce on him, not saying much, just waiting for dawn, which rises about a week later, pale and cold across the lake. Captain Louie's wife gets up, comes to the fire, yawns, puts coffee on for us. A blessed soul if there ever was one. She gives us a cup and we're glad to have it.

When daylight comes, Hillbilly hands me a knife and I slice into the meat and remove a small piece and chew it. That piece is good, done. But then I slice deeper and it's raw, soured, and we look at each other. The whole pig has ruined. We should have used charcoal instead of wood. We really messed up. We stagger to our beds and sleep a little. Later we throw the pig into the woods. Rob gets his Jeep mired in mud trying to launch my ski boat, and the lake is muddy, choppy with big waves. People get seasick. People start leaving early. A cold wind comes up and it's not a nice day. Before long almost everybody is gone. MA and I go back to our home, a house trailer in a pasture, and go to sleep, glad that it's over.

Item: Winter, cold, dark. Bringing wood in from the stacked lengths in the yard, red oak, mostly, some pin oak and white oak mixed in, but the red splits easiest. I buy a full load off a pulpwood truck from Harris Talley, a gigantic gentle black man, whose little children get up on the truck with him, his wife, too, and unload it in the yard. I saw it up with my Stihl 041 and split it.

The house is filled with the smell of woodsmoke. A good smell, a solid heat. Shane is around eighteen months old. Billy Ray about five, LeAnne not born or even conceived yet.

I work at a place called Comanche Pottery on my days off from the fire department. It's a few miles out from the north end of town. I go in at eight and get off at five, one hour for lunch, which I spend listening to music in my car, and eating the lunch MA has packed for me.

We pour liquid plaster into molds of different shapes, flower pots, Indian heads, leopards, elephants. We dip them in a wax solution to seal them from the weather and the elements. We package them with a machine that wraps hot plastic around them, then we load them into trucks.

Some of the people who work at this place are from Haven House, a home out near Old Sardis Road for recovering alcoholics and drug addicts, people who have come to the end of their road and are trying to get a new start. None of them stay long. They drift on out into their lives, maybe even back into their drugs and alcohol.

While I work I think of the things I'll try to write when I get home. And now I am home, in the kitchen, supper finished, MA and the boys up in the front room watching television, trying to let me alone, let me work, let me write. I sit at the typewriter, a new Smith-Corona that I will type on until it is completely useless, until the keys don't work, until the return carriage slips.

I'm writing something about a family of people walking down a road with their possessions in their hands, homeless people, fruit pickers, laborers, an old man, his wife, a boy, two girls. I know that it is the beginning of another novel, and in my mind I begin to call it *Nomads*. But later I will call it *Joe*.

I have chosen this thing to do, away from my family, the doors closed, characters who form in my head and move to the paper, black symbols on a white sheet, no more than that. It may seem senseless to anybody else, but I know there is a purpose to my work: the spending of years at the typewriter writing until I become better than I am now, until I can publish a book, until I can see that book in a library or a bookstore.

I love this thing, even if it does not love back.

# TIM MCLAURIN, *Keeper of the Moon: A Southern Boyhood*

Tim McLaurin was born in Fayetteville, North Carolina, in 1954 and grew up in Cumberland County. In addition to serving in the marines and the Peace Corps, McLaurin also worked as a carpenter and delivery driver and later toured the South as the star attraction of his own traveling snake show. After earning a degree in journalism from the University of North Carolina at Chapel Hill, McLaurin published his first novel, *The Acorn Plan,* in 1988 and another novel, *Woodrow's Trumpet,* in 1989. McLaurin survived a battle with cancer in 1990 and went on to publish his critically acclaimed memoir *Keeper of the Moon: A Southern Boyhood* the following year. While teaching writing at North Carolina State University, McLaurin published two more novels, *Cured by Fire* (1995) and *The Last Great Snake Show* (1997); the narrative poem *Lola* (1997); and the memoir *The River Less Run* (2000) before his death from cancer in 2002. His last novel, *Another Son of Man,* was published posthumously in 2004.

Roy Blount Jr. called McLaurin's *Keeper of the Moon* "an honest, absorbing memoir" in which "mortality is taken head-on."[1] This excerpt, about a legendary fighting dog and his downtrodden owner, offers a vivid, unexpectedly moving portrait of savage grace.

> The interpretation of literature is subjective. You might say that some Southern writers are lunatics who will pick up rattlesnakes. But, you might also say that some Southern writers have the guts to pick up serpents, and that is one reason Southern literature is held in esteem.[2]

FROM *KEEPER OF THE MOON:*

*A SOUTHERN BOYHOOD*

"Fire up," Jasper cried, holding aloft a half-fifth of El Chico tequila, the nub of a cigarette between two fingers. He nursed at the bottle, then threw his head back and shouted again, "Fire up, y'all."

The day was warm under a clear springtime sky, the air scented with the contrasting odors of two hundred pounds of hog slowly cooking, honeysuckle blossoms, dime-store perfume, and marijuana smoke. Nearly a hundred men, women, and children were scattered in bunches across a pasture of fescue, all enjoying the festivities of the fifth annual May Day Melee held in Cumberland County. I was in my mid-twenties and had come to swap lies with friends, swill beer, and eat good, greasy barbecued pork.

While May Day in most places was celebrated with people joining hands and minds to wish for peace, prosperity, and growth, the May Day Melee was an orgy of Budweiser and pit-bull fighting. The gathering was held at Wayne's house, a double-wide that sat a quarter mile off the road and out of sight of the sheriff's patrol. Here many of the residents of Fayetteville's east side released a winter's tension accumulated from layoffs, high heating bills, sick younguns, and long days working outside in the cold.

The community of east Fayetteville for decades had been the poor side of town, a collection of squat frame houses in need of paint, boarded-up stores, and bars with names like Thelma's Place and Little Reno. Most of the residents of the east side were a no-nonsense lot, born to a life of laboring by hand—plumbers, route salesmen, waitresses, sales clerks, roofers—hard-living people who had seen life from all angles except the top. Many of the men were veterans of the military and worked fifty-hour weeks. The women juggled part-time jobs, cared for the children, and kept up with the bills. They paid their taxes, stayed barely ahead of their creditors, and generally lived within the law. The people of this community, and ten thousand similar ones across America, constituted the backbone of our culture. For their daily sacrifice, these people believed fiercely in their rights in private life. If someone wanted to take a drink of untaxed liquor or smoke a joint, he felt he had earned that privilege as long as the bills got paid. And if he wanted to fight a chicken, wanted to see a dog-fight, he owned that animal, fed it, and watered it—by God, he felt it was his personal business and right.

Wayne was a mechanic, pushing forty, and had fought dogs most of his life. He admitted the practice was ugly and bloody. He also admitted that pit bulls were unpredictable and shouldn't be allowed unsupervised around children. Still, he defended fighting the dogs on several grounds.

"They love it. A pit bull would rather fight than eat," he explained. "We ain't making them fight. I've had dogs break their chain while I was working and tie up and fight till both couldn't stand up, with not a soul watching them or urging them on.

"As for the people who say it's cruel to fight dogs or chickens, that it should stay illegal," he continued, "I'll bet you a dollar that most of these same people defend abortion, say it's all right if they want to kill their own unborn babies."

Such was the logic of many dogfighters, tempered by a life of living hand to mouth, some dignity gained in the belief in a clear superiority of man over beast.

Jasper was in charge of cooking the hog. He took pride in that ability and had concocted his own sauce over the years, a potent blend of vinegar, hot peppers, and God knows what else.

Jasper pitched two no-hitters in his senior year in high school and was being scouted by the major leagues, but got busted with an ounce of pot a week before graduation. Things went downhill after that. He can still knock a bird out of a tree with a rock, and towards the bottom of a fifth he'll tell you what he could have done if it hadn't been for that rookie cop who nabbed him. He lifted the lid of the cooker, pierced the hog's skin with a knife, shook on a little more sauce, then slammed it shut.

"Getting there," he said. "'Bout another hour."

Powered by a drop cord, a stereo has been set up on the grass and tuned to the local country music channel. The air was filled with sounds of a good time: laughter, the clang of a horseshoe tournament, Emmylou Harris's melodic voice. Children shouted as they played tag between parked cars and pickup trucks.

Several of the trucks had pit bulls sitting in the cab or tied in the bed. The younger dogs yelped and pulled against their ropes; the older, experienced dogs saved their energy for later.

Pit-bull fighting at the Melee was not like the serious tournaments where thousands of dollars are bet, the dogs fought until one is dead or near dead. These dog owners were only out for local bragging rights—a little "roll," as they called it, a "scuff." Little or no money was bet. The dogs were only allowed to fight until one had clearly bettered the other—the owner called it when he thought his dog had had enough. Torn ears and facial cuts were usually the extent of the injuries, the pits good as new a couple of days later. The dogs were reflective of their masters, tough as nails for a few rounds, in for a quick knockout, but a little too soft in the belly to go the distance. As soon as the sun was lower, the crowd fed and well liquored, the fighting would begin.

A special buzz circulated among the dogfighters. Word was out that Tote Faircloth was coming to the Melee and bringing Roy Lee.

Years ago, Tote Faircloth sprang Roy Lee from the dog pound the day he got out of jail after tearing up the insides of a bar. The two had been inseparable ever since. Tote was an east-side legend. He was born Franklin Faircloth in the mountains of North Carolina and came to Fayetteville via the 82nd Airborne. In France during World War Two he won the Silver Star. After being discharged, Tote stayed in Fayetteville, married, sired a child, and settled into ordinary life as a welder.

His boy was three years old when he fell into a septic tank and drowned. The tragedy drove Tote and his wife to divorce, the war hero slowly turning to a life of hard drinking, fistfighting in bars, and catching canebrake rattlers that he sold to Special Forces at Fort Bragg.

Two theories circulated as to how his nickname began: one, that he often toted rattlesnakes around in a bucket in his truck; two, the more favored version, that he was christened by a lady friend who was impressed with what he toted around in his trousers.

Tote was a tall, barrel-chested man with big arms and lots of body hair. He wore licensed twin military .45s. Tote described Roy Lee as one-third pit bull, one-third crocodile, and one-third retarded. Roy Lee had one blue eye and one brown eye, a face full of scars, and yellow teeth, and might have been the fightingest creature on dry land. He had only one gear—forward. He let children ride his back, and hated all other dogs, from poodles to St. Bernards.

Several years before, I was riding one afternoon with Tote, searching the dirt roads of Cumberland County for snakes. Tote drove barely ten miles an hour, Roy Lee tied on a rope in back, yapping fiercely whenever we passed another dog. We were drinking Kessler's blended whiskey and iced tea, a Tote specialty. The sun was low, mourning doves calling from fields of cut hay, the air fragrant with overripe melons. "Where the hell is Roy Lee?" Tote asked suddenly, his eyes glued to the rearview mirror. "I thought he was tied in."

I craned my head around to see an empty truck bed. Tote jammed on the brakes.

Roy Lee was lying in the dirt behind the truck, the rope stretched tight between the spare tire and his collar. He wagged his tail but was slow getting up. The best we could figure out was that about three miles back, the harassment of two roadside dogs had got the best of Roy Lee. He had decided to "damn the rope" and jumped. The rope didn't snap and he had been dragged behind for a few miles while we exchanged small talk and sipped whiskey. Roy Lee had a bad collar burn around his neck and most of the hair on one flank was scraped off, but otherwise he was fine. Tote lifted the dog into the truck and shortened the rope, and within a mile, Roy Lee was barking again. Similar antics slowly magnified his reputation.

Jasper fussed over his hog, a second keg was tapped. Several melons were split for the youngsters, little hands grabbing gobs of sweet red flesh. The grumble of a low-geared motor sounded and another truck came into view—Tote, with Roy Lee riding shotgun. A murmur rolled through the ranks, and all the young bad-asses of east Fayetteville chewed their lips as the master arrived.

"Ain't it a goddam sight," Tote hollered through his window, easing his truck forward until he was parked close to the cooker. Roy Lee spied another dog, a tremor rolled up his spine, his ears perked forward. "Hide the pretty gals," Tote shouted. "Ole Tote likes them young and lean."

I hadn't seen Tote in nearly a year, but I had heard about his greatest battle—cancer of the lungs. The doctor had to cut out one to save him. When he swung out of his truck and took two steps, I understood why he had driven so close. Tote walked as if he balanced a crystal vase on his head, putting each foot down carefully, swinging his shoulders to balance each step. He was still a big man, but the operation, the chemotherapy, and the drugs had robbed him of his balance, stripped away his speed and muscle tone. Roy Lee followed at his heels, as if he sensed the old man might need to put his hand down and rest. They came slowly toward the cluster of people near the cooker.

"Lord, it's every hoodlum and sweetheart in Fayetteville," Tote said, calling names and shaking hands as he passed clusters of men and women.

"Roy Lee is looking tough," a man said.

"Tough as two alligators and twice as mean," Tote answered. "I fed him nails and gunpowder for breakfast."

"You gonna fight him today?" another asked.

Tote hesitated for a second. "I doubt there's anything here that would make him break sweat."

"Hey, you ain't got a rattlesnake in your pocket, have you?" one of the women called.

Tote continued until he was close to the cooker. Jasper grinned and lifted the lid and let him have a look, the steam rising in a cloud around both of their heads. The skin was starting to split on the hog's flanks, the fat bubbling.

"I ain't smelled it that good in a while," Tote said.

"You won't either," Jasper bragged. "This here is east Fayetteville gourmet hog."

Everyone formed a sort of semicircle around Tote, those who had never seen him awed by his presence, those of us who knew him pained at the sight of what cancer had done. One of the men sitting in a chair offered it to Tote. The old warrior thanked him, then sat slowly, grimacing like his knees ached. He turned down the offer of a beer, and it was then I noticed he held no cigarette in his hand; I had never before seen him when he wasn't chain-smoking. Roy Lee sat at the arm of his chair, the white hair around his muzzle obvious in the bright sunshine.

Tote folded his hands over his gut, clasped his fingers together, and looked as fragile and wounded sitting there as he had looked the time I went to see him in the hospital. I'd heard the story recounted many times over the past few years, but never like the first time as he lay there propped up in the bed, his words slow and pained, his eyes flat like a lazy sky in August.

"Bad blood had been between me and Earl Cooper for some time. I don't even remember how it started, but we had a few fights, me coming out the better each time. We started keeping out of each other's way, and I thought the trouble had ended. Then one afternoon I was driving into town and saw a car approaching. It swerved into my lane for a second, then out, and when it passed, the driver had his arm out the window, shooting me the bird. I looked in my rearview and saw his brake lights flare, thought for a second maybe it was one of my buddies kidding with me. Then I recognized the car as belonging to Earl's son, a smart-mouthed twenty-two-year-old who had started hanging around the bars. We'd already had some words.

"If I had just kept on going. God I've wished a many times I did, but I'd had a few drinks. If I just hadn't turned around.

"The car pulled to the shoulder of the road, so I turned around and drove up behind it. There was traffic on the road, so I got out on the passenger side and walked up to the car. Inside were four young men, beer cans in their hands. I could smell dope. They were all staring at me, the front window rolled down. I was leaning to look inside the window, to ask what their problem was, when I saw the glint of the barrel, and threw myself backwards a split second before the boy fired. He would have hit me square in the chest, but instead the slug ripped into my right shoulder.

"'You hit him,' I heard one of the boys holler, then I could hear them scrambling and ducking like they were afraid I'd shoot back. I rolled up close to the car where he couldn't hit me again, blood spurting from the big hole in my shoulder. After a second, the driver's door opened and the boy's tennis shoe appeared, then the second. He was coming to finish me off. I already had one of my .45s out, so I cocked the hammer and rolled to my belly, watching the steps under the car.

"I was praying he'd stop. All I wanted was for him to get back in the car and leave. I even hollered for him to stop. Told him to go from there. But he wouldn't stop; he was coming to kill me.

"I watched the boy's steps until they paused at the rear of the car. My finger was tight on the trigger, sweat trickling down the furrow between my eyes. I heard him take a deep breath, then he came in a rush.

"I was ready, had my arms locked. He jumped out cowboy-style, feet wide, had his gun held in both hands, raised over his head. He brought it down, had it almost leveled on me when I shot, hit him right between his eyes. Where the bullet went in, it made just a little round hole, but it blew out the back of his skull and slung blood and brains all over my truck windshield. He was dead before he hit the ground.

"Something died inside me that same day," Tote said slowly, "but if I hadn't killed him, he would have killed me. It drove me kinda crazy for a while."

Tote was cleared in a self-defense plea. For two years after the killing, he drove around with an inch-thick steel plate bolted to the rear window on the driver's side to prevent someone from shooting him from behind. I've read that some doctors think people let cancers start in their bodies when they allow stress and heartache to get the better of them, and I believe on that hot afternoon when Tote squeezed off that round, the first cell turned on him, starting growing strangely and multiplying into what was killing him today.

"Whoever eats the fastest, eats the most," Jasper finally yelled, waving aloft a steaming rib he had pulled from the hog.

Most of the men stood back and waited for the women and the children to fill their plates, some out of politeness, most out of reluctance to pile food on top of a good high. For the next half hour, the shouts and fits of laughter were muffled as people stuffed their bellies full of hot barbecue, coleslaw, and hushpuppies. Tote fixed himself a generous plate, but didn't eat much of it, instead shoveled bites off to Roy Lee, who thumped his tail in gratitude.

The first dogs were faced off when the trees were throwing shadows across the field. The pits were brother and sister, but family matters little to this breed once past adolescence. Mothers will fight sons, fathers their own daughters just as readily. Both dogs were brindle in color, both veterans, their ears notched and ragged, scars showing on their lips and snouts. They sat with ten feet of grass between them, heads lowered and eyes intent while their owners loosened their collars. The crowd had formed a wide circle, giving the animals plenty of room to turn, tumble, or run if inclined. Few ever ran.

On cue, the collars were slipped, and the dogs leaped forward on bunched muscles. When they were a yard apart, the male dog leaped, the bitch rose to her haunches to meet him head up in midair. They locked, jaw to jaw, a chorus of snarls coming from deep in their throats. The male's momentum knocked the bitch to her back, but she held her grip, her better leverage making him lose his hold. The male snapped at air, trying to twist his head enough to get another bite. Blood showed on his teeth.

"Eat that nose up," the bitch's owner encouraged her. "Tear that nose off."

"Skit 'er," the male dog's owner encouraged. "Pull loose, Demon. Skit 'er, boy."

The bitch held her bite for half a minute until the male was able to twist loose, his lip tearing as they came apart. Both dogs scrambled to their feet, the bitch grabbing the male by one front leg, the male nailing her on the ear. Both dogs had good holds; they stood on splayed legs and shook and growled and shook some more, tails wagging as if being caressed. After they held for two minutes with neither losing grip, the owners moved and pried the dogs' mouths open with wedged-shaped sticks. They were allowed to rest a minute, their breath flinging slobber flecked with drops of blood. The bitch's ear was cut again, the male's jaw bloody, one leg swelled at midjoint. When the dogs were released, they slammed together without hesitation.

The siblings fought through two more breaks, each time the bitch going for a leg hold, the male chewing into the loose skin covering her head and ears. Most people shouted for the bitch. When the dogs were broken apart a fourth time, although the bitch was bleeding worse, her wounds were only skin cuts. The male had fared worse, his sister having bit into muscle backed by bone, puncture wounds that were swelling rapidly. The male's owner studied the dog, a ring of observers gave advice. Finally, the man straightened.

"Let's face 'em for a second," he said. They turned the dogs, held them a couple of feet apart, both animals lunging to fight.

"Y'all see him now," the male's owner shouted. "He's game. He's got heart."

People in the crowd agreed, helping the man ease his pride. "Come on, Demon," the man said, leading the dog toward his truck. "You'll get her next time." In a lowered, scolding voice, "You can't slack off them ladies, boy."

Three more sets of dogs fought, all the fights ending the same way, a lot of blood but nothing that couldn't be cured with a shot of penicillin, a night's rest with food and water. The beer flowed, joints were rolled and passed. Jasper, who had passed out a half an hour ago in his garden chair, struggled to his feet and stood there on wavering legs, his eyes still closed, while urine darkened the front of his trousers. He sat back down, heavily, returning to whatever inning he was pitching, the cheers he deserved, oblivious to the guffaws and catcalls.

"Hey Tote," a man in his late twenties shouted. "My dog wants Roy Lee. He's calling him out."

He was a big guy, rawboned, with black hair greased back like Elvis. He had drunk heavily since noon, and his mean streak was starting to surface.

Tote eyed the young man from where he stood on the far side of the circle. "Buddy, I've done put Roy Lee in the cab. He's so full of barbecue he wouldn't fight a rabbit."

"Tote, nowwww. Tote, I don't want to hear it," the man said, walking into the open circle. "I been hearing half my life about Roy Lee. You brought him. Let him fight my dog."

"Let Roy Lee scuff," several other men joined in.

"Let him go, Tote," another said. "Roy Lee could fart and knock his dog down."

I could tell that Tote was against it the way he chewed at his lip, but there were just too many bright eyes turned on him, too many half-cocked smiles. Finally, he nodded once, turned, and started for his truck. A chorus of cheers erupted.

The younger man started for his own vehicle. He was back in less than a minute with his dog, a short-legged animal with a big head and massive jaws. His name was Repete—the son of Pete, a dog that had once fought Roy Lee to a standoff. Pete was dead from heartworms. Repete was fighting for the first time, barely past puppy stage, but he had good blood, looked fit and hard as a hickory knot.

Tote was gone a full five minutes, but he returned with Roy Lee walking beside him on a short length of chain, the dog acting different now, his head high and his eyes shiny as quarters. He knew damn well what was about to take place. Roy Lee searched the crowd, looking for his opponent, and when he spied him, his ears went back, his nostrils flared, a ridge of hair stood up on his back. The black dog was more interested in wagging his tail and looking at the crowd, but when his owner turned his head toward Roy Lee, he momentarily lunged against his chain and barked—the sign of a rookie.

Tote kneeled slowly beside Roy Lee, talked into his ear, and unhooked his collar. Across the circle, the other man was joined by his son, a seven-year-old who had played with the black dog since he was a weaned puppy. The man assured the boy that his dog would be all right, the kid's eyes shifting from his pet to Roy Lee and back again.

The dogs were faced off. "Roy Lee gonna put war on his ass," someone called. Roy Lee stared intently at his opponent, the black dog still interested in the excitement around him, licking the kid's hand when he reached to pat him one last time. Tote looked into the younger man's eyes, then nodded his head. Both dogs were released at the same time. Roy Lee hit the black dog while he was still gawking, slamming him to his back and grabbing a mouthful of throat.

The black dog learned quickly what closed fangs felt like, his world suddenly reduced to one fight. A guttural growl came from deep inside, all thoughts of the boy, of afternoons lying in the sun, erased. Using the strength in his big shoulders, the dog pivoted and got to his feet, twisted Roy Lee's neck until he lost his hold. Both dogs reared up on their hind legs and locked up jaw to jaw, gristle popping and slobber flying. Encouragement was shouted from the crowd on both sides. The dogs broke hold, backed off a foot, then slammed together again, the natural styles of fighting starting to emerge.

The black dog was by build and nature a "leg dog," using his shorter stature to bulldoze under Roy Lee to get at his legs or belly. Roy Lee was a "throat dog," instinctively going for his opponent's windpipe. The dogs feinted and parried, the younger dog using superior speed and strength, Roy Lee relying on his experience, leaning on his opponent, tucking his front legs far back to keep them out of his jaws. When both dogs got strong holds and kept them for a couple of minutes, they were broken apart. Roy Lee breathed hard, but was unhurt, just a small gash opened on his lower jaw. The black dog bled from his mouth and ear.

"Let's don't fight him no more," the kid said to his daddy, eyes wide at the sight of his bleeding pet. The man ignored him. A woman came up behind the boy and laid her hands on his shoulders.

Roy Lee hit the black dog again, slammed him to his back and got a good hold on his throat. The black dog gasped for breath and struggled to free himself. Roy Lee fought only with his mouth, lying limp while the other dog wasted energy trying to get loose. He choked and sucked at the air, unable even to growl. The boy whimpered and asked again for his father to stop them. Finally, the black dog broke Roy Lee's hold, but was behind on breath and short on energy. Roy Lee hit him again, this time bit into his soft belly. The black dog turned and snapped Roy Lee's leg, but he jerked it from his jaws and out of reach before he bit down. Roy Lee chewed at his belly, shook his head violently back and forth. Suddenly, the black dog yelped a shrill cry of pain and frustration.

"Stop them, Daddy," the boy cried, tears suddenly in his eyes. "He's getting hurt."

"Stop them, Larry," the man's wife said, a big-hipped woman in jeans. "You're scaring him."

"Y'all shut the hell up," the man said, his eyes still intent on his dog. "Damn dog was born to fight." An embarrassed murmur rolled through the crowd.

When the black dog squealed, Roy Lee fought harder, bit deeper into his belly and shook, then released his hold and sprang for his throat again. The black dog met him with open jaws, but Roy Lee feinted, let the dog's inexperience carry him by, then nailed him from the rear. He soon had his opponent on his back again in a throat hold. The black dog gasped.

"We ought to stop this," Tote said to the man. "Your dog's game. He's just young."

"He's gotta fight to learn," the man snapped. Roy Lee's tail twitched back and forth as he choked the younger dog. The black dog got weaker, unable to break the hold, his breath now coming in short gasps. He tried to squeal again, the sound high-pitched like a dying rabbit.

The boy sobbed. His mother pushed him toward the rear of the crowd and took a step toward her husband. "You don't stop them, I will, Larry," she shouted shrilly. "The dog's gonna die!"

The man whirled about and lashed out with one arm, slapped the woman hard across her face, caused her to pitch backwards to the ground. She put her hand to her mouth, her eyes stunned as she stared at her husband.

Tote stepped forward. He shouted, "Roy Lee!" and touched his dog's back. "Off now, off, Roy Lee," he said. "Ease off now."

Roy Lee broke his hold immediately, and Tote pulled him backwards by the tail. The black dog tried to get up once and attack, but his legs buckled. He rolled to the side and panted for air.

"Fight's over," Tote said to the other man, buckling the collar around Roy Lee.

"Let the damn dogs fight," the man said loudly. "My dog ain't finished."

"Mine's finished," Tote answered.

"You scared?" the man said. "I thought you were supposed to be so tough." His fist curled slowly at his side. "You look chicken to me."

A hush fell over the crowd, the only sound the boy crying. Tote stared deep into the man's eyes. "I ain't scared, son," Tote said. "But I ain't letting my dog kill yours."

The man pointed his finger at Tote. "I still say you're chickenshit."

I saw that same look enter Tote's eyes, the sheen I noticed when he was lying in the hospital bed, as if he was tallying up a life spent fighting and boozing, with only a fading reputation to show for it, a cancer in his chest that would eventually kill him. Any one of a dozen would have stepped in for Tote if it came to blows, but I feel Tote could probably still have taken the guy, fighting like Roy Lee had, on experience and guts and the grace God seems to give some people. I suspect as Tote stared across the ring, as the man's insult still rang in his ears, he saw the resemblance of another would-be warrior, one who'd still be living today if he'd had the sense to keep driving.

"I ain't scared of you, son," Tote finally said. "Not of a man who would slap his own wife."

The man's gaze faltered, his eyes flicked to the ground, then to his wife and son. Tote turned and led Roy Lee to the truck, the old dog limping slightly. Tote placed his feet carefully, like walking a beam. The two shuffled away from us, brushing together occasionally as if they leaned inward to one another for support.

# RICK BRAGG, *Ava's Man* and *All Over but the Shoutin'*

Rick Bragg was born in 1959 and grew up in Possum Trot, Alabama. After briefly attending Jacksonville State University, Bragg dropped out to work as a reporter for the *Birmingham News* and other newspapers where he wrote stories about "cockfights, speed trap towns, serial killers, George Wallace, Bear Bryant, and Richard Petty."[1] He later served as Miami bureau chief for the *St. Petersburg Times* before accepting a Nieman Fellowship at Harvard University in 1992. After joining the *New York Times* in 1994, Bragg was awarded the Pulitzer Prize for his coverage of the Oklahoma City bombing, the Jonesboro killings, and the Susan Smith trial. In 1997 he published *All Over but the Shoutin',* a best-selling memoir about his rural Alabama upbringing, and followed that with a memoir of his grandfather, *Ava's Man,* in 2001. Since leaving the *New York Times* in 2003, Bragg has taught writing in the journalism department at the University of Alabama. His other books include *Somebody Told Me: The Newspaper Stories of Rick Bragg* (2000), *Hank Williams: Snapshots from the Lost Highway* (coauthor, 2001), and *I Am a Soldier, Too: The Jessica Lynch Story* (2003). In 2008 Bragg published *The Prince of Frogtown,* a memoir of his father, and, in 2009, *The Most They Ever Had,* a profile of workers in an Alabama cotton mill.

"Sad, beautiful, funny and moving," Bragg's memoirs of his Alabama roots have been called "a report from the forgotten heart of 'white trash' America."[2] Included here are two sketches, the first from *Ava's Man* about Bragg's bootlegger grandfather; the second a revealing passage from *All Over but the Shoutin'* about the cousins on his father's side who had a talent for getting into trouble.

> I have often been asked if the poor and rough and tumble world I was born into had in some way held me back as a writer.
>
> I try hard not to laugh out loud. I have never found a cotillion to be half as interesting as a cotton field, or a fraternity or sorority half as compelling as an old woman who worked between the spinning steel of a cotton mill, or a young man who had to pound out some kind of self respect with his fists.
>
> My grandfather made whiskey and fought men with his hands. My father once plotted the murder of a brutal police chief. My mother worked on her knees to build a life with more dignity than I will ever attain or imagine.
>
> God protect me from the upper classes, at least as writing material.
>
> I will take my people, for better or worse.[3]

**FROM *AVA'S MAN***

Times was hard enough, Ava felt, without having to deal with the morons.

People still talk of the night the three drunk men kicked at the door in the middle of the night, shouting for him to come and drink some shine. One of the men was named Martin and everybody knew he didn't have the brains God gave a water bug. With his babies in bed, Charlie had too much good sense to let such men in his home, even in daylight.

"Y'all git," he said, loud, so his voice would carry through the pine. "These babies is sleepin'."

"Come on, Bundrum. We got a quart," growled Martin from the other side of the door. A whole country in need of food, but the clear whiskey still ran like water.

Before Charlie could swing his legs out of bed, all three men started hammering on the door.

"I said git," Charlie shouted, and reached for his overalls. Ava sat bolt up-right but still, a hurricane forming on her features, and the children looked from the door to their daddy, big-eyed.

"Let us in, Chollie," said Martin, his voice slurred, "or I'll kick it in." One man giggled as another, apparently Martin, kicked one, two, three times at the door, and then they all started kicking until the door trembled on its hinges.

Charlie's tool belt was inside, and he reached down and drew his ham-mer—about a pound of good iron on the end of an oak handle—from its loop.

"You got one more chance," Charlie said, but this time his voice was low, far too low to be heard by the men outside the wooden door. But then, most likely, it was way, way too late for second chances.

The men suddenly stopped pounding on the door, and it was deathly quiet. The littlest babies started to cry.

"Trash," Ava seethed, and she turned her eyes like two drill bits onto Char-lie, to let him know it was his fault for knowing such men.

Then, with a crash of breaking wood, the door slammed open, and Martin and the other men stood grinning and wobbling in the doorway, an open jar of likker held out, as if in apology.

As if in slow motion, the drunkards' heads traversed from the rage in Char-lie's face down, down to the hammer that swung back and forth, grim as a hanged man, at the end of his bony arm.

They fled. They stumbled over each other and spilt their whiskey, but they made it to their car and piled into it like a troop of circus clowns. And then, feeling safe, Martin cursed Charlie out the window as he turned the key, the motor started and the headlights winked on.

And there in the yellow glow, just a few feet from the hood, was Charlie, a scarecrow come to life in baggy red long-handles, his hammer held high in one fist, like a thunderbolt.

"Help me Jesus," Martin screamed, trying to find reverse.

The car lurched backward and Charlie threw his hammer with all his might, and the windshield shattered into a million glistening pieces. The ham-mer passed through and hit one of the men hard in the chest, and all three of them piled out, one wheezing, trying to get his breath, the two others cursing and screaming. They ran to the safety of the woods.

Charlie, his face still full of fury, walked into the house and loaded his Bel-gian 12-gauge, and walked back out on the porch. He stood, patient, until he saw one of the men run for their car, and tracked him across the dark yard like he was a pheasant. There was a half-moon, not good light to shoot by, but good enough.

He squeezed the trigger and the whole house shook, and out in the yard there was a yelp, like when you step on a little dog's tail.

"Damn, you shot me." It was Martin's voice.

"I shot you in the leg," Charlie said, correcting him.

"You still shot me," came the voice from the darkness, followed by some whimpering.

"Well, you ort not to kicked in my door," Charlie said.

For some reason Charlie considered it a point of pride that the men not be able to get back in their car, that they had to walk home. It seemed only reasonable, perhaps, after the trouble they caused.

Finally Ava, who had undergone another sea change, walked up and herded Charlie protectively back inside.

"I guess the law will be here in the morning," he said, all the anger draining out of him, leaving him empty.

"I reckon so," Ava said, and steered him over to the bed.

No one seems to remember what Hootie did, but more than likely he crawled under a bed.

Early the next morning, Walter Rollins came knocking on the door, which Charlie had hung back up before dawn. Walter was a full-time cotton farmer and a full-time police officer in Jacksonville, in Calhoun County, a respected man who did not cheat his pickers and did not complain if the women brought their children to the field. He let the small children play in the cotton wagon with his own boys, and paid in cash.

Walter had perhaps the most distinctive voice in Calhoun County. It was shrill and nasal and strung-out, all at the same time. Walter, a man who liked folks and liked talking, often accentuated the final word in his sentences a long, long time, like he wanted to make it last.

"My God, Char-lie," he said, sitting down at the table and taking a cup of coffee, "what'd you dooooo?"

Charlie told him straight.

Walter accepted a buttered biscuit, and a little daub of apple butter. It was all they had that morning.

"Next time," he said, brushing crumbs off his hands, "why don't ye just kill the little son of a beeetch."

Hootie, because he was weaker, because he needed a hero, brought out the light in Charlie's character. His children pulled it out of him, like taffy, when they crawled in his lap and felt his nose or tugged his ears. Ava could, still, if she wanted, with a cool hand on his sunburned neck. And in a way, sad as it may seem, the likker made him gleam, too, hiding his worries in a golden fog, loosening his tongue, numbing his mind and reminding him it had been a long, long time since he sang "Darling Nelly Gray."

But anger, temper, opened up the door on the hot, dark basement in Charlie's soul. His actions were so quick and so violent that people wondered how the two sides of his character lived in only one body, as if one leg would want to go one way and one leg go another, like a poor zombie conjured from goofer dirt. But the anger, dark as it seemed, was not meanness. Meanness just sleeps inside a man's brain, like a cancer. Anger is put inside a man, spins around in his guts and comes out like bile and razor blades. It looks the same, but only from a distance.

Some people blamed it on the times. Old men swear it even made the wild things meaner. Men who would have never stolen crept into the chicken houses and stole the eggs, and other men shot at them from the porch. But it wasn't the times, really. The willingness to hurt a man, when that man hurt or threatened you or your loved ones, was distinct, like fingerprints, to each man. In some men, it was tempered by reason and fear, and in others their rage overcame everything in one violent, terrifying moment. Charlie's temper did not blind him. He hit, and hit hard, because he believed he had to.

It is impossible to explain that to someone who has never hit in anger, who has never been hit, and known that the hitting would not end, could not end, until you'd hurt your enemy real, real bad. Jimmy Jim had taught it to Charlie, and Charlie taught it to his boys. Some men sent their children to military school, to learn war with honor. Charlie taught them how to war and win, and to go on living with their heads held straight up.

James learned it when he was about eleven or twelve. He was on his way to school when an older boy named Dahmer Jones, bigger and stronger, hit him in the leg with a rock. When his daddy saw James limping, he asked, "What happened to you, son?"

When James told him, Charlie just said, "Well, I reckon we can break him of that." He went to a big hickory tree and broke off a limb, and with his pocket knife he made James a big stick—about four feet long and about as big around as his wrist on the big end. "I want to see this stick when you get done with him," Charlie said as he handed James the weapon. "I want to see the bark tore off it."

"And son," Charlie said as his boy walked away, "use the big end."

Later, James told his daddy how it went.

"I went and hid in the culvert, and then I stepped out from it as Dahmer Jones went by. He said, 'Hah, you kind of hoppin', ain't you, Bundrum.' And I set into him, boy, and once I got started I just couldn't stop."

He laid the boy's head open to the skull.

The boys had grown up just like their daddy, unencumbered by too much school or civilization, and Ava wrote them both off as hooligans by the time they were eleven or twelve. His sons, who were becoming teenagers as the 1930s faded slowly into the 1940s, looked and spoke like Charlie, so much so that it was hard to tell them apart at a distance, just three tall, skinny men in overalls, walking the dirt roads and trails.

Charlie had, in the tradition of his own daddy, been hard on his two boys, but they respected him. "My daddy is a man," they would always say when somebody said something about him, about his drinking, his sideline whiskey making, his raggedy overalls. They learned to be men by watching him, the good and the bad.

Like a lot of brothers so close in age, they didn't like each other a lot. They drew blood. Once, in a wood pile, they battled with pine knots, which is like battling with baseball bats. Margaret ran and hid behind the house until it was over.

"They get it from you," Ava always said to Charlie, and he always nodded his head, no high ground to stand on.

But it wasn't hate. If it had been hate, one of them would have died. And, as is often the case, they sided with each other against the entire outside world.

James, with massive fists and arms of bone and sinew, was feared by the other boys. William would pick a fight with two and even three of them, and as they closed on him he would let out a single high whistle. James would come running, and the beating would commence. After a while, it occurred to James that William was whistling a real whole lot, that he was taking advantage of him. So one day, as the whistle came, he just looked up and smiled, and listened as the whistle grew more urgent, then plaintive, then finally faded to silence.

The things the boys remembered about their daddy were not always spoken things, which are just wind, really, but things he did. He always walked in front of them on a game trail or through tall grass, so that a snake coiled there would strike at him. He carried a long stick the size of a broom handle, but heavy and green, loose in his hand.

Once, as they pushed through high weeds, they heard a rattler's sing—they only bit you when you walked up on them but that didn't make you any less bit or any less dead—and Charlie and his sons looked around wildly.

A rattler was coiled at William's feet, and it struck even as Charlie stepped in front of his son and whipped his stick at its head, which made a sound like a pistol shot.

The snake thrashed, crazy-like, on the ground, dying, and Charlie kept walking, like nothing had happened, and the two little boys told it to anybody who listened that day, that week, until they led their own kids through the tall grass, stepping in front.

The snake, to Charlie, was just one more thing stabbing at his children, no more evil than drunk men at the door late at night, or an empty flour can or smokehouse. They could all get you, Charlie figured, but could get the children easier, because they were not as strong or fast.

He had to absorb it, like he would have absorbed the poison in those fangs, if that had been the only way to save his son.

He would not have seen it as heroic.

He just figured he could take it.

**FROM *ALL OVER BUT THE SHOUTIN'***

On Sunday evenings, we visited my daddy's people, strangers to me then, strangers to me now. But for one slender ripple in time I had a second family, a people unlike my momma's people. These were people, the menfolk anyway, without any governors on their lives, not even the law. They drove the dirt roads drunk, the trunks of their cars loaded down with bootleg liquor and unstamped Old Milwaukee beer, the springs squealing, the bumpers striking sparks on the rocks, the men driving with one hand and alternately lighting cigarettes and fiddling with the AM radio with the other, searching for anything by Johnny Horton.

They fought each other like cats in a sack, existing—hell no, living— somewhere between the Snopeses of Faulkner's imagination and the Forresters of *The Yearling*. It is a point of fact that the whole male contingent of the family got into a brawl in town—"they wasn't fightin' nobody else, just each other," my momma said—and, as a family, went to jail. One cousin by marriage—and I am not making this up—refused to wear shoes, even in winter. They were constantly bailing each other out of jail, not for anything bad, merely for refusing to march in step with the twentieth century. If they had been machines instead of men, they would have had just one speed, wide-open, and they would have run at it until they blew themselves apart. I guess, in a way, they did. They are all dead now, not from age, but misuse.

Against my will, I grew fond of them. I would have liked to have known them better.

What I know I learned from those Sunday evenings, when we visited my granddaddy Bobby and granny Velma Bragg's house to eat a meal that took hours to cook and a solid thirty minutes just to put on the table. I remember fine fried chicken, and mashed potatoes piled high with a small lake of butter in the middle, and cracklin' cornbread, and butter beans with a white chunk of fat pork floating like a raft in the middle, and sweet tea poured from gallon pickle jars. They lived in a big, rambling farmhouse, paid for with money from Bobby's steady job at the cotton mill, and they had a short, fat dog named Boots who was about 150 in dog years and moved stiffly around the yard, blind as a concrete block.

Bobby Bragg, a white-haired little man, was what we would now call an eccentric. He still had a horse and wagon, and it was not too uncommon then to see Bobby riding around the mill village in his long underwear, drunk as a lord, alternately singing and cussing and—it must be said—shouting out bawdy limericks to mill workers and church ladies.

The town's police officers seldom bothered the ornery old man, mainly because arresting him would would have left them not only with an unmanned horse and wagon but Bobby himself, and everyone with even a lick of sense knew Bobby would cut you as soon as look at you.

I was amazed by him. His hip bone was prone to come out of joint and when it happened he would not go to a doctor or do anything else that was remotely sensible, but he would limp and cuss and drink and limp and cuss and drink until all he could do was lie on the bed and cuss and drink. Until, one day, my granny Bragg had enough. She reached down and got his bad leg by the foot, and commenced to jerking and twisting and jerking and twisting until his hip bone popped back into place with a sound like, well, a pop, and he was cured.

When sober, he often dressed for dinner, not in a suit but in a fresh pair of overalls, and a white button-down shirt that was stiff as a board with starch.

"Clean as a pin," Momma said. Of the bad things that can be said about my granddaddy, no one could ever say he did not have a certain style. (It is widely believed in my family that a good many of my peculiarities, I most certainly got from him.)

My granny Velma Bragg was a sad-eyed little woman who looked very much like the part Cherokee she was, a sweet-natured woman with great patience who hovered over the men when they drank whiskey at a beautiful dining room table, trying to wipe up what they split before it ate away the varnish. I remember she was always kind, always gentle, especially to my momma. I guess, in a way, she had an idea what was in store for her. Momma and Granny Bragg still talk, every week. Survivors, both of them.

After supper the men went one way and the women went another. The old man, Bobby, would hold court on the porch, surrounded by his sons. The men drank—Lord, how they could drink—from endless cans of beer or from a jug when they had one. They even talked about drinking as they drank, and smoked Camels down to the barest nub before flipping them out in the dirt of the yard. When I close my eyes I can still see the trail of orange sparks it made. My momma often would holler for me to come inside, but I was enthralled. These men were what my momma's kinfolk called sinners, and it seemed to me like sinning was a lot of fun.

Listening to them, I learned much of what a boy should know, of cars, pistols, heavy machinery, shotguns and love, all of which, these men apparently believed, can be operated stone drunk. I learned that fighting drunk is better than sober because a clear-headed man hurts more when hit. I learned that it is okay to pull a knife while fighting drunk as long as you are cautious not to cut off your own head.

I learned that whiskey will cure anything from a toothache to double pneumonia, if you drink enough. (Once when I was bad sick with flu, they even gave it to me. They heated it in a pan, being careful not to let it get anywhere close to an open flame, and poured it over honey in a coffee cup. Then someone, my granny probably, squeezed a lemon into it. I drank it down in four gulps, took two steps, a hop, a skip and a staggering leap and passed dead out on the floor. From what I heard later, everyone except my momma thought it was pretty amusing. I cannot say it cleared up any congestion, but it made my head hurt so bad that I did not notice it so much.)

They talked about the mill. They talked about dogs. They talked about fist-fights and bootleggers and, a little, about war, but not my daddy's war. They talked about the new war, Vietnam, but my daddy never joined in, that I remember. He drank, smoked his cigarettes. Once, I recall, he came off the porch and walked off into the night for a long time. I remember it because Momma came outside, some time later, ready to go, and we had to search for him. We found him in the car, just sitting, smoking.

Now and then, the men talked of what they called "the nigger trouble," but I could not attach any significance to that. We had no contact with black people beyond a wave, now and then, from a car or from the side of a road. I was not of a world where there were maids, cooks or servants. When they picked in the cotton field beside white pickers, like my momma, they kept to themselves. There were no black people in my school, and at that time no black person had ever been in my house or in my yard. So how, I wondered, could there be trouble between us? They lived in their world, and we lived in our world. It became gradually clear, as I sat there listening, watching the orange comets of their cigarettes arch across the dark, what the trouble was about.

They were sick and tired of living in their world. They wanted to live in our world, too.

# LEWIS NORDAN, "A Body in the River"

Lewis Nordan was born in 1939 and grew up in the town of Itta Bena, Mississippi. After serving in the navy, Nordan earned degrees at Millsaps College, Mississippi State University, and Auburn University, where he wrote his doctoral dissertation on William Shakespeare. Along the way he taught high school and worked as an orderly and a night watchman before devoting himself full-time to writing when he was thirty-five. After publishing stories in *Harper's, Redbook,* and the *Southern Review,* Nordan published his first collection, *Welcome to the Arrow-Catcher Fair,* in 1983 and a second collection, *The All-Girl Football Team,* in 1986. His first novel, *Music of the Swamp,* appeared in 1991 and was awarded the Prize for Notable Fiction from the American Academy and Institute of Arts and Letters. He went on to publish three more novels, *Wolf Whistle* (1993), *The Sharpshooter Blues* (1995), and *Lightning Song* (1997); another story collection, *Sugar among the Freaks* (1996); and the memoir *Boy with Loaded Gun* (2000). After teaching creative writing at the University of Pittsburgh for more than twenty years, Nordan retired in 2005 and later moved to Ohio, where he lived until his death in 2012. His life and work have since been the subject of a collection of critical essays, *Lewis Nordan: Humor, Heartbreak, and Hope* (2012).

Nordan was sixteen years old when he heard that a black teenager named Emmett Till had been brutally murdered in nearby Money, Mississippi. Till's murder, and the outrage that erupted when the facts of the case hit the national news, marked the beginning of a lifelong obsession for Nordan, who began to question the morality of "the only home I had ever known."[1] In this chapter from his memoir *Boy with Loaded Gun,* Nordan reflects on that fateful summer of 1955 and the pivotal moment that later led him to leave home.

I look longingly at the place [his native Mississippi] at times, but I've found I'm a better Southerner outside the South than in the South. I don't want to be melodramatic, but writing as an expatriate, with a sense of longing and love and mythologized memories, took the place of some of the old anger I had about the racial violence. When I left the South, I had felt trapped for so long. . . . It is only by being away that I have understood the culture I was rejecting.[2]

## "A BODY IN THE RIVER"
### FROM BOY WITH LOADED GUN

One afternoon in early September, in our high school football locker room, I heard several boys on the team talking about a dead body that had been found in the Tallahatchie River. The room where the boys were putting on their practice uniforms was long and low-ceilinged. The floor was concrete. It smelled of sweaty socks and sweat-soaked pads and a backed-up toilet. The shower at the far end had a slow drain, and it carried its own unpleasant effluvium. I was the team "manager," a sort of hard-working waterboy and flunky. I busied myself taping ankles or changing cleats or helping this person or that person lace up his shoulder pads. I was not on the team myself only because of a knee injury, I told myself, but in truth I was skinny and slow-footed and uncoordinated, and was lucky to have been given this job of team manager in order to stay close to the more popular boys in school. The boys discussing the death, the body that had been discovered in the water, already seemed to know a good deal about the case—that the dead person's name was Emmett Till, that he was a black teenager who had insulted a white woman, that he had been killed and sunk in the river with a gin fan barbwired to his neck. This was such shocking information that it scarcely seemed real.

I was quiet, a little shy among these football guys—my social standing among the actual athletes was quite low—and so I added nothing to the conversation. Others were quiet too, I suppose; I am mainly remembering a few big talkers. Despite the horror of the content of the conversation, no one seemed horrified. People were laughing. It was a funny story, like a movie plot you remember as having scared you at the time, maybe, but now is a big joke. The tone of the conversation was one of general approval, and even hilarity. I worked hard at not seeming affected by what I was hearing. I added my share of approval by sitting quietly and listening. The theme of the conversation was that a "nigger" had done this thing, wolf-whistled this white woman. They seemed to be saying that this Chicago kid had learned his lesson, he sure got what he deserved! I wish I could report honestly that I was higher-minded and exempt from complicity in the general sense of approval and jocularity, but I cannot. I was jealous that I had no details to add and no social standing that would have allowed my participation in the first place. There was a terrible joke being told as well. The joke was that this "nigger" had tried to steal a gin fan and swim across the river with it and drowned himself. Probably I smiled at the joke, I don't remember. In any case, the thing that happened next remains one of my most vivid memories. The picture of the scene stands frozen in my mind's eye as clearly as a photograph on a table before me.

A boy putting on his shoulder pads turned to the rest of us and said, "I'm for the nigger." He was serious. I could see it in his face. He had not been smiling at the jokes, had not approved of anything that had been done or said. In my memory everyone else stopped talking and looked at him, frozen smiles on our faces. He said, "It ain't right. Kill a boy for that. I don't care what color he is."

When I have had occasion to tell this story in conversation over the years, I have often been asked, "Do you remember the boy's name? Where is he now?" I do remember his name, and I know the town he lives in. But I have always had to say that I am out of contact with him. I have had a fantasy of meeting him again someday and asking him about that moment, this act of unheard of courage when he voiced his disapproval. And courage is what it was. This was not the captain of the team, or the quarterback, who I suppose could have exhibited such outrageous individualism without fear of reprisal or ostracizing; and it was not the team geek, or waterboy, or manager, myself I mean—who had no status to lose anyway and could have been in that way impervious to ridicule. This was simply a boy on the team, a quiet country boy who had everything to lose and nothing except a lifetime of self-respect to gain, and he said, "I'm for the nigger. It ain't right." For forty years I have wished I had been the boy who spoke those courageous words.

The story of Emmett Till is a familiar one to most Americans. In the summer of 1955, traveling by train from his home in Chicago an African American teenager named Emmett (Bobo) Till journeyed to Money, Mississippi, in the Delta, for a visit with his uncle and aunt. Money was a little town just a few miles from my home in Itta Bena. Bobo was warned beforehand by his mother that the rules of etiquette were not the same in Mississippi as in Chicago and that he should be very careful of what he said and how he acted. Any small infraction could be serious.

Living in the same town Bobo visited was a big extroverted man known for violence, J. W. "Big" Milam. He owned a country store operated by his half-brother Roy Bryant and Roy's wife, Carolyn. The store was enough like Mr. Shiloh's in Itta Bena as to have become merged in my mind as one: big un-painted dungeons with bare-board floors and wide porches and a few groceries. Big Milam was admired for being good at "handling niggers." He carried a .45 automatic pistol wherever he went, which he said was "good for shooting or slugging." Shot through the chest in World War II, his body scarred with mul-tiple shrapnel wounds, Milam had pistol-whipped and killed German soldiers and prisoners in the war. He was an expert with the "grease gun" and all other weapons of short-range violence.

On a dare, in late August, Bobo Till went into the country store and asked Carolyn Bryant for a date. He made a couple of insulting remarks and wolf-whistled her, apparently. Later on, in reprisal, Roy and Big kidnapped the child from his Uncle Mose's and Aunt Lizzie's house, drove him around in the dark for several hours to scare him, tortured him, and finally shot him in the head and killed him. Then they barbwired him by the neck to a heavy fan from a cotton-gin motor and rolled his body into twenty feet of water in the Talla-hatchie River.

These details and others are available to us because many of them, includ-ing the kidnapping, were admitted to, even bragged about, by the defendants before the murder trial, and then the rest were revealed in a paid interview by the defendants to William Bradford Huie in *Look* magazine shortly after the trial. Both defendants were found not guilty of murder, and a grand jury in Greenwood failed to bring an indictment for kidnapping, despite the public admissions.

As a high school boy, in the days after the hilarity in the locker room, and then later, after I was a grown-up young man, I became obsessed with the case. I thought about it daily, I grieved it, but not with a social conscience, I'm sorry to say, and not with much compassion for Emmett Till or the loving mother who suffered this loss, but with a defensiveness that bordered on neu-rosis. To my mind, something had been done to me, to us, to the South. And not by Milam and Bryant but by the "Northern" media. I felt personally accused. The fact that what was being reported was essentially what had hap-pened did not mitigate my feelings of betrayal, as if an undeserved attack had been directed at me by the rest of the world. It's impossible for me to under-stand how I had for so long fantasized escape from the confines of my geog-raphy and now, suddenly, with the perfect moral excuse for full emotional detachment and rejection of the place, I clung to it, defended it against "outsiders." For a long time I focused on how "unfairly" Mississippi and the South were treated by other Americans. I hung out in public libraries and read accounts of the murder and of the trial over and over. The whole affair seemed unbelievable to me. Could those men, with familiar names, with a little country store, have really done what the magazines and newspapers were saying? I knew it to be true, but the truth was unacceptable to me. I began to feel torn apart by my loyalties, to what I knew of right and wrong and to the morality of the only home I had ever known.

The obsession was completely private. I talked about my feelings and beliefs with no one, neither friends nor family. My parents spoke not a word. In fact, just last year I asked my mother, who is eighty-seven, how we talked about the trial at the dinner table. Her answer: "Honey, we didn't talk about it at all. We never said a word." Years later, in the navy, and then in college, I still found myself going over the events in my mind. Once in about 1968—for reasons obscure even to me—I copied from microfilm, by hand, onto a legal pad, every word about the trial that *The New York Times* had reported during that summer and fall. The thing I could never admit, and that all my obsessive thinking seems now to have been covering up, was that I did indeed feel culpable. I had sat in the locker room and listened to the jokes. I had smiled. I had wished I had something to add and some status from which to enter the conversation. I had not been horrified at the word *nigger* or sought to correct anything at all, even by removing myself from it. I was as guilty as *The New York Times* had implied I was.

There is, I suppose, one more thing to tell. Forty years later, after publishing a novel based on the Emmett Till murder, I worked up my courage and called information and dialed the number of the boy in the locker room, the child who stood up for what was right when no one else even knew there was an issue of right and wrong. To my surprise, the voice on the other end of the line was not a sixteen-year-old boy, as I had foolishly expected, but rather a man in his middle fifties. I wondered how I sounded to him. He was easy to talk to, we were still friends, after so long. He was glad to hear from me. We talked for awhile. He told me he had three children, all grown and gone from home.

"Just me and my wife now," he said.

I asked about another friend, and he had some recent information, so we talked about him for a while.

I said, "Did you make it to the class reunion last year?"

He said no, that was cotton-ginning time, the fall, not the right time of year for him.

I said I was promoting books in the fall, so it was not a good time of year for me either. Though I did not say this to him, as it might have seemed to accuse my hometown of something it was not guilty of, I recalled that the death of Emmett Till had been the final reason, if I had needed one final reason, that I left Itta Bena to try to find a life in the larger world. I was running from myself when I left home, not from the people who loved me.

He said he had heard all about my books and was happy for me.

I said, "Did you know that my new book was about the murder of Emmett Till?"

He said, "Oh yes, I've heard all about it.

I said, "That's why I'm calling, actually. I'm calling to ask you what you remember about those days."

He said, "Well, I remember it, but I don't remember anything very specific."

I said, "Do you remember when you first heard of the murder?"

He said, "No, Buddy, I'm sorry I don't."

I said, "There were some terrible jokes being made, do you remember that?"

He said yes, he did remember, and then he recalled the same awful joke about the stolen gin fan.

I said, "I'm thinking of a day in the football locker room. The team was dressing out, and everybody was talking about the murder. Do you remember that?"

He thought for a few seconds. He said, "No, I don't think I do. I remember people talking about it."

I said, "The day I'm thinking of, we were all talking about the murder, and making jokes, and then you stood up for the dead boy. You said, 'I'm for the colored boy,' or something like that. Do you remember that?"

He thought again. He said, "No, Buddy. I'm sorry. I really don't."

I said, "The way I remember it, you said this and the rest of us just stopped talking. I thought you were so courageous. I wished I had said it. I think about that moment all the time. I've thought of you for all these years. You don't remember?"

His voice was thoughtful and kind. He said, "No, I'm sorry. I don't."

I said, "It took so much courage. I admire you for it."

He said, "Well, thank you. Thank you. Buddy."

We talked awhile longer. Finally he said, "I'm real glad you called. This has been nice."

I said, "I hope we can stay in touch."

He said, "Well, good. That would be fine. That would be real nice."

# FICTION

# HARRY CREWS, *A Feast of Snakes*

Choosing a selection from the many novels Harry Crews published over the years presented us with a considerable challenge. In the end we chose a generous excerpt from what may be Crews's most famous (and infamous) book, *A Feast of Snakes,* a bruising sideshow of a novel that hits all the pressure points as it burns through the darker recesses of the redneck psyche. Reading through it again, it is obvious why it remains, along with McCarthy's *Suttree* and Brown's *Joe,* one of the quintessential Rough South novels. It likewise reminds us why, despite Crews's undisputed reputation as the reigning godfather of the southern counter-canon, his fiction rarely appears in most anthologies of southern literature. Read it and you will soon see why. Four decades after it first appeared, *A Feast of Snakes* still connects like a punch to the gut.

> I think that blood, bone, mutilation, and being in extremis is wherein beauty, peace, and serenity lie, or that it is out of such things that beauty, peace, and serenity come. I've never learned a damn thing from peaceful or good things. I never have. But a writer or somebody who creates things stays in such things at his own risk and expense, because a creative life is not quiet and peaceful and serene. It is often chaotic and ugly.[1]

## FROM *A FEAST OF SNAKES*

She felt the snake between her breasts, felt him there, and loved him there, coiled, the deep tumescent S held rigid, ready to strike. She loved the way the snake looked sewn onto her V-neck letter sweater, his hard diamondback pattern shining in the sun. It was unseasonably hot, almost sixty degrees, for early November in Mystic, Georgia, and she could smell the light musk of her own sweat. She liked the sweat, liked the way it felt, slick as oil, in all the joints of her body, her bones, in the firm sliding muscles, tensed and locked now, ready to spring—to *strike*—when the band behind her fired up the school song: "Fight On Deadly Rattlers of Old Mystic High."

She felt a single drop of sweat slip from the small of her back, hang for an instant, and then slide into the mellow groove between the flexed jaws of her ass. When she felt the sweat touch her there, she automatically cut her eyes to see if she could pick out Willard Miller, the Boss Snake of all the Mystic Rattlers, *her* boss Snake, pick him out from the other helmeted and white-suited boys scrimmaging on the other side of the track. When they made contact, their soft, almost gentle grunts came to her across the green practice field.

She tried to distinguish the sound of him from the sound of the others, and she thought she could, thought how amazingly the sound was like the ragged snorts he made into her ear when he had her bent brutally back over the hood of her Vette. There was hardly any difference at all in the noise he made when he scored on the field or scored on her. In whatever he did, he was always noisy and violent and wet, tending as he did to slobber a little.

She saw the band director raise his baton and she tensed, rolled her weight forward to the balls of her feet, and then the music was crashing around her, the tubas pumping, the drums rattling, and she was strutting like it was the end of the world. From the sides of the field came the dry, awesome rattle of the diamondback. Some of the fans had come out and they had brought their gourds with them. The gourds were as big as cantaloupes, shaped like crooked-neck squash, and full of dried seed so that when they were shaken they vibrated the air with the genuine sound of a snake. During a game, the home stands of the Mystic Rattlers put everybody's hair on end. You could hear those dried gourd seeds two miles away, buzzing like the biggest snake den God ever imagined. During football season, nobody in Mystic was very far from his gourd. Sometimes you could see people carrying them around with them in town, down at the grocery store, or inside Simpkin's, the only dry goods store in Mystic.

The band was strung out now in the shape of a snake. The band members used the yard markers to position themselves, double timing in place, drawing their knees high and waving their instruments, so that the entire snake vibrated in the sun. The snare drums were under one goal post, rattling for all they were worth and she was under the other goal post, standing in the snake's mouth, her arms rigid as fangs. She was at one with the music. She did not have to think to perform. Of all the majorettes—and there were five others—she marched in place with the highest knees, the biggest smile, the finest skin, the best teeth. She was a natural, and as a natural her one flaw—if she had one— was that her mind tended to wander. She didn't have to think, didn't have to concentrate like the other girls to get her moves right. Consequently she sometimes got bored with the drills and her mind wandered. Even now as she pranced in place, her back arched, her pelvis thrust forward, she was winking at Joe Lon Mackey where he stood under the end zone bleachers.

That was where he usually stood when he watched them practice and she was not surprised to see him there, glad rather, because it gave her something to think about. He wasn't twenty feet from her, standing in the shadows, a burlap sack in one hand and a brown paper sipping sack in the other. From time to time he raised the sipping sack to his mouth. He'd winked at her when she first stopped under the goal post. She'd winked back. Turned her smile on him. She'd always liked him. Hell, *everybody* had always liked Joe Lon. But she didn't really know him *that* well. Her sister, who was going to school at the University of Georgia in Athens, her sister, Berenice, knew him *that* well.

Her sister and Joe Lon had been a number in Mystic, Georgia, in all of Lebeau County for that matter, and Joe Lon could have been going to the University of Georgia in Athens or anywhere else in this country he wanted to except it turned out Joe Lon was not a good student. That's the way they all put it there in Mystic: Joe Lon Mackey is not a good student. But it was worse than that and they all knew it. It had never been established exactly if Joe Lon could read. Most of the teachers at Mystic High who had been privileged to have him in their classrooms thought he probably couldn't. But they liked him anyway, even loved him, loved tall, blond, high school All-American Joe Lon Mackey whose exceptional quietness off the playing field everybody chose to call courtesy. He had the name of being the most courteous boy in all of Lebeau County, although it was commonly known that he had done several pretty bad things, one of which was taking a traveling salesman out to July Creek and drowning him while nearly the entire first string watched from high up on the bank where they were sipping beer.

She missed the band director's whistle signaling that the snake was about to strike and consequently the five other girls making up the snake's head almost knocked her over. She'd been standing, her arms positioned as fangs, winking at Joe Lon where he raised his sack in the shadows and wondering if Berenice would come home for the roundup, when the girl right behind her, high-stepping, hit her in the kidney with a knee and almost knocked her down. She caught herself just in time and hissed over her shoulder: "You want you ass kicked, do you?"

The girl said something back to her but it was lost in the pumping tubas. Under the stands Joe Lon Mackey took the last pull from a Jim Beam half pint and dropped the paper sack with the bottle in it into the weeds. He took out two pieces of Dentyne chewing gum and put them into his mouth. Then he lit a cigarette. He had been watching Candy—called Hard Candy by nearly everybody but her parents, Dr. and Mrs. Sweet—because she reminded him of Berenice and all the things that might have come true for him but had not. Two years ago Berenice had been a senior and head majorette and he, Joe Lon, had been Boss Rattler.

It was said that Joe Lon, on any given day of his senior year of high school, could have run through the best college defensive line in the country. But he had not. He had never set foot on a single college football field even though he had been invited to visit more than fifty colleges and universities. But that was all right. He'd had his. That's what he told himself about ten times a day: *That's all right. By God, I had mine.*

He reached into the back pocket of his Levis and pulled out a sheet of blue paper. It was almost worn through in the creases where it was folded. He shook it open and held it up to the light. It said: "I will see you at rattlesnake time. Love Berenice." There were some X's under the name. The letter had come to Joe Lon at the store three days ago. It had taken him most of the afternoon to be sure of the words and once he was sure of them, they had given him no pleasure. He had thought he was through with all that, had made his peace. He folded the letter and put it back in his pocket. But on the way to his pickup he took the letter out again and, using his teeth and his free hand, he carefully tore it into very small pieces and left them scattered behind him in the gloomy aisle underneath the stands.

He drove over to the little road that went by the practice field and watched Willard Miller run the ball. They were running him against the grunions, the smaller, second-string boys who came out for football for God knows what reason since they almost never got into a game and could only offer up their bodies as tackling dummies for the bigger, stronger boys. He watched Willard Miller fire three straight times up the middle. It was important to run him against grunions now and then. It gave him a chance to practice his moves without running the risk of getting injured. It also gave him great opportunities to run over people and step on them, mash their heads and their hands, kick their ribs good.

Joe Lon felt his own thigh muscles tick, as he watched Willard fake a grunion out of his shoes and then, after he had the boy entirely turned around and beaten, run directly over him for no reason at all. Well, what the hell, all things had to end, both good and bad. There were other things in this world besides getting to step on somebody. The main thing was to hold on and not let it bother you. Joe Lon turned on his lights and drove off into the early November dusk.

He had been drinking most of the day, but he didn't feel drunk. He drove out past the empty flag pole on the post office and past the jail, where he saw Buddy Matlow's super-charged Plymouth with the big sheriff's star painted on the door parked under a leafless Chinaberry tree, and on through town, where several people waved to him. He didn't wave back. Finally, two people shook their gourds at him though and he did raise his hand and smile but he only half saw them. He was preoccupied by the thought of going home to Elfie and the babies, that trailer where he lived in a constant state of suffocating anger.

He had the trailer just outside of town on the edge of a ten-acre field he'd bought and turned into a combination trailer park and campground. He drove slowly down the narrow dirt road leading to it and passed finally under a big banner that he himself had strung from two tall telephone poles he had bought secondhand from the REA. The banner was neatly printed in letters about two feet high: WELCOME TO MYSTIC GEORGIA'S ANNUAL RATTLESNAKE ROUNDUP.

The lights were on in his trailer, a double-wide with a concrete patio, and he could see the shadow of his wife Elfie moving behind the window in the kitchen. He parked the truck, took the burlap sack from the back, and walked out to a little fenced-in pen that had a locked gate on it. He took out a key and opened it. In the back of the pen were several metal barrels. The tops of the barrels were covered with fine-mesh chicken wire. He kicked two of the barrels and immediately the little enclosure was filled with the dry constant rattle of diamondbacks. He took a stick with a wire hook on the end of it from the corner of the pen, set the burlap sack down, and waited.

The mouth of the sack moved and the blunt head of a rattlesnake appeared. It seemed to grin and waved its forked tongue, testing, tasting, the air. There was an undulation and another foot of snake, perhaps four inches thick, appeared behind the head. Joe Lon moved quickly and surely and the snake was twisting slowly on the end of the hooked stick.

"Surprise, motherfucker," said Joe Lon, and dropped it into one of the barrels.

For a long moment, he stared into the barrel after the snake but all that appeared there was a writhing of the darkness, an incessant boiling of something thick and slow-moving.

He put the chicken wire back in place, threw the hooked stick in the corner of the pen, and headed for the trailer.

Elfie was at the sink when he walked into the kitchen. From the back she still looked like the girl he'd married. Her hair was red and glowed like a light where it fell to the small of her back. Her hips were round and full without being heavy. Her calves were high, her ankles thin. But then she turned around and she was a disaster. Those beautiful ball-crushing breasts she'd had two years ago now hung like enormous flaps down the front of her body. And although she was not fat, she looked like she was carrying a basketball under her dress. Two inches below her navel her belly just leaped out in this absolutely unbelievable way. The kitchen smelled like she had been cooking baby shit.

"Smells like you been cooking baby shit in here, Elf," he said.

There was a fat eighteen-month-old boy strapped into a highchair. Right beside him in a blue bassinet was a fat two-month-old boy.

Elfie turned from the sink and smiled. Her teeth had gone bad. The doctor said it had something to do with having two babies so close together.

"Joe Lon, honey, I been trying to keep your supper warm for you."

"Goddammit, Elf," he said. "You ever gone git them teeth fixed or not? I given you the money."

She stopped smiling, pulling her lips down in a self-conscious way. "Joe Lon, honey, I just ain't had the time, the babies and all."

There was no dentist in Mystic. She would have to go over to Tifton, and the trip took the better part of a day.

"Leave them goddam younguns with somebody and git on over there and git you mouth looked after. I'm sick and tard of them teeth like that."

"Aw right, Joe Lon, honey." She started putting food on the table and he sat down across from the two babies. "Don't you want to wash you hands or nothing?"

"I'm fine the way I am."

She took some thin white biscuits out of the oven and put them in front of him. Along with everything else she was a terrible cook. He took one of the lardy biscuits off the plate, tore it open, and dipped some redeye gravy on it. She sat with her plate in front of her without eating, just staring at him, her lips held down tight in an unseemly way.

"Was it a bad day at the store, Joe Lon, honey?"

He had been all right when he came into the trailer, but he sat at the table now trembling with anger. He had no idea where the anger came from. He just felt like slapping somebody. He wasn't looking at her but he knew she was still watching him, knew her plate was still empty, knew her mouth was trembling and trying to smile. It made him sick with shame and at the same time want to kill her.

"I left the nigger at the store," he said. "I went snake hunting."

The biscuit and gravy was sticking in his throat and a great gaseous bubble of whiskey rose to meet it. He wasn't going to be able to finish it. He wasn't going to be able to eat anything.

"What all did you git?" she said in a small voice. When he didn't answer, she said: "Did you git anything?"

The baby strapped in the highchair had a tablespoon he was beating the tray in front of him with. Then he quit beating the tray and threw it into the bassinet and hit the other baby in the head, causing him to scream in great gasping sobs. It so startled the baby in the highchair that he started kicking and screaming and choking too. Joe Lon, who had felt himself on the edge of exploding anyway, shot straight out of his chair. He grabbed the greasy biscuit off his plate and leaned across the table. Elfie didn't move. She left her hands in her lap. Her eyes didn't even follow him up. She kept staring straight ahead while he stuffed the dripping biscuit down the front of her cotton dress, between her sore, hanging breasts. He put his face right in her face.

"I got sompin," he shouted. "You want me to tell you what I got? I got god-dammit filled up to here with you and these shitty younguns."

She had never once looked at him and the only sign she made that she might have heard was the trembling in her mouth got faster. He kicked over a chair on the way out of the trailer, and before he even got through the door he heard her crying join the babies'. By the time he got to his truck the whole trailer was wailing. He leaned against the fender trembling, feeling he might puke. He almost never had an impulse to cry, but lately he often wanted to scream.

Screaming was as near as he could get to crying usually, and now he had to gag to keep from howling like a moon-struck dog.

Jesus, he wished he wasn't such a sonofabitch. Elf was about as good a woman as a man ever laid dick to, that's the way he felt about it. Of course getting married with her three months gone and then putting another baby to her before the first one was hardly six months old didn't do her body any good. And it ruined his nerves completely. Hell, he guessed that was to be expected.

But it didn't mean he ought to treat her like a dog. Christ, he treated her just like a goddam dog. He just couldn't seem to help it. He didn't know why she stayed with him.

He stood watching the ten-acre campground, knowing tomorrow it would fill up with snakehunters and blaring radios and noise of every possible kind and wondered if his nerves would hold together. He took a deep breath and held it a long time and then slowly let it out. There was no use thinking about it. It didn't matter one way or the other. The hunt was coming—the noise and the people—and whether he could stand it or not wouldn't change a thing. What he needed was a drink. He glanced once at the trailer, where the shadowy figure of his lumpy wife moved in the lighted window, and jumped into the truck and roared off down the road as though something might have been chasing him.

By the time he got to the store he had gone to howling. Through the open front door, he could see George sitting behind the counter on a high stool. There were no cars or trucks out front. Joe Lon sat next to the little store that was hardly more than a shed and howled. He knew George would hear him and it bothered him but George had heard him before. George would not say anything. That was the good thing about a nigger. He never let on that he saw anything or heard anything.

Finally Joe Lon got out of the truck and went inside. He didn't look directly at George because howling made him look just like he'd been crying, made his eyes red and his nose red and his face flushed. He was wishing now he had not torn up Berenice's letter. He wished he had it to look at while he drank a beer.

"Git me a beer, George," he said.

George got off the stool and went through a door behind the counter into a tiny room not much bigger than a clothes closet. Joe Lon sat on the high stool and hooked the heels of his cowboy boots over the bottom rung. He took out some Dentyne and lit a Camel. Directly, George came back with a Budweiser tallboy.

"What'd you sell today?" Joe Lon said.

"Ain't sell much," said George.

"How much?" he said. "Where's you marks?"

George took a piece of ruled tablet paper out of the bib of his overalls. The paper had a row of little marks at the top and two rows of little marks at the bottom. It meant George had sold twenty bottles of beer, five half pints, fourteen pints, and one fifth, all bonded. He had also sold ten Mason fruit jars of moonshine.

"Hell, that ain't bad for a Thursday," said Joe Lon.

"Nosuh, it ain't bad for a Thursday," George said.

"I got it now," said Joe Lon. "You go on home."

George stood where he was. His gaze shifted away from Joe Lon's face until he was almost looking at the ceiling. "Reckon I could take me a little taste of sompin? Howsomever, it be true I ain't got no cash money."

Joe Lon said: "Take yourself one of them half pints a shine. I'll put it on you ticket. Bring me one of them bonded whiskeys while you in there."

George brought the whiskey and set it on the counter in front of Joe Lon, dropping as he did the half pint of moonshine into the deep back pocket of his overalls.

Joe Lon had brought another ruled piece of tablet paper out of a drawer in front of him. "Damned if you ain't drinking it up bout fast as you making it, George."

"I know I is," George said.

"You already behind on the week and it ain't nothing but Thursday," said Joe Lon.

"It ain't nothing but Thursday an I already be behind on the week," said George, shaking his head.

George hadn't moved so Joe Lon said: "You don't want to borrow money too, do you? You already behind."

"Nosuh, I don't want no money. I already behind."

"What is it then?"

"Mistuh Buddy. He done locked up Lottie Mae again."

"Jesus."

"Yessuh."

"For what?"

"Say she a sportin lady."

"Jesus."

"Yessuh."

Buddy Matlow would take a liking to a woman and if she would not come across he would lock her up for a while, if he could. As soon as he had been elected Sheriff and Public Safety Director for Lebeau County he started locking up ladies who would not come across. They were usually black but not always. Sometimes they were white. Especially if they were transients just passing through, and a little down on their luck. If he got to honing for one like that and she wouldn't come across, he'd lock her up no matter what color she was, sometimes even if she had a man with her. He had been called to accounts twice already by an investigator from the governor's office, but as he kept telling Joe Lon, they'd never touch him with anything but a little lecture full of bullshit about how he ought to do better. Hadn't he been the best defensive end Georgia Tech ever had? Hadn't he been consensus All-American two years back-to-back and wouldn't he have been a hell of a pro if he hadn't blown his right knee? And hadn't he gone straight to Veet Nam, stepped on a pungy stick that had been dipped in Veet Nam Ease shit? Hadn't they had to cut his All-American leg off? Goddammit he'd paid his dues, and now it was his turn.

"I'll see about it," Joe Lon said.

"Would you do that, Mistuh Joe Lon? Would you see about it?"

"I'll talk to him tonight or first thing in the morning."

"I wisht you could axe him about Lottie Mae tonight."

"Tonight or first thing in the morning."

He cut the seal on the whiskey with his thumbnail and took a pull at it. George started for the door. Joe Lon waved the bottle in the air and gasped a little. He'd taken a bigger swallow than he meant to. He followed the whiskey with a little beer while George waited, watching him patiently from the door.

"Lummy git them Johnny-on-the-spots?"

Lummy was George's brother. They both worked for Joe Lon Mackey. They'd worked for Joe Lon's daddy before they worked for Joe Lon. They'd never been told what they made in wages. And they had never thought to ask. They only knew at any given moment in the week whether they were ahead or behind on what they'd drawn on account. Ahead was good; behind was bad. Everybody was usually behind on everything though and nobody worried about it much.

When George didn't answer, Joe Lon said: "The Johnny-on-the-spots, did Lummy git'm?"

Nothing showed in George's face. He said: "Them Johnny-on-the-spot." It wasn't a question. He'd just repeated it.

"Hunters'll start coming in tomorrow," said Joe Lon. "If the Johnny-on-the-spots ain't in the campground we in trouble."

"Be in trouble," said George.

"What? said Joe Lon.

George said: "What it was?"

"The shitters, George!" said Joe Lon. "Did Lummy git the goddam shitters or not?"

George's face opened briefly, relaxed in a smile. He did a little shuffle with his feet, took the moonshine out of his back pocket, looked at it, felt of it, and put it back. "Sho now. Lummy come wif the shitters on the truck all the way from Cordele."

"I didn't see'm on the campground," Joe Lon said. "I should've seen'm."

"He ain't taken them shitters offen the truck, but he have'm everone. I seen'm mysef. Mistuh Joe Lon, them shitters be fine."

"Just so you got'm, and they out there when the hunters start rolling in."

"You drink you whiskey, Mistuh Joe Lon. Don't think twice. Lummy and me is put our minds on the whole thing."

The screen door banged shut behind him, and Joe Lon poured another dollop of whiskey down. It wasn't doing any good much, didn't seem to be taking hold. He knew nothing was going to help a whole lot until he saw Berenice and either made a fool of himself or did not. He had the overwhelming feeling that he was going to make a fool of himself. Tear something up. Maybe his life. Well, at least he got the Johnny-on-the-spots. Last year it had taken two weeks to clean the human shit up in Mystic. There'd been about three times as many people as there had ever been before.

The rattlesnake roundup had been going on now as long as anybody in town could remember, but until about twelve years ago it had been a local thing, a few townspeople, a few farmers. They'd have a picnic, maybe a sack race or a horse-pulling contest and then everybody would go out into the woods and see how many diamondbacks they could pull out of the ground. They would eat the snakes and drink a little corn whiskey and that would do it for another year.

But at some time back there, the snake hunt had started causing outsiders to come in. Word got out and people started to come, at first just a few from Tifton or Cordele and sometimes as far away as Macon. From there on it had just grown. Last year they had two people from Canada and five from Texas.

Mystic, Georgia, turned out to be the best rattlesnake hunting ground in the world. There were prizes now for the heaviest snake, the longest snake, the most snakes, the first one caught, the last one caught. Plus there would be a beauty contest. Miss Mystic Rattler. And shit. Human shit in quantities that nobody could believe. This year, though, they had the Johnny-on-the-spots. Chemical shitters.

The telephone rang. It was his daddy. He wanted Joe Lon to send over a bottle with George.

"Ain't here," he shouted into the phone. "He already gone."

"Send somebody else then. Damn it all anyhow, I want a drink."

"Ain't nobody here but me. What happened to that bottle I left by this morning?"

"I drapped it and broke it."

"Bullshit."

"Joe Lon, I'm gone have to shoot you with a gun someday, talking to you daddy like that."

"Who'd run the store if you done that? Maybe Beeder could run the goddam store. Tote you goddam whiskey. Maybe she'd quit with the TeeVee and act normal. Send her over here right now and I'll give her a bottle for you."

"You a hard man, son, making such talk about you only sister. Lord Christ Jehovah God might see fit to strike you."

Joe Lon wanted to scream into the telephone that it was not Lord Christ Jehovah God that struck his sister. But he did not. It would do no good. They'd been over that too many times already.

"All right," he said finally, "never mind. I'll bring the whiskey myself. Later."

"How later?"

"When I git a chance."

"Hurry, son, my old legs is a hurtin."

"All right."

Just as he put the telephone down, a car drove up. It stopped but nobody got out. Carload of niggers. He sighed. Joe Lon Mackey carrying shine for a carload of niggers. Who would have thought it? He looked down at his legs as he was going into the little room behind the counter. Who would have thought them wheels, wheels with four-five speed for forty yards, would have come to this in the world. Well, anything was apt to come to anything in this goddam world. That's the way the world was. He spat as he took down the half pints of shine from the shelf.

During the next hour he sold more than had been sold all day, most of it to blacks who drove up and stopped under the single little light hanging from a pole in front of the store. He wished to God they were allowed to come inside so he wouldn't have to cart it out front to them. Of course, they *were* allowed to come inside. Except they were not *allowed* to come inside. It had been that way for the twenty years his daddy had run the store and it had been that way ever since Joe Lon had taken it over. He hadn't really *kept* it that way. It had just *stayed* that way. Nobody ever complained about it because if you wanted to drink in Mystic, Georgia, you had to stay on the good side of Joe Lon Mackey. Lebeau County was dry except for beer, and since Joe Lon had an agreement with the bootlegger, his was the only place within forty miles you could buy you a drink.

He worked steadily at the whiskey in front of him, chasing it with beer, and by the time Hard Candy's white Corvette car pulled up out front, he was feeling a little better about the whole thing. The Corvette was Berenice's old car and it reminded Joe Lon of everything he had been trying not to think about. Willard came in ahead of Hard Candy. He was an inch taller than Joe Lon and looked heavier. He had a direct lidless stare and tiny ears. His hair was cut short and his round blunt head did not so much sit on his huge neck as it seemed buried in it. He was wearing Levis and a school T-shirt with a tiny snake printed over his heart. His worn-out tennis shoes didn't have any laces in them. He sat on a stool across the counter from Joe Lon and they both watched Hard Candy come through the door stepping in her particular, high-kneed walk that always seemed to make her prance. She took a stool next to Willard. Nobody had spoken. They all sat, unsmiling, looking at one another.

Finally Willard said: "Me'n Hard Candy's just bored as shit."

Joe Lon said: "I got a fair case of the cain't-help-its mysef."

"I don't guess a man could git a goddam beer here," said Willard.

"I guess," said Joe Lon.

"Two," said Hard Candy.

Joe Lon said: "Hard Candy, if you don't quit walking like that somebody's gone foller you out in the woods and do sompin nasty to you."

"I wish to God somebody would," she said.

"*Somebody* already has," said Willard.

Joe Lon got up to get the beer. When he came back he said: "You want to hold this whiskey bottle I got?"

"We et us some drugs to steady us," Willard said. "I don't guess I ought to drink nothing harder'n beer."

"Okay."

"But I will," Willard said.

"I thought you might," Joe Lon said.

"You shouldn't do that," Hard Candy said.

Willard bubbled it four times and set it on the counter. Hard Candy took it up.

"We'll probably die," she said, a little breathless when she put it down.

"Probably."

They sat watching the door for a while, listening to the screenwire tick as bugs flew against it.

"I think it's gone be a shitty roundup," said Joe Lon.

"Will if this hot weather holds," Willard said. "Must be fifty degrees out there right now. Shit, it's like summer. Won't be a snake nowhere in the hole stays this warm."

They sat and watched the door again. A car passed on the road beyond the light now and then. Hard Candy turned and looked at Joe Lon.

"You reckon we could feed one?" she said.

"Let's wait a little while," Joe Lon said. "Maybe somebody'll come in we can take some money off."

"You got one back there that'll eat you think?" asked Willard.

"I try to keep one," Joe Lon said.

They watched the door some more.

"Hell, it ain't nobody coming," said Willard. "Git that rascal out here and let'm do his trick."

"I'll bet with you," said Hard Candy. She opened the little clutch purse she was carrying and bills folded out of the top of it.

"I don't take money from my friends," said Joe Lon.

"If you gone bet with him on the snake," said Willard, "You might as well go ahead and give him the goddam money anyway. You sure as hell ain't gone beat him."

"I lose sometimes," said Joe Lon, smiling.

"Git the goddam snake," said Willard. "Shit, I'll bet with you."

"You ain't bettin with me," said Joe Lon.

"I'll make you bet with me," said Willard.

They were both off their stools now, kind of leaning toward each other across the counter. They were both smiling, but there was an obvious tension in the attitude of their bodies.

"You ever come to make me do something," said Joe Lon, "You bring you lunch. You'll be staying awhile."

"Maybe I can think of something you'll *want* to bet on," said Willard.

"Maybe," said Joe Lon.

He went into the small room at the back of the counter and they followed him. There was a dim light burning. It took a moment for their eyes to adjust. Bottles of various sizes lined the shelves of both sides of the room. One middle shelf toward the back had no bottles on it. It held, instead, five wire cages that were about two feet square and about that high. Four of the cages held a rattlesnake. The fifth cage had several white rats in it. Joe Lon slapped the side of one of the cages with his hand. The snake made no move or sound. Nor did any of the other snakes.

"I've had these so long I probably could handle'm," said Joe Lon.

"Why don't you," said Willard Miller, showing his even, perfect teeth.

"Would if I wanted to," said Joe Lon.

"Hell, let's make that the bet then," said Willard. "The loser has to kiss the snake."

Joe Lon looked at him for a long moment. "You couldn't beat me at that either."

Willard Miller said: "I can beat you at anything." He was still smiling but something about the way he said it had no smile in it at all.

"You better back you ass out of here before you git it overloaded," said Joe Lon.

"If we don't never bet on nothing, how you know I cain't beat you?" said Willard.

"I know," said Joe Lon.

Hard Candy said: "I'll git the rat."

She went to the cage, opened the top, and reached in. When her hand came out she had a white rat by its long smooth pink tail. It hung head down without moving, its little legs splayed and rigid in the air. They followed Joe Lon out of the room to the counter, where he set the caged snake down.

"Ain't he a beautiful sumbitch?" said Joe Lon.

"Ain't nothing as pretty as a goddam snake," Willard said.

"I'm pretty as a snake," said Hard Candy.

They both looked at her. She was playing with the rat on the counter, holding its tail and letting it scratch for all it was worth. With her free hand she thumped the rat good-naturedly on top of its head.

"You almost are," said Willard, taking a pull at Joe Lon's whiskey bottle, "But you ain't quite."

Joe Lon took the bottle. "He's right, you ain't quite pretty as a snake."

"What would you two shitheads know about it anyway?" she said.

Joe Lon took a stopwatch from under the counter. It was the watch his coach had given him when he broke the state record for the two-twenty.

"Just for the fun what would you say?" asked Joe Lon.

"He'll hit the rat in a hundred and four seconds. He'll have it swallered in three and a half minutes."

"That's three and a half minutes *after* he hits it?"

"Right," said Willard.

Joe Lon bent down until his nose was only a half inch from the wire cage. The snake was in a corner, tightly knotted, with only its head and tail free. Its waving tongue constantly stroked in and out of its mouth. Its lidless eyes looked directly back at Joe Lon. The head was wide, wider than the body, and flat with a kind of sheen to it that suggested dampness. The tail was rigid now but still not rattling.

"This sucker'll hit right away, maybe twenty seconds. Yeah, I say twenty seconds. That rat'll be gone, tail and all, in two and a half minutes. That's total time. So I'm saying two minutes ten seconds after the hit." He had been staring into the cage while he talked. Now he straightened and backed off. "Drop that little fucker in."

"I'm playing," said Hard Candy.

"You already got the rat messed up and confused from thumpin him on the head," said Willard. "Stop thumpin him and do like Joe Lon says."

She held the rat up in the palm of her hand. She stroked its head with her thumb, gently. She pursed her lips and whispered to the rat: "Nobody's gone hurt you, little rat. We just gone let the snake kill you a little."

There was a spring-hinged door at the top of the cage that opened only one way. She set the rat on top of the door. It opened inward and the rat dropped through. The door immediately swung shut again. Joe Lon started the stopwatch. The rat landed on its feet, turned, and sniffed its pink tail. It looked at the snake in the corner, sat up on its hind legs, and started licking its front paws. The thick body of the snake moved and a high striking curve appeared below its wide blunt head.

None of them saw the strike; rather, they saw the body of the rat lurch as though struck by some invisible force. It sat for a split second without moving and then leaped straight into the air and landed on its back. The rattlesnake had retreated to the corner, its body again knotted and seemingly coiled about itself with only the dry flat head clear.

Almost immediately the snake came twisting out of the spot where it had withdrawn and very slowly approached the still rat. It touched the rat's back, ran its blunt head along the hairy stomach and legs, seemed to be taking the rat's measure. Finally, the snake opened its mouth, unhinged its lower jaw and, slow and gentle as a lover, seemed to suck the rat's head in over the trembling, darting tongue. Just as the head disappeared, the door of the store slammed open and a voice bellowed: "I caught you fuckers being cruel to little animals agin!"

They all turned together to see Buddy Matlow, wearing a cowboy hat and a wooden leg, standing in the doorway. When they looked back at the cage, there was nothing showing of the rat but the tail, long, pink, and hairless, sticking out of the snake's mouth like an impossible tongue.

"You degenerate sumbitches," Buddy Matlow said, watching the thin hairless tail disappear into the snake. "never could understand how anybody could stand doing things like that to little animals."

"Ain't done nothing yet," said Joe-Lon. "Snake et supper. We just watched."

"I ain't gone report you," said Buddy Matlow. "I just fed that snake of mine over at the jail not more'n an hour ago. You can git me a tallboy and a glass a that shine."

Joe Lon said: "How many times I got to tell you I don't sell nothing by the glass."

"I didn't think to pay for it," said Buddy.

"Makes a lot of noise for a goddam cripple, don't he," said Willard Miller. "I didn't have no more sense than to step on a stick with slopehead shit all over it, damned if I wouldn't say please when I asked for something." Willard's thin mouth was smiling almost shyly over the rim of his beer can, but his dark eyes were flat and hard and without light.

"You been running over too many grunions and reading about it in the *Wire Grass Farmer,*" Buddy said. He looked down and casually examined his stump. "One of these days I'm gone have to stick this piece a oak up you ass and examine you liver."

Sitting between them, Hard Candy took another pull at the whiskey bottle. She was flushed from the speed they'd eaten and a little lacquer of sweat beaded her upper lip. She was enjoying it all a lot and only wished it was real, wished they would suddenly lunge off the stools and lock up on the bare wooden floor one on one, wished she could smell a little blood. But she knew it wouldn't come to anything. They might as well have been talking about the weather.

"You want sompin back here, Willard?" Joe Lon stood in the door of the little room with a beer in one hand and a water glass full of moonshine in the other.

Willard drained the beer in front of him and set it down.

"Me'n and Hard Candy got to go." He smiled and blew Joe Lon a kiss as he and Hard Candy slid off their stools.

Joe Lon and Buddy Matlow watched Hard Candy leave. She might as well have been in front of the band with her baton. She was all high knees and elbows, her hard little body jerking rhythmically. When they were gone, Joe Lon brought the beer and the glass to Buddy.

"You don't reckon you could put this goddam snake up do you?" Buddy said. "I just soon do my drinking without it."

They both looked down at the cage at the place where the rat had stopped in a thick knot about four inches deep in the snake. Joe Lon stood listening to the Corvette go over the gravel and onto the highway in a great roar and squalling of tires, laying two hundred yards of rubber before it took second gear. Only then did Joe Lon take up the cage and put it in the back room. He brought another beer back for himself and sat on a stool across the counter from Buddy Matlow.

"That boy's sompin, ain't he?" Buddy said.

"Uh huh."

They drank in silence for a while, listening to the night tick against the screens.

"I wish you'd drink and git the hell out of here. Ain't no niggers gone come up here with you car parked out there."

But what he said was reflex. It was what he always said. He wasn't studying the car with the sheriff's star on the door or Buddy Matlow. He was thinking about that Corvette, the squalling rubber, squatting with power when you floored it. It had belonged to Berenice before she went off to college. He used to drive it, used to make it sing on all the highways of Lebeau County. He knew where Willard was headed right this moment. He used to go there himself. It was all part of the package, part of being the Boss Snake of all the Mystic Rattlers. Willard was headed for Doctor Sweet's drug cabinet to which Hard Candy would have a key, just as Berenice had had one. They would get in there and Willard would eat whatever he felt like—a little something to take him up, or maybe bring him down a bit—and she would fill her little pockets full and off they would go over the dark countryside trying to decide what to do with the night.

# BARRY HANNAH, "Ride, Fly, Penetrate, Loiter"

Barry Hannah was born in 1942 in Clinton, Mississippi. After graduating from Mississippi College with a pre-med degree in 1964, he earned a master's degree and a master of fine arts degree from the University of Arkansas and went on to teach writing at Clemson University. His first novel, *Geronimo Rex* (1972), won the William Faulkner Prize and was nominated for the National Book Award. After publishing his second novel, *Nightwatchmen,* in 1973, Hannah taught at Middlebury College and later at the University of Alabama, during which time he published the critically acclaimed story collection *Airships* (1978). In 1980 he published the novel *Ray* and moved to Hollywood to write screenplays for director Robert Altman, which resulted in the novella *Power and Light* (1983). Hannah returned to Mississippi in 1983 to teach at the University of Mississippi, where he directed the M.F.A. program in creative writing for several years. He went on to publish five more novels, including *The Tennis Handsome* (1983), *Hey Jack!* (1987), and *Never Die* (1991), and three well-received short story collections, *Captain Maximus* (1985), *Bats Out of Hell* (1993), and *High Lonesome* (1996), which was nominated for the Pulitzer Prize. After surviving a battle with cancer in the late 1990s, Hannah published his last novel, *Yonder Stands Your Orphan,* in 2001. He was at work on a new series of interconnected stories when he passed away in 2010, some of which appear in the posthumous collection *Long, Last, Happy: New and Selected Stories* (2010).

The majority of Hannah's work, which has been called everything from neo-Gothic to postmodern to postsouthern, is arguably no more Rough South than anything by Updike or Cheever. Still, when it comes to exploring the peculiar pathology behind the South's obsession with violence, there is no one better. How, then, do you choose a representative Barry Hannah story? Obviously you cannot. In this case we went with Hannah's provocative classic "Ride, Fly, Penetrate, Loiter," a story Brad Watson calls "a blues song on the page," a wild (and wildly parodic) portrait of the redneck zeitgeist in motion.[1]

> I've been labeled a violent writer, frankly I must like it. . . . My wife says, "You're a kind and gentle man, why don't you tell that kind of story?" I'm a pacifist, but I'm intensely interested in people under stress and combat. I wonder at violence itself—it's so far beyond and yet it's with you every day in the newspaper and in life.[2]

### "RIDE, FLY, PENETRATE, LOITER"

My name is Ned Maximus, but they call me Maximum Ned.

Three years ago, when I was a drunk, a hitchhiker stabbed me in the eye with my own filet knife. I wear a patch on the right one now. It was a fake Indian named Billy Seven Fingers. He was having the shakes, and I was trying to get him to the bootleggers off the reservation in Neshoba County, Mississippi. He was white as me—whiter, really, because I have some Spanish.

He asked me for another cigarette, and I said no, that's too many, and besides you're a fake—you might be gouging the Feds with thirty-second-part maximum Indian blood, but you don't fool me.

I had only got to the *maximum* part when he was on my face with the fish knife out of the pocket of the MG Midget.

There were three of us. Billy Seven Fingers was sitting on the lap of his enormous sick real Indian friend. They had been drinking Dr. Tichenors antiseptic in Philadelphia, and I picked them up sick at five in the morning, working on my Johnnie Walker Black.

The big Indian made the car seem like a toy. Then we got out in the pines, and the last thing of any note I saw with my right eye was a Dalmatian dog run out near the road, and this was wonderful in rural Mississippi—practically a miracle—it was truth and beauty like John Keats has in that poem. And I wanted a dog to redeem my life as drunks and terrible women do. But they wouldn't help me chase it. They were too sick.

So I went on, pretty dreadfully let down. It was the best thing offering lately.

I was among dwarves over in Alabama at the school, where almost everybody dies early. There is a poison in Tuscaloosa that draws souls toward the low middle. Hardly anybody has honest work. Queers full of backbiting and rumors set the tone. Nobody has ever missed a meal. Everybody has about exactly enough courage to jaywalk or cheat a wife or a friend with a quote from Nietzsche on his lips.

Thus it seemed when I was a drunk, raving with bad attitudes. I drank and smiled and tried to love, wanting some hero for a buddy: somebody who would attack the heart of the night with me. I had worn out all the parlor charity of my wife. She was doing the standard frigid lockout at home, enjoying my trouble and her cold rectitude. The drunkard lifts sobriety into a great public virtue in the smug and snakelike heart. It may be his major service. Thus it seemed when I was a drunk, raving with bad attitudes.

So there I was, on my knees in the pebble dust on the shoulder of the road, trying to get the pistol out of the trunk of my car.

An eye is a beautiful thing! I shouted.

An eye is a beautiful thing!

I was howling and stumbling.

You frauding ugly shit! I howled.

But they were out of the convertible and away. My fingers were full of blood, but it didn't hurt that much. When I finally found the gun, I fired it everywhere and went out with a white heat of loud horror.

I remember wanting a drink terribly in the emergency room. I had the shakes. And then I was in another room and didn't. My veins were warm with dope, the bandage on. But another thing—there was my own personal natural dope running in me. My head was very high and warm. I was exhilarated, in fact. I saw with penetrating clarity with my lone left eye.

It has been so ever since. Except the dead one has come alive and I can see the heart of the night with it. It throws a grim net sometimes, but I am lifted up.

Nowadays this is how it goes with me: ride, fly, penetrate, loiter.

I left Tuscaloosa—the hell with Tuscaloosa—on a Triumph motorcycle black and chrome. My hair was long, leather on my loins, bandana of the forehead in place, standard dope-drifter gear, except for the bow and arrows strapped on the sissy bar.

No guns.

Guns are for cowards.

But the man who comes near my good eye will walk away a spewing porcupine.

The women of this town could beg and beg, but I would never make whoopee with any of them again.

Thus it seemed when I was a drunk.

I was thirty-eight and somewhat Spanish. I could make a stand in this chicken house no longer.

Now I talk white, Negro, some Elizabethan, some Apache. My dark eye pierces and writhes and brings up odd talk in me sometimes. Under the patch, it burns deep for language. I will write sometimes and my bones hurt. I believe heavily in destiny at such moments.

I went in a bar in Dallas before the great ride over the desert that I intended. I had not drunk for a week. I took some water and collected the past. I thought of my books, my children, and the fact that almost everybody sells used cars or dies early. I used to get so angry about this issue that I would drag policemen out of their cars. I fired an arrow through the window of my last wife's, hurting nothing but the cozy locked glass and disturbing the sleep of grown children.

It was then I took the leap into the wasteland, happy as Brer Rabbit in the briars. That long long, bloated epicene tract "The Waste Land" by Eliot—the slide show of some snug librarian on the rag—was nothing, unworthy, in the notes that every sissy throws away. I would not talk to students about it. You throw it down like a pickled egg with nine Buds and move on to giving it to the preacher's wife on a hill while she spits on a photograph of her husband.

I began on the Buds, but I thought I was doing better. The standard shrill hag at the end of the bar had asked me why I did not have a ring in my ear, and I said nothing at all. Hey, pirate! she was shrieking when I left, ready to fire out of Dallas. But I went back toward Louisiana, my home state, Dallas had sickened me so much.

Dallas, city of the fur helicopters. Dallas—computers, plastics, urban cowboys with schemes and wolf shooting in their hearts. The standard artist for Dallas should be Mickey Gilley, a studied fraud who might well be singing deeply about ripped fiberglass. His cousin is Jerry Lee Lewis, still very much from Louisiana. The Deep South might be wretched, but it can howl.

I went back to the little town in the pines near Alexandria where I grew up. I didn't even visit my father, just sat on my motorcycle and stared at the little yellow store. At that time I had still not forgiven him for converting to Baptist after Mother's death.

I had no real home at all then, and I looked in the dust at my boots, and I considered the beauty of my black and chrome Triumph 650 Twin, '73 model, straight pipes to horrify old hearts, electricity by Lucas. I stepped over to the porch, unsteady, to get more beer, and there she was with her white luggage, Celeste, the one who would be a movie star, a staggering screen vision that every sighted male who saw the cinema would wet the sheets for.

I walked by her, and she looked away, because I guess I looked pretty rough. I went on in the store—and now I can tell you, this is what I saw when my dead eye went wild. I have never been the same since.

The day is so still, it is almost an object. The rain will not come. The clouds are white, burned high away.

On the porch of the yellow store, in her fresh stockings despite the heat, her toes eloquent in the white straps of her shoes, the elegant young lady waits. The men, two of them, look out to her occasionally. In the store, near a large reservoir, hang hooks, line, Cheetos, prophylactics, cream nougats. The roof of the store is tin. Around the woman the men, three decades older, see hot love and believe they can hear it speak from her ankles.

They cannot talk. Their tongues are thick. Flies mount their shoulders and cheeks, but they don't go near her, her bare shoulders wonderful above her sundress. She wears earrings, ivory dangles, and when she moves, looking up the road, they swing and kiss her shoulders almost, and the heat ripples about but it does not seem to touch her, and she is not of this place, and there is no earthly reason.

The men in the store are stunned. They have forgotten how to move, what to say. Her beauty. The two white leather suitcases on either side of her.

"My wife is a withered rag," one man suddenly blurts to the other.

"Life here is a belligerent sow, not a prayer," responds the other.

The woman has not heard all they say to each other. But she's heard enough. She knows a high point is near, a declaration.

"This store fills me with dread. I have bleeding needs," says the owner.

"I suck a dry dug daily," says the other. "There's grease from nothing, just torpor, in my fingernails."

"My God, for relief from this old charade, my mercantilia!"

"There is a bad God," groans the other, pounding a rail. "The story is riddled with holes."

The woman hears a clatter around the counter. One of the men, the owner, is moving. He reaches for a can of snuff. The other casts himself against a bare spar in the wall. The owner is weeping outright.

He spits into the snuff in his hands. He thrusts his hands into his trousers, plunging his palms to his groin. The other man has found a length of leather and thrashes the wall, raking his free hand over a steel brush. He snaps the brush to his forehead. He spouts choked groans, gasping sorrows. The two of them upset goods, shatter the peace of the aisles. The man with the leather removes his shoes. He removes a shovel from its holder, punches it at his feet, howls and reattacks his feet angrily, crying for his mute heels.

"My children are low-hearted fascists! Their eyebrows meet! The oldest boy's in San Diego, but he's a pig! We're naught but dying animals. Eve and then Jesus and us, clerks!"

The owner jams his teeth together, and they crack. He pushes his tongue out, evicting a rude air sound. The other knocks over a barrel of staves.

"Lost! Oh, lost!" the owner spouts. "The redundant dusty clock of my tenure here!"

"Ah, heart pie!" moans the other.

The woman casts a glance back.

A dog has been aroused and creeps out from its bin below the counter. The owner slays the dog with repeated blows of the shovel, lifting fur into the air in great gouts.

She, Celeste, looks cautiously ahead. The road is still empty.

The owner has found some steep plastic sandals and is wearing them—jerking, breaking wind, and opening old sores. He stomps at imagined miniature men on the floor. The sound—the snorts, cries, rebuffs, indignant grunts—is unsettling.

The woman has a quality about her. That and the heat.

I have been sober ever since.

I have just told a lie.

At forty, I am at a certain peace. I have plenty of money and the love of a beautiful red-haired girl from Colorado. What's more, the closeness with my children has come back to a heavenly beauty, each child a hero better than yours.

You may see me with the eye-patch, though, in almost any city of the South, the Far West, or the Northwest. I am on the black and chrome Triumph, riding right into your face.

# BREECE D'J PANCAKE, "The Scrapper"

Breece Pancake was born in 1952 and grew up in the town of Milton, West Virginia. After graduating from Marshall University with a bachelor's degree in English, Pancake taught for two years at the Virginia Military Institute before enrolling in the English master's program at the University of Virginia. In 1977 he published his first story in the *Atlantic Monthly*, which incorrectly accented his middle initials as "D'J," a misprint he would later adopt for all of his published works. Despite his early success, Pancake struggled with his own insecurities and in 1979 died, an apparent suicide. In 1983, Little, Brown and Company published a posthumous collection of Pancake's work, *The Stories of Breece D'J Pancake,* which was nominated for the Pulitzer Prize. A new edition of the book was published in 2002.

Andre Dubus III praises Pancake's bleak, wondrous stories about his native West Virginia for their "fearlessness on the page, an inherent willingness to go as deeply as the story and the character require."[1] That certainly applies to "The Scrapper," Pancake's New South take on the classic southwestern fight tale, which reads like a mountain cousin to Hemingway's Nick Adams stories.

> About Pancake, Dominic Luxford writes, "He wrote in a language that could be lean and raw, graceful and poetic in a single stroke. In this way, Pancake had the ability to turn stories into memories. . . . Their power gives one a sense of being in the privileged company of someone who was truly wise beyond his years."[2]

### "THE SCRAPPER"

In the silence between darkness and light, Skeevy awakened, sick from the dream. He rolled over, feeling his head for bumps. There were only a few, but his bones ached from being hit with chairs and his bloody knuckles stuck to the sheets. The shack was dark and hollow as a cistern, and he heard his voice say, "Bund."

The dream had been too real, too much like the real fight with Bund, and he wondered if he had really tried to kill his best friend. His mother begged him to quit boxing when they brought punchy Bund home from the hospital. "Scrap if'n you gotta," she had said, touching the bandage over Skeevy's eye, "but don't you never wear no bandages again. Don't never hurt nobody again."

Trudy mumbled softly in her own dreams, and he slipped from under the covers slowly, trying not to make the springs squeak. He felt empty talking to her, and did not want to be there when she woke up. He dressed and crept to the refrigerator. There was only some rabbit left; still, it was wild meat, and he had to have it.

Outside, a glow from the east was filtering through the fog and turning the ridge pink. Skeevy knew Purserville was across that hill, but he knew the glow could not be from their lights. He started up the western hill toward Clayton wishing he was farther away from Hurricane, from Bund.

As he crested the first knoll, he looked back to the hollow, where he knew Trudy was still sleeping, and far beyond the horizon, where he knew Bund would be sitting on a Coke case in front of the Gulf station begging change, his tongue hanging limp. Skeevy felt his gut skin, and he figured it was just a case of the flux.

At the strip mine, Skeevy sat on a boulder and ate cold rabbit as he looked down on the roofs of Clayton: the company store, company church, company houses, all shiny with fog-wet tin. He saw a miner steal a length of chain from the machine shop where Skeevy worked during the week, promised himself to report it, and forgot it as quickly. Around the houses, he could see where the wives had planted flowers, but the plants were all dead or dying from the constant shower of coal dust.

Just outside of town, across the macadam from the Free Will Church, was The Car, a wheelless dining car left behind after the timber played out. The hulk gleamed like a mussel shell in the Sunday sun.

Skeevy threw his rabbit bones in the brush for the dogs to find, wiped his hands on his jeans, and went down the mountain toward The Car. As he crossed the bottle-cap-strewn pavement of the diner's lot he looked back to where he had sat. The mountain looked like an apple core in the high sun.

Inside, the diner still smelled of sweat and blood from the fight the night before. He shoved the slotted windows open and wondered how ten strong men could find room to fight in The Car. He rubbed his knuckles and smiled. He yawned in the doorway while he waited for the coffee-maker, and through the fog saw Trudy's yellow pantsuit coming down the road.

"Where you been?" he asked.

"You're a'kiddin' me, Skeevy Kelly." She came through the lot smiling, and hooked her arm around him. "You don't show me no respect. Just up an' leave without a good-mornin' kiss."

"I bet you respect real good. I'd respect you till you couldn't walk."

"You're a'kiddin' again. What you want to do today?"

"Bootleg."

"Stop a'kiddin.'"

"I ain't, Trudy. I gotta work for Corey," he said, watching her pout.

"Them ol' chicken-fights . . ."

"Well, stick around and talk to Ellen."

"Last time that happened, I ended up smellin' like a hamburger." Skeevy laughed, and she hugged him. "I'll go visit the preacher or somethin.'"

"You watch out that 'somethin' ain't about like that," he said, measuring off a length with his arm. She knocked his hand down and started toward the road, until he could only see her yellow slacks pumping through the fog. He liked her, but she made him feel fat and lazy.

"Hey, Trudy," he shouted.

"What?" came from the foggy road.

"Get respected," he said, and heard "I swan to goodness . . ." sigh out of the mist.

A clatter came from the church across the road as two drunken miners dusted themselves down the wooden steps and drifted up the road toward the houses.

Skeevy took two cups from the shelf, filled them, and crossed the road to the church. There was only a shadow of light seeping through the painted window. The old deacon was sweeping bottles from between the pews, talking softly to himself as the glass clanked in empty toasts.

"Here, Cephus." He offered the heavy mug. "Ain't good to start without it."

The skinny old man kept to his chore until the mug grew too heavy for Skeevy and he set it on the pew.

"They had a real brawl," Skeevy offered again.

"Ain't right, drinkin' in a church." The old man looked up from his work, his brown eyes catching the hazy light. He took up his coffee and leaned on his broom. "How many?" he asked, blowing steam from his brew.

"Even 'nough. 'Bout twenty-five to a side."

"Oooowee," the old man crooned. "Let's get outa here. Lord's abotherin' me for marvelin' at the devil's work."

Once outside, Skeevy noticed how the old man stood straighter, making an effort, grimacing with pain in his back.

"Who won?" Cephus asked.

"Clayton, I reckon. C'mon, I gotta show you a sight."

They crossed the blacktop to the abandoned mill basement beside the diner. There, with its wheels in the air, lay Jim Gibson's pickup truck.

"Five Clayton boys just flipped her in there."

"Damn" was all Cephus could say.

"Nobody in her, but she made one hell of a racket."

"I reckon so." He looked at Skeevy's knuckles.

Skeevy rubbed his hands against his jeans. "Aw, I just tapped a couple when they got bothersome. Those boys fight too serious."

"I usta could," Cephus said, looking back to the murdered truck.

Skeevy looked to the yellow pines on the western hills: the way the light hit them reminded him of grouse-hunting with Bund, of pairing off in the half-day under the woven branches, of the funny human noises the birds made before they flew, and how their necks were always broken when you picked them up.

"You chorin' the juice today?" Cephus kept looking at the truck.

"Sure. Where's the cockfight?"

"I figger they'll meet-up someplace or another," he said, handing Skeevy the cup with "'Preciate it" as he started for the church. Skeevy side-glanced at the old man to see if his posture drooped, but it did not.

He returned to the diner, plugged in the overplayed jukebox, and threw a few punches at his shadow. He felt tired, and only fried one cheeseburger for breakfast.

Because the woman's back was toward him, Skeevy kept looking at the soft brown scoops of hair. It was clean. Occasionally the man with her would glance at Skeevy to see if he was listening. Being outsiders, they shouted in whispers over their coffee.

Tom and Ellen Corey pulled up in their truck. Ellen's head was thrown back with laughter. Before coming in, they reviewed the upended truck in the neighboring basement. Ellen kept laughing at her short husband as they entered, keeping to the upper side of the counter and away from the customers.

As he leaned over the counter to catch Corey's whispers, Skeevy noticed how Corey's blue eyes were surrounded by white. He had seen the same look in threatened horses.

"Jeb Simpkin's barn," he whispered. "One o'clock."

"Okay."

"Was he all right when he left?" Corey asked.

"Who?"

Skeevy kept his face straight while Ellen sputtered beside him, her hand over her mouth. The outsiders were listening.

"Gibson, dammit. How hard did I lay him?"

"Too hard. You used the club, remember?"

"Oh, shit."

"Yeah," said Skeevy as Ellen broke out laughing.

Skeevy took the keys and went to the Coreys' truck. Across the road, children, women, and old people were shuffling to church. Rev. Jackson and the deacon greeted them at the door, shaking hands. Cephus shot Skeevy a crude salute, and Skeevy made the okay sign as he climbed into the cab. He wondered if Cephus could see it.

As the truck rumbled down the blacktop, Skeevy leaned back behind the wheel, letting his eyes sag, and he could feel his belly bouncing with the jolts of the truck. He took the revolver from beneath the seat, and watched the roadside for groundhogs to shoot. Between the diner and Corey's coal-dust driveway he saw nothing.

From the cellar of Corey's house he loaded the truck with pint cases of Jack Daniel's and Old Crow: four-dollar bottles that would sell for eight at the cockfight. When he first came to Clayton, he had hated bourbon. He noticed the flies were out, and in Hurricane they would be crawling quietly on Bund's tongue. He opened a case, took a bottle, and drank off half of it. Before the burning stopped, he was at Simpkin's barn, and could hear the chickens screaming.

Warts Hall, a cockfighter from Clayton, came from the barn with a stranger, catching Skeevy as he finished the pint.

"Got any left?" Warts asked. His face was speckled with small cancers.

"More than you can handle," said Skeevy, throwing back the blanket covering the cases. Warts took out two Crows, handing Skeevy a twenty.

"Kindy high, ain't it?" the stranger asked, seeing the change.

"This here's Benny the Punk from Purserville."

"Just a Pursie?" Skeevy asked.

Benny looked as if to lunge.

"Well," Skeevy continued, "I don't put no price on it."

The Punk pretended to read the label on his bottle.

Gibson came out of the barn and Skeevy sidestepped to the cab where the revolver was hidden.

"Got one for me, Skeev?" Gibson asked.

"Sure," Skeevy answered, moving to the truck bed. "I reckon I forgot my cigarettes."

Gibson offered one from his pack and Skeevy took it, handing the man the bottle and pocketing the cash. He noticed the yellow circle around Gibson's eye and temple where the club had met him. Gibson stood drinking as Skeevy counted cases and pretended to be confused.

"Where's the mick?" Gibson asked.

Skeevy turned back smiling. "Ain't got no idy."

"You see him, you tell him I'm alookin.'"

"Sure."

The Punk followed Gibson back into the barn, where the gamecocks were crowing.

A wind was rising, pushing the clouds out of the hollow and high over head. Cally, Jeb's daughter, stood on the high front porch of the farmhouse. Skeevy watched her watching him. He had heard Jeb talk of her at work and knew she had been to college in Huntington; he believed Trudy when she said college girls were all looking for rich boys. He watched her clomp down the steps in chunky wooden shoes, and as she crossed the yard between them, he saw how everything from the curve of her hair to the fit of her jeans was too perfect. She looked like the girls he had seen in *Playboy*, and he knew even if she stood beside him, he couldn't have her.

"Your name's Kelly, isn't it?" Her voice was just like the rest of her.

"Yeah," he said, not wanting to say his first name. He knew she would laugh.

"Mom said you were related to Machine Gun Kelly . . ."

He pulled a case out onto the tailgate as if to unload it, wishing somebody had shot the bastard the day he was born.

"He was a cousin of mine—second or third—ever'body's sort of ashamed of him. I don't know nothin' 'bout him."

"I thought you might know something. I'm doing a paper on him for Psych."

"Say what?"

"A paper for Psychology."

Skeevy wondered if she collected maniacs the way men collect gamecocks. He hoisted the case. "Comin' to the main?" he asked.

"Gross."

"They don't have to fight if they don't want to," he smiled, carrying the case inside. Seeing Cally standing at the door, he went back for another. She followed him slowly on her chunky shoes.

"Where do you live?" Cally asked.

"In the holler 'twixt Purserville an' Clayton."

She looked puzzled. "But there's nothing there."

"Sure," he said, and wondered if she would add him alongside his cousin in her collection.

They watched as Cephus's truck bounced through the creek and climbed, dripping, up to the barn. Cephus rushed in without speaking, and Skeevy left Cally standing as he followed with another case. When he came out, Corey had her cornered.

"Gibson's lookin' for you," he said to Corey.

"Been talkin' 'bout that very thing to Cally, here—"

"All Mr. Gibson wants is to restore his dignity," she interrupted.

"So I thought we'd arrange a little match. Since you got boxin' in your blood, I'd be willin' to let you stand in. Loser pays for the truck—'course I'd be willin' to do that, but I know you won't lose."

"I quit boxin' five years ago," Skeevy said, playing with the chain on the tailgate.

"You're quick, boy. I seen you. Don't even have to box. Just dance Gibson to death," Corey laughed. "'Sides," he said to Cally, "Skeevy loves to scrap."

She giggled.

"Hell, scrappin's different. This here's business."

Cally giggled again.

He looked to the pasture field where wind-pushed clouds were blinking the sun on and off. He spotted a holly tree halfway up the slope. His mother had always liked holly trees. He had never told anybody about his promise to her; he knew they would laugh.

"Two-huntert bucks," he heard himself say.

Corey's eyes grew white rims, but they receded quickly. "Half profit on the booze," he bartered.

"Take it or leave it," Skeevy said, watching Cally smile.

"All right," Corey said. "Cally, you talk good to Jim. Get him to agree on Saturday."

Watching her walk into the barn, Skeevy knew Cally could probably make Jim forget the whole thing. But he was glad for the fight, and began starving for wild meat.

"Where's lunch?" he asked Corey.

In the pit, two light clarets rose in flapping pirouettes. Skeevy neither watched nor bet: newly trained cocks had no form and spent most of their time staying clear of one another.

"Lay off," Cephus yelled. "Ain't no need to make no bird fight. Break for a drink."

For ten minutes, Skeevy and Corey were run ragged handing out bottles and making change. Suddenly there were no more takers, and they still had half a truckload.

"The Pursies ain't buyin' from me after last night," Corey whispered. They loaded all but a half-case into the truck, and Corey took it back to his house.

Leaving the half-case unguarded, Skeevy walked to the pit to examine Warts's bird, a black leghorn with his comb trimmed back to a strawberry. Warts had entered him in the main against a black-breasted red gamer. Skeevy watched as the men fixed two-inch gaffs to the birds' spurs. The Punk stood by him, cleaning his nails with a barlow knife.

"What you want laid up, Benny?"

"Give you eight-to-ten on the red," he said, his knife searching to the quick for a piece of dust.

"Make it," said Skeevy. They placed their money on the ground between them, watching as the two owners touched the birds together, then drew them back eight feet from center.

"Pit!" Cephus yelled, and the cocks strutted toward each other, suddenly meeting in a cloud of feathers.

Warts's rooster backed off, blood gleaming from a gaff mark beneath his right wing.

"Give me—" But before the bettor could finish, the two birds were spurring in midair, then the gamecock lay pinned by the leghorn's gaff.

"Handle!" said the judge, but neither owner moved; they were waiting to hear new odds.

"Dammit, I said 'handle,'" Cephus groaned. The birds were wrung together until they pecked, then set free.

"Even odds," someone shouted. Benny leaned forward for the money, and Skeevy stepped on his hand.

"Get off!"

"Leave it there."

"You heard. It's even."

"You made a bet, Punk. Stick it out or get out."

The Punk left the money.

The birds spun wildly, and again the leghorn came down on the red, his gaff buried in the gamer's back.

"Handle." Cephus was getting bored.

The red's owner, a C&O man from Purserville, poured water on his bird's beak, and blew down its mouth to force air past the clotting blood.

"He's just a Pursie chicken," Skeevy grinned. Benny threw him a cross look.

Warts rubbed his bird to the gamer but got no response.

"Ain't got no fight left," Cephus grumbled.

"Don't quit my bird," the C&O man shouted, his hands and shirt speckled with blood.

"If I's as give out as that rooster, I'd need a headstone. Break for a drink."

"Pleasure," Skeevy said to Benny as he picked up his money and returned to the half-case. After selling all but the two bottles in his hip pockets, Skeevy started out the door to look for Cally. Gibson stopped him, smiling.

"I'll make you fight like hell," he warned.

"Well," said Skeevy, "anytime you get to feelin' froggy, just hop on over to your Uncle Skeevy."

"See you Saturday," Gibson laughed.

Outside, he looked for Cally, but she was not around. He went down the farm road, across the blacktop, and up the hills toward his shack. When he topped the first hill, he could see rain coming in from Ohio; and looking back on the tiny people he had left behind, he could see Benny standing with Cally. He wondered if Benny would have to clean his nails again.

Trudy's silence was building as he poured another bourbon and wondered why he gave a good goddamn. When he switched on the light, he disturbed the rest of a hairy winter-fly. He watched it beat against the screen, trying to get to another fly somewhere to breed and die.

"It ain't like I'm boxin' Joe Frazier . . ." He watched her cook and could not recall when she had cared so much about her cooking. "You done tastin' them beans, or you just run outa plates?"

She granted a halted laugh, turned and saw him grinning, and broke into a laughing fit.

"I swan, you made me so mad . . ." she snorted, sitting.

"Ain't nothin' to get mad over."

"Ain't your fight, neither."

"Two-huntert bucks makes it pretty close." He had meant to keep quiet and send the money to Bund. For a moment he saw her eyes open then sag again, and he knew she was worried about the hospital bills. He went back to watching the fly.

Outside the rain fell harder, making petals in the mud. He saw his ghost in the window against the outside's grayness and felt his gut rumble with the flux. Lightly, he touched the scar above his eye, watching as his reflection did the same.

He got up, opened the screen, and let the black fly buzz out into the rain. When he saw the deep holes the drops were making, he wondered if the fly would make it.

"Why don't winter-flies eat?" he asked Trudy.

"I figger they do," she said from the stove.

"Never do," he said, going to the sink to wash.

Taped to the wall was a snapshot of a younger self looking mean over eight-ounce gloves. That was good shape, he thought, fingering the picture. Because it was stained with fat-grease, he left it up.

Trudy put supper down, and they sat.

"You reckon that money would do for a weddin'?" she asked.

"Maybe," he said. "We'll think on it."

They ate.

"Did I ever tell you 'bout the time me an' Bund wrecked the Sunflower Inn?"

"Yeah."

"Oh."

In the stainless steel of the soup machine, Skeevy could see his distorted reflection—real enough to show his features, but not the scar above his eye. His mouth and nose were stuffed with bits of torn rags for padding, and breathing through his mouth made his throat dry.

"Too tight?" Corey asked as he held the bandages wrapped around Skeevy's knuckles. Skeevy shook his head and splayed his fingers to receive the gray muleskin work gloves. He twisted his face to show disgust, and sighed.

"Well, you're the damn boxer," Corey said. "Where's your gloves?"

Skeevy made a zipping motion across his lips and stuck out his right hand to be gloved. He knew it would hurt to get hit with those gloves, but he knew Gibson would hurt more.

A crowd had formed around Corey's truck, and he had Ellen out there to guard it. She was leaning against the rear fender, talking to a longhair with a camera around his neck. Cally came out of the crowd, put her arm around the longhair, and said something that made Ellen laugh. Skeevy squeezed the gloves tighter around his knuckles.

When Skeevy and Corey came outside the crowd howled with praise and curses; the longhair took a picture of Skeevy, and Skeevy wanted to kill him. They cornered the diner and skidded down the embankment to the newly mown creek-basin. The sun was only a light brown spot in the dusty sky.

Jim Gibson stood naked to the waist, his belly pooching around his belt, his skin so white Skeevy wondered if the man had ever gone shirtless. He grinned at Skeevy, and Skeevy slapped his right fist into his palm and smiled back.

It was nothing like the real fight: Cephus rang a cowbell, Gibson threw one haymaker after another, the entire crowd cursed Skeevy's footwork.

"Quit runnin', chickenshit," someone in the crowd yelled.

In his mind the three minutes were up, but nobody told Cephus to ring the bell. Six minutes, and he knew there would be no bell. Gibson connected to the head. And again. Cheers.

Skeevy tried to go low for the sagging belly, made heavy contact twice, but was disappointed to see the results. He danced some more, dodging haymakers, knowing Gibson could only strike thin air a number of times before weakening. When he saw the time come, he sighted on the man's bruised temple, caught it with a left hook, and dropped him. Then came the bell.

Skeevy felt a stinging in his eye and knew it was blood, but this was nothing like the real fight. This was crazy—Gibson wanted to kill him. Gotta slow him, he thought. Gotta stop him before he kills me.

Cephus rang the bell. Can't believe that goddamned bell, he thought. What the hell is this? Can't see shit. Chest. Wind him. He sighted on the soft concave of Gibson's chest and moved in.

As he threw a right cross to Gibson's chest, Skeevy felt the fine bones of his jaw shatter and tasted blood. Gibson did not fall, and Skeevy danced with the flagging pain. He went again with a combination to the temple. He wanted to tear the eye out and step on it, to feel its pressure building under his foot . . . pop.

As he went down he could hear Trudy screaming his name above the cheers. He lay for a time on the cold floor of the Sunflower Inn: the jukebox played, and he heard Bund coughing.

He rolled to his side.

Cephus threw water on Skeevy, and he spat out the bitten-off tip of his tongue. Gibson waited as Skeevy raised himself to a squat. His head cleared, and he knew he could get up.

# LARRY BROWN, "Samaritans"

Any number of Larry Brown stories would qualify as Rough South classics, from "Wild Child," a fine example of honky-tonk noir, to the semiauto-biographical "92 Days," with its portrait of that new breed of backwoods bohe-mian for whom the novels of Faulkner and McCarthy are as essential to life as whiskey and cigarettes and beer. Here we chose one of Brown's personal favorites, "Samaritans," which he insisted was not a "message story" but an ironic and admittedly "contradictory" tale about the perils of judging others and the hazards of doing good.[1]

> You just try to lay it out straight the way it is, and let the reader form his or her opinion about it. You know, you can't be influenced either way. And that's why . . . I get whatever negative things I get said about my work. It usually refers to how brutal it is, and I say well that's fine. It's okay for you to call it brutal, but just admit by God that it's honest.[2]

## "SAMARITANS"

I was smoking my last cigarette in a bar one day, around the middle of the after-noon. I was drinking heavy, too, for several reasons. It was hot and bright out-side, and cool and dark inside the bar, so that's one reason I was in there. But the main reason I was in there was because my wife had left me to go live with somebody else.

A kid came in there unexpectedly, a young, young kid. And of course that's not allowed. You can't have kids coming in bars. People won't put up with that. I was just on the verge of going out to my truck for another pack of smokes when he walked in. I don't remember who all was in there. Some old guys, I guess, and probably, some drunks. I know there was one old man, a golfer, who came in there every afternoon with shaky hands, drank exactly three draft beers, and told these crummy dirty jokes that would make you just close your eyes and shake your head without smiling if you weren't in a real good mood. And back then, I was never in much of a good mood. I knew they'd tell that kid to leave.

But I don't think anybody much wanted to. The kid didn't look good. I thought there was something wrong the minute he stepped in. He had these panicky eyes.

The bartender, Harry, was a big muscled-up guy with a beard. He was washing beer glasses at the time, and he looked up and saw him standing there. The only thing the kid had on was a pair of green gym shorts that were way too big for him. He looked like maybe he'd been walking down the side of a road for a long time, or something similar to that.

Harry, he raised up a little and said, "What you want, kid?" I could see that the kid had some change in his hand. He was standing on the rail and he had his elbows hooked over the bar to hold himself up.

I'm not trying to make this sound any worse than it was, but to me the kid just looked like maybe he hadn't always had enough to eat. He was two or three months overdue for a haircut, too.

"I need a pack a cigrets," he said. I looked at Harry to see what he'd say. He was already shaking his head.

"Can't sell em to you, son," he said. "Minor."

I thought the kid might give Harry some lip. He didn't. He said, "Oh," but he stayed where he was. He looked at me. I knew then that something was going on. But I tried not to think about it. I had troubles enough of my own.

Harry went back to washing his dishes, and I took another drink of my beer. I was trying to cut down, but it was so damn hot outside, and I had a bunch of self-pity loading up on me at that time. The way I had it figured, if I could just stay where I was until the sun went down, and then make my way home without getting thrown in jail, I'd be okay. I had some catfish I was going to thaw out later.

Nobody paid any attention to the kid after that. He wasn't making any noise, wasn't doing anything to cause people to look at him. He turned loose of the bar and stepped down off the rail, and I saw his head going along the far end toward the door.

But then he stuck his face back around the corner, and motioned me toward him with his finger. I didn't say a word, I just looked at him. I couldn't see anything but his eyes sticking up, and that one finger, crooked at me, moving.

I could have looked down at my beer and waited until he went away. I could have turned my back. I knew he couldn't stay in there with us. He wasn't old enough. You don't have to get yourself involved in things like that. But I had to go out for my cigarettes, eventually. Right past him.

I got up and went around there. He'd backed up into the dark part of the lounge.

"Mister," he said. "Will you loan me a dollar?"

He already had money for cigarettes. I knew somebody outside had sent him inside.

I said, "What do you need a dollar for?"

He kind of looked around and fidgeted his feet in the shadows while he thought of what he was going to say.

"I just need it," he said. "I need to git me somethin."

He looked pretty bad. I pulled out a dollar and gave it to him. He didn't say thanks or anything. He just turned and pushed open the door and went outside. I started not to follow him just then. But after a minute I did.

The way the bar's made, there's a little enclosed porch you come into before you get into the lounge. There's a glass door where you can stand inside and look outside. God, it was hot out there. There wasn't even a dog walking around. The sun was burning down on the parking lot, and the car the kid was crawling into was about what I'd expected. A junky-ass old Rambler, wrecked on the right front end, with the paint almost faded off, and slick tires, and a rag hanging out of the grill. It was parked beside my truck and it was full of people. It looked like about four kids in the backseat. The woman who was driving put her arm over the seat, said something to the kid, and then reached out and whacked the hell out of him.

I started to go back inside so I wouldn't risk getting involved. But Harry didn't have my brand and there was a pack on the dash. I could see them from where I was, sitting there in the sun, almost close enough for the woman to reach out and touch.

I'd run over a dog with my truck that morning and I wasn't feeling real good about it. The dog had actually been sleeping in the road. I thought he was already dead and was just going to straddle him until I got almost on top of him, when he raised up suddenly and saw me, and tried to run. Of course I didn't have time to stop by then. If he'd just stayed down, he'd have been all right. The muffler wouldn't have even hit him. It was just a small dog. But, boy, I heard it when it hit the bottom of my truck. It went WHOP! and the dog—

it was a white dog—came rolling out from under my back bumper with all four legs stiff, yelping. White hair was flying everywhere. The air was full of it. I could see it in my rearview mirror. And I don't know why I was thinking about that dog I'd killed while I was watching those people, but I was. It didn't make me feel any better.

They were having some kind of terrible argument out there in that suffocating hot car. There were quilts and pillows piled up in there, like they'd been camping out. There was an old woman on the front seat with the woman driving, the one who'd whacked hell out of her kid for coming back empty-handed.

I thought maybe they'd leave if I waited for a while. I thought maybe they'd try to get their cigarettes somewhere else. And then I thought maybe their car wouldn't crank. Maybe, I thought, they're waiting for somebody to come along with some jumper cables and jump them off. But I didn't have any jumper cables. I pushed open the door and went down the steps.

There was about three feet of space between my truck and their car. They were all watching me. I went up to the window of my truck and got my cigarettes off the dash. The woman driving turned all the way around in the seat. You couldn't tell how old she was. She was one of those women that you can't tell about. But probably somewhere between thirty and fifty. She didn't have liver spots. I noticed that.

I couldn't see all of the old woman from where I was standing. I could just see her old wrinkled knees, and this dirty slip she had sticking out from under the edge of her housecoat. And her daughter—I knew that was who she was—didn't look much better. She had a couple of long black hairs growing out of this mole on her chin that was the size of a butter bean. Her hair kind of looked like a mophead after you've used it for a long time. One of the kids didn't even have any pants on.

She said, "Have they got some cold beer in yonder?" She shaded her eyes with one hand while she looked up at me.

I said, "Well, yeah. They do. But they won't sell cigarettes to a kid that little."

"It just depends on where they know ye or not," she said. "If they don't know ye then most times they won't sell em to you. Is that not right?"

I knew I was already into something. You can get into something like that before you know it. In a minute.

"I guess so," I said.

"Have you got—why you got some, ain't you? Can I git one of them off you?" She was pointing to the cigarettes in my hand. I opened the pack and gave her one. The kid leaned out and wanted to know if he could have one, too.

"Do you let him smoke?"

"Why, he just does like he wants to," she said. "Have you not got a light?"

The kid was looking at me. I had one of those Bics, a red one, and when I held it out to her smoke, she touched my hand for a second and held it steady with hers. She looked up at me and tried to smile. I knew I needed to get back inside right away, before it got any worse. I turned to go and what she came out with stopped me dead in my tracks.

"You wouldn't buy a lady a nice cold beer, would you?" she said. I turned around. There was this sudden silence, and I knew that everybody in the car was straining to hear what I would say. It was serious. Hot, too. I'd already had about five and I was feeling them a little in the heat. I took a step back without meaning to and she opened her door.

"I'll be back in a little bit, Mama," she said.

I looked at those kids. Their hair was ratty and their legs were skinny. It was so damn hot you couldn't stand to stay out in it. I said, "You gonna leave these kids out here in the sun?"

"Aw, they'll be all right," she said. But she looked around kind of uncertainly. I was watching those kids. They were as quiet as dead people.

I didn't want to buy her a beer. But I didn't want to make a big deal out of it, either. I didn't want to keep looking at those kids. I just wanted to be done with it.

"Lady," I said, "I'll buy you a beer. But those kids are burning up in that car. Why don't you move it around there in the shade?"

"Well." She hesitated. "I reckon I could," she said. She got back in and it cranked right up. The fan belt was squealing, and some smoke farted out from the back end. But she limped it around to the side and left it under a tree. Then we went inside together.

The first Bud she got didn't last two minutes. She sucked the can dry. She had on some kind of military pants and a man's long-sleeved work shirt, and house shoes. Blue ones, with a little fuzzy white ball on each. She had the longest toes I'd ever seen.

Finally I asked her if she wanted another beer. I knew she did.

"Lord yes. And I need some cigrets too if you don't care. Marlboro Lights. Not the menthol. Just reglar lights."

I didn't know what to say to her. I thought about telling her I was going to the bathroom, and then slipping out the door. But I really wasn't ready to leave just yet. I bought her another beer and got her some cigarettes.

"I'm plumb give out," she said. "Been drivin all day."

I didn't say anything. I didn't want anybody to think I was going with her.

"We tryin to git to Morgan City Loozeanner. M'husband's sposed to've got a job down there and we's agoin to him. But I don't know," she said. "That old car's about had it."

I looked around in the bar and looked at my face in the mirror behind the rows of bottles. The balls were clicking softly on the pool tables.

"We left from Tuscalooser Alabama," she said. "But them younguns has been yellin and fightin till they've give me a sick headache. It shore is nice to set down fer a minute. Ain't it good and cool in here?"

I watched her for a moment. She had her legs crossed on the bar stool and about two inches of ash hanging off her cigarette. I got up and went out the door, back to the little enclosed porch. By looking sideways I could see the Rambler parked under the shade. One of the kids was squatted down behind it, using the bathroom. I thought about things for a while and then went back in and sat down beside her.

"Ain't many men'll hep out a woman in trouble," she said. "Specially when she's got a buncha kids."

I ordered myself another beer. The old one was hot. I set it up on the bar and she said, "You not goin to drank that?"

"It's hot," I said.

"I'll drank it," she said, and she pulled it over next to her. I didn't want to look at her anymore. But she had her eyes locked on me and she wouldn't take them off. She put her hand on my wrist. Her fingers were cold.

"It's some people in this world has got thangs and some that ain't," she said. "My daddy used to have money. Owned three service stations and a sale barn. Had four people drove trucks fer him. But you can lose it easy as you git it. You ought to see him now. We cain't even afford to put him in a rest home."

I got up and went over to the jukebox and put two quarters in. I played some John Anderson and some Lynn Anderson and then I punched Narvel Felts. I didn't want to have to listen to what she had to say.

She was lighting a cigarette off the butt of another one when I sat down beside her again. She grabbed my hand as soon as it touched the bar.

"Listen," she said. "That's my mama out yonder in that car. She's seventy-eight year old and she ain't never knowed nothin but hard work. She ain't got a penny in this world. What good's it done her to work all her life?"

"Well," I said, "she's got some grandchildren. She's got them."

"Huh! I got a girl eighteen, was never in a bit a trouble her whole life. Just up and run off last year with a goddamn sand nigger. Now what about that?"

"I don't know," I said.

"I need another beer!" she said, and she popped her can down on the bar pretty hard. Everybody turned and looked at us. I nodded to Harry and he brought a cold one over. But he looked a little pissed.

"Let me tell you somethin," she said. "People don't give a shit if you ain't got a place to sleep ner nothin to eat. They don't care. That son of a bitch," she said. "He won't be there when we git there. If we ever git there." And she slammed her face down on the bar, and started crying, loud, holding onto both beers.

Everybody stopped what they were doing. The people shooting pool stopped. The guys on the shuffleboard machine just stopped and turned around.

"Get her out of here," Harry said. "Frank, you brought her in here, you get her out."

I got down off my stool and went around to the other side of her, and I took her arm.

"Come on," I said. "Let's go back outside."

I tugged on her arm. She raised her head and looked straight at Harry.

"*Fuck* you," she said. "You don't know nothin about me. You ain't fit to judge."

"Out," he said, and he pointed toward the door. "Frank," he said.

"Come on," I told her. "Let's go."

It hadn't cooled off any, but the sun was a little lower in the sky. Three of the kids were asleep in the backseat, their hair plastered to their heads with sweat. The old woman was sitting in the car with her feet in the parking lot, spitting brown juice out the open door. She didn't even turn her head when we walked back to the car. The woman had the rest of the beer in one hand, the pack of Marlboro Lights in the other. She leaned against the fender when we stopped.

"You think your car will make it?" I said. I was looking at the tires and thinking of the miles they had to go. She shook her head slowly and stared at me.

"I done changed my mind," she said. "I'm gonna stay here with you. I love you."

Her eyes were all teary and bitter, drunk-looking already, and I knew that she had been stomped on all her life, and had probably been forced to do no telling what. And I just shook my head.

"You can't do that," I said.

She looked at the motel across the street.

"Let's go over there and git us a room," she said. "I want to."

The kid who had come into the bar walked up out of the hot weeds and stood there looking at us for a minute. Then he got in the car. His grandmother had to pull up the front seat to let him in. She turned around and shut the door.

"I may just go to Texas," the woman said. "I got a sister lives out there. I may just drop these kids off with her for a while and go on out to California. To Los Vegas."

I started to tell her that Las Vegas was not in California, but it didn't matter. She turned the beer up and took a long drink of it, and I could see the muscles and cords in her throat pumping and working. She killed it. She dropped the can at her feet, and it hit with a tiny tinny sound and rolled under the car. She wiped her mouth with the back of her hand, tugging hard at her lips, and then she wiped her eyes.

"Don't nobody know what I been through," she said. She was looking at the ground. "Havin to live on food stamps and feed four younguns." She shook her head. "You cain't do it," she said. "You cain't hardly blame nobody for wantin to run off from it. If they was any way I could run off myself I would."

"That's bad," I said.

"That's terrible," I said.

She looked up and her eyes were hot.

"What do you care? All you goin to do is go right back in there and git drunk. You just like everybody else. You ain't never had to go in a grocery store and buy stuff with food stamps and have everbody look at you. You ain't never had to go hungry. Have you?"

I didn't answer.

"Have you?"

"No."

"All right, then," she said. She jerked her head toward the building. "Go on back in there and drank ye goddamn beer. We made it this far without you."

She turned her face to one side. I reached back for my wallet because I couldn't think of anything else to do. I couldn't stand to look at them anymore.

I pulled out thirty dollars and gave it to her. I knew that their troubles were more than she'd outlined, that they had awful things wrong with their lives that thirty dollars would never cure. But I don't know. You know how I felt? I felt like I feel when I see those commercials on TV, of all those people, women and kids, starving to death in Ethiopia and places, and I don't send money. I know that Jesus wants you to help feed the poor.

She looked at what was in her hand, and counted it, jerking the bills from one hand to the other, two tens and two fives. She folded it up and put it in her pocket, and leaned down and spoke to the old woman.

"Come on, Mama," she said. The old woman got out of the car in her housecoat and I saw then that they were both wearing exactly the same kind of house shoes. She shuffled around to the front of the car, and her daughter took her arm.

They went slowly across the parking lot, the old woman limping a little in the heat, and I watched them until they went up the steps that led to the lounge and disappeared inside. The kid leaned out the window and shook his head sadly. I pulled out a cigarette and he looked up at me.

"Boy you a dumb sumbitch," he said.

And in a way I had to agree with him.

# TIM MCLAURIN, *The Acorn Plan*

"Bubble Riley decided to drink all the wine in the world the night Billy cut the soldier's lung in half."[1] That opening sentence tells you all you need to know about Tim McLaurin's novel *The Acorn Plan,* a raucous, brutal study of honor and excess, desperation and redemption.

> I grew up in a community where alcohol was the central social event—the hard-living, hard-playing community, of particularly men—overindulging in life and alcohol and all aspects of life. Yet the theme of religion runs through my works too. I've often said that some people find salvation in church, others in a bottle of Jim Beam. Both are an escape—something to guide you—of course, alcohol in a downward spiral. It is something that gets hold of your life.[2]

**FROM *THE ACORN PLAN***

Bubble Riley decided to drink all the wine in the world the night Billy cut the soldier's lung in half. He made the pledge right after the Fayetteville police had gone, standing alone in front of Jerry's Burger Barn, staring at the puddle of blood and wishing they hadn't gotten so drunk.

Most of the crowd had left; seeing someone cut was not unusual at Jerry's, especially when Billy was around. They'd gone back to their cars, to their hot beer, cold hamburgers and nooky. But Bubble stood motionless for several minutes, his head lowered, mumbling, noticing how the soldier's blood was already congealing around the edges and how, against the black asphalt, it looked so very red.

Bubble walked to the curb and sat. Slowly he rocked, cradling his gut, which burned from all the wine. "Goddamn dumb-ass boy," he mumbled, shaking his head. He knew Billy hadn't set out to cut the soldier. They hadn't even planned on coming to Jerry's, but had considered going to the river and fishing for bullheads.

"Naw, not that. Bubble," Billy had said. "Last time you got so drunk I had to tote you back up the bank."

"You got a better idea?"

Billy took another swig of wine from the bottle they shared.

"We could go over to Marge Thompson's house. I saw her today, and she said to stop by."

"She ain't wanting to see the two of us, old fart I am."

"Margie? Shit. She'd want the four of us if we were that many."

"Thought you said she's a claptrap."

Billy nodded while taking another guzzle of wine. "What about some pool? We could go over to Earl's Place and take them schoolboy's quarters."

"You forgetting you still owe Earl for that busted window?"

Bubble took the bottle from his nephew. He knew Billy was getting drunk. He was a damn good boy when sober, but lately Billy got a mean streak in him when he drank too much. That bothered Bubble.

"I wish your car was running," Billy said. "We could buy a case of beer and go to the drive-in flick."

Bubble nodded his head and felt sad. Just this week he had sold the battery. "What about the walk-in?"

"Naw, I don't like sitting in them nasty seats."

Bubble measured the bottle against the street light. Half empty. He felt even sadder.

"What say I run over to the grill and get another?" Billy asked.

"You don't need no more wine."

Billy laughed. "Man that's twenty-one don't have to drink milk." He scooted across the street and returned with another quart bottle. They sat on the up-turned Pepsi crates for half an hour more, passing the bottle and debating.

"We could go to the bowling alley on Raeford Road."

"Naw. The bus line is fixing to shut down."

"You hungry?" Billy asked.

"Yeah, come to think of it," Bubble answered. He tried to drink on an empty stomach. That way, the wine went further. Bubble emptied the bottle. It amazed him how quick bottles seemed to go these days.

Both were close to knee-walking when they left, so they weaved a course through backyards and alleys to keep out of sight of the cops. They reached the white cinder block, neon-lit diner, just as the car-privileged crowd was returning from downtown, mostly local people who leaned on their horns while backing into parking spaces. The people shouted to one another, drinking beer and tossing empty cans on the pavement.

More than a few lowered their voices when Billy stumbled by. Some even shut up altogether and sat quietly in their cars, a sensible practice when Billy was noticeably drunk.

Billy stepped onto a picnic table bench. "Sons of bitches," he roared. "Daughters of queers, Billy boy is here."

"Hush that kind of talk," Bubble grumbled.

"Why?"

"Cause the law will think you're drunk."

"I am drunk." Billy stepped on top of the concrete table. "Sons of sluts. Come here to Billy, and he'll slice your butts."

Billy jerked back his head and laughed, but no one in the cars did. They looked at their food. Bubble frowned until Billy stepped down, then went to the window and ordered a couple of hamburgers with fries.

"You sit down and eat this and sober up some," Bubble ordered.

Billy squeezed catsup on his fries, joked with Bubble, and watched cars circle the diner. He shouted at people he knew and at some he didn't know. Trouble rode in on the loud-motored '57 Chevy, candy-apple red, jacked high in the rear and sporting polished Crager mags. Billy watched it pass. The cam went whump, whump, whump and the stereo was cranked up loud.

"Bad ride, ain't it," Billy said.

The driver backed into a space, the engine revved several times, then shut down. The stereo kept blasting. A tall man with a soldier's short hair and bearing stepped out. He wore tight jeans and a T-shirt that revealed the legs of a nude lady tatooed on his right bicep. He bopped along to the diner, snapping his fingers to the music.

"Hey, buddy," Billy shouted. "What you pay for that rod?"

The soldier stopped and turned toward Billy. He peered over the rim of his shades, then walked on.

Billy squinted one eye at Bubble. He shouted louder. "I said there, my man, what you pay for that thing?"

"More money than you'll ever have," the soldier called over his shoulder. Then he leaned into the order window.

Billy tried to stand, but Bubble grabbed his arm. "Let it be," he warned.

"Hey, fuck you, grunt," Billy shouted at the soldier.

The soldier finished his order before he came over. "You got a problem, man?" He cocked one hand over his back pocket.

"Naw, not me," Billy said, carefully inspecting his fingernails. "Why you ask? You looking for a problem?"

"No. I just thought maybe you had a problem, that's all." The soldier turned to go.

"Hey, you with the airborne?" Billy asked.

"What if I am?"

"Cause I think the airborne sucks."

The soldier whirled back. Clutched in one fist gleamed the hooked blade of a paratrooper's knife. "Hey, fucker. I came here minding my own business. Might be best for you to do the same."

A crowd was quickly gathering in a semicircle, some grinning, but most watching with nervous eyes.

Slowly, Bubble stood. "Look, friend," he started.

"I ain't your friend, motherfucker."

"Well then, look here, mister. I'm sorry 'bout my nephew here. He's just real drunk. Why don't you go ahead and enjoy your food. We're real sorry."

The soldier hesitated before lowering the hand that held the knife. He tapped the side of the blade against his thigh. "O.K. Ain't no problem, pop. Just tell your boy to shut up his foul mouth."

"I'll do that. I sure will." Bubble turned and shook Billy's shoulder. "You stop it now, hear me?"

Billy leaned back on the bench against the table. His hands were behind his back. The soldier gave him a long, hard stare over his shades, then wheeled smartly about-face. "Dumb-ass hick," he said loudly.

"You suck. Airborne sucks. Your mama sucks," Billy taunted.

The soldier spun around on one heel and sliced in a wide arc. Billy came off the bench smooth and quick, slipping underneath the blade, and slashed across with his hawk-billed blade, catching the soldier under his armpit between two ribs. The sound was easy, just the rip of cloth, but the blade didn't surface until it reached the sternum and brought out chunks of pink lung.

The soldier looked very surprised. He dropped his blade and knelt slowly, holding his ribs and moaning. Blood flowed from between his fingers, ran down his shirt and dripped on the pavement. He was still kneeling when the ambulance arrived.

Billy knew there was no sense in running. Too many people there knew him, and besides, he felt a curious interest in the way the man knelt, his face white and his palm jammed tight against his chest. Somehow he seemed much more human now than when he was a bopping, juke-walking bad ass.

Billy slipped the knife to Bubble, then sat down on the curb and waited for the police to come screeching up.

The officers didn't rough him any; all the ones who worked the east side of Fayetteville had known Billy's father. They just snapped on a set of handcuffs and drove him to Central Station.

He was locked in a cell along with several drunks, where he bent forward on a cot and drummed his fingers against the side of his head. An hour later, he was led into a small office for questioning.

"Why'd you cut him?" asked the detective.

Billy shrugged. "I don't know. I guess I was trying to save his life."

"Don't be a wise ass with me, Billy. I've known you since you were knee-high."

Billy shrugged again. He was led back to the cell.

Billy knew that Bubble had already made the call, and that Wallace Bain would be down in the morning to pay his bail, so he stretched out on the filthy bunk, watched the drunks cry and cuss, and chewed on his fingernails. Later, he slept the dreamless, snoring sleep that comes from too much wine.

It seemed Billy had just closed his eyes when he awakened to naked, electric lights, his tongue thick and temples throbbing. Someone was calling his name. He sat up and before him stood the jailer with Wallace Bain, stiff and out of place in his gray linen suit. Wallace wasn't frowning, but his eyes said he was fed up and worried. He stood over Billy's cot for several seconds. Then he did frown, so Billy frowned back and wished his head didn't hurt.

"He'll be all right," Billy said. "Lung meat always heals fast."

Wallace exhaled heavily. "Maybe, maybe not. We don't know for sure yet. One thing I do know, is that you're not all right."

"Yeah? As in why?"

"Jesus Christ, Billy! Three times in four months." Wallace lowered his voice. "The prosecutor says he's going to ask for attempted murder."

"Bull. For cutting someone? Hey, he swung first." Billy swallowed, the sound of it loud in his own ears. "If I'd wanted to kill him, I'd gone for his neck."

Wallace shook his head deliberately and stared at the concrete floor. The drunks watched Billy with new respect. "I can't figure you out anymore," Wallace said. "Just can't." He walked to the bars, then spun back. "I'm just glad your dad doesn't have to see this. It would kill Mike deader than that heart attack."

"Oh, he probably sees all right," Billy answered, narrowing his eyes. "Ain't you supposed to be able to see everything from up there?"

"For God's sake, Billy. You're nearly twenty-two. A grown man. What the hell is going on?" Wallace pulled out a handkerchief from his back pocket and mopped his forehead. "You know," he said quietly, "you might get time for this. Six months is a real possibility."

"Just get my bail, how 'bout? You're a lawyer, remember? Not a preacher."

"Yeah, well maybe I ain't no preacher, but I was your dad's best friend. And I've known you since you were shitting yellow."

"Just get my bail, O.K.?"

"If I was about five years younger right now, I'd bust your ass good."

Wallace's face colored deep red and a thick vein stood out on his forehead. Then Billy smiled, the smile that could take anyone, his face lighting up and his eyes sparkling like troubled water. "Hey, you're sounding like you're back on the corner with my old man."

Wallace smacked fist into palm. He sighed. "I wish to hell you had another couple of years in the Marines. You still don't have any discipline."

"Get me out of here, Wallace," Billy repeated, the smile erased from his face. "I don't like it in here."

"It's going to take some time. I've got some convincing to do."

"I swear. I'll go straight as a hoe handle."

"The judge said no bail until they know this guy is going to be O.K."

"He'll make it. I wasn't cutting to kill."

Wallace left then, but didn't return for five days.

On Monday morning Bubble walked out on his job. He marched into the boss's office and put it right on the line.

"I'm quitting, Harry. As of this very minute," he said to the pot-bellied, balding man behind the wide, metal desk. "Just give me my time and what other, and I'll be gone."

The boss rubbed his fleshy chin. He sat forward. "Quit? Why do you want to quit?"

"Personal reasons, sick of this place, running for mayor. Take your pick."

"My God, Bubble. You better give this some thought."

"I've thought."

The boss stood, then walked to the window overlooking the guts of the mill. Over his shoulder, Bubble saw bodies scurrying between the huge, whining machines. He turned and looked Bubble in his eyes. "What do you think Mike would have said about this?"

Bubble's top lip curled slightly. Twenty years he had been in the plant, but had never been promoted above general floor help because of his week-long drunks. "Mike can't say nothing now. Jobs don't matter much to dead men."

So Bubble left the drab interior of the cotton mill for the last time, punched the clock and heard it snap neatly through the paper card, and strode out through the shadows of the twin smokestacks. He was given three day's back wages, a week's vacation pay, and the cashed-in value of his insurance plan—a little more than six hundred dollars all totaled. He hid most of it in a sock in a hole in the bottom of his mattress. Then he headed downtown with two tens in his pocket.

Ordinarily, the squat, sad houses of east Fayetteville would have held nothing new for Bubble. Years back, he had ceased to mark how every day the buildings settled closer to the dirt and concrete, turned grayer like mushrooms that have passed their prime. The community was just home to him and all the others at the mill, to the truckers and plumbers and waitresses and route salesmen. But today, he did notice, now a liberated man, shocked at how the houses were rickety as wet cardboard, the brief spots of color from flowers planted inside discarded tires, and candy-striped, rusty swingsets, only highlighting the decay. Billy was decaying too. Bubble picked up his gait at the thought as he hurried to Willie's Bar and Grill. He took the shortcut that skirted the river through the back lot where the winos hung out.

"Hey, Bubble," a drunk shouted from the shade of a tree. "What brings you here on a Monday?"

"Got business with Willie," Bubble answered.

The winos exchanged glances. Six of them rested in various stages of drunk, but even the drunkest managed to prop himself up on one elbow. Bubble was good drinking company because he was generous and hated to be alone.

"Kind'a early for ya, ain't it?" asked Shorty Bullard, a stocky, red-faced man with bad teeth.

"Don't matter none," Bubble said. "I've turned over a new leaf." Deep down, Bubble realized he was an alcoholic, and had been for years. So far he had managed to keep his drinking within reason, limiting it to weekends except for occasional binges. He wasn't in the same league as those who spent their days and nights behind Willie's bar, having kept up a house and held onto his job until now.

"A new leaf, huh?" Shorty's eyes widened. "You ain't giving up drinking?"

"No. Nothing like that. I'm aiming to drink more."

That jolted everyone. Several managed to sit up and rub their eyes. Shorty smiled. "Well, I think I can speak for all of us in saying we'd be glad to have you join us if you're planning on pulling a drunk. We've got some sardines and crackers, and I've got a snort here to get you jump-started."

Shorty passed him a green bottle containing two fingers of wine. Bubble sniffed the top, then took a swallow. The wine was hot and acidic, but he swallowed quickly and wiped his mouth on his sleeve. Shorty took the bottle and drained the last drop. Bubble stood in silence, gazing at the failed men.

"I need some professional advice from you fellows," he said finally.

Shorty nodded, then looked at the other winos who nodded as well. "Well, there ain't no PhD in the whole lot here, but we'll give you our best."

"I need to know this. What is the worst wine in the world for making a fellow crazy? You know, shooting and cutting crazy."

"That's a tough one. Why d'ya want to know?"

"Cause I aim to drink all of it."

"All of it?"

"Yeah, if it's in me, I aim to drink all the wine in the world."

The winos stared blankly at Bubble, wondering if they had heard him right. Then Shorty chuckled and the others joined him in a chorus of laughter.

"Can't nobody drink all the wine in the world. Bubble," Shorty said. "Hell, I been trying all my life and ain't made a dent."

Their laughter galled him, but Bubble faked a chuckle of his own.

"I mean it," Bubble said. "I want to know what is the worst wine in the world. Crazy-making wine."

The winos put their heads together and discussed the matter intensely, each one arguing for his favorite brand.

"You want to get crazy, you ought to drink 'bout a fifth of Richard's Triple Peach," said Chubby Watts. "That shit'll make you run rabbits."

"Bullshit," said Larry Cooper, his brimmed fishing hat pulled even with his eyebrows to hide a recently stitched-up forehead. "Richard's wouldn't make my dick hard. You want to raise hell, drink you a gut full of Thunderbird."

Punk Davis spit in the dirt. "Shit, Larry. All Thunderbird did for you was get your ass whupped. Ask me, Roma Rocket is best. Don't make you sleepy, either."

"Ain't nobody asked you," Larry answered, and pulled his cap a little lower.

Shorty held his arm and shouted for silence. "Quit the arguing. Hell, we'll ask Clarence. He's the authority on hell raising."

Shorty walked to where Clarence Hubbard lay passed out in the edge of some bushes. He shook him several times and slapped his face. Clarence moaned, then spoke several unintelligible words. Shorty felt under the man's belly and pulled out a nearly empty bottle of wine. He held it away from his face and read the label.

"M.D. 20/20. 'da Mad Dog. If Clarence drinks it, it's gotta be bad," he said, handing the bottle to Bubble.

"Yeah, Clarence would know," said Chubby, a half-burned cigarette jiggling between his lips as he talked. "He's cut a lot of people."

"Shot a nigger once, too," another said.

Bubble nodded. He crunched on a saltine cracker. Then he marched into Willie's and bought a case of Mad Dog.

The early fall weather was good, clear days without rain and nights warm enough to prevent much dew. Bubble lounged with his new friends, drinking much wine, dining off sardines and potted meat and crackers and liver pudding. He drank under the shade of a willow tree and slept there, cushioned with a long piece of cardboard and musty pillow, only returning home to take more money from the hole under his mattress. He tried to forget that Billy was three days now in jail, but still called Wallace, the family lawyer, regular to see if bond had been set.

Bubble stuck to drinking Mad Dog, and for a while he thought it might actually be possible to drink all the crazy-making wine in the world, or at least all in Willie's Bar and Grill. Anyway, his real objective was to show Billy just how disgusting and wasted alcohol could make a man. Bubble realized he hadn't cared about his own life for years now, but he cared about the boy, and he'd show him. He'd show him goddamn well what wine would do to you. That afternoon a delivery truck arrived and loaded Willie's shelves with wine again, and Bubble realized what a task he had. He set to with renewed vigor, and soon word spread to every drunk east of the river that a real party was going on.

Bubble had always likened the drunks behind Willie's to autumn leaves a cold rain has plastered against sidewalks and car tops, their colors muted and leeched. They wore mismatched and ill-sized clothes snatched from backyard lines and Salvation Army bins: checkered trousers paired with striped shirts, old coats with busted sleeves, one wing-tip loafer teamed with a tennis shoe laced up with fishing line. Their teeth were bad, the men's chins unshaven, skinned elbows and infected insect bites slow to heal, then leaving white scars. Their eyes were dimmed by wine and the personal griefs they chose years before to never see again. Yep, like old leaves, fading fast but slowly dying.

Among the dying were Chubby Watts, so skinny he tied his trousers with a length of rope, and Punk Davis, and Wilma, Punk's old lady, who would screw anyone for a bottle, and Shorty, who was short, and Milton and Larry Cooper, who had once run a fish market before they began drinking up the rent, and Clarence, who was half Cherokee Indian and half crazy and had killed a nigger once, and Mary the Queen, a fat woman from somewhere up north who sold queenly blow jobs, and Harry Little, who had lost a leg in Viet Nam and would cry "In coming! In coming!" when he was very drunk. They clustered within the shade of the tree with about a dozen others who drifted in and out, and drank and ate and slept and puked and fucked and coughed there, and shit in the blueberry bushes growing on the banks of Cape Fear. Sometimes they fell backwards from their squat and rolled into the deep, gray water and drowned. They were all bums, had been, would be.

But not Bubble. He knew he wasn't a bum, just a man with a weakness for drink, prone to fall hard occasionally for a few days, only to get sick and spit up blood and be cared for by his sister Ruby until he could return to work. But this time was different. He wasn't drinking from weakness, he was drinking with conviction.

Ruby came on the morning of the fourth day. She was wearing her starched, white waitress uniform, her red hair piled high in its usual coil, her meaty arms folded over her bosom while she frowned.

"What in hell do you think you're doing?" She towered above where Bubble sat; her words had the ring of one scolding a child.

Bubble cocked an eye from where he was eating a can of cold pork and beans. He took a moment to focus his vision. "Hey there, little sister."

Ruby grunted. "Couldn't you have at least let someone know where you were?"

"I know where I am," Bubble finally answered. He spit a bean into the grass. "So does the gang here."

Ruby squinted a mean eye at the bums under the tree. She wrinkled her nose. "I meant human beings. Not a bunch of hogs."

"They ain't hogs. They're my buddies."

"Yeah," Chubby answered. "We're his friends."

Ruby stared at the red creases across Chubby's thin face from sleeping squashed against the ground. His fly was open, his shirttail pulled through the hole.

"I take it back. I don't mean hogs. Hog shit is a better description."

"Somebody should slap her face," said Wilma. "Who is she to be so high and mighty?"

"Watch your mouth," Bubble warned. "This here's my sister."

Ruby stared at the small woman till Wilma dropped her eyes to the ground, then turned her anger back to Bubble. "I'm ashamed to claim you right now. I hear you even quit your job."

"Wasn't much of one."

"It kept you living, didn't it?"

"No." Bubble took another swig from his bottle. "Actually, I think it kept me dying."

Ruby watched a trickle of wine leak from the corner of Bubble's mouth and drip from his jaw to the front of his shirt. His shoes were off, one big toe poking through a hole in his sock.

"I suppose you think all this wine you're drinking is gonna do you good?"

"Damn right," said Milton Cooper. "See the bloom in his cheeks?"

"Yeah, I see it, hog shit, bloom in his cheeks with bloodshot eyes, stinking, sitting there eating cold pork and beans. I see it."

"You're looking at it all wrong, Ruby," Shorty said. "Bubble ain't killing himself, he's healing himself. Timothy 5:23, and I quote Saint Paul, 'Drink no longer water, but use a little wine for thy stomach's sake and thine often infirmities.'"

"He didn't mean lay around drinking rot gut."

"If you don't like it, hit the road, honey," said Mary the Queen, crossing her arms and cocking her head to one side. A grimy crease between her double chins made her throat look slit.

"I said for ya'll to shut up," Bubble hollered. "I can handle my own sister."

"Make me leave, whore," Ruby said to Mary. Ruby stood at five-foot-ten and weighed 170 pounds, with thick calloused hands that were capable of pulling out gobs of hair. Mary snorted, then spit on the ground, but shut up.

"You even been to see Billy yet?" Ruby asked.

"No," Bubble mumbled, then ducked his eyes. "I been in touch with Wallace, though, and he's taking care of everything."

"Well, he's got his work cut out for him this time. That soldier nearly bled to death."

Several bums moved away from the argument to sleep. Bubble fiddled with a loose button on his shirt.

"I talked to Harry today, and he said to tell you that if you'll be at work tomorrow, he'll give you one last chance."

"I can't do that," Bubble said while slowly shaking his head. "I got to do this thing for Billy."

"For Billy?" Ruby cried, her eyes wide. "For Billy?"

"Yeah, for Billy."

"How do you figure laying up drunk and losing your job is gonna help Billy?"

"That boy has got to see right damn soon what drinking will do to ya." Bubble raised his chin. "I plan to drink every drop in the world."

The few drunks still conscious grinned.

"All the wine in the world, huh? You're a fool." Ruby turned and started for her car. "A damn fool." She shouted this over and over before reaching her battered green Plymouth and driving away.

Bubble and his followers slept through the hot afternoon, awakening at twilight with rat nests and cobwebs filling their heads and mouths. They pooled their money, Bubble providing most of it, and purchased another case of wine. An old tire was doused with kerosene and lit. They sat in the dancing light, eating from cans and smoking, passing the bottles until drunkenness again swept over them like a soft, warm wave. One of the bums had a coughing spell, and the sound of him starving for breath reminded Bubble of how Mike had sounded in his last few weeks.

"This is a free way to be, ain't it?" Bubble said to anyone listening. "Being a bum is a free way for a man to live."

A pause. "Yeah," Chubby answered. "Free to work a little, or never work, sleep when you feel like it, and drink when you can. Hell, I could up and thumb down to Florida tomorrow."

"Free way to die, too, ain't it," Bubble continued, looking into the fire. "Men let lots of things kill them, but usually they suffer too long. Shit, a man could drink himself to death in six months if he tried."

"Quicker than that," Chubby answered. "I knew a fellow who had been drunk just five days when he passed out, puked and croaked."

"After just five days?"

"Yep, young guy. Wasn't no bum, neither. Had just split up from his wife. Went to sleep on his back and that was it."

"I don't wanna drown in wine puke."

"Me neither, but you got to admit, it's quicker than laying up with your liver gone."

Bubble nodded. "Good to know there's a few things we can control in this old world."

Soon most of the bums were sleeping, curled on their pads like babies, what valuables or money they owned stuffed in their crotches. Bubble sat alone by the fire, thinking drunk, jumbled thoughts. For a second, he imagined he saw Mike's face in the flames, not a bad face, but the way his older brother had looked in his good days. The face disappeared with a twist of the flames and Bubble shook his head.

"Strong-ass wine." He took another swig. "Crazy-making wine." Bubble stood, rubbed his knees, then headed for his cardboard pad beside the bushes, wavering with his feet striking the ground heavily and flat. "Goddamn strong-ass wine," he mumbled again. He flopped down and began pulling at his shoes. He jumped when a second face appeared in the darkness.

"Damn, Wilma! Scare me to death." Bubble slapped at his chest and coughed.

"Sorry, Bubble. Just thought I would say goodnight."

"Yeah? That's nice of 'ya. Well, good night. Say, where's Punk?"

"Over there passed out."

Wilma was short and skinny with a sharp face and large front teeth like a rodent's. Her breasts were too large for her body. She was wearing a stained pair of white painter's pants and a ridiculous laced blouse that might have been part of some rich woman's evening suit. Her hair was mostly gray.

"Yeah? Well, sleep tight, hear," Bubble said. He continued taking off his shoes.

Wilma sat down heavily on the grass. She hugged her knees. "Punk was telling me you got a house?"

"Yeah. Sort of. I rent it."

"Then why you sleeping out here with these bums? Might rain even tonight."

"Houses don't mean nothing to me 'cept a place to sleep."

"Then sleep there."

Bubble wrenched off his second shoe. He picked at the goo between his toes. Wilma slid closer. She traced one finger across his arm.

"Bubble honey. You ought not to be sleeping outside like this. Gonna be cold soon. You'll get sick." She leaned a little closer, then smiled. "Say, what if

I was to move in with you? I can cook real good, and clean up, and be good company at night."

"You already got Punk."

"The hell with Punk. He's always lying in his puke."

"The last thing I need right now is a woman."

"Why? You're a man." Wilma slid her finger down his arm across his leg, lightly drawing circles around his crotch. "Think about it, baby. We could have a real nice time together." The circles she drew pressed heavier and heavier until she was vigorously rubbing his penis.

"Oh God," Bubble whispered, feeling the heat gather. Wilma took his hand and placed it between her thighs. "Oh shit," he said.

Wilma slid off her pants in seconds, then helped Bubble off with his, and pulled him on top of her upon the cardboard bed.

"You might have a point," Bubble said. "It's been awhile."

They had barely begun to grind together when Bubble felt hot stinging on his rear end. "Goddamn it," he yelped and jumped to his knees, turning to see Punk waving the neck of a shattered wine bottle in small circles.

"I got something right here you can fuck," Punk growled.

Bubble felt his buttocks with one hand, the other stretched up before him. "Goddamn. Hold on now, Punk," he said backing up. "I was just leaving."

Bubble took off running, his pants down around his ankles, arms pumping, leaving the good life behind him in back of Willie's Bar and Grill.

"Goddamn it, blow, blow," Bubble hollered later that night while Ruby cleaned his wounds with alcohol. He craned his head back from where he lay on her green vinyl couch, trying to watch what she was doing, his butt bare and streaked with two long, red wounds. Ruby swabbed the cuts and swore right back at him.

"I hope it burns. Laying around like some cur dog. How the hell did you do this, anyway? Must've had your pants off. Ain't no cuts in your pants."

"I was shitting and fell back on a busted bottle."

"I really believe that one."

"You believe what you want. Just get me fixed up."

"You ought to have stitches. A couple of places look bad."

"Naw, they don't. Just stick on some Band-Aids and let it go."

"Stupid drunk. Stupid asshole drunk."

Bubble fell asleep that night on his belly in Ruby's living room. The next morning there was fire across his backside, but after soaking in a bathtub of hot water and epsom salts, he felt better and was capable of walking, though stiffly. Ruby fed him eggs and fatback, grits and coffee, lectured him, then pitied him, and finally left for the diner after making him swear to stay put.

Bubble thought about staying for a while as he sopped up the last of the egg yolk, even considered hobbling back down to the mill to ask Harry for that job. Then he remembered the animal looking out of Billy's eyes the night he slit the soldier. He laid down the scrap of toast and went out to buy another jug of wine.

# DOROTHY ALLISON, "River of Names"

"What I try to bring to the lives I steal is significance and respect," writes Dorothy Allison. "What I demand is for attention to be paid to those who are mostly not seen, not acknowledged." Such a story is Allison's "River of Names," a survivor's tale haunted by the memories of those who did not make it as told by one who did.

> I know the awful impact of poverty, the damage of despair and the self-fulfilling nature of stunted aspirations. But knowing all that, I developed the conviction that those of us born poor, or queer, or people of color, or simply different in any of the many ways this culture holds the different in contempt—that we were intrinsically better than those who had never been tested by adversity. It is no advantage to realize that as a culture we have this same schizophrenic notion—that Americans fear and hate the poor even as we drape over them an idealized veil of awe and sentimental fantasy.[1]

## "RIVER OF NAMES"

At a picnic at my aunt's farm, the only time the whole family ever gathered, my sister Billie and I chased chickens into the barn. Billie ran right through the open doors and out again, but I stopped, caught by a shadow moving over me. My Cousin Tommy, eight years old as I was, swung in the sunlight with his face as black as his shoes—the rope around his neck pulled up into the sunlit heights of the barn, fascinating, horrible. Wasn't he running ahead of us? Someone came up behind me. Someone began to scream. My mama took my head in her hands and turned my eyes away.

Jesse and I have been lovers for a year now. She tells me stories about her child-hood, about her father going off each day to the university, her mother who made all her dresses, her grandmother who always smelled of dill bread and vanilla. I listen with my mouth open, not believing but wanting, aching for the fairy tale she thinks is everyone's life.

"What did your grandmother smell like?"

I lie to her the way I always do, a lie stolen from a book. "Like lavender," stomach churning over the memory of sour sweat and snuff.

I realize I do not really know what lavender smells like, and I am for a moment afraid she will ask something else, some question that will betray me. But Jesse slides over to hug me, to press her face against my ear, to whisper, "How wonderful to be part of such a large family."

I hug her back and close my eyes. I cannot say a word.

I was born between the older cousins and the younger, born in a pause of babies and therefore outside, always watching. Once, way before Tommy died, I was pushed out on the steps while everyone stood listening to my Cousin Barbara. Her screams went up and down in the back of the house. Cousin Cora brought buckets of bloody rags out to be burned. The other cousins all ran off to catch the sparks or poke the fire with dogwood sticks. I waited on the porch making up words to the shouts around me. I did not understand what was happen-ing. Some of the older cousins obviously did, their strange expressions broken by stranger laughs. I had seen them helping her up the stairs while the thick blood ran down her legs. After a while the blood on the rags was thin, watery, almost pink. Cora threw them on the fire and stood motionless in the stinking smoke.

Randall went by and said there'd be a baby, a hatched egg to throw out with the rags, but there wasn't. I watched to see and there wasn't; nothing but the blood, thinning out desperately while the house slowed down and grew quiet, hours of cries growing soft and low, moaning under the smoke. My Aunt Ray-lene came out on the porch and almost fell on me, not seeing me, not seeing anything at all. She beat on the post until there were knuckle-sized dents in the peeling paint, beat on that post like it could feel, cursing it and herself and every child in the yard, singing up and down, "Goddamn, goddamn that girl . . . no sense . . . goddamn!"

I've these pictures my mama gave me—stained sepia prints of bare dirt yards, plank porches, and step after step of children—cousins, uncles, aunts; myster-ies. The mystery is how many no one remembers. I show them to Jesse, not saying who they are, and when she laughs at the broken teeth, torn overalls, the dirt, I set my teeth at what I do not want to remember and cannot forget.

We were so many we were without number and, like tadpoles, if there was one less from time to time, who counted? My maternal great-grandmother had eleven daughters, seven sons; my grandmother, six sons, five daughters. Each one made at least six. Some made nine. Six times six, eleven times nine. They went on like multiplication tables. They died and were not missed. I come of an enormous family and I cannot tell half their stories. Somehow it was always made to seem they killed themselves: car wrecks, shotguns, dusty ropes, screaming, falling out of windows, things inside them. I am the point of a pyramid, sliding back under the weight of the ones who came after, and it does not matter that I am the lesbian, the one who will not have children.

I tell the stories and it comes out funny. I drink bourbon and make myself drawl, tell all those old funny stories. Someone always seems to ask me, which one was that? I show the pictures and she says, "Wasn't she the one in the story about the bridge?" I put the pictures away, drink more, and someone always finds them, then says, "Goddamn! How many of you were there, anyway?"

I don't answer.

Jesse used to say, "You've got such a fascination with violence. You've got so many terrible stories."

She said it with her smooth mouth, that chin that nobody ever slapped, and I love that chin, but when Jesse said that, my hands shook and I wanted nothing so much as to tell her terrible stories.

So I made a list. I told her: that one went insane—got her little brother with a tire iron; the three of them slit their arms, not the wrists but the bigger veins up near the elbow; she, now she strangled the boy she was sleeping with and got sent away; that one drank lye and died laughing soundlessly. In one year I lost eight cousins. It was the year everybody ran away. Four disappeared and were never found. One fell in the river and was drowned. One was run down hitchhiking north. One was shot running through the woods, while Grace, the last one, tried to walk from Greenville to Greer for some reason nobody knew. She fell off the overpass a mile down from the Sears, Roebuck warehouse and lay there for hunger and heat and dying.

Later, sleeping, but not sleeping, I found that my hands were up under Jesse's chin. I rolled away, but I didn't cry. I almost never let myself cry.

Almost always, we were raped, my cousins and I. That was some kind of joke, too.

"What's a South Carolina virgin?"
"'At's a ten-year-old can run fast."

It wasn't funny for me in my mama's bed with my stepfather; not for my Cousin Billie in the attic with my uncle; nor for Lucille in the woods with another cousin; for Danny with four strangers in a parking lot; or for Pammy, who made the papers. Cora read it out loud: "Repeatedly by persons unknown." They stayed unknown since Pammy never spoke again. Perforations, lacerations, contusions, and bruises. I heard all the words, big words, little words, words too terrible to understand. DEAD BY AN ACT OF MAN. With the prick still in them, the broom handle, the tree branch, the grease gun . . . objects, things not to be believed . . . whiskey bottles, can openers, grass shears, glass, metal, vegetables . . . not to be believed, not to be believed.

Jesse says, "You've got a gift for words."

"Don't talk," I beg her, "don't talk." And this once, she just holds me, blessedly silent.

I dig out the pictures, stare into the faces. Which one was I? Survivors do hate themselves, I know, over the core of fierce self-love, never understanding, always asking, "Why me and not her, not him?" There is such mystery in it, and I have hated myself as much as I have loved others, hated the simple fact of my own survival. Having survived, am I supposed to say something, do something, be something?

I loved my Cousin Butch. He had this big old head, pale thin hair and enormous, watery eyes. All the cousins did, though Butch's head was the largest, his hair the palest. I was the dark-headed one. All the rest of the family seemed pale carbons of each other in shades of blond, though later on everybody's hair went brown or red, and I didn't stand out so. Butch and I stood out—I because I was so dark and fast, and he because of that big head and the crazy things he did. Butch used to climb on the back of my Uncle Lucius's truck, open the gas tank and hang his head over, breathe deeply, strangle, gag, vomit, and breathe again. It went so deep, it tingled in your toes. I climbed up after him and tried it myself, but I was too young to hang on long, and I fell heavily to the ground, dizzy and giggling. Butch could hang on, put his hand down into the tank and pull up a cupped palm of gas, breathe deep and laugh. He would climb down roughly, swinging down from the door handle, laughing, staggering, and stinking of gasoline. Someone caught him at it. Someone threw a match. "I'll teach you."

Just like that, gone before you understand.

I wake up in the night screaming, "No, no, I won't!" Dirty water rises in the back of my throat, the liquid language of my own terror and rage. "Hold me. Hold me." Jesse rolls over on me; her hands grip my hipbones tightly.

"I love you. I love you. I'm here," she repeats. I stare up into her dark eyes, puzzled, afraid. I draw a breath in deeply, smile my bland smile. "Did I fool you?" I laugh, rolling away from her. Jesse punches me playfully, and I catch her hand in the air.

"My love," she whispers, and cups her body against my hip, closes her eyes. I bring my hand up in front of my face and watch the knuckles, the nails as they tremble, tremble. I watch for a long time while she sleeps, warm and still against me.

James went blind. One of the uncles got him in the face with home-brewed alcohol.

Lucille climbed out the front window of Aunt Raylene's house and jumped. They said she jumped. No one said why.

My Uncle Matthew used to beat my Aunt Raylene. The twins, Mark and Luke, swore to stop him, pulled him out in the yard one time, throwing him between them like a loose bag of grain. Uncle Matthew screamed like a pig coming up for slaughter. I got both my sisters in the toolshed for safety, but I hung back to watch. Little Bo came running out of the house, off the porch, feetfirst into his daddy's arms. Uncle Matthew started swinging him like a scythe, going after the bigger boys, Bo's head thudding their shoulders, their hips. Afterward, Bo crawled around in the dirt, the blood running out of his ears and his tongue hanging out of his mouth, while Mark and Luke finally got their daddy down. It was a long time before I realized that they never told anybody else what had happened to Bo.

Randall tried to teach Lucille and me to wrestle. "Put your hands up." His legs were wide apart, his torso bobbing up and down, his head moving constantly. Then his hand flashed at my face. I threw myself back into the dirt, lay still. He turned to Lucille, not noticing that I didn't get up. He punched at her, laughing. She wrapped her hands around her head, curled over so her knees were up against her throat.

"No, no!" he yelled. "Move like her." He turned to me. "Move." He kicked at me. I rocked into a ball, froze.

"No, no!" He kicked me. I grunted, didn't move. He turned to Lucille. "You." Her teeth were chattering but she held herself still, wrapped up tighter than bacon slices.

"You move!" he shouted. Lucille just hugged her head tighter and started to sob.

"Son of a bitch," Randall grumbled, "you two will never be any good."

He walked away. Very slowly we stood up, embarrassed, looked at each other. We knew.

If you fight back, they kill you.

My sister was seven. She was screaming. My stepfather picked her up by her left arm, swung her forward and back. It gave. The arm went around loosely. She just kept screaming. I didn't know you could break it like that.

I was running up the hall. He was right behind me. "Mama! Mama!" His left hand—he was left-handed—closed around my throat, pushed me against the wall, and then he lifted me that way. I kicked, but I couldn't reach him. He was yelling, but there was so much noise in my ears I couldn't hear him.

"Please, Daddy. Please, Daddy. I'll do anything, I promise. Daddy, anything you want. Please, Daddy."

I couldn't have said that. I couldn't talk around that fist at my throat, couldn't breathe. I woke up when I hit the floor. I looked up at him.

"If I live long enough, I'll fucking kill you."

He picked me up by my throat again.

"What's wrong with her?"

"Why's she always following you around?"

Nobody really wanted answers.

A full bottle of vodka will kill you when you're nine and the bottle is a quart. It was a third cousin proved that. We learned what that and other things could do. Every year there was something new.

You're growing up. My big girl.

There was codeine in the cabinet, paregoric for the baby's teeth, whiskey, beer, and wine in the house. Jeanne brought home MDA, PCP, acid; Randall, grass, speed, and mescaline. It all worked to dull things down, to pass the time.

Stealing was a way to pass the time. Things we needed, things we didn't, for the nerve of it, the anger, the need. You're growing up, we told each other. But sooner or later, we all got caught. Then it was When Are You Going to Learn?

Caught, nightmares happened. "Razorback desperate" was the conclusion of the man down at the county farm where Mark and Luke were sent at fifteen. They both got their heads shaved, their earlobes sliced.

What's the matter, kid? Can't you take it?

Caught at sixteen, June was sent to Jessup County Girls' Home, where the baby was adopted out and she slashed her wrists on the bedsprings.

Lou got caught at seventeen and held in the station downtown, raped on the floor of the holding tank.

Are you a boy or are you a girl?

On your knees, kid, can you take it?

Caught at eighteen and sent to prison, Jack came back seven years later blank-faced, understanding nothing. He married a quiet girl from out of town, had three babies in four years.

Then Jack came home one night from the textile mill, carrying one of those big handles off the high-speed spindle machine. He used it to beat them all to death and went back to work in the morning.

Cousin Melvina married at fourteen, had three kids in two and a half years, and welfare took them all away. She ran off with a carnival mechanic, had three more babies before he left her for a motorcycle acrobat. Welfare, took those, too. But the next baby was hydrocephalic, a little waterhead they left with her, and the three that followed, even the one she used to hate so—the one she had after she fell off the porch and couldn't remember whose child it was.

"How many children do you have?" I asked her.

"You mean the ones I have, or the ones I had? Four," she told me, "or eleven."

My aunt, the one I was named for, tried to take off for Oklahoma. That was after she'd lost the youngest girl and they told her Bo would never be "right." She packed up biscuits, cold chicken, and Coca-Cola; a lot of loose clothes; Cora and her new baby, Cy; and the four youngest girls. They set off from Greenville in the afternoon, hoping to make Oklahoma by the weekend, but they only got as far as Augusta. The bridge there went out under them.

"An Act of God," my uncle said.

My aunt and Cora crawled out downriver, and two of the girls turned up in the weeds, screaming loud enough to be found in the dark. But one of the girls never came up out of that dark water, and Nancy, who had been holding Cy, was found still wrapped around the baby, in the water, under the car.

"An Act of God," my aunt said. "God's got one damn sick sense of humor."

My sister had her baby in a bad year. Before he was born we had talked about it. "Are you afraid?" I asked.

"He'll be fine," she'd replied, not understanding, speaking instead to the other fear. "Don't we have a tradition of bastards?"

He was fine, a classically ugly healthy little boy with that shock of white hair that marked so many of us. But afterward, it was that bad year with my sister down with pleurisy, then cystitis, and no work, no money, having to move back home with my cold-eyed stepfather. I would come home to see her, from the woman I could not admit I'd been with, and take my infinitely fragile nephew and hold him, rocking him, rocking myself.

One night I came home to screaming—the baby, my sister, no one else there. She was standing by the crib, bent over, screaming red-faced. "Shut up! Shut up!" With each word her fist slammed the mattress fanning the baby's ear.

"Don't!" I grabbed her, pulling her back, doing it as gently as I could so I wouldn't break the stitches from her operation. She had her other arm clamped across her abdomen and couldn't fight me at all. She just kept shrieking.

"That little bastard just screams and screams. That little bastard. I'll kill him."

Then the words seeped in and she looked at me while her son kept crying and kicking his feet. By his head the mattress still showed the impact of her fist.

"Oh no," she moaned, "I wasn't going to be like that. I always promised myself." She started to cry, holding her belly and sobbing. "We an't no different. We an't no different."

Jesse wraps her arm around my stomach, presses her belly into my back. I relax against her. "You sure you can't have children?" she asks. "I sure would like to see what your kids would turn out to be like."

I stiffen, say, "I can't have children. I've never wanted children."

"Still," she says, "you're so good with children, so gentle."

I think of all the times my hands have curled into fists, when I have just barely held on. I open my mouth, close it, can't speak. What could I say now? All the times I have not spoken before, all the things I just could not tell her, the shame, the self-hatred, the fear; all of that hangs between us now—a wall I cannot tear down.

I would like to turn around and talk to her, tell her . . . "I've got a dust river in my head, a river of names endlessly repeating. That dirty water rises in me, all those children screaming out their lives in my memory, and I become some-one else, someone I have tried so hard not to be." But I don't say anything, and I know, as surely as I know I will never have a child, that by not speaking I am condemning us, that I cannot go on loving you and hating you for your fairy-tale life, for not asking about what you have no reason to imagine, for that soft-chinned innocence I love.

Jesse puts her hands behind my neck, smiles and says "You tell the funniest stories."

I put my hands behind her back, feeling the ridges of my knuckles pulsing. "Yeah," I tell her. "But I lie."

# PINCKNEY BENEDICT, "Pit"

Born in 1964, Pinckney Benedict grew up on his family's dairy farm in the Greenbrier Valley near Lewisburg, West Virginia. After graduating from Princeton University, where he studied writing with Joyce Carol Oates, Benedict published his first story collection, *Town Smokes* (1987), at the age of twenty-three while earning his master of fine arts degree at the University of Iowa. His books include the story collection *Wrecking Yard* (1992) and the novel *Dogs of God* (1995), both of which were named Notable Books by the *New York Times*. He is the recipient of Britain's Steinbeck Award and the *Chicago Tribune's* Nelson Algren Award, and he has been honored with appearances in *New Stories from the South, O. Henry Prize Stories, The Pushcart Prize* anthology, and *The Oxford Book of American Short Stories*. Benedict has taught writing at a number of universities, including Ohio State, Oberlin, Southern Illinois, and Princeton. He has also edited the anthologies *Surreal South* (2007) and *Surreal South '09* with his wife, the novelist Laura Benedict. His third collection, *Miracle Boy and Other Stories,* was published in 2010.

"Emerging from the harsh realities of difficult lives," writes Mary Morris, "[Benedict's] stories do not spare us the violence of love or the love of violence."[1] In "Pit," Benedict offers up an unconventional view of the Rough South with a fugitive tale that takes an unexpected detour into the macabre.

> The "Rough South" for me: I recall, when I was a boy, reading an article in the newspaper about a fellow who was killed in one of the towns around Charleston; Nitro, maybe, or Hurricane. He died of gunshot wounds in a vacant lot that everybody in the neighborhood called "the ape yard," which was not far from a regionally famous watering hole where this fellow had

been drinking heavily. The guy was described by everybody who knew him as "the meanest old man in West Virginia," which would have made him, especially back in those days, one righteous mean old man. The gun that killed him was his own, which he carried on him at all times. All of the eyewitnesses—there were a number—swore that the shooting was self-inflicted. I believe that God has kept me alive in the years since I read that article so that I can write a short story in which I fully imagine the series of events that led up to the "suicide" of the meanest old man in West Virginia in a place called the ape yard. Everything I have written and everything I will write, until I write that story, has just been training.[2]

**"PIT"**

Brunty thought that Paxco was going for a gun, so he went into his jacket and jerked out the thin-bladed fillet knife, stuck it right into Paxco's chest. Paxco folded up against the plywood barrier around the dog pit, coughing blood.

The dogs in the pit, the little spitz and the big black mutt, just kept on going at it, with the slow mutt taking most of the damage. The spitz was awful quick and a better fighter than his size might make you think. He was out of King Generator up in Pocahontas County, and King Generator was a dog that was born to fight.

The two motorcycle crazies and the out-of-town high roller just stood and watched the whole thing happen. The high roller had expected some excitement but he hadn't figured on anything like this. He hadn't figured on seeing the pit owner get knife-murdered during the fights. He stood back against the wall of the barn while Paxco died.

Brunty tried to pull the knife out of Paxco's chest but it was stuck on a rib and wouldn't come. He was about crying, watching blood come out of Paxco's mouth. The fillet knife had cost Brunty two and a half bucks at the True Value in town. He had started carrying it for protection a couple of months earlier, when Paxco's boys had threatened to break his fingers for not paying Paxco what he owed, and the first time he ever pulled it was when he shoved it into Paxco's lung.

The handle of the knife was orange so you could see it if you dropped it in the dark. It looked strange to Brunty, the day-glo handle, designed to float in the water, the fisherman's friend, sticking out of Paxco. It looked like a lever you might pull to start some machine going.

"Christ Amighty," Paxco said to Brunty. His fingers feathered the butt of his police .38 but he wasn't strong enough to pull it out of its holster so he could kill Brunty. He felt the breath going out of him. He felt it going out through the hole that Brunty had made in his chest, and he wanted to smoke Brunty for that.

Paxco had done a lot of things in his life that he figured were bad enough he should die for them, if you were a Christian that believed in such things. Divine retribution. Still, he was surprised to get it from a little bastard like Brunty.

He tried again to pull the gun out of the leather shoulder holster but just dropped it down in the sawdust next to his leg. It was a flat black revolver with fancy rubberized Pachmayr grips, a gun like a quick-draw artist might have. Paxco held his hands up in front of him, tried to close them but couldn't. They felt like they were swelling.

Brunty leaned close over Paxco, trying to figure out what to do about the knife. He felt stupid and slow, knew he had to get out of there quick. It was just luck that none of Paxco's boys were there that evening, just good luck that Brunty wasn't spread out dead on the floor already.

Paxco had three big boys that worked for him, collecting money and busting heads, just generally keeping the peace. They all three carried cut-down shotguns that they called *lupos,* which was a name they had heard in some movie about the Mafia. They would have killed Brunty without thinking twice about it, dumped his body in a lime pit up on the mountain and been done with it. They had done things just like it and worse before.

"Kiss my ass, Brunty," Paxco said, and shivered. Brunty looked at him, saw the spirit leave out of his body. It was like watching a light go out in somebody else's house.

Paxco's hands rested in his lap, folded one over the other, very white and clean-looking. Paxco didn't have any dirt under his fingernails, which were neat and trimmed. He had always been careful about how his hands looked. Brunty watched the eyelids close down over Paxco's dead empty eyes.

The dogs on the other side of the barrier quit their fighting. For a minute Brunty thought it was because they sensed Paxco's passing. He was struck by that, the fact that dogs could tell when a man died and take note of it, stop what they were doing.

When he looked, he saw that the big black mutt had killed the fast little spitz in spite of the predictions. The spitz had taken an ear off of the mutt. The ear lay in the middle of the pit, looking dull and chewed and wrinkled. Brunty had seen nights when there were four or five ears left in the sawdust of the pit, lying there like winter leaves. The black dog had its square head down in the open belly of the spitz. Its thick bald tail whipped from side to side.

"You are in for a world of hurt," one of the motorcycle crazies said to Brunty. He was a fat man with a little goat beard that he held together with a rubber band. He wore a long black raincoat. His partner had a pair of little round dark glasses which made him look like he was blind.

Brunty snatched up the heavy revolver next to Paxco's body, pointed it to cover the two men. "Stay still and just don't move at all," Brunty said. He kept the .38 mainly on the guy with the beard. The black raincoat looked like a good place to keep a piece. He didn't want any more surprises.

The high roller was still in his corner. He couldn't take his eyes off of Paxco. He was surprised at how bright the blood was on Paxco's shirt. He was a candidate for state senate and didn't think this kind of thing would be good for his campaign. He couldn't be sure though. Sometimes it was hard to tell what the voters would get behind.

It took Brunty a couple of tries to thumb back the hammer on the revolver. You're gonna have to do them too, he kept hearing in his head. They seen you put steel to Paxco. It was like a nightmare, that he was going to have to kill three more people just because he had killed Paxco. Brunty was panicked. He couldn't think of a way around it.

The guy with the glasses laughed. "You'd best to get out of here quick, man. You got some trouble coming down." He gestured at Paxco, who looked like he was sleeping, except for the blood and the orange handle of the knife. "You got worst enemies than us," the guy said. Brunty thought of the three bruisers with the double-barreled *lupos*. He didn't know where they were but it was a bet they wouldn't be gone all night. The stink from the dead dog's guts—or maybe it was Paxco—was getting to him.

"Nobody leave here for ten minutes after I go," he said. The motorcycle riders just looked at him. They didn't care what he said. The high roller looked like he was crying. Seeing that made Brunty feel strong for a second, knowing he could make a man cry. "I could kill you," he told them. "I could of killed all of you but I didn't." Keeping the revolver on them, he backed out of the barn.

Outside in the cool early morning air, Brunty looked around for where he had parked his car. The rusted-out Dodge Dart was where he had left it, near the door. Two other guys, young kids from the county, sat in the back of an old Ford pickup, waiting for their time in the pit. They didn't know what had happened inside, stared at Brunty with his cocked revolver.

They had their dog chained to the bumper of the truck. It was just a block-headed yellow hound with big paws and a long whip tail. Brunty remembered a dog like that. He remembered drinking from a jar, dragging on a butt, waiting for a dog like that to circle rabbits around to him. That memory was strong in Brunty.

He paused as he was getting into the Dodge. "Get out of here," he said to the kids. "You don't want to be here." They just looked at him. They didn't know about anything bad. They had heard about the high roller and his money and they wanted their chance at some of it.

Brunty uncocked the revolver, tucked it inside his jacket where he had kept the fillet knife. He started the Dodge, pulled around Paxco's old dented Continental and the Harley hogs the motorcycle boys had come in on. The block-headed dog yelped and scrambled under the truck, pelted by gravel from Brunty's spinning tires. The two kids put their arms across their faces to keep from getting cut by the rocks as Brunty pulled out of the lot.

Inside the barn, the two motorcycle crazies stuck around just long enough to pull out their flick knives and take all the money off the high roller. They also made him swear to tell the police and Paxco's shooters that it was Brunty who killed Paxco, and not them. They knew the assumptions that people make about other folks that ride motorcycles, and they wanted to be sure they were protected.

They left the one-eared black dog behind only with regret. When they left he was pulling the heart out of the little spitz. They would have taken him if they could have figured a way to get him on one of the bikes without falling off. They liked his style, and there was no telling how much a dog that could kill a son out of King Generator was worth.

Brunty pulled up in front of Sister Sue's. Sister Sue was a woman that ran a place up in the hills of Pocahontas, and Brunty figured she would put him up for a while, only until he worked out what he could do, where he could go. It was sure as hell he could not go home again, not after he had murdered Paxco.

"Yo Sue," he called as he got out of the Dodge. Sister Sue's was a blue two-story house about a hundred yards off the mountain road. It had taken Brunty forty-five minutes to get up there. The sun was rising, and a cool breeze blew through the pine trees that surrounded the place. A couple of ragged yellow-colored chickens scratched and pecked in a patch of bare dirt in front of the porch.

"Sister Sue," Brunty yelled at the house. The front door opened and she stepped out onto the porch. She was a tall, handsome woman with a nose that had been broken some years ago. She pulled her bathrobe tight around her, looked at Brunty like she didn't know who he was.

"It's Brunty," he said to her. Suddenly he wasn't sure whether Sister Sue's was the place to be. He didn't think she owed any love to Paxco, but it was hard to tell. A lot of things got confused when you stuck a knife into the chest of a man like Paxco.

"Hey Brunty," she said. "You got any money?"

Brunty looked down. "Got a lot of trouble, Sue," he said. "Figured I might could put up here for a little."

Sister Sue laughed at him. It was the kind of laugh she gave men just before she told them to get out. She liked Brunty pretty well because he was a small man and fairly clean and seldom a wicked or brutal drunk. "How come you always come to me when you got no money," she said to him. "You think I can eat trouble?"

"I busted caps on Paxco," Brunty said. He figured it was best to come right out with it. No use to cover anything up.

Sue snorted. "Bullshit," she said. "How come you ain't dead then?"

"I swear to God," Brunty said. "His boys was out running shine or something is why they didn't kill me. I run a knife right through his chest. He sat down and spit blood and then he died."

Sue stood and looked at Brunty for a couple of minutes. The bathrobe she had on was thin and he could see the solid flesh of her legs through the material. Her hair was long and the dull copper color of an old penny. She had it tied behind her neck with a broad black ribbon.

"You sure do look good, Sister Sue," he said.

"I never been flattered by a man that was dead and still walking around," Sister Sue said. She stepped to one side, motioned for him to come up on the porch. "I guess you best to come on inside."

Brunty followed her into the old house, which smelled to him like eggs over easy, like clean bedclothes. Sister Sue led him into the kitchen, sat him down at the table. There was a red-and-white-check plastic tablecloth on it. He rested his arms on the table, looked around at the enamel-white stove, refrigerator, sink. It didn't seem to him like this could be the same world where he had killed Paxco. He couldn't see this place with his blood spilled all over the clean white appliances. He relaxed a little.

"You ought not to of called me a dead man," he said to Sue. It was the first time this thought had occurred to him, that he should be insulted by her calling him that. She had her back to him, putting together an egg sandwich for him. She knew he liked an egg sandwich when he was hungry.

"I ain't dead yet," he said to her. He took the plate with the sandwich on it out of her hands. He felt more like eating now. He hadn't been sure he wanted to eat before, but with the sandwich in front of him he felt like he could put something down after all.

"I guess not," she said, looking at him. "But what kind of future you figure you got, the man that put the knife into Paxco?"

"I might do okay," he said. He took a bite of the sandwich and it tasted good to him. He figured that a man that had an appetite was a man that could go on living for a while. "There's more places than just around here. I could take the Dodge and go up to Pennsylvania, Maryland maybe. Lots of places a man could go."

"What would make you do a thing like stabbing Paxco? You know they got to kill you for trying something like that," she said. "You never did a thing like that before that I knew of."

He looked at her, held his right hand up in front of him. He stared at it like it was the cause of all his troubles. "I went up to the pit to ask him for some more time," he said. Sue shook her head at him.

"He moves like he's going for his gun, don't want to talk to me but just wants to waste me on the spot. So I stuck him. It was the fastest thing I ever done, like I didn't do it at all. I swear, it was like somebody else just jumped into my skin and done it for me."

"You crazy bastard, Brunty," she said to him. He mopped his plate with the crust of the sandwich. "They'll catch up to you," she said.

"Maybe," he said. "I figure."

"So how do you figure to keep alive when they do?" she said. "Them three boys with the *lupos* will cut you to pieces."

He thought about that. It was a good question. He reached inside his jacket, pulled out the .38 with the Pachmayr grips. He put it down on the table in front of him. It looked funny, the flat black steel next to the plate with egg on it. He picked it up again, hefted it. The gun had a good balance to it. "I took this off of Paxco," he said.

Sister Sue looked at Brunty sitting at her table with the revolver in his hand, playing with it like he was some kid. "Didn't seem to benefit him overmuch," she said. She picked the plate up from in front of him, put it in the sink so it could soak clean.

Brunty was in Sister Sue's bed when Paxco came to him. He was relaxing on the clean cool sheets, stripped down to his shorts. He was thinking about Sister Sue, wondering if she was going to sleep with him. He wanted that a lot, for Sue to walk into the room and shed that bathrobe she was in. He figured that would be a good way to spend the last of his time in the area. He had made love to Sue before and she was good at it. Better than he was. He could hear her cleaning up in the kitchen downstairs.

As he was thinking this, Paxco came into the room and sat down on the edge of the bed. He sat down in a patch of light that came through the blue curtains on the window. He turned to look at Brunty lying there in the comfortable bed, and there was blood on his lips and down his chin. The blood was dark and dried.

"Hey Brunty," Paxco said. When he spoke Brunty could see that there was blood on his teeth too. He was a mess of blood.

"Don't I know it," Paxco said. He nodded at Brunty. "I never would of knowed I had this much inside me. Something about busting a lung though is what I understand. When you get into a lung, you get a lot of blood." He laughed. The orange knife handle coming out of his chest bobbed up and down when he laughed like that, and Brunty wished he wouldn't.

"You got a piece of the heart too," Paxco said. He didn't sound angry or anything. Paxco had always been a calm character. That had been a big part of his success in the rackets, that he never got mad on the outside, never let his emotion slow him down. Brunty could tell that he hadn't died in terror.

He couldn't see through Paxco or anything. The man wasn't like a ghost at all. He listened and he could still hear Sue in the kitchen down below. He wanted to call out to her, scream out that Paxco was in here with him. He thought maybe Paxco had come to kill him. Paxco was still wearing his leather holster. It hung empty under his armpit.

"You ain't alive, are you," he said to Paxco. His voice came out small and weak, and he knew there was no way that Sister Sue would hear him.

"Christ," Paxco said. He sounded exasperated. He put his hand on Brunty's knee. Brunty could feel the weight of Paxco's hand on his knee through the sheet. He could feel the grip in the hand. It felt like he figured Paxco's hand would of felt, if Paxco had ever touched him like this when he was alive. "You ain't very smart, Brunty," Paxco said. "Plus you are just about dead."

"Who's going to kill me, Paxco?" Brunty said. "You going to do it?"

"You know who," Paxco said. "They can't let you go. They can't afford to. Folks would start to figure maybe they could get away with something too."

Brunty reached around next to him, put his hand on the night table for the revolver. He couldn't find the gun, knocked the little lamp off the table onto the floor. It didn't bust when it hit the floor, rolled around for a couple of seconds.

"You know," Paxco said, "the man that owns old King Generator lives a couple miles from here." He frowned. "That whelp wasn't worth too much was he?"

"I guess not," Brunty said. "I didn't have nothing to bet on him anyway."

"You could go see that guy," Paxco said. "Tell him his pup got eat up by some mongrel. But you ain't got the time." He smiled. Brunty didn't have anything to say.

"Anyhow," Paxco said, "I just wanted to come and see you. See the man that killed me." He patted Brunty's knee, studied his face for a couple of seconds. "I can't believe it was a little son of gun like you that did it. You come at me so fast I didn't know what was going on."

"Were you going for the .38?" Brunty asked.

"Hell yes," Paxco said, and he smiled. "I was going to put a couple through your forehead, just because I didn't like you. I would of cooked you if you hadn't of got to me first." He stood up from the bed.

"That's good then," Brunty said. He hoped Paxco was going. He couldn't stand to look at that knife handle anymore.

"Or maybe I was just going to scratch myself," Paxco said. His voice was mean. "Or grab a cigarette. You ain't got the time to find out, Brunty."

On his way out, Paxco kicked his foot against the little table lamp. "You ought to be more careful, Brunty," he said. Paxco seemed to find that pretty funny. Brunty couldn't see the humor in it.

Paxco walked out of the room. Brunty closed his eyes. Outside the window a woodpecker drilled a hole into a hard old oak. He had read somewhere that a woodpecker hits a tree with its head at nearly a hundred miles an hour, over and over again, half a dozen times a second. He didn't see how it was possible for something to live through that kind of punishment.

"Sue," he called out. His voice was still weak. He had forgotten about having sex with her. He wanted to ask her about Paxco. He wanted to see what she thought about him coming in like that. He wanted to see if she thought that such a thing was able to happen. He kept his eyes closed so he couldn't see the patch of light on the bedspread where Paxco had been sitting.

Sister Sue woke Brunty up when it got dark outside. She put the lamp back on the table and turned it on before she shook his shoulder. When he looked at her she handed him a newspaper. "Take a look at that," she said. "I thought you might want to see it."

Brunty spread the paper out on his lap. *"Local Man Murdered"* was a headline on the front page. They had a picture of Paxco next to the column of newsprint, Paxco in a leather jacket sitting on the hood of his Continental. The front page told about him, his record and running the dog pit and all. The story was continued further back in the paper and Brunty turned to the page.

There was an old picture of himself as a volunteer fireman. He looked like a kid with the big fire helmet sitting on his head. He figured they had got the photo from his ex-wife. It was funny that she still had a picture of him after all that time. He had enjoyed the fires he had helped to fight. That had been some excitement.

"You didn't tell me about no motorcycle gang," Sue said. "They don't figure it was just you killed Paxco. They think them motorcycle boys was in it too." There was a picture of the high roller on the page with Brunty's. He had told a story that got Brunty and the motorcycle crazies all mixed up in the killing. Brunty scanned the page for something about the two kids and their yellow dog, but there was nothing. That meant they had got away from it. He was glad of that.

He read in the paper where the cops had killed the one-eared mongrel. They said it was too vicious to do anything with. The rest of the dogs, the ones out back of the barn in the wire hutches, were at the pound. Brunty wondered what Paxco would think of that, his dogs dead or heading to the gas chamber.

"Paxco was in here a while ago," he said to Sister Sue. She didn't say anything back. He was really interested in how she felt about it. "I wanted to yell out for you but I couldn't," he said.

Sue stepped back away from Brunty, toward the door. There was something funny about the way she looked at him. "We got to move your car," she said. "Setting out in front like that, somebody is bound to see it." She was gone out the door before Brunty even realized what was going on. The three shooters had sent Sister Sue in to see if she would try to tip him off, to see if they had to kill her too. They were waiting just outside in the hall.

He was scrambling around on the night table for the revolver when the first of them shot him. The gun wasn't anywhere that he could see it. In his rush to find it, he knocked the lamp off the bedside table again, and this time the bulb busted on the floor.

The three boys with the double-barreled *lupos* blew him out of bed and onto the floor. The heavy shot cut tight patterns in the sheets. They were close enough that powder burned the weave black.

Brunty rolled across the floor and the three men came on across the room, fired into his body again. Buckshot tore up the board floor of the place. The last thing he knew was that his legs were tangled in the sheets and that he had to get them loose if he wanted to run. He died trying to get his legs out of the sheets.

"He ain't near as tall as I thought from his picture," one of the boys said, poking at the body with his 12 gauge. Out in the hall, Sister Sue listened to them and felt sad and sick, in spite of the fact that she had managed to save herself from the ugly situation that she was in.

The killers brought Brunty's corpse out of the house wrapped in the bedsheets. He was a mess to carry and they were pretty much disgusted with the job. "We cleaned his clock," one of the boys said. He was glad to see Brunty dead. He had thought a lot of Paxco.

They dumped the body in the trunk of Brunty's own Dodge. The motorcycle crazy with the little black glasses was already in there, as dead as Brunty. They figured to drive the car off a cliff further up in the mountains. It was a good six-hundred-foot wooded drop into a narrow gorge that they knew about. It would probably be months or years before some hiker tripped across the old car and the dead bodies.

They figured to get the other motorcycle rider if they could find him. Somebody would give him up to them after a while, like Sue had given them Brunty.

"This's okay because it's vengeance, but the next one's got to be neater," the biggest of the killers said. "We got to be businesslike about this stuff." He wiped his hands on a clean part of the sheet, wiped them again on his jeans. The other two nodded.

"Did you hear what he said about Paxco?" one of the other killers asked.

"Off his nut," the biggest one said. "Paxco's stiff as a poker." The big one was in charge now. He figured that maybe Paxco had got what was coming to him. He figured that with him running things they all stood to do a lot better. He was grateful to the corpse in the trunk of the Dodge, in a strange way.

"You boys have killed a lot of people," Sister Sue said from the porch of her house. The biggest boy looked at her as he stepped into the Dodge to drive it up the mountain, and his eyes on her made her feel cold.

"We didn't kill anybody that didn't need killing," he said to her. He started the Dodge, guided it down her driveway. The other two shooters followed a safe distance behind him and the two dead men, stayed about five car lengths back, driving Paxco's big old Continental up the mountain.

# LEWIS NORDAN, *The Sharpshooter Blues*

*Publishers Weekly* calls Lewis Nordan's voice "a melodious, bittersweet yawp, pulsating with love, grief, rage, and a thirst for redemption."[1] In this pivotal chapter from Nordan's novel *The Sharpshooter Blues,* a half-wit grocery clerk named Hydro meets his destiny when a couple of Bonnie and Clyde wannabes hold up his store.

> I became a comic writer, but I was always writing from the same place, that is that deeply serious, melodramatic horror that's at the heart of my work. Something about me believes that comedy comes out of darkness and that all comedy is underpinned by loss.[2]

### FROM *THE SHARPSHOOTER BLUES*

The sun had set now. Supper dishes were stacked in the sink, the hotplate was unplugged, like Mr. William Tell showed Hydro he must always do. Hydro was standing out by the pumps looking across the sugarcane fields. The Delta sky was streaked with red and gold. Louis was inside William Tell, sitting on the floor of the pantry, reading *Mr. Magoo.*

Hydro went in the store and mashed the No Sale key and opened up the cash drawer of the register and pulled out the bills and counted them and turned them so the faces were all looking out in the same direction, like Mr. Tell showed him, and smoothed them flat with his hand.

He said, "Louis, you doing okay?"

Louis said, "Uh-huh." He sounded like he was in a cave, back in the pantry, with the groceries and whiskey and the broom and the mop and dustpan and buckets.

Hydro counted up the change and wrote down the numbers on a little pad with the date. He folded the bills up and bound them with a rubber band and put the heavy change in a leather pouch with a drawstring and then stuck them both in a metal cash box with a lock and key and put the strongbox in the false bottom of a steamer trunk. He felt like a regular storekeeper. Mr. Tell was nice as he could be, but particular about his money. He told Hydro, "Don't let nobody steal my money."

Back behind the counter Hydro reached up and pulled a string on a light cord and a bare light bulb blazed on, no telling how many watts, and sent shadows running all around the store. It was dark outside now.

Hydro took the shovel with him, out in back of the store, and crossed the fence into the sugarcane field, and spaded him a hole in the ground between cane rows and shoveled the watermelon and the cantaloupes into the hole and then put dirt on top again.

There were still a few things to do, though. He washed the few dishes and the pan he'd used to heat up the stew in, and put them on a rack to dry, like Mr. Tell showed him.

He went up to the front of the store and looked out the door to see was anybody coming. He pulled the door shut and shot the bolt, goodnight, Irene, I'll see you in my dreams. Sometimes Hydro's daddy came out and sang to him.

Hydro knew Louis had most of the *Gerald McBoing Boings* with him in the pantry, but that was all right. Hydro had him a stack of comic books up underneath his army cot. *Heckle and Jeckle* and *Little LuLu* and *Casper the Friendly Ghost*. He had some more in a bound trunk of Mr. William Tell's. He didn't keep scary comic books out at William Tell, *The Crypt* and *Ghoulish Tales*. Casper was scary enough for Hydro.

He looked in his basket to see was there another peach pie in there, but they wasn't. It was a shame, since all of his spoons were clean. He wondered if Plastic Man wasn't Gerald McBoing Boing's daddy in real life. It did make sense, if you thought about it.

About the time Hydro got good and settled in, though, here came somebody up the gravel driveway in a car, a 1953 Mercury with Hollywood mufflers and headlights blaring all through the front windows. Happy Hour's done come and went, he hoped whoever it was understood that.

He listened to the car stop and to the deep throat of the glasspacks shut down, out by the pumps. Hydro walked out into the front part of the store and peeped out the window to see who it was.

When he saw them, all dressed up in black like they was, girl and a boy, he thought, Well I declare. What are them two doing in Arrow Catcher, Mississippi? He couldn't believe his own two eyes. This must be Morgan's Texas friends, from the diner.

Hydro stood beside the front window, real quiet, just watching them. The boy flung his door open and got out of the car and stood there. He stretched himself real good. He walked back and forth in the gravel a little bit and looked at the gas pump and then said something back into the car, to the girl in there.

The boy was dressed in a baggy black suit of some kind, looked like a zoot suit, with blousey legs and wide lapels. He had his hair well-greased and slicked back like a Mexican.

Hydro wished he could tell what they were talking about. He once read a little bitty advertisement about a lip-reading school. You could order lip-reading lessons by mail from the back of a *Gerald McBoing Boing* comic book. He wished now he'd written off for it.

He'd ordered plenty of other things, including a ventriloquist's dummy that he named Joseph of Arimethea, but he never could make it talk, so he traded it to old Mr. O'Kelly in Arrow Catcher for one of his soap carvings of wild animals. He got him a yellow Dial soap lion but forgot and left it out in the rain and it foamed up and melted and got ruined. You couldn't tell if it was a lion or a dog. Now poor old Mr. O'Kelly believed Joseph of Arimethea was his grandson. Ain't you glad you use Dial soap? Don't you wish ever-body did?

The other door of the car opened up and the girl stepped out in the gravel and stretched herself, too. The girl was dressed up in black, same as the boy, hot as it was, and had red lips.

Black skirt, black turtleneck, black stockings, even a little black hat of some kind, although Hydro couldn't think of the name for her hat. What was it called? It might be a boo-ray, or maybe boo-kay, something another.

Hydro shot the bolt and opened the front door to greet them. It startled them a little bit, looked like.

Hydro said, "I ain't got no tortillas. We plumb out of tortillas." He thought he'd bring up the subject real gradual, then pop the question: What is a tortilla, anyhow?

The boy and girl looked at each other, and then back at Hydro.

Hydro said, "Morgan ain't here. He's done already went home."

For a while the boy and girl still didn't talk.

The boy said, "Let me see if I have this straight. You ain't got no tortillas and Morgan has done gone home."

The girl with the red lips giggled when he said this.

Hydro said, "That's it, that's right."

The girl said, "You open?"

Hydro said, "I was just fixing to read *Heckle and Jeckle.*"

The boy said, "We need some gas. Pump us some gas."

Hydro said, "Oh. Okay"

He went out to the car and took the hose off the pump.

He said, "How much?"

The boy said, "Fill it up."

Hydro never had filled up a tank all the way to the top before. He was more used to selling gas in one-dollar two-dollar installments. Sometimes one-gallon, two-gallon.

Hydro said, "Say which?"

The boy gave him a look. Then he turned away and talked to the girl some more.

When the tank was full, Hydro was amazed at how much it cost. He never had seen such a big gas bill.

The boy opened up the screened door of the store and went on in, un-invited, while Hydro was still out by the pump. The girl followed him inside.

Well, Mr. Tell wouldn't like it, strangers inside the store while he was out at the pumps, but Hydro guessed it was all right this one time.

Hydro wiped off the windows with a rag and checked the oil and checked the radiator and the air pressure in the tires.

He remembered a couple of cans of hot tamales on the shelf in the pantry. He'd have to disturb Louis. That boy ought to be headed on home, anyway; it was after dark. So, anyway, he could fix them the tamales, fire up the hot plate, if they wanted it. Maybe open up some saltines and a bottle of Tabasco sauce.

When Hydro walked inside the store to explain about the tamales and saltines, the boy and girl were standing behind the counter with the cash drawer of the register wide open. They looked up when he came inside.

The girl said, "Where is the money?"

Hydro said, "I won't charge y'all what the pump says. It's too much. A couple of dollars ought to about cover it."

Hydro came walking on up to the counter where they were standing.

The next time the girl spoke, she was holding a pistol in Hydro's face.

She said, "Listen to me, you fucking moron."

Hydro said, "I shot a lope off Morgan's head because I'm so hopeless. We all are."

The girl said, "You're hopeless all right."

The boy said, "Where do you keep the money? We know you've got money in here somewhere."

The girl said, "I'm just aching to cover these walls with hair."

Hydro said, "Hair?"

William Tell was way out in the country, beneath starry-starry skies, and between wide Delta fields of fragrant sugarcane, and so on a Sunday night, when the roads were all quiet except for a pulpwood truck crossing between Money and the river, where the wood would be loaded onto a barge and floated down to Vicksburg to a papermill, or New Orleans, and the sun had gone down and the golden moon was just beginning to rise up out of the gum and cypress trees in the loblollies in the flatwoods, you could hear far away, if the wind was just right, like it was tonight, the big farm bell ringing vespers in the parish yard of St. George by the Lake, a deep clear distant sound, like a dream, or a memory, or a prayer.

Hydro was listening to this sweet music while looking down a gun barrel at the counter of William Tell Grocery, as the big yellow light bulb above his cot swayed and cast comic shadows across the faces of Gerald McBoing Boing and Mr. McGoo and the bare boards of the floor. Back in the darkness, down at the end of the gun barrel, Hydro thought he could see his mama, who was a long time dead.

And Hydro's daddy, Mr. Raney, far away, out at the fishcamp on the island in Roebuck Lake, beneath the same rising moon, heard the Sunday music, too, just as Hydro was hearing it.

Mr. Raney was cleaning fish, out on the island, where the fishhouse stood. The lake below him, where he looked down between his feet, through worn planks, was like a black mirror catching gold and silver traces of lamp light from the pier and moonlight and starlight from the sky.

Each fish in its turn Mr. Raney laid on the cleaning table beneath his knife and bore down and took the head off with a single stroke and a soft crush of severed bone. He turned each fish, and split it up the bottom, from the tail to the head, and reached into the cavity with his fingers and brought out the bright guts and eggs and slung them off his fingers, over the rail and into the water.

With the knife blade then, he scrape-scrape-scraped a fish, first one side and then the other, until it was clean of scales, and then dropped it into a great tub of chipped ice with the other cleaned fish. His arms were covered with the scales of crappie and bluegill, and in the moonlight they looked like silver.

He thought about taking a small mess of fish out to Hydro at William Tell. They could dig a pit out in back of the store and open a can of lard and a bag of cornmeal and chop up an onion and stir up a batch of hushpuppies and have a regular fish fry. He could sing a song or two.

Well, no, not tonight. It was late. Hydro had already eaten, probably. But maybe it wasn't too late to go out and sing to him, though. Maybe that's what he would do instead.

Hydro said, "Y'all ain't from El Paso, are you?"

The boy said, "He saw the Texas plates."

The girl said, "He won't be talking to anybody."

She cocked the hammer of the pistol.

She said, "Where do you hide the money?"

Hydro said, "In the trunk."

She said, "In the trunk?"

He said, "Mr. Tell's trunk, over yonder."

The boy said, "Open it up."

Hydro walked over to the trunk and unbuckled the belts around it and opened the latches.

When it was open, the three of them stood looking at Hydro's stash of comic books.

Hydro said, "Plastic Man is Gerald McBoing Boing's daddy. It's a theory I've got."

The boy took the pistol away from the girl and held it to Hydro's head.

He said, "Listen here. We want the money. Where is it?"

Hydro said, "Pull out the shelf. It's got a bottom up underneath the bottom."

The boy said, "You pull it out."

Before Hydro could move, the girl ripped the comic books out of the top of the trunk and flung them all over the store. She jerked the false bottom out of the trunk and revealed the roll of bills and the bag of change.

Back in the pantry, Louis heard this and laid down his comic book and peeked around the edge of the half-open door.

The girl said, "Jackpot."

Hydro looked around at the comic books, where they lay in pieces on the floor. Louis eased the door shut and stepped back inside the pantry. He saw the pistol the boy was holding. He reached up and turned the switch on a hanging light bulb and made the pantry dark. He listened at the door again.

Hydro said, "Mr. McGoo ain't Gerald's daddy. Some people might say he is, but he ain't."

The girl took the money out of the trunk and snapped the rubber band off the roll. She wet her thumb and peeled off bills, counting them.

She said, "There's a lot of money in bootlegging, looks like."

The boy said, "Get a couple of cases of whiskey and some food while you're at it."

The girl said, "You get it."

The boy was still holding the gun. He looked at her.

She threw the roll of loose bills down in the bottom of the trunk and dropped the bag of silver down beside them. She picked up a clean croaker sack from a stack and started raking canned goods off the shelves into it. She took peanut butter and cheese and sardines, too. She found a drawer with ammunition in it, and picked out all the boxes of .38 caliber cartridges and put them in the sack.

Hydro said, "That Dinty Moore is extra tasty."

The boy said, "Have you got a shovel?"

Hydro said, "I buried a watermelon this evening."

The boy said, "You going to be burying something bigger than a watermelon tonight."

Louis eased back inside the pantry again and tried to make his breathing more regular.

The girl said, "Have you got a can opener?"

Hydro said, "Yessum."

He reached in a drawer and pulled out the can opener.

The boy fidgeted with the pistol. He was nervous watching Hydro open a drawer.

Hydro handed the can opener over to the girl.

She took it out of his hand.

She said, "We ain't got time to be digging a hole."

She took a loaf of bread and some cold beers and that filled up the second croaker sack.

She said, "Bring the money. And the whiskey. I can't carry a case of whiskey and all these groceries."

The boy followed her out of the store, both of them loaded down, and they put the supplies in the trunk of the car.

Hydro followed them out the front door and tagged along out to the car.

Louis stayed in the pantry. He didn't know what to do.

Hydro said, "I never did understand what a streetcar was."

The girl slammed the trunk shut and looked at Hydro.

She said, "A streetcar?"

Hydro said, "Look like all cars are streetcars."

The girl and the boy looked at each other.

The boy said, "Let's do it. We got to get out of here."

The girl said, "Can a big-headed idiot like this get it up, do you suppose?"

The boy said, "If we don't have time to dig a grave, we sure as hell don't have no time for you to be pulling down your pants for this fool."

The girl said to Hydro, "Do you know what sex is?"

Hydro said, "A grave?"

The boy said, "Let's go. I'll take him out back and do it, and then we'll go." He said to Hydro, "Get back in the store. Get moving, right now."

The girl said, "I'll do it."

The boy stopped. He said, "You want to do it?"

She said, "Give me the gun. I'll do it."

The boy handed over the gun.

He said, "What else are you going to do?"

She said, "You wait in the car."

He said, "We don't have time for this, Cheryl."

She said, "You've given him my name and address, why don't you give him my telephone number, too."

He said, "We got to get moving."

She said, "You keep watch over these groceries. Me and Gerald McBoing Boing here got some talking to do."

He said, "Be sure he's dead."

Mr. Raney finished up out on the pier and turned on the water at the spigot and stuck his hands and arms up under the stream and let the fish scales wash away. Up on the railing there was a thin red sliver of Lifebuoy soap, which he took and lathered up under the cold water as well as he could and used that to wash off more of the scales and fish slime.

When he was finished he slung the water off his hands and was careful not to wipe his hands on his overalls, so he wouldn't have to start all over washing them again. He went inside the fishhouse then, and stepped out of his boots and then out of the overalls and hung them on a nail and pulled on his regular boots, the brogans. He was wearing clean khakis and a white shirt underneath his overalls. He checked himself in a cracked piece of mirror hanging up on the fishhouse wall and ran his fingers through what was left of his hair.

He had a little pistol that he kept on the sideboard, .25 caliber, so he picked it up now and fired off a couple of shots into the refrigerator, up against the wall. It was an old refrigerator, unplugged, worthless. Shooting it once or twice a day was just something Mr. Raney liked to do. It relaxed him, made him remember the old days, when his mama and daddy were still alive.

He had one more peach pie in the good refrigerator, the one that worked, so he took the pie out and put it in a burlap bag and stuck the pan of newly cleaned fish in the lower pan of the icebox and then switched off all the lights in the fishhouse and headed down the stairs to the landing. It wouldn't hurt Hydro to have an extra peach pie on hand, if he woke up hungry.

Darkness had fallen across the Delta, and it was especially dark down on the landing, near the boats and under the trees, where the moon didn't shed much light, but Mr. Raney knew the way, he didn't stumble. There was a board sidewalk, made out of washed-out, silver-gray two-by-fours, down to the water, onto the dock. Sometimes it was slick, but not tonight.

He made his way along the walk, in the dark, carrying the peach pie in the sack. He might sing "Rescue the Perishing" to Hydro. It was Sunday, after all. Maybe not. Hydro wasn't partial to church music. He might sing "Money Honey" or "Sixty Minute Man" instead.

He knew where the boat was, the one he would take through the bayou over to the mainland, the leaky old wood boat with nets and poles and tackle boxes and his daddy's little motor on the back. It was dark, dark down by the water.

He couldn't see much. He said, "Where are you, boat?" He bent down and felt around in the dark, this way and that way, until he found the bow. He said, "Here you are."

He pulled it up alongside the landing and stepped in the front end. He unwound the rope from a spar on a creosoted post and picked up a Feather paddle in the bottom of the boat and poled along in the shallow water until he couldn't reach bottom anymore, then he sculled behind the boat with the paddle.

The dark lake water buoyed him up and lapped softly against the gunwales, as he drifted backwards into the moonlight and rocked back and forth like a baby in a cradle.

He found the pull-rope for the little Evinrude engine, down in the floorboards, and wrapped it around the crankshaft, one-two-three, and set the throttle and pulled out the choke and leaned back and gave the rope a good yank.

The little motor started up on the first pull, putt-putt-putt, rattle-rattle-rattle. A fragrant, familiar mixture of warm oil and gasoline filled his nostrils.

Mr. Raney turned the bow out into the bayou and pushed the throttle over to High and set out in a cloud of oily smoke, slow as a turtle, under the moon and stars, across the swamp and towards the Runnymede bridge and town.

In the narrow channel he had to steer a little. He slid around a cypress knee, he avoided a stob sticking up out of a bream bed, he slid alongside a trotline and didn't get it tangled up in the propeller.

Then, out in the wide bayou, he drifted past a log filled with sleeping turtles, past alligator nests and snowy egrets and blue herons sleeping on one foot out in the bulrushes and willows, a water moccasin swimming, gar rolling in the moonlight.

For a little while two small dolphins slid in alongside the boat and swam as slow as he was going. Then they swam far out from the boat, they rolled like wheels and showed their oily humps, they dived, they disappeared, they surfaced near him, they swam in circles around him, and then they were gone.

In a minute he saw the Roebuck bridge, and then before long he was tying his boat to one of the stanchions, and laying the pie on the front seat of his pickup truck, which he left up on Harper's Road every day where nobody ever bothered it.

He reached up under the seat and found the ignition key, right where he left it, and started up his truck and headed out Highway 49 to William Tell.

The boy in the zoot suit saw the lights of Mr. Raney's truck coming, as it pulled off the highway and headed down the gravel road to the store.

He said, "Shit."

He flung open the car door and went running up past the gas pumps and then up the steps and inside William Tell.

He said, "Somebody's coming."

Cheryl was naked, standing beside the cot where Hydro lay. Hydro was naked too, not looking at her, or at anything.

Louis could see this from behind the pantry door. He was trembling. He took off his little pink-rimmed glasses and cleaned the lenses on his shirt and put them back on. He stared at Cheryl. The sight of her nakedness, this girl's flesh and bones, her milky skin, her skeleton-thin frame and tiny breasts, the wide, womanly patch of hair between her legs, broke his heart. He tried to ease away from the door again, but he was so nervous he pushed too hard and it closed with a click of the lock.

The boy in the zoot suit looked up.

Cheryl was holding the pistol to Hydro's head, his temple, where he lay on the cot. The hammer of the pistol was cocked.

She turned away from Hydro and looked at the boy in the zoot suit.

She said, "What?"

He said, "Did you hear something?"

She said, "What?"

Louis was standing in black darkness.

He said, "A truck. Somebody just pulled up, out front"

She said, "Shit."

She lowered the gun, and let the hammer down, real careful, with her thumb. She didn't dress yet, she only moved swiftly past the boy, around the counter.

She hurried across the store to the front window and looked out. There was somebody coming, all right. It was an old pickup, bouncing serenely down the road from the highway with its headlights jiggling.

She said, "Goddamn."

The boy trailed behind her to the window and looked out, too, but now she was already gone, already moving. She raced back to the rear of the store. Louis could hear her standing just outside the closed pantry door. He knew she was naked. He was afraid she would try to hide in the pantry.

Hydro had not moved.

Cheryl laid the gun on a chair and started pulling on her clothes.

The boy said, "If you'd gone on and done it, we'd be out of here by now."

She said, "Put your clothes on." Talking to Hydro.

She grabbed up Hydro's pants and shirt and threw them in his face.

Hydro did not move, did not seem to have heard her.

She said, "Somebody's coming. Get moving. You're going to see who it is."

The truck stopped out in front of the store. The tires ground to a halt in the gravel when the brakes were applied, and then something in the bed of the truck seemed to shift forward, a toolbox or an ice chest, something heavy, and made a loud metallic sound when it did, a scraping, and then a thump, or clunk, when it stopped.

The girl said to Hydro, "Put your clothes on. Right now."

Hydro pulled on his pants, then his shirt.

Louis hoped to get one more look at the naked girl. He opened the pantry door again and peeked around the side.

Just then a light turned on in the little store, where Hydro and the boy and girl stood. The light was as bright as the sun. The whole store lit up. You never saw such an amazing and sudden light. It might as well have been the center ring of the bigtop at the Ringling Brothers and Barnum & Bailey Circus, it got so bright in that little grocery and whiskey store, William Tell. It was like the spotlight at the air show, one time, when two-winged cropdusters did loops and turns above the fairgrounds at night.

What an incredible and magical light, like sunshine! Louis felt almost good about his life, peeking around the doorjamb and seeing such a light. Cobwebs in the ceiling corners, the labels on soup cans, a broom that had been lost, misplaced, days before—everything became visible, all of a sudden. Nothing in that store was hidden anymore when that light turned on.

That's what seemed like had happened, when the first shot was fired. Not just Louis thought this, either. The boy in the zoot suit thought it, too. He thought somebody had turned on a bright light, or maybe that the sun had started to shine indoors all of a sudden.

Partly this was because a flame a foot long leaped out of the end of the gun barrel. It did provide a certain amount of sudden and unexpected illumination, that was the truth.

And partly, also, it was because only sudden light, or maybe sudden insight, was ever so startling as the sound of that elemental and unexpected explosion in this small room, especially in this well-dressed boy's mind, in his ringing ears.

Everything became suddenly so clear to him, so crystal clear. Things the boy had never understood were now, all of a sudden, plain as day, past and present, the meaning of life and death, how to break into show business. Suddenly, and for the first time, he understood the expression "This sheds a whole new light on things."

He turned just in time to see the back of Cheryl's head blow off and go flying past him, blood and hair and bone, and onto the wall of the store, in amongst the canned goods. Louis saw this, too. It was almost like Plastic Man's head was stretched halfway across the room. Cheryl didn't fall backwards, though, and not even forwards. Louis all of a sudden remembered that expression "fell in a heap." He remembered the expression "like a sack of potatoes." That was Cheryl. That was how she died. With a bullet between her eyes and her hair all over the walls and Vienna sausages, and then, flop, like a heap of potatoes.

Louis opened the pantry door all the way. He might as well get a good look at this. He wiped his glasses on his shirttail again, and then fitted the earpieces around his ears and pushed the glasses up on his nose.

The boy in the zoot suit imagined another bright light then, and more clear vision and lucid insights into the past and present and future, and for maybe one one-millionth of a second he thought he might have heard a repetition of the phrase "We are plumb out of tortillas."

And then he even imagined his own hair all over the walls, and another sack of potatoes in a heap, similar to Cheryl, but he may have been mistaken about most of this. In fact he probably was, because before he could have heard or seen anything like it, Hydro, the big-headed lover of peach pie who had just killed Cheryl, had already turned a few degrees to his left, in his hopeless way, and had already swung the pistol around, out in front of him, straight-armed. The hammer was already cocked again.

And in fact, the boy in the zoot suit was already dead with a bullet in his forehead, so there is little chance that he might have had these insights, no matter how clear they might have seemed. The boy in the zoot suit was dead before the light and shape of the foot-long flame of the second shot could have registered on his optical nerve; his brain pan was already resting among the canned corn beef and Dinty Moore and Campbell's pork and beans before any such insights or even firelight might have reached it for interpretation.

Louis saw it, though, and regretted that he had no one to tell this to. This was by far the most interesting thing that he had ever seen, and it seemed to him impossible that the sight of it would not ruin his whole life forever if he did not tell someone. He could tell his sister Katy, except just hearing it might ruin her life too, he supposed.

Hydro wondered how an elephant might feel at the end of a long day, after toting all that extra weight around with him. He's just got to be tired, don't he? That's how tired Hydro was. Tired as a durn elephant. He felt like his legs all by theyself must weigh two three tons.

He was still holding the pistol out in front of him, but now he let his arm ease down, real slow, to his side. He turned again, another few degrees, and faced the front door of the store. The gun was just hanging there on his fingers for a minute, while Hydro let his breathing become regular. It didn't fall, though, the pistol, he didn't let it drop to the floor.

Hydro was dressed, in a careless sort of way. He was still barefoot. Just standing there, with the gun dangling by his side, as if at ease. The whole store smelled like cordite and burned gunpowder. The air seemed thick with something, maybe smoke, maybe only portent. There was another smell, too—blood, he thought. He hadn't given the first thought to how much blood there would be when he pulled the trigger, let alone what it would smell like.

Hydro held onto the pistol and didn't let it fall out of his hand, because he wasn't quite done with it yet. He was about to use it one more time. He had heard the truck pull up out front. He didn't recognize the sound of it. Don't blame Hydro for not recognizing his daddy's pickup truck. He didn't recognize much of nothing. He was under a right smart amount of stress.

He didn't know who was coming up the drive, in the store. It could be anybody. It might be friends of the boy and the girl. Well, see, that was the thing.

He wasn't planning on taking any chances. Hydro was fixing to shoot the next person who walked through the door of William Tell.

He heard the pickup door open and slam shut. He heard steps in the gravel. He heard boots on the wood steps. He cocked the pistol a third time and held it out in front of him, aimed at the door. Come right in, can I help you? We are plumb out of tortillas.

Mr. Raney, coming down the drive-road in his truck, had heard the two shots, loud, too. He saw the flash. It looked like lightning inside the store.

He was already pumping on the brakes, hoping he could get this sorry old truck stopped. Morgan or some of the other boys from Arrow Catcher must be out here visiting, keeping Hydro company, wasn't that nice. They were shooting up the store a bit, having some fun.

But even before that, before he heard the shots or saw the flash, Mr. Raney saw the boy in the black zoot suit, scurrying out of a strange car with Texas plates, and in through the front door of the store.

Well, wasn't that nice, too. You don't see many zoot suits in this modern day and age of ours. He might ask this boy for some fashion tips, pass them along to Hydro. You couldn't go wrong befriending a man in a zoot suit. That was Mr. Raney's own personal appraisal of the current fashion scene.

Then he saw what looked like two faces inside the front window of the store, neither of them Hydro.

Mr. Raney thought Hydro was pretty lucky to have friends with a pistol, every man needed a friend, it didn't matter how big his head was. A friend with a firearm was a special blessing. And a zoot suit! He couldn't remember the last time he saw one. Hydro himself would look mighty fine in an excellent suit of clothes like that.

Mr. Raney carried a gun, too, and not just the little .25 on the sideboard. A big gun, ten-inch barrel. He kept it in a locked toolbox out in the bed of his truck. So he knew firsthand the value of firepower in friendship.

Sometimes there was just nothing as satisfying as shooting a gun inside a house. It didn't have to involve a refrigerator. It relieved stress. It cemented relationships, strangers or partners in marriage. It helped most anybody, the least of these my brethren, as Preacher Roe might say. It cleared the air.

You wouldn't want to be careless with it, you wouldn't want to hurt anybody, but to fire a shot out your bedroom window, say, into a neighbor's garage, or in your own kitchen, into a large appliance, maybe, or just through the ceiling, when you were singing the blues, when you had lost your dear wife in childbirth and your only son had come out a waterhead, well, there was not a thing in the world to criticize about shooting off a pistol in that case, now was there, nothing but a good idea to spread a few rounds through the house, nail a few nails in the wall, so to speak, melt a little ice cream.

When Mr. Raney was a boy he worked behind the soda fountain in old Mr. Durham's drug store. There was a man back then named Childe Harold who Mr. Raney used to admire greatly, lived in Arrow Catcher in a house called The Green Door, for some reason, out near the dump.

Childe Harold was a fat man, with a long white beard, and sweated bad. He smelled like Korea, once he got started sweating. He wore a red bandanna around his neck, and for some unknown reason, he wore a silk stocking tied around one ankle.

Every day when Childe Harold came into the drug store, with Red Man stains in his beard, and had flopped his big old sweaty fat butt down in a booth, Mr. Raney, just a boy working behind the big marble soda fountain, would go up to him and he'd say, "Can I get you some coffee, Mr. Childe Harold?"

Childe Harold would stroke his beard with one hand and give his silk stocking a good yank with the other hand, and then he'd drag his enormous old fat ass out of the little booth, pulling and straining, heaving and puffing, sweating, and the gun in his holster would be swinging this way and that way, knocking up against the booth, getting stuck up underneath his leg and poking him in the butt.

He talked through his nose. He would say, "Goddamn."

Then, once he did finally get himself pulled out of the booth, he'd yank the pistol out of the holster, ten-inch barrel Colt .45, fully loaded, and hold it out in front of him. He did this every day.

In his nasal way, Childe Harold would say, "Hold my gun, son, I got to shit."

Dooney Man Drake, the town lawyer, wrote Mr. Raney a letter one day, when he was still in high school, told him Childe Harold was dead, died of a heart attack, and Mr. Raney had inherited his pistol. Dooney Man said in the letter he hated for a bearded man to die and never learn to talk right.

Mr. Raney's daddy said, "A letter? You got a letter?" His mama said, "Well, but ain't that nice, though."

They were more interested in the letter than in the inheritance.

Later on, Mr. Raney showed the pistol itself to his folks.

His daddy said, "And a letter to boot. I swanee goodness."

His mama said, "Don't shoot it off in the house without asking first, honey."

His daddy said, "A schoolboy—*my* boy—receiving his very own letter, through the United States Post Office. I'm just so proud of you, son, I could almost cry."

When Mr. Raney thought these old friendly thoughts of his childhood, he also thought, well, he might as well get in on the fun. He wouldn't shoot another man's refrigerator, even an old friend's, that could be considered pushy, he understood that, but it sure couldn't hurt nothing to put a plug in one of Mr. William Tell's cans of pork and beans, now would it, nobody could blame you for shooting the pork and beans.

So he reached back in the bed of the truck and dragged the heavy old toolbox over to the side and opened it up and reached around in the dark and found the leather bag.

The pistol was so big, it was about the only thing that would fit in the toolbox, though there were a few other things in there, a couple of wrenches anyway, a half-pint of whiskey, a claw hammer, and a box of ten penny nails. He hauled the leather bag out and pulled open the drawstring.

He took the pistol out of the bag, real careful, because it was covered with grease, packed in it, and he didn't want to get grease all over his shirt. He pulled a big rag out of his back pocket and wrapped the pistol in it and rubbed it good, to get some of the grease off.

He wiped the long blue barrel and the checkered handle grip; he seesawed the rag through the trigger guard. It was still pretty greasy, but you could handle it. He wiped grease off the hammer.

He let the cylinder drop, to see if the gun was loaded; the sound of metal on metal was like the sound of silk on silk. He wiped grease off the cylinder too, and the gate, and clicked it back in place and gave it a spin, for good measure.

He stomped on the board steps on his way into the store; he pounded each step hard, in case there was still some mud from the island caked onto his boots. He didn't want to be tracking up Mr. William Tell's floor with gumbo.

When the front door of the store opened, Hydro was already holding the dead girl's pistol out in front of him, straight-armed. It was no small caliber weapon itself. The hammer was already cocked. His hand did not tremble. The large figure that filled up the door frame was unrecognizable to Hydro.

The first shot was Hydro's. He let the hammer fall. It was like simultaneous lightning and thunder.

The second shot was Mr. Raney's, Childe Harold's ancient enormous side-arm, and the sound and blaze that erupted from it were even more elemental, essential, volcanic than the crash and yellow illumination of the pistol in Hydro's hand.

The report from this ancient weapon was so large, so impressive and heartfelt, you had to say it was historical, it was geological, geographical, it was the Army Corps of Engineers, it was the dam on Grenada Lake with the locks open, it was so loud, and the light it produced was the hydroelectric generators in the dam as they turned on all the electricity in Grenada County, or Buffalo, New York, with one switch, lights on. The echo lasted a century, it seemed like; eyes that saw the fire from the barrel were seared permanently, like eyes that had looked straight into the sun. The sulphur and cordite, burning, might have come from the bowels of hell, they stunk so bad, they produced such a cloud of noxious smoke.

There were no other shots, only those two. The firefight was finished.

Far across the sugarcane fields, across acres of water, deep in the swamp, wild creatures heard the gunfire. Some of them might have thought it was thunder, the innocent didappers who looked for rain, the gentle alligators who were too bored to care, the nutrias who stood on gum stumps and shook water out of their fur like slinging silver coins in many directions at once.

But turkey vultures, roosting in the tops of dead trees in sight of the Indian mound, where stone-age civilizations lay quiet for so long, they heard it and opened one eye, perhaps, and shrugged their big poultry shoulders, shivered, as if to shake off a bad dream, and slept again.

Sly foxes heard it, and wrapped their red tails across their half-sleeping eyes and crept an inch deeper into their dens.

Wild dogs heard it, and dreamed of armadillos without shells.

Louis McNaughton heard it, the fat little boy with pink-rimmed glasses, and stepped back into the pantry and turned on the overhead light. He wished there were more choices for a person whose life had probably just been ruined by what he had seen. If there were choices, he couldn't think what they were right now. He sat down again to try to finish reading *Gerald McBoing Boing*.

Mr. Raney said, "What a racket! Wasn't that something special! My eyes are still seeing black spots."

Hydro said, "Daddy?"

Mr. Raney said, "Let's get some lights on in here. Let's see what we hit. I probably should have warned you about shooting Mr. William Tell's refrigerator. Them things are expensive."

Hydro said, "Daddy? Are you all right?"

Mr. Raney said, "I'm not promising nothing about my marksmanship. I was only half-remembering where them pork and beans used to set. No telling what I put a plug in."

Hydro dropped the gun to the floor. It sounded like a tire iron.

Mr. Raney said, "Turn on some lights, son. Let's see what we got here. If I hit one of them cans of Campbell pork and beans, I'll buy you a Co-Cola."

Hydro said, "I missed you. How did I miss you?"

Hydro reached up above him and yanked on the light cord. The door directly behind his father had a piece missing as big as a wedge of pie.

Mr. Raney's eyes were still getting adjusted to the light. He said, "Introduce me to your friends, son, let's don't be rude. I saw them through the window. I got to tell you, I admire your young man's sense of style, sure do."

It wasn't until right then that Mr. Raney noticed that Hydro was barefooted and there might be some dead folks in the room.

Mr. Raney said, "Sugarplum?"

He walked through the store, closer to Hydro.

Mr. Raney said, "What has happened? Why are these two lovely children laying here dead on the floor with their heads blowed off? Where are your shoes?"

# JIM GRIMSLEY, "Your Daddy in Time"

Born in 1955 in Rocky Mount, North Carolina, Jim Grimsley attended the University of North Carolina where he studied creative writing with Doris Betts and Max Steele. He spent the next two decades working at a hospital in Atlanta and writing several plays while serving as playwright-in-residence at the 7 Stages Theatre. Grimsley's first novel, *Winter Birds,* was initially published in German in 1992; when the English edition finally appeared in America two years later, it was named a finalist for the PEN/Hemingway Award and received the Sue Kaufman Prize from the American Academy of Arts and Letters. Over the next decade Grimsley published a collection of plays, *Mr. Universe and Other Plays* (1998), and several novels, including *Dream Boy* (1995), *My Drowning* (1997), *Comfort and Joy* (1999), *Boulevard* (2002), and *Kirith Kirin,* which won a Lambda Award in 2000. Since then he has published three more novels, *The Ordinary* (2004), *The Last Green Tree* (2006), and *Forgiveness* (2007), and a story collection, *Jesus Is Sending You This Message* (2008). A film adaptation of *Dream Boy* premiered in 2010. Grimsley currently serves as director of the creative writing department at Emory University in Atlanta.

"[Grimsley] can portray the life of poor people, especially poor people in the South, in a way that is not condescending, and I think that's extremely rare in contemporary American fiction," says Lynna Williams. "He writes about suffering and pain in language that serves the story first—the result can literally make you hold your breath."[1] In this excerpt from *Winter Birds,* a young boy and his family struggle to survive the wrath of their abusive, alcoholic father.

> These memories are often very unpleasant and lead to stories that are cathartic to read, but hard to sell to publishers. I think you see people

writing now from a class that hasn't spoken at all. Larry Brown is amazing and *Push,* by Sapphire, is an extraordinary book. But the attitude toward that class of people, until recently, has been that poor people were just like everybody else, only with fewer things. Nobody dealt with just how animalistic your life can become when you don't have *anything.*[2]

**"YOUR DADDY IN TIME"**
**FROM *WINTER BIRDS***

When Allen crawls under the house to bring Mama a sweater, she sends you away, because of the glass, she says, though she will not look you in the eye. You are bound to cut yourself in the dark if you stay, she says. You should find Grove and take care of him. Allen watches you solemnly. He whispers that Papa is hiding at the front of the house. He keeps his distance from Mama. When you turn away she does not watch you go; she whispers, "Be careful," to the air.

You crawl slowly through the litter of jagged glass. Old cobwebs drift into your hair. You set down your hand onto the doll's foot and the air whistles out. Once you look back at Mama and Allen, but their shapes are indistinct in the darkness; you can hardly tell which gray mass is which. At the edge of the house you hurry into the light. You do not see your Papa until his shadow crosses your hands.

He is drinking from the bottle, long sucking swallows that make his throat muscles slide and convulse. He squints as if the whiskey hurts going down. Only when he tears the bottle from his jaw does he see you.

You freeze. He replaces the bottle in the bag without hurry. Soon it rests in the pocket of his coat. When he reaches for you he smiles. The good hand descends onto your shoulder. As he lifts you, a pain flashes through your arm. Maybe you squirm, or maybe he is afraid you will fall because the one hand can't keep you steady. His grip on your shoulder tightens and tightens. You try to keep from looking at his face though you can smell his breath and feel the stubble of his beard. You do not make a sound. "You thought you were smarter than your Papa, but he caught you, didn't he?" He hoists you higher, till you are level with his gaze. He curls his lips. "Ain't you got nothing to say to me? You can hide with your Mama under a filthy house, but you don't even want to talk to your Papa."

He gathers you so close you squirm to get away. In his eyes you see glittering light that makes you cold. You bend back your head to escape that sweetish smell of his breath that reminds you of clotting blood.

"You hurt my shoulder," you say softly.

"I didn't mean to," he says.

"You grabbed me too hard."

"I did not. Does it still hurt?" He gives you a dull stare, stroking your shoulder with his bearded chin. He sways with your weight, once nearly falling, catching himself against the corner of the house with the piece of arm. He pulls you close and stoops to see under the house. "Where is your Mama?" he asks, but you don't answer. Your shoulder throbs more sharply with each pulse of blood. Once you see Duck behind Papa, pointing at you and calling. Out in the fields you see Queenie nosing among the cornstalks, belly swaying like a bruise. "You wouldn't have got hurt if you hadn't tried to be smart like your Mama. It probably won't me who hurt you. You probably hurt your shoulder under that house."

"You grabbed me too hard, I felt it," you say, counting the veins in the whites of his eyes, a red lace. Papa touches you with the piece of his arm and studies you. Suddenly you think he is sad. "You don't want to talk to me, do you?" he asks.

From far off you hear Amy shouting. You shiver, bare-armed in the November wind.

"Answer me," Papa says. "You ought to like me, because I'm your Daddy. But here I been carrying you for five minutes and you ain't hardly said a word."

You feel the funny feeling in your belly that you get from the smell of whiskey. You say, "I don't like it when you yell."

"I ain't been yelling at you," Papa says.

"You been yelling at Mama all day."

He asks, in a softer voice, "Does your arm still hurt?"

You touch it with your hand. The big ache is gone, leaving only the little, underneath ache that will gather and swell against the bone. The blood leaks out of the vein where he grabbed you. But you say, "It's better now."

Queenie, at the edge of the yard now, pauses at the sight of Papa and walks slowly toward him, wagging her tail.

"My arm hurts sometimes," Papa says. "But I don't say nothing, I don't want nobody to think I'm crazy. The doctor can't do nothing about it, because my arm's not there." He laughs. His teeth are yellow and flat. The sleeve swings idly. Queenie wags her tail and lopes forward, tongue quivering.

Softly you ask, "Does it hurt now?"

He hears you from far away. He shakes his head, not watching you, though you can see yourself in his black pupils. "It don't mean anything," he says. He nudges Queenie with his foot. "Bitch," he says, "get away." Queenie gazes up at you both, confused that no one will pet her. When she comes back he only pushes her away again, more roughly, his work boot pressing the place where her fat puppies sleep. She watches mournfully as Papa turns to the house again, stooping to search for your Mama. "There she is, at the front," he says, and runs toward her with you bouncing against the bone of his shoulder, the pain in your arm increasing.

At the front of the house Papa stops beneath the sycamores that guard the house from the road. The branches darken the light falling from the gray table of clouds. The wind rushes through you, cooling even the ache. Can Papa feel the wind even in the arm that isn't there? The sleeve streams back, hangs useless against the wind, and slowly falls. When Papa has a coat on, does the arm that isn't there feel like it has a coat on? Does it feel naked? Does it hurt when another arm passes through its space?

"Has she got out already?" Papa asks.

He isn't asking you. On the porch stands Amy Kay with Grove beside her, both watching you with fear on their faces.

"You put my brother down," Amy says.

"I asked you a question. You better answer it."

"I ain't telling you nothing."

Grove whispers past his fist, "You better leave him alone," his voice so hoarse and soft the wind almost drowns it to nothing.

"Put me down," you say in Papa's ear, and when he stares at you, you rest your fists against his neck as if you can push yourself away.

Seeing the fists, he tightens his embrace till you can hardly breathe. "I'm still your Daddy," he says.

You make no sound, you hold your face perfectly still.

"You don't tell me what to do," he says, "you don't tell me to put you down."

You draw shallow breaths, you pretend the pain in your shoulder and ribs is for someone else.

"Leave him alone!" Amy shouts, and then she hollers for Mama; but you only watch Papa, pressing your fists against the veins of his neck.

Allen crawls out from under the house and runs to the porch, with Duck behind him.

They call Mama now, watching you fight to breathe, and soon she comes out herself. Hands on hips, she watches Papa, the shadows of tree branches woven over her face.

At once Papa takes on a look of expectancy.

"Turn Danny loose," Mama says.

"I ain't hurting him," Papa answers, smiling.

"No, you're not hurting him, you're squeezing him so tight he's turning blue."

"Are you going to start your shit again, Miss High-and-Mighty?"

"I said put him down, Bobjay. He can't breathe."

He only smiles and squeezes you tighter. You dig your knuckles hard against his bones and arch your back, sipping the air since you can't drink it. Papa gives you an ugly look that passes through you, but still your expression stays the same. You stare at the vein you have gathered in your hands. You count the slow swing of the empty sleeve back and forth in the air. "Put him down," Mama says. "You hurt that youngun and I swear I'll make you sorry."

"If he gets hurt it won't be my fault. You're the one had him crawling under that house."

"Who had me crawling under there? You son of a bitch, put him down!"

Papa looks at you and laughs. "Look at his face. He ain't scared, he hates his Daddy."

You turn your face to the sky.

"Bobjay Crell, you put my youngun on the ground right now, you dirty one-armed son of a bitch."

Papa smiles a slow wide smile. "What did you call me?"

"Put him down."

"No, what did you call me? You called me a one-armed son of a bitch. I want you to call me that again."

Slowly his grip on you loosens and you slide to the earth. Your shoulder throbs and you gasp for air, you kneel in the pale grass and breathe, breathe.

Mama pushes back hair and says, "Danny, come over here now," motioning toward the porch. But Papa steps toward her and she backs away.

His face is darker than the clouds. "Go ahead and run."

"I can't run. You hurt my leg."

After a moment he laughs. "Oh boy. You're sorry you said it now, ain't you?"

"I was mad, Bobjay, I didn't mean it." She steps back. "Please leave me alone." She backs up the steps, hands reaching for support she doesn't find. There is only air, and Papa laughs, and takes a step each time she does, and says, "You can't go anywhere else, honey."

The hand rises.

A cry from the porch, Amy.

Mama makes a low sound from the belly.

"No, leave her alone," Allen says.

But the sound comes to you from such a distance, there is a hush on this grass where you are still catching up with air. Duck jumps off the porch and runs away crying, his hands on his ears. Papa is shouting something. Mama has already fallen, and is raising her arms to cover her face. Her voice surrounds you, entering like a knife, and you feel as if you bleed from the hearing. You look away from them, at the trees swaying serenely in the wind. But even then you can picture her face when he slaps her, and the sounds she makes rise round you in spirals.

He makes her crawl into the house since she crawled under it.

Says *Don't ever call me no one-armed sonofabitch baby.*

She says *Please, please, I didn't mean it.*

While Amy says softly Mama, Mama, sags against the porch post saying Mama, and Mama disappears into the house on her hands and knees with her hair falling over her face.

The wind descends onto the house and fields, onto your face, onto Mama's vanishing skirt and legs and new bruises, descends onto the trees and the river, a noise, a rushing that almost makes you cold enough inside that you don't want to follow them into the house, that you don't want to see her after he finishes with her.

But when the door closes you stand. Their shouts are muffled by the house. You watch Allen and Amy and Grove. Allen goes to the door and opens it, and then Amy rushes inside with a strangled cry, only to run into Papa's legs.

Over you he hovers a moment, and a new cold rushes through you as he watches you. He has swept Amy to one side and Allen to the other. He gives you a long strange look. "My arm hurts now," he says, and walks to the truck. Fishing the bottle from his pocket, he drains it and throws it in the grass. He starts the truck and backs down the driveway, and clatters away down the road, between two dark banks of trees.

# CHRIS OFFUTT, "Melungeons"

Born in 1958, Chris Offutt grew up in the clay-mining town of Haldeman in the mountains of eastern Kentucky. After attending Morehead State University, Offutt left to become an actor in New York, then later drifted around the country working as a mover, roofer, truck driver, housepainter, fruit picker, nature guide, and an all-purpose circus animal helper before attending the University of Iowa, where he received his master of fine arts degree. In 1992 he published his first story collection, *Kentucky Straight,* which was honored with awards from the Guggenheim Foundation and the American Academy of Arts and Letters. He followed that in 1993 with the acclaimed memoir *The Same River Twice.* Since then Offutt has published a novel, *The Good Brother* (1997), another story collection, *Out of the Woods* (1999), and the memoir *No Heroes* (2002). His stories have been published in *GQ* and *Esquire* and have appeared in both *Best American Short Stories* and *New Stories from the South.* In 2005 he made his comic-writing debut with *Michael Chabon Presents: The Amazing Adventures of the Escapist, No. 6.* Offutt has also written episodes for HBO's *True Blood* and Showtime's *Weeds* and is the cocreator and executive producer of the Epix TV series *Tough Trade.*

In the stories of Chris Offutt, writes Mark Lucas, "brief flickers of insight or tenderness are earned with blood and trouble." So it goes in "Melungeons," Offutt's tale about the last vestiges of an old blood feud. "As with his evocation of Kentucky in general," Lucas writes, "Offutt's use of the mysterious Melungeon people is just the opposite of local color; he goes straight for the deep archetype in this tale of exile, revenge, and liberation."[1]

The popular view of Appalachia is a land where every man is willing, at the drop of a proverbial overall strap, to shoot, fight, or fuck anything on hind legs. We're men who buy half-pints of bootlegged liquor and throw the lids away in order to finish the whiskey in one laughing, brawling night, not caring where we wake or how far from home. Men alleged to eat spiders off the floor to display our strength, a downright ornery bunch.

The dirt truth is a hair different. The men of my generation live in the remnants of a world that still maintains a frontier mentality. Women accept and endure, holding the families tight. Mountain culture expects its males to undergo various rites of manhood, but genuine tribulation under fire no longer exists. We've had to create our own.[2]

## "MELUNGEONS"

Deputy Goins sat in his office and watched the light that seeped beneath the door of the jailhouse. When it reached a certain pock in the floor, it would be time to go home. Monday was nearly over. In the town of Rocksalt, the deputy doubled as jailer to balance each job's meager pay. Goins had come in early to free his prisoners in time for work at the sawmill. They'd left laughing, three boys who'd gotten drunk through the weekend. Goins had spent all day in the dim office. He was tired.

Something outside blocked the light and Goins wished the county would buy a clock. A man opened the door.

"Time is it?" Goins said.

The man shrugged. He peered into the dark room, jerking his head like a blackbird on a fence rail. He looked older than Goins, who was sixty-three, and Goins thought he'd probably come for a grandson.

"Nobody here," Goins said. "Done turned them loose."

"I heard tell a Goins worked here."

"That's me. Ephraim Goins."

"Well, I'm fit for the pokey. What's a man got to do to go?"

"Drunk mostly."

"Don't drink."

"Speeding."

"Ain't got nary a car."

"Stealing'll do it."

"I don't reckon."

The man kept his head turned and his eyes down. Goins decided that he was a chucklehead who'd wandered away from his family.

"Why don't you let me call your kin," Goins said.

"No phone." The man jerked his chin to the corridor where the cells were. "What if I cussed you?"

"I'd cuss back."

"Ain't they nothing?"

"Let's see," Goins said. "Defacing public property is on the books, but it'd be hard to hurt this place."

The man walked to the door and stood with his back turned. "Come here a minute," he said.

Goins joined him. The man had unzipped his pants and was urinating on the plank steps leading to the door. Goins whistled low, shaking his head.

"You've force put me, sure enough," he said, hoping to scare the man away. "Looks like you're arrested. Lucky they ain't no lynch mob handy."

The man inhaled deeply and hurried down the hall to a cell. Goins opened the heavy door. The man stepped in and quickly pulled it shut behind him.

"Name?" said Goins.

"Gipson. Haze Gipson."

He lifted his head, showing blue eyes in rough contrast with his black hair and smooth, swarthy skin. They watched each other for a long time. The name Gipson was like Goins, a Melungeon name, and Goins knew the man's home ridge deep in the hills. He glanced along the dim hall and lowered his voice.

"Say you're a Gipson?"

"Least I ain't the law."

"What's your why of getting locked up?"

"You been towned so long," Gipson said, "I don't know that I can say. I surely don't."

"Why not?"

"Don't know which way you're aimed at these days."

Goins stepped close to the bars.

"You know," he said. "If you're a Gipson, you do. But you ain't making it easy."

"It never was."

Gipson lay on the narrow cot and rolled on his side, turning his back to Goins. A mouse blurred across the floor.

"I'm a done-talk man," Gipson said.

Goins returned to his desk. He stared through the window at the courthouse and remembered his fourth-grade teacher threatening a child who was always late to school. "If you don't get up on time," the teacher had said, "the Melungeons will get you."

Melungeons weren't white, black, or Indian. They lived deep in the hills, on the most isolated ridges, pushed from the hollows two centuries back by the people following Boone. The Shawnee called them "white Indians," and told the settlers that they'd always lived there. Melungeons continued to live as they always had.

Goins wasn't born when the trouble started between the Gipson and Mullins clans, but he'd felt the strain of its tension all his life. Members of his family had married both sides. To avoid the pressure of laying claim to either, Goins had volunteered to serve in Korea. Uniforms rather than blood would clarify the enemy.

When a dentist noticed that his gums were tinged with blue, the army assigned Goins to an all-black company. Black soldiers treated him with open scorn. The whites refused to acknowledge him at all. Only one man befriended him, a New Yorker named Abe, whom no one liked because he was Jewish.

On a routine patrol Goins became separated from the rest, and was not missed until the sound of gunfire. American soldiers found him bleeding from two bullet holes and a bayonet wound. Five enemy lay dead around him. Goins was decorated with honor and returned to Kentucky, but stayed in town. He didn't want to live near killing. Out of respect for its only hero, the town overlooked which hill he was from. Now the town had forgotten.

Goins rose from his desk and walked to Gipson's cell, his boots echoing in the dark hall. The smell of human waste and disinfectant made his nose sting. The walls were damp.

"How long you aim to stay?" Goins said.

"Just overnight. Hotel's too risky."

"Why stay in town at all?"

"Man gets old," Gipson said. "You don't know who I am, do you?"

"No," Goins said. "I ain't been up there in thirty years."

"Longer for me. I'm the one that left and went north."

"Plenty of work?"

"As many taxes they got laying for a man, it don't hardly pay to work."

"What'd they take you for up there?"

"Went by ever who else was around. Italian mostly. Couple times a Puerto Rican till they heard me talk. Sometimes it never mattered."

"Why come back?"

"I got give out on it," Gipson said. "I'm seventy-six years old. Missed every wedding and funeral my family had."

"Me, too."

"By choice." The man's voice was hard. "You can walk back out your ridge any day of the year. Don't know why a man wouldn't when he could."

Goins gripped the cell door with both hands the way prisoners often stood, shoulders hunched, head low. He didn't hunt or fish anymore, had stopped gathering mushrooms and ginseng. Being in the woods was too painful when he didn't live there. The last few times he'd felt awkward and foreign, as if the land was mocking him. He wondered if Gipson's exile was easier without the constant reminder of what he'd lost.

Goins unlocked the cell and pulled the door open an inch. Gipson's face twisted in a faint smile. One side of his mouth was missing teeth.

"I'm going," said Goins.

"I'll be here come daylight."

"Hope you know what you're doing."

"Some of my grandkids have got kids," Gipson said. "You don't know what it's like to see them all at once. And them not to know you."

"You were up to the mountain?" Goins said.

The man nodded.

"Bad as ever?"

"Not so much as it was. They're married in now and don't bother with it no more. The kids have got a game of it, play-acting. I look for it to stop when the next bunch gets born. Still ain't full safe for me. I'm the last of the old Gipsons left alive."

He moved to face the wall again. Goins walked quietly away, leaving the cell open, hoping Gipson would change his mind. He left the front door unlocked. The dusk of autumn cooled his face and he realized that he'd been sweating. The fading sun leaned into the hills with a horizontal light that made the woods appear on fire.

A gibbous moon waned above the land when Beulah Mullins left her house. Though she hadn't been off the mountain in fifty years, she found the old path easily, and followed it down the final slanting drop to the road beside the creek. The road was black now, hard and black. She'd heard of that but never seen it. Beulah stayed on the weedy shoulder, preferring earth for the long walk to Rocksalt. The load she carried was easier on flat terrain.

Beulah had never voted or paid taxes. There was no record of her birth. The only time she'd been to town, she'd bought nails for a hogpen. Her family usually burned old buildings for nails, plucking them hot from the debris, but that year a spring flood had washed them away. Beulah had despised Rocksalt and swore never to return. Tonight she had no choice. She left her house within an hour of learning that Haze was on the mountain. He'd slipped away, probably after hearing that she was still alive, and headed for town. Beulah walked steadily. The air was day-white from the moon.

Sixty years before, five Mullins men were logging a hillside at the southern edge of their property when a white oak slipped sideways from its notch. The beveled point dug into the earth. Instead of falling parallel with the creek, the oak dropped onto their neighbor's land and splintered a hollow log. Dislodged tree leaves floated in the breeze. When the men crossed the creek, they found a black bear crushed to death inside the hollow log. They built a fire for the night and ate the liver, tongue, and six pounds of greasy fat.

In the morning, a hunting party of Gipsons discovered the camp. The land was theirs and they demanded the meat. Since the Mullins men had already butchered the bear, they offered half. The Gipsons refused. Three men died in a quick gunfight. The rest crept through the woods, leaking blood from bullet wounds. Over the next two decades, twenty-eight more people were killed, a few per year.

Ground fog rose to the eastern sky, streaked in pink like lace. Beulah's face was dark as a ripe paw-paw. Checkered gingham wrapped her head, covering five feet of grey hair. She wore a long coat that smelled of oil and concealed her burden. Her legs hurt. A flock of vireos lifted from a maple by the creek, a thick cloud of dark specks that narrowed at the end like a tadpole. Beulah watched them, knowing that winter would arrive early.

She scented town before she saw the buildings. Rocksalt was bigger now, had spread like moss. Frost in the hills was heavy enough to track a rabbit, but here the ground was soft. Town was suddenly all around her. Beulah moved downwind of a police car. She couldn't read, but knew that an automobile with writing on its side was like a tied dog. Whoever held the leash controlled it. She stalked the town from the shade. Her shins were damp from dew.

Railroad Street was empty. The muddy boardwalk was gone, and the cement sidewalk reminded her of a frozen creek, shiny and hard in the shade. Beulah leaned against the granite whistle post in the morning sun. On her last trip this had been the center of town, busy with people, wagons, and mules. Now the tracks were rusty and the platform was a bare gantry of rotted wood. Beulah looked past it to the tree line, listening to a cardinal. The hollow was glazed by mist like crystal.

She turned her back and headed into the silence of improvement. Sunlight crept down the buildings that faced east. She walked two blocks out of her way to avoid a neon diner sign glowing in the dawn. No one here would take Haze in. There was only one place he could have gone.

A bench sat in front of the jail with one side propped on a concrete block. The load she carried prevented her from sitting and she moved to shade, leaning against the southern wall. She was eighty-four years old. She breathed easily in the chill air.

Goins slept rough that night, listening to the building crack from overnight cold. At dawn he rose and looked at the hills. He missed living with the land most in autumn, when the trees seemed suddenly splashed in color, and rutting deer snorted in the hollows. There were walnuts to gather, bees to rob. Turkeys big as dogs jumped from ridgelines to extend their flight.

He rubbed his face and turned from the window, reminding himself of why he'd stayed in Rocksalt. Town was warm. It had cable TV and water. He was treated as everyone's equal, but his years in town had taught him to hide his directness, the Melungeon way of point-blank living.

After breakfast, he reached under his bed for a cigar box that contained his Purple Heart and Bronze Star. They were tarnished near to black. Beneath them was an article he'd cut from a Lexington paper a few years back. It was a feature story suggesting that Melungeons were descendants of Madoc, a Welsh explorer in the twelfth century. Alternate theories labeled them as shipwrecked Portuguese, Phoenicians, Turks, or one of Israel's lost tribes. It was the only information Goins had ever seen about Melungeons. The article called them a vanishing race.

He slipped the brittle paper in his pocket and walked to work. Strands of mist haloed the hills that circled the town. The jailhouse door was unlocked, and Goins hoped the cell would be empty.

Inside, Gipson sat silently on his bunk, making a cigarette. Goins gave him a cup of coffee. The cigarette hung from Gipson's mouth. Once lit, he never touched it.

"Sleep good?" Goins said.

"My back hurts like a toothache."

Goins unfolded the newspaper article and handed it through the bars. Gipson read it slowly.

"Don't mean nothing," he said. "They're just fighting over who come to America first. Damn sure wasn't you and me."

"I kindly favor that lost tribe of Israel idea."

"You do."

"I've give thought to it. Them people then moved around more than a cat. Your name's off Hezekiah and mine's Ephraim. I knowed a Nimrod once. Got a cousin Zephaniah married a Ruth."

Gipson shook his head rapidly, sending a trail of ash to the grimy floor.

"That don't make us nobody special," he said.

"We're somebody, ain't we."

"We damn sure ain't Phoenicians or Welshes. We ain't even Melungeons except in the paper. It don't matter where we upped from. It's who we are now that matters."

"Man can study on it if he's a mind to."

"You're a Goins."

"I'm a deputy."

Goins returned to his desk. He wanted to ask for the article back but decided to wait until the man wasn't twitchy as a spooked horse. A preacher had donated a Bible for the prisoners and Goins hunted through Genesis for his namesake, the leader of a lost tribe who never made it to the land of milk and honey. He hoped it was hilly. He turned to Exodus and thought of Abe, his army buddy from New York. Goins wondered if he had a phone. Maybe Abe knew where the lost tribes went.

The jail's front door slowly creaked open and a woman's form eclipsed the light that flowed around her. She stepped inside. Goins didn't know her, but he knew her. It was as if the mountain itself had entered the tiny room, filling it with earth and rain, the steady wind along the ridge. She gazed at him, one eye dark, the other yellow-flecked. Between the lines of her face ran many smaller lines like rain gulleys running to creeks. She'd been old when he was young.

"You look a Goins," she said.

He nodded. He could smell the mountain on her.

"They a Gipson here?" she said.

Goins nodded again. He swallowed in order to speak, but couldn't.

The woman shifted her shoulders to remove a game bag. Inside was a blackened pot, the lid fastened with moonseed vine. She looked at him, waiting. He opened a drawer for a plate and she removed the lid to reveal a skin of grease that covered a stew. She scooped a squirrel leg onto his plate, then a potato. The musk of fresh game pushed into the room. Her hands were misshapen from arthritis but she used them freely, her lips clamped tight. Goins understood that she was following the old code of proving the pot contained no file or pistol. He relaxed some. She wasn't here for trouble.

The woman shifted her head to look at him. The blink of her eyes was slow and patient. She stood as if she could wait a month without speech or movement, oblivious to time and weather. Goins tried again to speak. He wanted to ask her where they'd all come from, but knew from looking at her that she wouldn't know or care.

When he realized what she was waiting for, he opened his pocketknife, sliced some meat from the leg, and lifted it to his mouth. It tasted of wild onion and the dark flavor of game. He nodded to her. She straightened her back and faced the hall and did not look at him again.

She walked to the cells, moving stiffly, favoring her left side as if straining with gout. The long coat rustled against her legs like brush in a breeze. Goins pivoted in his chair to give them privacy. He looked at the strip of light below the front door, knowing that as the sun passed by, the light would get longer, then shorter, before he could leave. Outside, someone laughed while entering the courthouse. A car engine drowned the sound of morning birds. Goins stared at the closed door. He swallowed the bite of meat.

Behind him he heard the woman say one word soaked in the fury of half a century. Then came the tremendous bellow of a shotgun. The sound bounced off the stone walls and up the hall to his office, echoing back and forth, until it faded. Goins jerked upright in the chair. His legs began to shiver. He held his thighs tightly and the shivering traveled up his arms until his entire body shook. He pressed his forehead against the desk. When the trembling passed, he went down the hall to the cells.

Gun smoke stung his eyes and he could smell cordite. The left side of the woman's coat was hiked across her hip where she'd hidden the gun. Its barrel was shiny and ragged at the sawcut. Her legs were steady. She tossed the weapon into the cell, looked at Goins and nodded once, her expression same as before.

The cigarette in Gipson's cell still trailed smoke. Blood covered the newspaper article and flowed slowly across the floor. The woman stepped to the next cell and waited while he unlocked the door. Her face seemed softer. She stepped inside. When the door clanked shut, her back stiffened, and she lifted her head to the gridded square of sky visible through the small window.

People were running outside. Someone shouted his name, asking if he was hurt. Goins used the phone to call an undertaker who doubled as county coroner. It occurred to him that coroner was a better job than jailer. The coroner would receive twenty-five dollars for pronouncing the man dead, but Goins got nothing extra for cleaning the cell.

He put the Bible away and found the prisoner's log and wrote Mullins. Under yesterday's date he wrote Gipson. Goins rubbed his eyes. He didn't write Haze because the man was down to a body now, and the body was a Melungeon. Goins covered his face with his hands. It was true for him as well.

He opened the door and stepped into the sun. People ducked for cover until they recognized him. He looked at them, men and women he'd known for thirty years, but never really knew. Beyond them stood the hills that hemmed the town. He began walking east, toward the nearest slope. There was nothing he needed to take. The sun was warm against his face.

# GEORGE SINGLETON, "Jacksonville"

Born in Anaheim, California, in 1958, George Singleton grew up in Greenwood, South Carolina, and graduated from Furman University with a degree in philosophy. Inspired by the writing of Thomas Pynchon, John Barth, and Donald Barthelme, Singleton began writing fiction in college and later received his master of fine arts degree from the University of North Carolina at Greensboro. In addition to teaching, Singleton has worked as a pharmacy clerk, garbage truck driver, roofer, and housepainter. His stories have appeared in numerous magazines and journals, including *Harper's, Atlantic Monthly, Five Points, Zoetrope, Playboy, Story,* and the *Georgia Review,* as well as several editions of the anthology *New Stories from the South.* Singleton is the author of four story collections, *These People Are Us* (2001), *The Half-Mammals of Dixie* (2002), *Why Dogs Chase Cars* (2004), and *Drowning in Gruel* (2006); the novels *Novel* (2005) and *Work Shirts for Madmen* (2007); and a writer's guide, *Pep Talks, Warnings, and Screeds: Indispensable Wisdom and Cautionary Advice for Writers* (2008). He is the recipient of a Guggenheim Fellowship and the Hillsdale Award for Fiction from the Fellowship of Southern Writers. Singleton lives in Pickens County, South Carolina, and teaches writing at the South Carolina Governor's School for the Arts and Humanities.

Tony Earley calls Singleton "a big-hearted evil genius who writes as if he were the love child of Alice Munro and Strom Thurmond."[1] Singleton's characteristic wit is on full display in "Jacksonville," which introduces us to Harry, a Nietzsche-quoting flea market jockey on the run from the law and the memory of his late father.

My South might be a little different than the ones depicted between, say, Reconstruction and 1972. I don't have a whole lot of grandmothers rocking on their front porches, or men spitting tobacco at the general store. I don't write much about guns or confederate flags. What I'm usually trying to show is the tension between the old Old South and the New South, or the New South and the New New South, with characters trying to slog through day to day dilemmas, against all odds. I might have a hard-working character in overalls sitting at a bar, thinking things through—but he's not half as frightening, to me, as a character in that same bar, dressed in a suit, daydreaming hard to develop some nearby land. I don't write so much about the plight of uneducated textile workers as I do undereducated, unemployed sons and grandsons of ex-textile workers. There are quite a few ways to insert "seething" into the situation.[2]

#### "JACKSONVILLE"

If my father still lived I'd've inadvertently gotten him thrown into jail overnight on grand theft charges twice, I suppose, seeing as I got booked for receiving stolen goods and attempting to sell hot merchandise—which I didn't think was all that uncommon or unlawful in Jacksonville what with all the naval personnel and their ways. One time I ran across this little submarine guy who sold plastic roulette wheels fitted for urinals he'd swiped from bachelor officers' quarters restrooms down in Key West. You pissed in the center and an arrow spun around to "little squirt," "straight shooter," "should've been a girl," "for large women/small heifers," like that. The guy wanted five bucks each, and they were obviously stolen government property provided by taxpayer money. I bought two, and sent one to my ex-wife and another to her daddy, a man I still admired seeing as he had a sense of humor. When I stood there that day examining each used urinal pad for shape, contour, line, color and the like it never occurred to me that the law might show up and throw handcuffs on the guy like what happened to me at the same flea market within the same year. I thought one of my cohorts—probably Fagen, or Madame Tammy—got somebody to don a realistic uniform and bust me for a table of hotel ashtrays my father took from the 1950s until his death on the day Reagan got sworn in the second time.

"Do you own the Desert Inn in Las Vegas?" this cop named Marion Pelt asked me. I had a table between a guy selling goddamn gamecock hatchlings and another fellow selling bongs he'd disguised as miniature bassoons.

I laughed, of course. I said, "Used to. Lost it in a big poker game. Who'd've thought Bugsy held four tens to my full house, kings over jacks?" I said, "I'm asking ten dollars for that particular ashtray. It's an old one. Some of the Holiday Inns and Ramadas are only a dollar. I'm asking fifty for the yellow and black Playboy Club ashtray, and the Tropicana one. The rest are in between." I swept my arm over the table like a gameshow model and continued the motion to my open car trunk where another thousand or so ashtrays waited, wrapped in newspaper, for their turns on the wooden-topped display case.

The cop looked up and down my rows. He said, "You must be a crummy poker player, Cuz. You lose the Magnificent Riviera, Caesars Palace, Howard Johnson's, the Lake Tahoe Inn, the Thunderbird Hotel, and," he picked up a nice embossed glass ashtray, "Edgewater Hotel and Casino, Laughlin, Nevada?"

It was at this point that I understood what would happen in America once the law gave up on the drug dealers, gun-runners, and illegal alien smugglers. If I were more of a scholar I'd've made some kind of connection between the American educational system, the dwindling support for liberal arts, and perhaps the American Cancer Society's ad campaigns equating smokers with members of the Untouchable caste. I said, "Bubba, I never owned Beaver Falls Savings or the Brass Rail in New York City, but I got their goddamn ashtrays in the back of my car. Businesses order ashtrays so people *will* take them, you idiot. It's advertising. I never owned Tom Taylor Motors DeSoto dealership, but I got Tom's ashtray, and it'll cost you forty dollars. It's old."

The guy selling gamecocks loaded up his wire cages in the back of his pickup, and it was obvious how he kept looking peripherally. The cop said to me, "If you didn't own those places, then these must be stolen merchandise," as if he didn't hear me.

I said, "My father was a traveling salesman. When he wasn't moving around the entire country selling textile supplies, he was at a convention somewhere. He was an officer in the Elks, too. He brought back ashtrays all the time and told me they'd be worth money one day. He knew."

More than a few passersby stopped. No one came up to my table wanting to haggle over my Handlery Hotels collection. The cop said, "A traveling salesman. And a prophet. Well, it looks like your daddy's right in one respect. Oncet we sell off all them ashtrays at auction they'll be worth money. To the state."

Later on I thought about saying how everyone selling paperbacks at the flea market didn't own a publishing house or book store or write them outright under pseudonyms. I thought about how the guy selling hubcaps wasn't Henry fucking Ford. Later on I made up a bunch of analogies, too late. I'm not sure if they'd've helped, though, seeing as I ended up behind bars overnight the first time for resisting arrest, creating a public disturbance, threatening and then bribing an officer of the law, and tax evasion. Actually I never really understood which charges stuck and which ones Officer Marion Pelt only listed off as possibilities. Finally—this will prove that Jacksonville's not much more than south Georgia—I got nailed for contributing to the delinquency of a minor.

I'd been under surveillance, evidently. I sold some kid an ashtray, and he wasn't old enough to buy cigarettes. The cop planned some kind of cause-and-effect argument to the magistrate, I suppose.

So did I, but it didn't have anything to do with jurisprudence in general, or a Jacksonville magistrate in particular. No, it had to do with the IRS, the memory of my father, and a constant peckish stomach I couldn't escape ever. It had to do with what I *thought* was the stability of driving back roads, always.

I'm almost certain my father kept a stash of Gideon's Bibles, too. It's not like he could come home those twelve or however many weekends a year, hand me a box of shoeshine strips and towels, and still appear the prodigal hunter/gatherer hero. Even ashtrays didn't seem much to me—especially during my pre-teen years—until I realized that my mother only got packs of matches and paper room service menus. When I turned about sixteen I nailed thin shelves across the walls of my room, row after row, and balanced each ashtray upright. When my friends came over I shut the blinds, closed the door, and turned on a strobe light while listening to the Grateful Dead—not a real chart topping band in South Carolina in the early to mid-70s. My senior year I got voted most likely to visit Antarctica. That was supposed to be a compliment.

I didn't mention to Marion Pelt anything about the Bibles, et cetera. I figured he had the will power to check up on my dead father, do investigative work involving hotel registers and their dwindling supplies, and somehow get the IRS to send back tax notices to my mother, et cetera.

Madame Tammy and Fagen bailed me out, or at least got a bondsman who'd take ten per cent of the grand I needed. "They must not like your type around here," Fagen said to me. "A thousand dollars ain't shit for bail, Dale. Hell, my first DUI cost me five grand to walk out the next morning."

Fagen and I only knew each other from flea markets between Florida and Virginia. We didn't camp out together or anything, and I'm not sure he ever knew my real name. Fagen had this quirk about saying any given name in any given language so that it rhymed with the last part of his last question or statement during a conversation. I heard him say, "You know what I mean, Gene?" more often than not, is what I'm saying.

I said, "Fuck that cop. It's like they always say—there's somebody getting murdered right down the street and this cop's bugging me about ashtrays. Even my mother says it." I signed a paper and got a receipt about when to show up in court. The half-cop behind the cage handed me a manila envelope that held my watch, wallet, and shoelaces. Outside I said, "Did they tow away my car, or take all the ashtrays for evidence?"

Madame Tammy wasn't wearing her palm-reading attire. "You're in good shape," she said. She wasn't wearing a muumuu with silver and gold orbs spread all over it. She wasn't wearing make-up, or a thin cotton scarf wrapped around her head. Madame Tammy wore jeans and a UGA t-shirt. She looked like the kind of woman who owned an antique store, on her way to an estate sale. She said, "You owe me. You owe me big. Let me say this—even I know that maybe I don't have the best psychic abilities, but from way across the flea market I felt like someone was in trouble. I closed early, and packed my crystal ball, and came over to your table just as they put you in the cruiser." We walked through a parking lot.

I said, "Thanks. I didn't see you."

"You were in a way, Jay," Fagen said. "You were hollering something about cheese, what cheese said."

I had probably yelled out something about Nietzsche, but didn't remember. Madame Tammy said, "Let me just say that I happened to have some dirt on the cop that came to back up the one giving you so much shit. It didn't take much talk for me to get him to load up every ashtray and put them back in your car. I only had to look that old boy in the eye and offer him one image: lace panties. Your car's back over at the campground. I drove it over there myself, and Fagen here picked me up."

I said, "I got money. If y'all can give me a ride back over there I'll get you the money you put up for me getting out."

Fagen put his arm around my shoulder. Madame Tammy walked in front of us a few steps. Fagen squeezed, and nodded towards her butt. He said, "Where else we going to go, Antonio?" and laughed. I didn't answer, 'cause I needed to look at the map. "In the movies I'd take you to a whorehouse, but this ain't the movies."

Fagen slapped my back. Madame Tammy didn't respond, even with her eyes. I needed to get out the Rand McNally, I knew for sure.

"What you got packed going north?" Fagen asked around the campfire. This was Florida and hot, sure, but a fire helped evaporate humidity. Only fires kept us from drowning nightly.

I passed two beers his way. We had driven straight from jail to a place in Fernandina Beach that specialized in longnecks. I set the empties in a circle around the fire in order to make novelty ashtrays to sell once my real ones sold out. I said, "Tell him, Tammy. You're the seer. You know all."

Tammy spun a bottle on her index finger like a car hop spins trays. She spun it like some poor work-study college kid does in the school cafeteria. Tammy said, "I know all, and I'm about to tell all, Harry. Don't make me blackmail you like I did that cop yesterday."

Tammy and I'd gotten drunk and fooled around the season before, up near Pound, Virginia. I'd gotten ahold of about five hundred hardbacks—some first editions, too—at an estate sale over in Whitesburg, Kentucky the week before. Whoever died either retired as an English professor or thought it hip to read poetry, probably to impress a bunch of coal miners' widows who in turn, I imagine, made fun of the guy and beat the shit out of him. There were a couple books by that Ezra Pound fellow and, being drunk and in a place called Pound, it seemed only reasonable that Tammy read a couple cantos while mounted atop me, her head working overtime as an unstable third tent pole.

I said to Fagen, "Sometimes I read poems. I don't write them or anything. I'm not a total pussy, I just read the things."

Madame Tammy said, "You bought lard buckets in Alabama and took them to a mini-storage warehouse unit on the Maryland-Pennsylvania border to sell up north. You bought those wind-up newspaper log rollers up north and took them to Alabama. In Georgia you keep a little six-by-ten foot space filled with face jugs and pottery bought in North Carolina. In Asheville you keep your collection of used tools and farm implements that you bought in Georgia to sell to all the yuppies wanting realistic-looking mountain homes. In South Carolina you got your cigarette advertisements bought up in Virginia and North Carolina, and in Virginia it's strictly stock car paraphernalia bought down around Darlington. How'm I doing so far?"

Fagen said, "Poems like 'On the shores of Gitchy-goomy'? I have to say I like that poem, too. 'By the shining big sea waters.' I forget it now."

I couldn't spin my bottle right. I stuck it in the fire pit mouth-end down to experiment. Tammy said, "It's going to fuck up your schedule for a year, but you need to go ahead and leave for halfway up north. You need to drop off some ashtrays in Georgia and both Carolinas, pick up your pottery, bush axes, and whatever else, and go ahead up north for fall and winter. Don't think about it as going against the tide, Harry. Think of it as being the first settler."

We all knew she was right. Although Fagen specialized in selling rabbit pelts, raccoon tails, and Davy Crockett hats—and only rabbit pelts, raccoon tails, and Davy Crockett hats—I said, "You wouldn't want to buy my collection of ashtrays, would you? They're old. People are feeling nostalgic for the old days. For summer vacations spent on two lane roads driving around with their folks. I got more than a few ashtrays with Route 66 somewhere printed on the address, and U.S. 1, too."

Fagen nodded. He said, "I counted them all when Tammy's cop wrapped them back up." Then he offered me a nickel apiece.

I didn't bother telling him how he'd be the coolest flea market vendor on the circuit once he attached shelves to the inside of his tent, and got a strobe or black light going every night beside the fire. I said, "For the entire collection I've been asking five grand. There's a thousand in all. Where you going to find antique hotel ashtrays with advertising on them for five bucks each, man?"

Madame Tammy said, "Russia. From old brave ex-hotel workers in Russia."

Fagen turned his coonskin hat sideways. He said, "It doesn't matter what they're worth if you can't sell them. Hell, I'm not in this business just to find things to only carry, Harry. Goddamn, it seems to me you'd want to get rid of them like anyone would want to get rid of evidence. It ain't worth it to your nerves to keep these things, in your trunk or in a storage unit, man. I'll give you a dime each."

Two hours later we settled on a quarter. I pulled the empty half-melted bottles out of the fire bare-handed, and didn't feel a thing. I packed my tent before dawn, and drove away with a light trunk.

I'm not sure what most fathers leave behind for their sons, outside of a house, business, insurance payment, car, and the occasional boat. I'm not complaining, but my father only left me a certain sense of movement, a way to know when I've worn out what might not've been a welcome originally. The first thing my father did after retirement, of course, was to leave my mother. By that time I'd already ruined three separate career tracks—teaching, advertising, amateur real estate—two wives, and a credit record. I took my father's gift humbly, and whether I knew it or not each day perfected that which he only worked as a hobbyist. After all, he returned home at least once a month, plus our vacation times each summer. Me, I couldn't set up my wares at the same jockey lot two weekends in a row.

"You will meet a stranger wearing galoshes long before any of us will," Madame Tammy told me before I left. She crawled out of her tent, and looked as if she hadn't slept. I laughed. "Good luck, Harry. Maybe we'll see you in Scranton or some place."

"I guess you know where I'm going," I said. "Hey, could you tell me where I could find a joker poker machine that's ready to pay off its jackpot? I've always wondered why those women who work on psychic hotlines didn't hang out their own shingle and just go to where more money came their way. Hell, a real psychic could just go to Las Vegas or Atlantic City and walk up and down the one-armed bandit aisles until they got the feeling, you know what I mean." I turned the radio on an all-night AM radio station talk show that came out of Miami. For some reason I thought I could somehow pick up knowledge of the Spanish language by listening as often as possible. The word for telephone seemed to be *telefono*.

Madame Tammy walked to my car and slapped my arm lightly. She said, "Slot machines don't have souls, Harry. A psychic can't predict anything about something without a soul." She took my left hand from the steering wheel and stroked my palm lightly.

I said, "Well, if you do figure it out and end up in one of those places, think about me. Steal the ashtrays."

Madame Tammy nodded. In the dark I made out a slight smile on her lips. She said, "In a week I want you to go sit down by yourself somewhere. Go into a diner, and take a booth all by yourself. I want you to think about those ashtrays that your father gave you. I want you to decide whether they were worth selling off to Fagen, or if you should've taken a chance of driving around with them in your trunk. That cop did you a favor, Harry. That cop came to you out of nowhere in order to give you a test, and not the kind of test you either pass or fail."

I thought to myself, Fuck—don't get all cosmic on me. The one thing I can't stand is driving from point A to point B while thinking about cosmic questions. Every time it'd happened in the past I ended up on the side of the road looking up and down intersections, wondering which direction to take. I said, "Oh, I can give you an answer right now, Tam."

Actually, I couldn't. I wasn't able to concentrate. Madame Tammy let go of my hand and bent down in such a way that her body could be used as a square. Her breasts bobbed and dangled a half-reach away like two conical moons. I said, "There's no way to write or anything. You don't by any chance have a schedule you know, do you? I mean, are you going to be anywhere for Labor Day, or Halloween?"

Madame Tammy stood back up. She said, "If you still smoked cigarettes it would seem like a sign, wouldn't it? But you don't. It still might be, though." And with that she walked away, past her own tent, and out into a copse of mangrove. Her back was turned, but I swear I made out, "I'll see you tonight or tomorrow morning."

I closed the atlas on my front seat and drove forward. I said out loud to myself, "Stop thinking and start doing." The host of the talk show said, *jubileo,* I think.

Jacksonville's in the civics books only because the county and municipal governments are one or something, and in square mileage it's the biggest city in the United States. At least that's what Fagen said one night. I know that a person trying to get out of town might still be doing so two or three hours later, depending on traffic across the St. John's River, incoming fog, and whether or not naval maneuvers occur somewhere in the western hemisphere. Wrecks, road blocks, detours, and sinkholes might slow a near-felon from simple escape. The haphazard and reckless braking of unsure drivers might make someone veer onto an unknown circuitous route, frustrated that it's taking him longer to get from the southern part of the city-county to the state line than it would to drive from Savannah to, say, New Hampshire on a normal weekday.

I took an exit off U.S. 1 and ended up still behind people sending messages to each other via brake light Morse code, semaphore, or whatever it's called. It was just past dawn, and I realized that the yard and garage sale shoppers were out. The Hispanic talk show hostess down in Miami seemed angry and excited about something, and the only word I could make out over and over happened to be *intruso.*

I wondered if Officer Marion Pelt would return to the flea market in hopes of finding me out selling my ashtrays again. I wondered if Fagen had the balls to unwrap the only concrete things my father ever gave me, and then sell them from fifty cents to a dollar each for a quick turnover. I'd done it before. I'd talked a man into believing his End of Day 3/4" Onionskin marbles weren't worth but a penny each since they were nothing more than machine-made dearies, bought his entire stock, then re-sold them for an average of ten dollars apiece to a woman from Pakistan who was educated in London and swore she feared marbles in such a way that she wanted to destroy each one on this planet. I'm no psychologist, but I'd bet she lacked friends as a child. I wondered if somehow somebody who either feared or hated cigarettes—I'll be the first to admit paranoid tendencies—wanted a monopoly on old advertising ashtrays, paid off the cops, and ended up losing out on the deal after all. I found myself driving through a residential area, following Magic Markered posters giving directions to a yard sale offering children's clothing, furniture, china, odds and ends, and wondered if I'd still be teaching high school had I agreed to take on driver's ed when the fucking principal gave me an ultimatum.

When I pulled into a multi-family yard sale I realized how I should've proposed to Madame Tammy before I left, or at least made a case that there was more to me than camping gear. A woman dressed in a University of Florida sweatsuit shined her flashlight in my face and said, "We got us some real nice toys. They's baby clothes over at Marlis's table. My husband's still putting together one of them big plastic kitchens ain't ever been used. Our little girl never got old enough." She didn't seem fazed. I knew that trick. "I got some pots and pans cheap, too."

Later on I knew that I should've proposed to any woman selling off her high school yearbooks, or flatware, or her ex-husband's pistols and golf clubs. I was a scared, lost, little man, and didn't like that feeling. I wanted to get back in the car, turn on the radio, and find an AM station with one of those psychologist women who give advice, what the hell.

I shaded my face so the yard sale woman would take her light off of me. She had one Howard Johnson ashtray out. I said, "You didn't lose your cookbooks, too, did you? Let me guess: you're selling all your pots and pans because the gas company cut off your propane after not paying the bill."

The woman turned around as if to call for help. Two or three carloads of early yard sale rovers piled out in the driveway. The woman said to me quietly, "I'm just trying to do the best I can. I don't need no more trouble in my life. I'm serious." I could see how I'd misjudged her.

A woman wearing bicycle shorts and a t-shirt with *Mom* printed on the front—in case she got struck with amnesia, I supposed—said, "How much are these placemats?" She held one up and put her heavy palm down on the others. She'd driven up in a new 4 x 4.

"All six are there. Fifty cents," said the woman.

"Two possess stains. Two look like someone dyed spaghetti sauce into them. I'll give you a quarter. It's not right setting company down over these and two people feeling like lepers or something," Mom said. She held one eyebrow up. I hated her, and knew that she owned an antique store somewhere, that the placemats must've been worth something I couldn't see.

"Well, okay I guess," said the woman selling.

I picked up the ashtray—a beautiful, clear square with Howard Johnson's light blue and orange sign printed on it. I paid for it later, after I'd thrown it through the 4 x 4's windshield, but before anyone got out a cell phone. The ashtray wasn't even chipped. I picked it up off the ground and walked towards the haggling Mom. I said, "The last thing you need to worry about is your guests' feelings, Mom. Quit being so goddamn cheap. There are homeless people everywhere, and women like this one not too far behind. Not everyone's got health insurance. Colleges aren't hiring full-time faculty so they don't have to offer benefits. Fuck you, lady."

I think I went on about declining standardized test scores, treatment of farm animals, and the audacity of some states and people to fly Confederate flags. When the cops caught up with me some four hours later—at another yard sale entirely—I'm pretty sure I mentioned my stance on speed traps, sting operations, and existential choices, like an idiot. They seemed perplexed that I only owned camping gear and the two dozen new ashtrays I'd bought that morning in the lower middle-class district in which I shopped, where every other house's owner sold off his or her possessions. After the arresting officer called in my license plate, et cetera, he came back to me and asked if I'd already dropped off my black market cartons bought up in North Carolina. For some reason—and not intending to be enigmatic—I told him I'd dropped off more than he could comprehend.

Later on, I knew, one of two things would happen: either they'd find another way to charge me for stolen merchandise, or let me loose in order to harass me more so in time. That night a trustee slipped one generic cigarette into my cell, but offered no match. I wondered how I could sue Madame Tammy for about a minute, then turned my thoughts toward friction and fire.

# DALE RAY PHILLIPS, "What It Cost Travelers"

Born in 1955, Dale Ray Phillips grew up in Haw River, North Carolina, where he spent his summers working at the local cotton mill and reading the stories of John Cheever. ("I read Cheever the way Baptists read the Bible," he says.)[1] After graduating from the University of North Carolina at Chapel Hill, Phillips studied writing at UNC Greensboro and Hollins College before earning his master of fine arts degree at the University of Arkansas. In addition to working a variety of odd jobs over the years—bartender, banquet waiter, respiratory therapist, and journeyman housepainter—Phillips has taught writing at several universities, including the University of Arkansas, Clemson University, Southern Illinois University–Carbondale, and Murray State. His stories have been published in *Harper's, Atlantic Monthly, GQ,* and *Zoetrope,* and they have been honored with appearances in *New Stories from the South* and *Best American Short Stories.* His story collection, *My People's Waltz* (2000), was nominated for a Pulitzer Prize.

Phillips's wry, carefully observed stories read like compact novels on the lost and the left behind, the "owners of used cars and second mortgages," and shady, "stouthearted pilgrim[s]" schooled in the ways of "thievery and love."[2] In "What It Cost Travelers," a down-on-his luck divorced father and sometime scam artist drifts along the Gulf Coast looking for a way back home.

> I'm somewhat confused by the terms Rough South and even the New South, as I consider myself a writer who happens to be Southern. I also believe the phrase dysfunctional family is redundant. I simply write about

the small world I know and have manufactured, and I've long since stopped worrying about the real from the imagined. If my stories move a reader, it's because our hearts beat the same rhythms in most any environment and inside any chest.[3]

## "WHAT IT COST TRAVELERS"

When I was thirty-five and freshly separated and still a stouthearted pilgrim to myself, I took a job on the Gulf Coast swindling people. I sold fake trailer lot deeds to investors with souls more crooked than my own. This stint was my father-in-law's brainchild and his prescription for what I needed—a working vacation designed to clear myself of debt while I charted the direction of my life and tenuous marriage. Three divorces had taught him this tactic. My own marriage had floundered after a drunken night when my son's rocking horse sailed through the picture window. I had been convinced my wife, Lisa, had cuckolded me with the young Hispanic groundskeeper of the apartment complex she managed. I wish I could confess that my character was roomy enough to dismiss my suspicions or that I had proof of her infidelity, but I didn't. Instead, I got the guy deported as an illegal alien, and in recompense Lisa moved me to a vacant apartment and changed the locks on our door. She called a lawyer who ran No Contest Divorce ads on Houston TV. When I began canceling the night classes I taught to conduct surveillance on my own home and love, I felt like a changeling. My dreams filled with sirens—both police and nymph—so I made some excuses and headed south.

"Why are you sending back *arrowheads*?" Lisa asked the first time I called. "Most fathers would mail stuffed animals or fairy tale books." The fake lots sat on an old Indian burial ground, and after rooking clients, I poked with a mattock for relics. The souvenir flint pieces seemed a roundabout way of explaining what I was searching for. I posted packages of small ones designed to down birds and deer and larger ones fashioned for humans.

"I'm not most fathers," I said.

"You got that right. That window cost two-hundred-fifty to replace."

"They're nice arrowheads," I said. "Besides, I thought maybe we could mount them on gold chains and market them as necklaces."

"Damn you, have you gone into cahoots with Daddy again?" Lisa believed I was fishing and airing my soul for the required separation period. Also, her father and I had once summoned some quick money by creatively adjusting insurance claims.

"No, honey," I lied.

"I have a *suitor* at the door." Vivaldi's *Four Seasons*—the tape we listened to before making love—was playing. "Don't call back tonight." She hung up and unhooked the phone.

After that, I only called when I was desperate to hear her voice quicken my pulse. She didn't want me back—of that she was sure. Sometimes she put our son on the phone to illustrate the new sounds learned in my absence, and his babbling reminded me of happier times when I owned the best love had to offer.

"Who is this Rob Roberts guy?" Lisa asked after one of those conversations. "Why is he calling *here* for you all the time?" I feared I had swindled him until I remembered I'd had a car accident with him on the way down, outside Houston. He could have been my double, except for his red hair and Vandyke. During heavy rains, his car had planed, and my Winnebago with the eighteen-foot Wellcraft boat in tow left his car totaled. The Winnebago lost a headlight, but we were both unscratched. The police decided no fault, and Rob Roberts and I exchanged insurance cards. He asked for a ride to Angleton, the nearest town. I told Lisa that Rob Roberts quickly located the Winnebago's bar and helped himself to my Old Crow. Then he produced a wallet and showed pictures of his children from different marriages. I suspected the kids weren't even his, that they came with the wallet like those pictures in the frames at K-Mart. Lisa and I called these people laminites, and I was smart enough not to tell her his wallet was filled with people he didn't know.

"I guess I gave the guy our home number without thinking," I said.

"Don't get any ideas about coming back before the thirty days are over," she said. "And by the way, I'm sure that whatever it is you're doing down there, it's illegal. Do you want your son to visit you behind bars?"

The investors I fleeced were savings and loan officers who would write off the loss rather than risk prosecution and the embarrassment of an audit. Their hands were slick with ill-gotten oil rights and other people's money. The real estate was called Paráiso, and some days I sold as many as twenty parcels of paradise to people convinced they were stealing from me. The land was a short half-mile off Galveston Bay—in La Porte—and after a week I didn't notice the stink of the dioxins or the sulfuric smell from the chemical plants and many refineries. The breeze from the bay kept what I called the furies (botflies and mosquitoes) farther inland, and in the mornings—which is the time for sweet-heart deals—the salty air was laced with diesel odors as tugboats ferried tankers into port or back to the gulf. After selling unreal real estate, I'd jig with mud minnows for flounder off sandbars which the tide would sink.

Certain afternoons, I drank at Marybelle's, where astronauts once cele-brated before getting shot into outer space. The owner of the bar could remem-ber Neil Armstrong drunk and pointing heavenward as he bellowed that, by God, he would travel to the moon and bring back a piece of it. The story went that John Wayne, on a lost weekend, held the record at Marybelle's for the most crabs eaten at a single sitting. Outlined holes in the ceiling tiles proved he had fired his six-shooter raucously in Texas fashion, before the Hollywood helicop-ter whisked him away to make the movie about the grit it took to tame Amer-ica. By the time I drank there, in the early 1990s, the clientele were mainly just-paid oil riggers and shrimpers and wealthy widows who preferred rough, impermanent men. I drank beer bumped with schnapps while people formed couples, feeling guilty my love was not Hollywood material. I was a man with a failed marriage, sitting in a bar lined with signed pictures of men who had ridden into sunsets and left footprints on the moon. Behind me, newly formed couples laughed as they understood they would spend a quick night together. That sound and the smell of Creole-seasoned crabs and the first evening stars on the water made me feel like a missing person.

This French leave feeling prompted me to buy some beer and shrimp and drive to Sandy's house. She worked as my secretary to add a legitimate quality to my dealings. She claimed she didn't mind my job required that I deceived people as I quickly passed through. Her two grade-school kids—little Glen and Glenda—still attended the special school in Johnson City built to accommo-date the children of astronaut trainees and engineers who worked at the Space Center. Her husband, Big Glen, had been an engineer who helped with the tile work on *Challenger* before suffering a nervous breakdown. He now thought Sandy was his sister and his children were orphans she had kindly adopted. We all sat at the table layered with newspapers and tossed the shrimp shells in a central heap like any normal family. We passed garlic butter and cocktail sauce while the kids crawled all over me and searched my pockets for the Hershey's Kisses I brought as booty. Big Glen even deferred the largest shrimp to me, as if *he* were a moocher in *my* house. He slept in a little pop-up camper in the backyard, working late into the night on balsa wood airplanes constructed meticulously to scale. Sandy and I were careful to keep the bedroom door locked when we made love. The situation was indecent, but I wasn't her first lover since Glen's breakdown, and I had misplaced the scrupulous part of myself which could care. The Gulf Coast was like that—full of people whose luck had tricked them into risking anything in order to rediscover what they had lost.

I married up in life, and Lisa would have disapproved of Sandy. She lived in a cul-de-sac in a frame house nearly identical to the other one hundred in a development no one had bothered to name. A few hopelessly wind-crooked pines or a spindly poplar ornamented the more industrious renters' yards, along with ceramic flamingoes and birdbaths and a rock garden or two. Each house had a carport and a slab concrete patio. A few yards boasted above-ground swimming pools because the bay there was unfit for swimming. The poor soil yielded few vegetable gardens—just crabgrass and sandburs. This was one step up from a trailer park. The women had jobs and the men were often bandaged or in casts as they bent over the hood of a car, inspecting its guts.

Certain mornings, the whole place made me melancholy for my childhood and the life I had outdistanced. I'd say the hell with swindling people and piddle around the house sipping coffee laced with Old Crow as I sat by a window investigating these people's lives. Dressed in Sandy's checkered robe and her furry bunny slippers, I felt like a man on vacation who had abandoned the rules of home. These were people like those from my childhood, and they brought forth rummaged memories. Once, just after dawn, I witnessed one neighbor scooping a shovel full of dog shit from his yard. He plopped it on the dog owner's car hood. Then he pulled out Old Jake and shot a fine stream on the fender and back tire. His wife admired him from the patio door, urging him to hurry and to arc it higher. Another time, a man pulled a woman from a car and stripped off her shirt. He lay back on the trunk and begged her to squirt milk in his face. She was still plump with maternity's weight, and she screamed she wanted more money. My only conversation with one of Sandy's neighbors involved dimes. I had gone to the Winnebago for more bourbon. A portly man hurried over as I crossed the yard. He claimed to have quit drinking for a month, until that morning, when he had found the dimes. He held out a coffee cup and asked for straight whiskey. He said his first or second wife—he couldn't remember—wore bunny slippers like mine. When he asked to try one on, I obliged. Neither of us thought the moment odd.

"I must have done this, but I don't remember." He showed me a cigar box full of dimes, grouped in hundreds in sandwich baggies. "See here, there's my name on the box."

He said he'd decided to quit the booze and tidy up his life, and he found— of all things—plastic baggies full of dimes stashed at the back of his closet, where he kept girlie magazines and mateless socks. These were simply dimes—

not collector's items—and he had two cigar boxes full of these things he had no reason to save. *Why dimes,* he kept asking. He was afraid to look in his freezer—hell, it might be stacked with dead cats! He confessed he had never collected anything but wives and trouble and once, as a kid, some wishbones. He asked me what type of desperate person would sit up late nights drinking and putting dimes in plastic bags? When I gave him another drink, he tried to pay for it with a baggie of hoarded silver.

I shut Sandy's curtain and tried to imagine these people in happy moments —grilling fat porterhouses over a perfectly laid fire, or as honored guests at a wedding party where everyone smiled awkwardly in rented formal attire while the photographer snapped a group picture. What I wondered most was why good fortune was rented too. This thought sent me wandering through Sandy's house. The urge to protect my surrogate family and the real one I had left behind was as startling as any quickening. I peeped in on sleeping Sandy, then checked on little Glen and Glenda, tucking the sheets around their chin if the air was too cool or easing back the bedcovers if sweat had beaded on their foreheads. Once, I caught myself kissing those two kids on their cheeks, as I had done to my own son. Of all the things to think about, I remembered a day in Arkansas when Lisa and I were newlyweds. We were snowed-in and happy. On a bet, I had run outside naked and made a snow angel in the nearest drift. Lisa stood by the living room window with her hands on her hips as she shook her head approvingly at my tomfoolery. My flannel shirt she wore had fallen open, exposing her breasts and the half-moon marks her bikini top had hidden from the summer sun. She looked my way thoughtfully, studying her reflection and my nakedness against the winter landscape. I thought: I am somehow contained in her image. Back inside, she warmed me up with lazy winter love in a chair by the gas heater. Sex always made her sleepy, while it fueled me. She slept, and I dressed and went outside and held my cupped face to every window. The slipcover of the chair still held our rough imprint, and the scented candles Lisa lit for such occasions reminded me of hopeful birthdays. At each window I breathed on a pane and wiped through my breath like a kid in front of a department store display. A neighbor walking by to check his mail at the bottom of the mountain hailed me. Did he think I was checking for cracked panes or air leaks, or had he ever walked outside his own happiness and cased it like a burglar? I had stood there, a traveler to myself, wanting only to safe-keep this good feeling and to delay its passage. This was how I felt watching Sandy's kids sleep. What would I have said if either child had awoken and asked what I was doing there in their mother's robe and slippers? That I was a man on the mend passing through their lives? A more honest response would have included the fact that I was caught up in a motion which was no one's to own.

Saturdays, my father-in-law rendezvoused with me at Marybelle's to counsel me on thievery and love. Sandy gave him his share of the money wrapped as a gift with festive paper and a bright bow. He insisted she be present at these exchanges.

"That way, you'll be less likely to rat on us. Conspiracy to commit fraud is a crime too, and what we have here is a conspiracy."

Each week he gave me a list of investors he had scouted and a new fake ID. I was Yancey McCalister, Bucky Earl Mays III, Thurgood Owens, and Parker T. Wiley. He selected the names from the *Houston Chronicle*'s obituary section and credit-checked them to insure that the investors would be pleased with net worth and solvency. Their wills had yet to be probated; these were souls so newly dead they still received mail. Using these assumed names, I baited greedy loan officers with a forged dual contract for deed and asked them for 10 percent of the property's value. Then I allowed them to haggle me down to 5 percent so that they could sense desperation in my situation. "Let them smell foreclosure," my father-in-law always said. "Sign a default clause promising the land is theirs if you don't pay back the loan in a month."

Sandy's job was to shuffle the paperwork and flirt and mix the drinks as he and I drove the bankers to appraise the property. I'd hint of a possible divorce—a lie must be seasoned with a little truth—and they sympathized. I posed as a man selling what he could before misfortune visited, and they offered me no more than 5 percent for my misery. The month I toured the Gulf Coast, I swindled two loan officers a week, but I could have easily fleeced more. Of the eight, seven used appraisers they had bribed, and all of them asked point-blank if a quick roll with Sandy were part of the deal. One banker bragged that, before the advent of his second divorce, he'd sold his custom bass boat for fifty cents to an old man who sold minnows at a bait shop he frequented—just so his wife would be furious. "Two quarters," he'd said to her. "Enough to cover your eyes when you're dead." He claimed the old man's dream was to die happily in that boat, a big bass running while the drag screamed like a blender. The banker confided it was the one good thing he'd done in his life except adopting ten starving children advertised on TV. "And I did it for vendetta," he said. This was the only time I felt remorse as I signed a certified check.

"Don't go moral on me," my father-in-law said when I recounted the story. "Fleece two a week—no more—and we won't get caught. We're a little part of something bigger than Texas." He was right; we were a small part of what would be named the savings and loan scandal.

"Look at the seal on that baby," my father-in-law said that second Saturday at Marybelle's. "That's impressive work, isn't it?" He handed me a forged contract for deed and my weekly identity. Paperclipped to the edge of the document was a snapshot of Lisa and me on our honeymoon, sunburnt and happy and hoisting a forty-pound king mackerel.

"What's this supposed to mean?"

"Richard." The use of my real name jolted me. "She's throwing things like this out. I'm sorry. It's not a good sign. When I told Lisa we were going speckled-trout fishing this weekend, she asked me to get you to sign these." He handed me a preliminary copy of the divorce and a waiver of my right to contest. The child support and visitation rights were generous, but when I signed the documents I fought the crazy urge to use a name resurrected from the dead. Then he gave me a letter from my insurance company stating Rob Roberts was claiming back injuries from the car accident. Wasn't I hurt too? Allstate queried. If so, we could countersue. The business card of a chiropractor not mentioned in the letter was inside the envelope. Sandy read the letter with interest.

"You can't sue him," she said.

"She's right." My father-in-law tore up the letter and card. "That's how people get caught. One scam at a time." He winked at Sandy. "Right?"

"But the guy wasn't hurt. He's a goddamned crook. He's swindling people." The anger in my voice surprised me. Sandy and my father-in-law laughed; what did I think *we* were doing? By evening, when Venus and the first stars were mirrored in the heavens and on the water like a string of cheap lights, we had only to repeat *he's a swindler* and we'd laugh until we lost our breath. After my father-in-law left, Sandy and I lingered to watch sailboats motor toward the pass leading to the gulf. Flashing beacons warned of pilings which each year claimed the lives of wreckless boaters. Above us a rainbow-shaped bridge carried the highway toward Houston and old feelings and broken vows. For a quick second or two, I tortured myself with an image of Lisa, legs hoisted in the crooks of some stranger's arms as she demanded him to love deeper, harder.

"Men like you like them beautiful, don't they Richard?" Sandy had removed the photograph of Lisa and me from my shirt pocket. She stood there, one woman appraising the image of another. The swiftness of my reflex to stop her when she pretended to shred the picture startled me.

"I won't tear up your honeymoon picture of things." She stuffed the snap-shot back in my pocket. "I can't be her—hell, I don't want to be. I like my men rumpled and on the lam. Like you." We kissed under a moon imprinted with a wanderer's urge. She laughed, bit my lips, pulled away. "The guy before you once bet me in a poker game as part of the pot. I didn't get mad, Richard. I *liked* it. Part of me wanted his full house to lose, so I could watch his face as I left with the winner."

"And if his full house had gotten beat?" I asked. "What then?"

"I would have gone back to him the next day and shown him what he had wagered and lost. I would have screwed him silly. Which is what I'm going to do to you tonight."

We took the back roads to a stretch of the gulf between Freeport and San Luis Pass, past broken and twisted windmills known locally as President Carter's Folly. High winds had thwarted the Utopian idea that electricity could be produced cleanly here. Sandy drove the Winnebago while I mixed drinks and adjusted the radio to pleasant stations. We found an access road and drove up the beach. The way was lined with groups of cars parked side-by-side like drive-in moviegoers. Tires, lumber, and stumps of great trees washed down from the Trinity River or another tributary burned in bonfires around which people—mostly teenagers and migrant workers who couldn't afford a motel room—gathered. Here and there lonely men angled for big skate and gafftop and cast purse nets for bait fish. At night the gulf seemed a substantial paradise; the oil balls and garbage were hidden. Naked lovers proud of their sport raced through our headlights to the surf. When Sandy asked had I ever made love in the gulf, I was ashamed to admit I hadn't. We parked the Winnebago along a deserted stretch.

"Leave your clothes on," she said. "We'll undress each other in the water."

We waded past the breakers, to our chests. Schools of skittish mullet splashed and jumped. "Throw it all away," Sandy whispered as we embraced. She helped me with my shirt, whirled it around her head like a lasso, and let it fly. I stepped out of my pants and boxers as soon as she ripped them down. My lips and hands tested the difference between this woman's geography and the image of the one drifting away with my shirt. For an instant I panicked; the wallet floating away contained no money but my one true ID. Then Sandy guided me inside her, and I didn't care. Midway through love she pulled my face from her breasts and held it breath-close to hers.

"We could run away together and start fresh somewhere out west where we have no history." She licked and bit my nipples.

"What about your kids?"

"We'd take them, of course."

"And Glen?"

Sandy's mouth tugged my earlobe. "Glen doesn't know who he is. We could stick him in an institution. Or we could carry him with us, if you feel that guilty."

"So I'm your ticket out of here?"

"Wasn't Lisa *your* passport? Didn't *you* marry up?" Then she moved hard against me and whispered, "Lisa has felt this with other people." The mention of Lisa coupled made me come.

"Good?" Sandy guided my hand to our joining, which felt borderless.

"Oh, Richard," she said. "Why do people get so possessive about this feeling? Love is lent. Hell, it's usury."

A week after my wallet drifted away, the Coast Guard—not an FBI investigator—nearly arrested me for fraud. By midweek I had swindled my quota and decided to go offshore fishing. Sandy insisted I take Glen; he had once loved to fish, and the time alone with the kids would allow her to explain the trip out west to which I had halfheartedly conceded.

"We'll fly to Reno, gamble some, and scout out the prospects there." She said Glen would watch the kids until we returned for them. We would do a few quick land deals, then live an honest life in Wyoming or Montana, where property was reasonable and there was space enough to start over. "Just like pioneers," she claimed. The kids would frolic on horseback through streams and summers my son would visit and stouten himself on the trout we would catch. All this happiness could be ours if we simply traveled there. Sandy was beside me in the Wellcraft helping stow away enough gear for two nights on the water as she said this.

"Too much of my life has been like this trailered boat, Richard. All packed and ready to go with no place to put in. You *do* believe we can make a go of it?"

"Yes."

"You wouldn't con me, would you?" Her laugh rasped as she walked her fingers up my chest and poked my nose. "You'll learn to love me." Though she didn't say *state's evidence,* we both thought it.

"You can't con an honest person," I said.

"You remember that."

"We can't forget *these.*" Glen trotted from the house with cartridges for his .22-caliber pistol. He liked to shoot sharks at night.

"It would be terrible if someone got hurt with that gun," Sandy said.

"What's that supposed to mean?" I asked.

"It means careless people get hurt on boats all the time. Don't *you* be one of them."

As we left. Sandy and the kids formed a little group on the patio and called our names. The kids still called Glen Dad, but he was none the wiser for it.

"I don't know why they call me that," he said as we drove away from the cul-de-sac. "But I like it." Sandy had claimed that being with Glen was like living with a ghost. He had gone to a place where he couldn't be reached, she'd said.

Which was exactly how I felt about my own life and marriage as we launched at dusk from Texas City. Along the way Vietnamese families washed their shrimp boats and picked crabs and conversed in their twangy language. The restaurants along the wharf were lit with festive lanterns under which couples sat with heads bent together. On the jetties, teenaged boys with their dates fished for whatever would bite. Glen mixed us drinks and sat beside me at the console pointing at the beacons and absently naming the first constellations. Another big drink convinced me we all had selective amnesia, and I joined in his naming of the heavens. He scrunched his brow and remembered from somewhere that men on boats drinking whiskey liked to sing.

"What do you like to sing?" I asked.

"Hymns." He was as chock-full of them as a Methodist hymnal, and I joined in where I could. He had been a baritone in a barbershop quartet, so mainly I drank whiskey and listened. We were far enough out that land had fallen from sight, and our wake turned phosphorescent as night spilled from the crown of the sky. Glen's hymns reminded me of my father's stories that the New World had been an Eden before the Europeans ruined it. My father said the entire East Coast had been covered with vines whose roots were a single Eve of a wild grape plant. My father got excited when he imagined that plant and the settlers who saw it that first morning the ship made landfall. They knew they had arrived somewhere—but where? So much of this New World was uncharted. They didn't even know if the inhabitants would shower them with gifts or arrows. Most of those settlers were escaping debts back home or seeking their fortunes. All of them saw in the tangled landscape whatever happiness their hands could carve. They were at that point in their lives where terra incognita—that's how it was listed on the old maps—became the life they would own. Amidst the good cheer of bottles uncorked to toast their arrival, they would wonder if something were beginning or ending. Sitting beside Glen as he sang hymns, I wondered: Had they truly discovered a New World, or had they simply wandered closer to the source of their troubles?

We tied up to a working oil rig with floodlights and a warning horn which sounded at lugubrious intervals. I fished for small bonita which I sliced into ribbons and tossed overboard for chum. Soon enough, the sharks came in shadowy droves, and the larger ones made a mess of the tackle, but the sixty pounders were ours for the taking. Glen peppered them with his .22 when I got them alongside the boat.

"I got your number, you bastard." He jerked the trigger so rapidly the shots sounded like a string of firecrackers. He emptied whole clips into them. How could he remember hymns or how to shoot sharks, but not the feel of his wife? He had a loaded gun, and now was not a good time for his memory to return.

Two bored oil riggers came down the catwalk to investigate the noise. I apologized if our sport disturbed their sleep. "Should we find an uninhabited rig?" I asked.

"The day's the same as the night out here," the one with thick glasses said. He explained they slept in windowless rooms so dark they needed flashlights to find the light switch. "We're just two geologists getting in some offshore time. The company requires it. The rig runs itself." Then he asked if they could join in the fun; his buddy had snuck a .38 aboard the platform.

"Back in a minute!" the owner yelled. The one with glasses asked could he run a shark on our tackle.

"I've never caught a fish before." He cleaned his glasses on his shirt as he confessed. "I got a stuffed sailfish on my wall, big sucker, five feet—even my wife thinks I caught it." When he lay down on the catwalk, I handed up a big Penn reel on a broomstick-thick rod, baited and ready to go. He fumbled puzzledly with the equipment. "Don't tell my buddy—he thinks I caught that fish."

"I won't. Hell, I'll never see you again." I winked and he followed my instructions expertly. By the time his co-worker returned, the rod was bowed mightily with a big hammerhead. They called the fish "Jaws" and passed the rod back and forth so that each could share this pull-you-down feeling.

"I told you fishing was a spiritual thing," the guy with the store-bought sailfish said to his buddy. When the big shark's white underside thrashed on the surface, we cheered as Glen filled it with holes. The guy with the .38 fired like a carnivalgoer at a shooting gallery.

"Offshore time!" I couldn't tell if he were praising or cursing his fate. I had read somewhere that the fear of sharks is nearly universal, and looking into those obsidian eyes, I didn't doubt it. A shark could chop you in half and not care. It could blindside your dear grandmother as she floated past the breakers and called for the family to come join her—the water was perfect for a swim. Here was something primordial, before evil itself, colder than the ice at the center of the world. You could lose yourself in a shark's eyes.

What brought me back from the realm of the dead was what it cost travelers. At sunrise we unhitched from the rig after the geologist explained our position on his topographical maps. The sailfish guy asked sheepishly if he could buy my rod and reel; he'd left *his* gear on the mainland, and they had three more days to kill here at the edge of the world. They had strung two big sharks from the catwalk like huge crows on fence posts, and they had tired of taking pictures.

"Keep the rod," I said. "What good is money out here?" Besides, the rod and reel belonged to my father-in-law. When he produced his wallet, I repeated I didn't want any money.

"Go get some of the canned goods we got upstairs," he commanded his buddy. Then he handed me a picture of himself with a woman and kid, bunched in a department store photo booth, clowning at the camera. "That's who I am," he said. "That's my family."

When I started to reciprocate, I remembered my lost wallet. "I don't have anything like that to give you."

He misunderstood. "I'm glad I have a family." He said he didn't see them enough, but he would soon. A promotion, and he'd move back with them at home base, in Dallas, where they were living. His co-worker lowered down a garbage bag full of canned pâté and Danish hams and fancy crackers.

"Everything's in cans here—it lasts longer," my friend with the fake sailfish said. "When I get back, I'm not eating anything in cans for a goddamned month."

"Luck!" everyone yelled as we cast off. The less talkative geologist was an opera buff who had brought tapes and a jam box, and we got under way to the preternatural sound of some Italian tenor broadcasting tragedy across the waters. At twenty miles out, the gulf was a sparse forest of oil platforms, some inhabited, some not. Glen drove, and I set out two rods with Rapalas as big as the catfish of my childhood.

"Pick a rig and make a slow loop around it." I poured a bourbon and Coke and settled back to wait for the reels to sing. When I dozed, Lisa appeared, in the bathtub, shaving her legs with one hand in long, lazy strokes, while her other arm cradled our nursing son. I was trying to get into that tub and make zany faces at my dreaming self when Glen awoke me, holding a broken key in my face. The motor had stalled, and he had tried to start the boat with the lever in forward.

When I let loose with a string of invectives, he cowered like a kid and sulked with his back hunched away from me. To worsen our predicament, the Wellcraft had floated into an acre of sargasso. I got under the console to hot wire the engine, and I heard him splashing.

"What are you *doing?* Get back in the goddamned boat. This isn't the time for swimming." He whumped against the engine, and when I raised my head from under the console to see where he was, the wires connected and the engine fired. Glen was untangling the gulfweed from the motor—he'd climbed back into the boat and was leaning over the transom—and the propeller sheared his hand.

"Would you look at that," Glen said as I hurried to him. In shock, he inspected the stump bemusedly. As I fashioned a tourniquet, I remembered the Latin for left hand—*manus sinistra.* We were slammed against the stern, watching it tumble from memory and sight. That hand had held Sandy tightly, and it had formulated the precise mathematics required to shoot men into space and snatch them back safely. Was it waving hello or farewell or pointing a finger in accusation? Though unattached, that hand seemed to be grasping at things unseen.

Glen began vomiting and shaking, so I covered him with my poncho and screamed "Mayday" over the radio. When a crackly voice answered, I gave our position from the Loran. As I iced Glen's arm in the fish cooler, I thought of phantom limbs which itched and ached and must be soothed, though they beckoned from a part of yourself which no longer existed.

The Coast Guard cruiser which answered our Mayday took us back to Texas City, where an ambulance waited. The dispatcher had called Sandy, who was en route. I was asked to stay behind to answer the questions the report required. When the Coast Guard seaman asked for some identification, I said I might have lost it during the confusion of the accident.

Just then Sandy rocketed into the parking lot, left the driver's door open, and hurried toward me. "Oh, Richard, when they called and said there'd been an accident, I thought it was *you.* The dispatcher didn't know the name of the injured person."

"Hold on here," said the seaman. "How come she calls you Richard, but the boat's registration number is listed in Jack McQueen's name?"

"He's my father-in-law. He lent me the boat to do a little fishing."

"But you signed Parker T. Wiley on the report. What's going on here?"

"Wait." Sandy went to the car and rifled through her glove compartment, then came back. "Here's his ID," said Sandy. "He left it in my car. You know how men misplace things."

"I still have to check." The seaman trotted off to his boat to call.

"Shut up. Let me do the talking." Then she commanded me to kiss her and squeeze her breasts and not stop. We were still like that when the seaman returned.

"Excuse me," the seaman said. "Okay. This Jack McQueen vouches for you, and your ID checks out clean as a whistle, but the name you signed is listed as dead. Now why would you want to use a dead man's name?"

"He just made up the name," said Sandy. "It's the name we always use when we check into hotels. You see he's down here fucking me and he doesn't want his wife or her lawyers to know." She stared at him. "Haven't *you* ever told someone you were who you weren't?"

This softened him. "While I was back at the boat, the hospital called and said your fishing buddy will be all right. He confirms it was an accident, but he's a little disoriented."

"He's not quite right," I said. "He sometimes forgets who he is."

"Seems to me like you got that problem too," said the seaman. "Now if you'll just scratch through that dead man's name and put your own, I'll file the report."

"How in the hell did you get my real ID?" I asked Sandy once we were driving to the hospital.

"I make duplicates of everything, in case something like this happens."

Glen was released from the hospital five days later, and we hired a domestic to watch over his recovery. A relative would take care of the kids while Sandy and I went west. The plane tickets were bought and rooms were booked when, on the afternoon of the night I was to board a plane with Sandy, I had a change of heart. Or rather, I met a part of myself I had run into on the way down. I was drinking at Marybelle's while Sandy did some last-minute shopping, when Rob Roberts walked in wearing a neck brace and settled on the bar stool beside me.

"Remember me? We had ourselves a little accident outside Houston." He brushed back his thinning red hair and ordered a round.

"You're suing me, right?"

"Not you. Your insurance company." When he asked had my divorce come through, I told him that today was the day the required separation period was over. When I remembered those laminites in his wallet, I felt embarrassed for him. He kept adjusting his neck brace like an uncomfortable tie.

"I'll level with you, I'm not really hurt. The chiropractor and my lawyer make me wear this to court. When I saw your Winnebago in the parking lot, I slipped the brace on. You mind if I take the damned thing off?" When I said I didn't, he unbuckled it and placed it out of sight by his feet. He winked. "The women they think you've got love problems when you wear this thing." When he asked if I were doing business down here or what, I answered I was taking a little vacation from myself.

Three drinks later, he said he would let me in on a little secret. His old girl-friend was in on a good scam. He couldn't quite figure out the whole deal, but his share in it was mildly lucrative.

"She's hooked up with this guy—she won't tell me who he is but they do something with these fake IDs." He showed me an old one I had used with his picture on it. His ex-girlfriend—Sandy was her name—had once worked for the highway department and knew all about such things. "I think she's fallen for the sap. Says he's her ticket out of here. Anyway, do you realize all the things a guy can do with an ID like this?"

"I've got to be going," I said.

"No hard feeling about the insurance thing?"

"None. It's just insurance money."

"You're a *decent guy.*" When he said those two words, I knew what I would do. I left Marybelle's, where men had gone before they walked in space. Then I stopped by Western Union and wired money to Reno in Glen's name. I collected Glen and the kids and took them to the airport, where I had promised to meet Sandy. I got them first-class tickets and left before Sandy arrived.

Driving away, I envisioned the surprised look Sandy's face would register when the stewardess directed her to the aisle where Glen and the kids were waiting. When Glen handed her my note which told of the money wired and waiting in Reno, she'd weigh that against my deception and strap on the seat-belt. Once airborne, she'd order the drinks it took to gain perspective. She had her family sitting beside her, and most everything in the landscape she was leaving behind was rented. Arrangements could be made for a neighbor to send the necessities. Besides, the hotel was booked for two weeks, and I *had* delivered more than she expected—thirty-five thousand dollars—all of my gains. Around the Continental Divide, perhaps she'd start explaining to Glen who he was and what they had shared. This was wishful thinking, but I hoped the next morn-ing in Nevada they'd all eat cold pizza—the kids' favorite breakfast—while chuckling at funny lines from old comedies as they plotted ways to invest their grubstake in happiness. What would keep Sandy from abandoning them? Would it be the thirty-five thousand that only Glen could collect, maternal instinct, or the way she searched her face in the hotel mirror the next morning and realized she had arrived where there were no easy answers. I never heard from Sandy again, and all I know of the Gulf Coast, I have confessed. Rob Roberts settled out of court for a meager two thousand. In my account of things—I was imagining now—Sandy tripled their money at Reno, and the God of travelers resurrected Glen's memory and their love, and they lived happily ever after. Only a swindler of dreams would allot them less, and I wasn't that. I was a man, headed home, wondering why his heart never fit inside its wanting.

Past Angleton, the road widened into four lanes with silhouettes of farmhouses. I eased upward through Texas into the uncharted feel of whatever lay just past the headlights. I thought of North Carolina—where I hailed from— and the grief my people's appetites brought them. My ancestors who were indentured paid for their passage with a portion of their lives. Imagine it—all the people who risked ocean crossings because they believed in a place where they could reinvent themselves. I kept envisioning my son's squeals of recognition when he saw me, and my hands and lips testing Lisa's familiar geography.

Then Houston appeared on the horizon like a city of lights. I pulled over to get a beer from the Wellcraft's cooler, and I sat at the boat's console drinking. There was no moon that night, or clouds, and I had an unobstructed view of the same heavens the old-timers had used for navigation. Another beer convinced me there was no difference between their situation and mine; no amount of traveling can save us from ourselves. We simply people new places with old sorrows and hopes. I began to see myself for who I was—a man struggling upward through a Leviathan dream called America. This thought drove me from the boat into a field of knee-deep roadside clover. I don't know why, but I started dancing. I even pulled out Old Jake, whooped up at the stars, and peed my initials like a kid. I began to formulate what the Gulf Coast would mean. It would be a place where I had swindled people and lost Lisa and any arrogant identification I would ever have with innocence. Why is it that, once you understand a place in the landscape of yourself, you've already left it behind?

Back on the road to Houston, I imagined my homecoming. For all I knew, some stranger could have settled into the apartment, and if this were the case, I would not start a scene. But suppose Lisa—not some sleepy-eyed lover— answered the door. Let's even say she left the porch light burning on the off chance that tonight was the night I'd wander back home. I'd ease up in low gear and strangle the urge to honk and disturb the nosy neighbors. I'd have another sack of arrowheads with me—not Cupid's flowers—and that would take some explaining. Rather than ring the bell, I'd knock to hold the full weight of my love in my hand. Maybe she'd be sewing as she did late nights, and she'd look through the peephole and recognize, through no fault of our own, we'd lost sight of the life we'd embarked upon. Locks would tumble as she opened the door.

"It's you," she'd say—something I couldn't deny. Then she'd invite me in to sleep on the couch, because our love had wandered and returned home more of a beggar than a prince. I'd do the wink trick with my eyes that was our secret, and when she returned the gesture, I'd be grateful but confused and filled with a sensation that even returning heroes could not deposit. This moment we were up against would be as real as bagged dimes and fake sailfish and the rest of our lives. Somehow, we would have to learn to inhabit this new space our love and its dissolution had created, where counterfeit promises were not acceptable payment for safe passage. We'd stand there under that left-on porch light, unsure, two people struggling to unknot what pilgrims called grace from their tangled hearts. This flat-footed moment is what it costs travelers. Before stepping over the threshold, I'd take Lisa's hand—not in marriage this time—and place it over my sternum, so she might at least understand the human racket my chest was making.

"Honey," I said that night. Somehow my voice had lost its ability to con. "Please, feel this."

# LEE SMITH, *Saving Grace*

Born and raised in the mountains of southern Appalachia, Lee Smith grew up in the small coal-mining town of Grundy, Virginia, where her father ran the local dime store. By the age of nine, Smith was already writing stories, a passion she took with her to Hollins College where she began work on the book that would become her first novel, *The Last Day the Dogbushes Bloomed* (1968). She went on to publish several more novels, including *Fancy Strut* (1973) and *Black Mountain Breakdown* (1981), and a story collection, *Cakewalk* (1981), before the publication of *Oral History* (1983), which became a Book-of-the-Month Club featured selection. Since then Smith has published six more novels, including *The Devil's Dream* (1992) and the national best seller *The Last Girls* (2002), as well as three more story collections, including *Mrs. Darcy and the Blue-Eyed Stranger: New and Selected Stories* (2010). Her honors include numerous appearances in *New Stories from the South* and the *O. Henry Prize Stories* anthologies, the Southern Book Critics Circle Award, and the Academy Award in Literature from the American Academy of Arts and Letters. She has also collaborated with Jill McCorkle, Marshall Chapman, and Matraca Berg on the musical *Good Ol' Girls,* which premiered on Broadway in 2010. A retired professor of English at North Carolina State University, Smith lives in Hillsborough, North Carolina, with her husband, essayist Hal Crowther.

Though not typically known as a Rough South writer, Smith has never shied away from the grittier side of life, often writing stories that, while frequently humorous, are, as the *Village Voice* noted, just as "dark, winding, [and] complicated as the hill country itself."[1] In this excerpt from her novel *Saving Grace* (1995), Smith follows the misadventures of Florida Grace Shepherd and her fugitive father, Virgil, a self-destructive, snake-handling prophet of doom.

Though I was born into an old mountain family in a remote coal-mining Appalachian community, my mother was a "foreigner," a home economics teacher from the faraway Eastern Shore of Virginia who had certain aspirations and was "raising me to leave." Which I did, eventually, for school and marriage, though in another way, I never left at all. For I was always in love with the place and the people, and when I started writing, these were most often the voices I heard whispering in my ear, theirs were the stories I wanted to tell. I especially wanted to write about the older mountain women I'd been privileged to know, ladies who had grown up hard, with too little education and too many children, and spent their lives taking care of others, just "keeping on keeping on." These were heroic lives, and I have tried to honor them. I got the idea for Florida Grace Shepherd when I was doing research on serpent-handling over in eastern Kentucky and ran into a woman exactly my own age who even looked like me—except that she was raising up a double handful of copperheads. What would it be like to be her? I wondered. I wrote the book to find out.[2]

**FROM *SAVING GRACE***

I was never to learn what happened to Daddy while he was in jail, but something did. He was wilder and moodier after that. About a day later after we left Chattanooga, as he was driving along smoking a cigarette, he hollered out, "Oh, Jesus! Sweet Jesus!" and ground the cigarette out into his own cheek while the truck jerked all over the road. We ended up in the other lane, but luckily there was nothing coming. Daddy got a terrible sore on his cheek which lasted for weeks and looked awful. Once he yelled at a lady in a parking lot for wearing gold jewelry, and another time he dumped a rack of potato chips on the floor of a Zippy Mart because a boy gave him back the wrong change. In meeting, he'd take up any serpent, anytime. He got bit repeatedly, and did not seem to mind or even notice. He was never hurt. At a camp meeting in Crab Orchard, Tennessee, a crown of flames sat on his head, and yet another time, a dancing green light shone in the trees by a river where he was baptizing. All these months have run together in my mind, since we traveled from one place to another, all over the South. We were traveling with three coolers full of serpents in the back of the truck, plus several boxes. In Coldwater, Tennessee, Daddy healed a woman that was about to die from internal bleeding, and drove the demons out of a poor young man that crawled into church on his hands and knees, speaking nonsense. After his healing, he walked out the door like a man, talking like anybody else. I was there. I saw these things. I read the Bible out loud for Daddy at each location. I did not offer to drive the truck, though. I did not mention that I could drive. I did not want to displease Daddy, for he was a real power in those days, and I could not have gone against him.

But Daddy did not seem to appreciate or even realize what all I did for him. He never said thank you. He took my help for granted, though others remarked to him in my presence how lucky he was to have such a nice big girl. Daddy's attitude hurt my feelings, even though I knew he had more important things on his mind, such as saving souls. It was not for me to call the shots. I told myself that Daddy was giving me as much attention as he could, as much as I deserved. I knew I did not deserve much, due to what I had done. I was sure everything was my fault. I often dreamed that I was being swept along down a great flooded river, and I'd feel that it was really true even when I woke up, like the earth was moving, turning to water beneath my feet. Still, Daddy and I did okay, I reckon, until we got back to Tennessee and Daddy got hooked up with Carlean.

He met her at church, which was where he met all of them. In Piney Ridge, it was the Hi-Way Tabernacle of God, though there wasn't any highway anywhere around that I could see. Somebody said they were going to build the highway through there, but then did not. Anyway, that was the name of the church. In looks it resembled so many others where we had preached in the past months, a little white frame building set up on cinder blocks, very plain, up a dirt road on a muddy lot beside an abandoned coal tipple. A slag heap on the mountain above it smelled like rotten eggs. It was some kind of an independent church with a mournful pastor named Travis Word. It used to have two pastors, but the other one, who was Travis Word's brother-in-law, had died. I believe Daddy saw this situation as an opportunity, and planned to seize it. Travis Word gave me the creeps. He was big and tall and looked like Abraham Lincoln. He could scare people into Christ, it was said. When we showed up in Piney Ridge, Travis Word seemed glad to see us at first, for his church had been declining, as there were a lot of people put off by his gloomy ways, while Daddy was ever one to get folks jacked up, laughing and shouting in the Spirit, full of joy. Daddy could bring them in. It was a church that used to follow the signs, but had not done so in years. This is something that comes and goes among congregations, depending upon who the preacher is, and how long he stays with them. Anyway, there were those that appeared to be just *waiting* for Daddy to show up. They all jumped out of the woodwork when we came.

One of these was Carlean Combs.

Carlean Combs was a tall redheaded woman as big as a man, as big as Daddy himself, with a jutting nose and a jutting chin and dark eyes set too close together. She looked like a witch. She had a big hard white body, and the longest legs. Her breasts jutted straight out, pointy as ice cream cones. At first I thought this was because of the bras she wore, but later when we lived with her I saw her breasts all the time and they were like that. They were really like that. Everything about Carlean was big except for her mouth, small and narrow as a slit in her face.

She showed up on the fourth or fifth night of the revival. Word had got out by then, so the church house was packed. Daddy had had me read from Peter Number Two as he called it, about false prophets and modern times. Daddy said he felt that he had been called to Piney Ridge for a special purpose, to bring the people back to the old-time religion and the old-time ways.

"Now I know there is churches down the road here that's got padded seats and wall-to-wall carpet," he said. "They've got colored windows and Lawrence Welk music and kitchens in the basement, Lord, Lord. They have got all these things, my beloved, but they ain't got the Lord Jesus Christ in their hearts tonight. No sir! And I'll tell you why not. Because the Lord don't need all them fancy things, that's why not. Why looky here, beloved, Hebrews tells us flat-out that God is the same yesterday, today, and forever. Yesterday, today, and forever! Now, don't that tell you something? Don't that tell you something important? Why, them old-timey people, they didn't have nothing like folks has today in their church houses. They didn't have nice rostrums nor gold crosses on the altar of God, nor fancy new cars to carry them to church. No sir. Them old-timey people, if they didn't have no way to get there, they'd walk miles down the muddy road. *Miles,* beloved, a-carrying the old lanterns in their hands, a-singing the old songs, with the knowledge and love of God in their hearts. And when they got to the church house, my beloved, why, it'd be the same thing. They'd fall on their knees where they was at, and pray till their hearts was *full,* praise God, full of that old-timey Spirit that Jesus loves. Now, I know that this old-timey Spirit has gone away from you-uns over here, but we're fixing to get it back. Well, we're *a-going* to get it back, praise Jesus! Praise Jesus, beloved—"

This was the first time I saw Carlean Combs, who kept working her way slowly forward through the crowded little church house, shouldering people aside. I noticed that whenever anybody turned and saw who it was, they would step back mighty fast to let her pass. She never took her squinty eyes off Daddy. When she finally got to the front, everybody was singing and dancing and clapping, and Daddy held a little copperhead in each hand. Two or three other men were dancing and handling in addition to Daddy, and the hot air in there was just crackling as the Spirit moved among them. I stood over by the wall watching, though I could not keep my feet still, the music was so good in that church.

Carlean—of course I didn't know her name yet—danced up into the cleared space at the front of the church. She was wearing a tight aqua-and-white-striped top, and aqua pants that looked like they'd been glued on her. Her hair was pinned up on top of her head.

It was easy to tell she had not been saved.

Everybody was singing "Jesus on the Main Line." Carlean moved her whole body as she danced forward. She didn't look at anybody but Daddy. A heavy woman to the right of her began shrieking out in tongues and sank to the floor, and several came forward to help her, but Carlean just stepped to the side, closer to Daddy, and kept on dancing. Her body rippled all over in rhythm. Then she let her head fall back, like a rag doll. In the light from the dangling bulb, her white neck and chest were slick and shining with sweat. It made me feel funny to see her neck exposed that way. It was like her throat had been cut.

I kept watching her. By then, Daddy was watching her too. Suddenly she let out a big whoop and reached up and started pulling bobby pins out of her hair and throwing them down on the floor. Her heavy hair flew out around her face, bouncing down her back in rhythm as she danced. Now she was right in front of Daddy, not yelling anymore but kind of whimpering, and I couldn't see her face, all I could see was that hair, which was like a live thing, as real and as alive as the copperhead she took from Daddy's hand and wrapped around her white wrist like a bracelet. I could see its markings real plain, and its triangular head, which darted back and forth in rhythm as she danced. The copperhead appeared to be jived up too.

Now the Spirit spread all over the room as visible as paint, so that even the skinny little guitar player cast his instrument down and ran forward to grab up a serpent. Daddy lit a kerosene rag stuck in a Pepsi bottle and held the flame to his face. People were screaming. Several women in the back fainted dead away and had to be carried out. So a lot was going on as you might imagine, but at some point during this meeting I glanced over to find the Reverend Travis Word staring at me steadily with a look I could not fathom. He stood near the opposite wall, right across the church house from me, comforting a pudgy woman who was clinging to him and crying, but he looked across her gray head at my face. I realized that he was younger than I'd thought, and not scary, just stiff and serious, the kind of preacher that could never bust loose like Daddy no matter how much he might wish to. It made you wonder how in the world he'd ever gotten called to be a preacher in the first place. When Travis Word saw me looking at him, he looked down and then away.

The Spirit moved off then, which left everybody praying at once, Daddy up at the front in a big gang of the newly saved, Carlean Combs among them. I looked back as I was going out the door to see Daddy with his arms outstretched like Jesus on the cross, his shirt front and neck and face blackened by the fire, in wild contrast to his white hair.

I went home with a family named Rogers that we were staying with. Daddy never did come back that night, nor the next day.

Rose Rogers, a nice sickly woman, kept casting glances at me while I was helping her can some beans, but she didn't say anything. It was after supper the next night, almost dark, when Daddy finally came driving up to the house in the Arnold's Electric truck with Carlean Combs in the front seat. She stayed in the truck.

But Daddy came in like gangbusters, hugging Rose and Lucius Rogers, tousling the kids' hair and saying how pretty they were. The kids got to laughing and Rose and Lucius lost their sour look. Nobody could stay mad at Daddy when he was right there in the room.

"Come on, Grace," he said to me as he had said so many times before. "Get your things," though he knew that they were mostly in the truck.

But I made no move to come. "Where are we going?" I asked him straight-out. "Are we going someplace with her?" I pointed out the front door at the truck.

Lucius Rogers cleared his throat and looked at Rose, who nodded.

"Brother Virgil," Lucius began, "we feel, me and Rose, that there is things you ought to know, sir, before you go rushing off into something." He held his head up and seemed determined to have his say.

"Such as what?" Daddy straightened up from where he'd been bent over tickling a child. He stared at Lucius Rogers.

"We have been knowing that there woman for a long time around here." Lucius spoke out strongly. "She does not go to our church, nor to any church, and she is not fit for a preacher like yourself. You will do us all harm, sir, to take up with such as that."

I felt a stab of fear at these words.

But Daddy gave Lucius a look that had made many before him quake. "Do you propose to tell me who is *good* and who is *not good* in the eyes of the Lord, Mr. Rogers? For there is only one that can say these things, and that one is our Lord and Savior Jesus Christ. And let me tell you another thing, Mr. Rogers.

Jesus ain't stuck-up. Oh no, beloved. Oh no. He ain't too stuck-up to stoop for a poor sinner woman who has given herself over to Him in the hope of glory and the chance for a better life. Oh no, honey! Oh no! He has got a big house, beloved, and He's got a room for us all. Why, He's got a room for you-uns, and a room for me, and a room for my daughter Grace here, and a room for Carlean Combs. Yes, He has! Don't you doubt it! Why, don't you-uns remember the words He spoke to Simon the Pharisee, concerning that sinner woman? 'I entered your house,' He said, 'but you didn't give me no water for my feet, and here she has wet my feet with her tears and wiped them with her hair. You didn't give me no kiss, but from the time I came in here, she has not stopped a-kissing on my feet. You did not anoint my head with oil, and here she has come along and anointed my feet with ointment. So I'll tell you what. Her sins, which are many, are forgiven this minute, for she has loved much; but who is forgiven little, loves little.' Now what about that, my friends? Oh, you had better be careful now! You had better watch out! Remember the woman that they brought to Him in John Eight, why, she had committed the sin of adultery, beloved, and they was all ready to stone her, but Jesus said, 'Let him who is without sin among you be the first to throw a stone at her.' And you know what? They couldn't do it, beloved. And we can't do it today either!"

Daddy thundered at Rose and Lucius, who clung together as they listened to him. A picture of Jesus Himself hung on the wall behind them. They were good, God-fearing people, and their faces changed as they listened.

Finally Daddy lightened up. "But He will forgive you, beloved, just as He forgives us all for our manifold sins and wickedness on this earth, for His mercy is everlasting. Now let us pray together—Grace, have you got your things?—before we go." Daddy prayed a long prayer asking God's forgiveness for Rose and Lucius, who knew not what they'd done. He said that he himself had already forgiven them. Then he stood and beamed at everybody.

If he had left it at that, it would have been all right, but he could not resist saying one more thing from the door, and Lucius Rogers's conscience was so strong he could not resist answering.

"And I'll tell you what!" Daddy was smiling. "Carlean Combs is just as happy as she can be today, as a newborn child of God. Why, she's been shedding tears of pure joy! She will be joining the church directly, for she's just crazy about Jesus!"

"Sir, she is just crazy," Lucius said quite plain as Daddy closed the door. Daddy paused on the stoop but did not go back. He charged off down the steps muttering, and unlocked the back of the truck, and I had to get in there and ride amongst coolers and piles of stuff, while Carlean Combs rode up in the front with Daddy.

She *was* crazy, as it turned out. She had been in the hospital several times, and had had shock treatments. She took nerve pills. She had been married three or four times, nobody was exactly sure, nor was it clear where she had come from. I learned all this from the fat old man named Mister Harnett Bean who ran a truck stop called the Volunteer Café, and employed Carlean as a waitress. When I asked him where the husbands were now, thinking of our own safety, he grinned at me in a funny way, shaking his head. He was so fat that his jaws flapped, and fat rose up on his neck like those collars on English queens. "Gone," he said. "She wore 'em out."

I nodded. I could see that. I was hoping she would wear Daddy out before long too. I hated Carlean, and I hated living out in the woods behind the Volunteer Café, in the little old beat-up trailer which Mister Harnett Bean had given her. Nobody decent would have lived out there. We did not even have water. We had to walk up the sandy path to the café to take a shower. We hauled our drinking water out there in plastic jugs.

The trailer itself was dark green, with brown rusted-out places all over it. It looked like camouflage. One of the blocks it sat on had sunk into the swampy ground, so that the whole trailer was on a slant. I had to walk uphill to get to the tiny back room where I slept on a mattress on the floor, and all night long I'd feel like I was slipping off of it, and wake up numerous times, and in the mornings I'd be real tired.

Whenever I woke up in the night, I'd hear Daddy and Carlean Combs, still up, and still at it. Talking and carrying on. They never seemed to sleep. Whatever was wrong with her, it was wrong with him too. It was wrong with both of them. In the morning I'd find cigarette butts and clothes strewed all over the slanted linoleum floor, and sometimes beer bottles.

I knew that Daddy was backsliding, and that Carlean had not really been saved.

But the folks over at the Hi-Way Tabernacle had not figured it out yet, as both Daddy and Carlean put on a real show of holiness when they went over there for meeting, Carlean with her wild red hair pulled back so tight it gave her slant-eyes, in long plain dresses that made her look like she was in disguise. These dresses had belonged to Mr. Bean's dead wife, Belle. There was no end to them, as he was rich and had never touched a one of her things since she had died eight years before. Mr. Bean appeared to get a kick out of seeing them on Carlean.

Carlean became the one that read the Bible out for Daddy to preach, though she pronounced about half of it wrong.

I didn't even care. Sometimes I didn't even go to meeting. I felt that God didn't have much use for the likes of me, anyway. Mr. Bean had given me a job waiting tables at the truck stop, which made me real nervous at first, but then I started enjoying it. At least I enjoyed it when Carlean wasn't there, for she'd swoop by like an eagle, keeping an eye on me.

"I know what you're up to," she told me more than once. "You might fool your daddy, but you can't fool me." Close up, Carlean was cross-eyed. The awful thing was, I thought she might be right. For I felt that Carlean *did* know me, like Lamar had.

And it was true that I liked to talk to the truckers and the local men that came in there, I liked to kid with them all. I had also bought myself some pink Tangee lipstick and some Maybelline blush-on and mascara at the drugstore. I'd go in the ladies' room at the café and put them on to work my shift. I had a cute pink waitress uniform, and I knew the men were looking at me. Carlean was right. One of them was looking at me a lot. His name was Davey Street, and he was tall and gangly, with a big grin. He drove a truck for Wonder Bread, and came by four days a week, in the late afternoon. I knew he was going to ask me for a date before long, but he kept not quite doing it. He was not much older than me, and shy, though he liked to talk once you got him started. He'd order a piece of pie and a Pepsi and ask me a lot of questions, which made me real nervous, as I did not want him to find out anything much about my life. I did not intend to get into what Daddy did, nor what our situation was.

Over at the Tabernacle they were having a power struggle. This is what Daddy called it. What it was, was that some of the elders had begun to have their doubts about Daddy, but Daddy had the rest of them in the palm of his hand. So there was serious dissension among them, which is not good for working the signs. A woman named Lois Montreal was hurt at a home meeting by a canebrake rattler which Daddy handed to her, and then she went to the hospital and talked about it, with the result that Daddy was arrested in front of the Tabernacle one Sunday morning before the meeting even got started. They drove him away in an unmarked police car, while the church people gathered around by the church house steps, praying and talking among themselves. When the police car was out of sight, some people turned to go inside, which Travis Word was urging them to do, but a lot or them—the ones that had come just to see Daddy work the signs—turned around and left. Me and Carlean left too.

She drove me back to the trailer in the Arnold's Electric truck, with her skirt hiked way up on her thighs. It was hot that morning, and she had rings of sweat under the arms of Mr. Bean's dead wife's long-sleeved brown dress. She took it off the very minute she got inside the trailer, and dropped it on the floor. Then she walked over to the refrigerator in her half-slip and pointy bra to get a beer. She opened the bottle and looked at me. "You want a beer?" she asked.

"Yes," I said.

"I knew it." Carlean handed me one, and I opened it and licked off the foam, which tasted bitter and not at all the way I'd thought it would taste. I acted like I liked it, though. I took a big swallow and carried the bottle back with me, walking uphill to my room, where I figured I would change clothes and then go to the Volunteer Café and get the funny papers from Mr. Bean, who saved them for me.

I was putting my dress on a hanger when I heard the lock click behind me. I ran right over to the thin metal door and pounded on it. "Carlean!" I yelled. "Carlean! What are you doing?" I hadn't even known that my door could be locked.

Carlean was laughing and laughing on the other side of it. "Don't you go noplace now, you hear?" she cackled. Then I heard her moving around out there for a while longer, singing "This Ole House." Then I heard her slam the trailer door, and a little later I heard the truck start, way up the path where they kept it parked.

I did my best to get out of that place, but there was no way. There was no window, and though the door rattled, it would not give. Finally I got so hot and tired from pushing at it that I just laid down on the mattress and drank the rest of the beer. Everything began to spin around. Since all this was happening on a big slant anyway, I started to feel like I was going crazy. I swore I would not do it, that I would not go crazy like the rest of them, I swore it on the Bible which lay on the floor at my feet. The only light in the room came from a forty-watt bulb in the ceiling, so it was very dim in there. The walls were painted aqua. I laid there on the mattress and imagined myself as a fish swimming around in an aquarium. This was peaceful. But with another part of my mind I was thinking it was simply a matter of time until I did go crazy, whether I swore on the Bible or not. I prayed hard to God, saying that if He would just get me out of there, I would give in to Him and do His bidding from that day forward. I would open my heart to Him and let Him in, and join the church. I meant it too. I felt Him move in my heart then, a little flutter like a baby bird just learning how to fly. Then it started to rain, drumming on the trailer's metal roof. This was a sound which I loved. I took it as a sign that God had heard me, a sign of His care. I let Him comfort me with the sound of the rain. I closed my eyes and let go of everything until I was swimming free, beyond the aquarium, in and out of undersea caverns through shafts of light that pierced the beautiful blue water of the sea.

I don't know how long I slept, nor when they came back, nor why I didn't call out when I woke up and heard them. They were making a lot of noise, banging things around in the big part of the trailer. I was instantly, totally awake. It had quit raining. I felt all rested, like I had slept for hours and hours. I had to go to the bathroom real bad, but something made me hold it and lay still. It came to me that they were packing.

They were going to leave me.

Sure enough, it was not long before I heard the rusty front door of the trailer slap and then slap again, as they carried things out to the truck. One time there was a crash over in the kitchen part of the trailer, and the sound of breaking glass. Carlean yelled, "Shit!" Daddy said, "Leave it. What do you want all this stuff for, anyway? You ain't gonna need it. I've got all the stuff you need." Then there was a lot of laughing and breathing noise while, I guess, they kissed.

They took some more things out to the truck, and then I heard the jingle of keys. You can always tell what keys sound like. *Go, go, just go,* I was thinking. *Go to Hell.* The door slammed one more time and I could hear their voices getting fainter, moving away. I sat up on the mattress.

Then I heard the door again, and Carlean yelling, "Where the hell are you going?" and Daddy's voice saying, "Just a minute, honey, I forgot something," and Carlean saying, "Come on now, Virgil, you didn't forget nothing." The trailer shook as Daddy strode across it and up the slant toward my room. I lay back down on the mattress and closed my eyes. His footsteps stopped, and I could hear his heavy breathing outside the door. I thought he must have come back for the Bible. Then it crossed my mind that he might kill me. But what he did was flip the lock on my door. The trailer shook again as he went out.

"Never mind, I couldn't find it," he hollered to Carlean.

"You asshole," she yelled back.

As soon as I heard the truck leave, I jumped up and ran out into the dark, wet woods, not too far, and peed like crazy. The woods smelled wonderful, the way they do after it rains. I breathed in deep. I had been dying for air in that little room. Then I walked back to the trailer and sat on the steps enjoying the cool sweet smell of the night. After a while I went inside and ate some saltine crackers, which was all that I could find. I didn't care. I felt real good. But I did not want to sleep in the room where she had locked me for so long. I walked down the slope to the other end of the trailer and looked at their unmade bed, which was nasty. I found a half a pack of Camel cigarettes on the floor and went out on the steps to smoke them. Then I went inside and lay down on the old sofa and fell immediately asleep.

In the morning I got dressed and went to the Volunteer Café, where I took a shower and washed my hair and put on my uniform and makeup. Carlean was supposed to work that shift, not me, but I was here and she was gone.

Mr. Bean raised his eyebrows when he saw me come out of the washroom. He sat in his big chair by the cash register reading the paper, with his belly balanced on his spread-apart knees like a beach ball. "Where's Carlean?" he asked, and I told him.

"Son of a gun!" he said, slapping his leg. He laughed his wheezy laugh. "I never did think all that religion had took with her."

"Can I eat something before I start working?" I asked, and he looked at me good and then hollered at Don to fix me whatever I wanted. But he told me to bring him the phone first, and I did. Mr. Bean never got up if he didn't have to. I ate two fried eggs and some sausage and three pancakes while he talked on the phone. Then he asked me if there was anybody I wanted to call, and I said no. Even now I am not sure why I said that, or why I felt that way. I simply thought that I had come too far along the road that I was on, to turn back now. I had to keep on going. I could not imagine going back to live with Ruth and Carlton Duty and Billie Jean and that baby I had never seen, back there where everything awful had happened. I thought about it and thought about it, but I just could not bring myself to call them. Some truckers came in and I took their orders, and before long here came two elders from the Hi-Way Tabernacle that I had to talk to, and then the police, who were real respectful, calling me "Miss." I liked that. Daddy and Carlean had run off with as much Tabernacle money as they could lay their hands on, which did not surprise me, but I couldn't give the police any leads. I didn't have a clue as to where they'd gone.

Mr. Bean told everybody that I was welcome to stay out in his trailer and work at the Volunteer Café as long as I wanted to. This was a big relief to me, since I was broke, of course. Daddy had not left me a dime. I thought Mr. Bean was real nice. But then the next Wednesday when I got done with my shift, Marcia told me Mr. Bean had said for me to come over to his house and see him for a minute before I left for the night. He lived right next to the café in a nice white house, and so I walked on over there, thinking nothing of it, bone-tired but enjoying the early-evening breeze and the fireflies rising from the scrub grass along the path that went to his house. Out on the road, cars and trucks flashed back and forth. I enjoyed seeing them, too. I had big plans right then. I hoped it would not be very long before I could save up enough money to get some kind of a car myself. Then I would drive over to Scrabble Creek for a visit before heading out for parts unknown, where I would get a job, and make my fortune. For I had learned to be a good waitress at the café, and I could do that anywhere.

Now that things seemed to be working out, I had conveniently forgotten the promise I had made to God in my hour of need. It is real funny how strong you can mean a thing, and then how fast it will slip your mind. But I was young, and thought I could do anything, and have it all.

I walked across Mr. Bean's front porch and pushed his screen door open. By now it was pretty dark. "Mr. Bean," I hollered. "Mr. Bean?"

"Come on back here, honey," he wheezed out of the darkness. I could see a sliver of light under a door at the back of the room, so I walked toward that, through a dim parlor which smelled old and musty. I could barely make out the dark shapes of the furniture. When I opened the door, I could tell right off that there was a big difference between Mr. Bean's dead wife's parlor and that back room where I guess he stayed all the time. He sat on a ratty old sofa covered by a ratty old quilt, watching TV. He had the TV close enough so he could reach over and change the channels without getting up. Of course, he didn't get up when I came in either. He just looked at me, with something new and lively in his hooded eyes. "Sit down," he said. "*Sit down!*" cried a loud, cracked voice which made me jump, but it turned out to be only Mr. Bean's parrot, which sat in a big cage on top of a dresser in the corner. It was a scraggly, bad-looking parrot.

Mr. Bean patted the seat beside him. So I did sit down, but as far away from him as I could get, which was not too far since he took up most of the couch.

I looked around the room. He had a refrigerator in there, and a desk piled up with papers, and piles of clothes and papers all over the floor. It was a mess. That day's newspaper lay on the floor by his feet, with some pictures of naked girls spread out on top of it. At first I couldn't believe it. I looked again to see if that could possibly be right, which it was, and then I saw his old red thing hanging out of his pants. "Hiya, hiya," the parrot said. Mr. Bean leaned forward, grunting, to turn the sound all the way down on the TV. Then he looked at me.

"Now Gracie," he said, "there's some things I need for you to do."

I was out of there so fast I don't even remember leaving! I don't remember anything until I was back in the trailer, where I slammed the door shut and pushed the sofa up against it even though I knew that was stupid, that Mr. Bean was not able to walk all the way out there. It was all he could do to get back and forth between his house and the café. But I was scared he would send somebody to get me, like Don the skinny cook with tattoos all over his arms. Of course I could not imagine Don doing this, but Mr. Bean was a rich man, in a place of poor people. People will do a lot for money. I didn't have any money myself, and wasn't supposed to get paid until Friday. Now I knew I would never get paid. I sat curled up in a ball on the couch wedged against the door, and sure enough, not ten minutes had passed before somebody was there, knocking at first and then banging on the door.

# ROBERT MORGAN, "Sleepy Gap"

Born in 1944, Robert Morgan was raised on his family's farm in the Blue Ridge Mountains, where he developed an early interest in poetry and music. After studying math and engineering at North Carolina State University, Morgan transferred to the University of North Carolina at Chapel Hill where he took a degree in English before going on to earn a master of fine arts degree from UNC Greensboro. He published his first poetry collection, *Zirconia Poems,* in 1969 and later accepted a teaching job at Cornell University. Over the next twenty years, Morgan published several books of poetry, including *Red Owl* (1972), *Groundwork* (1979), and *At the Edge of the Orchard Country* (1987), before publishing his first story collection, *The Blue Valleys,* in 1989. Another story collection, *The Mountains Won't Remember Us,* followed in 1992, along with the novels *The Hinterlands* (1994) and *The Truest Pleasure* (1995), which was named a Notable Book by *Publishers Weekly.* Morgan's best-selling third novel, *Gap Creek* (1999), was named an Oprah Book Club selection and won the Southern Book Critics Circle Award. Since then he has published two more novels, *This Rock* (2001) and *Brave Enemies* (2003); a story collection, *The Balm of Gilead Tree* (1999); and four collections of poetry including *The Strange Attractor* (2004) and *Terroir* (2011). He is also the author of two nonfiction books: *Boone* (2007), a biography of Daniel Boone, and *Lions of the West: Heroes and Villains of the Westward Expansion* (2011). A recipient of the Academy Award in Literature from the American Academy of Arts and Letters, Morgan currently serves as Kappa Alpha Professor of English at Cornell, where he has taught since 1971.

"At their finest," says Dwight Garner, "[Morgan's] stripped-down and almost primitive sentences burn with the raw, lonesome pathos of Hank Williams's best songs."[1] In "Sleepy Gap," Morgan offers an ironic variation on the classic chain-gang tale—in this case, the confrontation between an unrepentant bootlegger and the prison warden determined to break him.

When I began as a writer, I really wondered what I had that I could write about. My favorite writers wrote fiction set in Moscow, Paris, London. All I knew was this little farm in the Blue Ridge Mountains and the university. Over the years, as I've worked at writing, developed as a writer, I kept discovering this material that I had. I discovered that instead of having a dearth of material, I have an overwhelming amount of stories, information, characters, to write about, and I'm still amazed by that discovery: that I can turn a family story, my own low experience, killing hogs or carrying water from the spring, into literature.[2]

**"SLEEPY GAP"**

"The thing is," the warden said, "if there are ever a man among you that takes a drink while serving time, he will be throwed into the Outhouse." The Outhouse was the box in the prison yard where they locked somebody for solitary confinement. It was a stinking hole of a place full of spiders and ticks. On a hot day it roasted you and on a cold night you froze with one threadbare blanket to wrap around your shoulders.

"But I can't blame a man for taking a drink," the warden said and picked his nose. "Any man would want a drink while going to school for the government. This ain't supposed to be no resort." The warden spit on the grass. "But the fact is that I find the man that brought him that liquor, and sold him that liquor, I will break him. Ain't no man that can't be broke, and I will do whatever it takes to break him."

We knowed what the warden meant. There was nothing subtle about his punishments. His methods was simple and direct. He didn't practice any advanced psychology, and he didn't worry about modern theories of rehabilitation.

"Show me a man that thinks he's tough, and I will show you somebody that can be broke," the warden liked to say. "You are here at the taxpayer's expense, and I mean to see that the public gets its money's worth."

If somebody broke the rules they had to sit in the Outhouse for a couple of days. If they broke the rules again they got whipped. And when a man got whipped he was led out into the prison yard and stripped naked. Then he was tied across a big oak log with his hands strapped to rings at either end of the log. From the windows of the block it looked as if he was taking a swan dive.

And there was nothing fancy about the instruments the warden used for whipping either. He didn't keep bullwhips or sticks that could break bones. He had a collection of sourwood and maple limbs, lean and supple. And every time we worked along the country roads he made the trusty gather more shoots and limbs, willow and hickory, as well as maple and sourwood. In a whipping he might break half a dozen switches and he wanted to keep a generous supply on hand.

The warden did the whipping himself. "I wouldn't ask any man to do something I wouldn't do," he said. "And I want it to be clear the punishment is official, that the punishment comes from the top."

When the warden talked to us over the intercom or in the cafeteria, he usually ended up by saying, "You all don't know it, and you may never believe it, but I'm the best friend you have. The only salvation for a man incarcerated is hard work, to get his mind right so he can respect hisself. And I'm here to help do that. I can guarantee that you will work hard, and I will do my best to help you begin to respect your sorry selves. A man can't respect hisself until he pays his debts. And the only way you can pay your debt is hard work."

The day I'm talking about was a cool summer day. You know the kind of day we have in the mountains. It had rained the day before and cleared off during the night. Puddles stood muddy as coffee in the road, but the air was so clear it bit your eyes, and every leaf on every tree looked waxed and polished. Shining white clouds drifted over the mountains, and the mountains was so blue their tops whispered to the blue sky.

My friend Mike was in the prison for making liquor. A lot of people in the county made liquor back in the 1920s and 1930s. It was the only way to wring a few dollars from the steep mountain acres. Mike had made blockade since he was a boy. And I guess his daddy had made it before him, in a spring hollow on the back of their place. But Mike got caught because he sold a quart to a tourist that was arrested for drunk driving. They promised the tourist they would let him off light if he told where he got the booze.

Mike liked to tell about the trial. When he saw they was going to send him to the pen, he told the judge, "I've been stilling corn for spirits since I was a shirt-tail boy, and my pappy stilled it before me. And long as the sun shines or grass grows green in spring I will be making it, judge, reckon on it."

"We'll see," the judge said, and rapped his hammer. Mike got two to five, and they took his cow and horse to pay the fine. The sheriff even took his wife's chickens.

"The thing is, don't never sell to a stranger," Mike said.

We climbed into the truck early that morning, and they drove us way up the valley toward Sleepy Gap. The bouncing truck made me belch the watery oatmeal we had for breakfast. It tasted better the second time. "This is my end of the county," Mike said, looking out the back of the truck. "When we get out one day I'll give a party for you all."

They put us to clearing brush off the high bank of the road near the gap. Every man had an axe or a brush hook. It was going to be a long hard day. The only comfort was the air was dry and the breeze cool.

"Watch out for poison oak in this brush," Freeman, the guard, said.

"Hell, poison oak will die when it touches me," I said.

"Look who's bragging," Mike said.

"And there's poison ash along the ditch," Freeman said.

"Maybe we can find something sweeter in these weeds," Mike said.

"Like a rattlesnake," Gosnell said. Gosnell was a glue sniffer. He saved every nickel he made to buy airplane glue. During the night you could hear him snuff up and giggle. He would laugh to hisself in the dark for hours.

"Maybe the tooth fairy will leave something under a bush for us," Mike said. Mike had lost an eyetooth and if he laughed you seen the gap. He looked ten years older when he opened his mouth.

"Maybe the angel Gabriel will step out of a cloud and call us to glory," Gosnell said.

"That would be one hell of an escape," Coggins said.

"Except you would be called to hell," Gosnell said.

"The hell you preach," Coggins said.

"That's exactly what I preach," Gosnell said.

"Stay out of the trees!" Freeman called. He held his shotgun pointed at the sky. It was loaded with buckshot. "Just work in the brush where I can see you." Freeman had a high-powered rifle in the truck cab, and he carried a .44 magnum on his hip. But the 12 gauge was his primary weapon. "Buckshot will cripple but it won't kill," he liked to say.

To this day I don't know exactly how Mike done it. I mean I know in general what happened. But none of us saw a thing. And I know Freeman didn't see a thing. We were scattered out along the bank chopping bastard pines and slashing locust sprouts, poplar bushes and whips of sourwood. The bank was tangled up with blackberry briars and honeysuckle vines. Some of Mike's kin must have followed the chain gang truck up the road toward Sleepy Gap. They couldn't have knowed beforehand that's where we'd be working. They must have slipped along the edge of the woods and somehow signalled to Mike, and put a jug behind a stump or under a pine bush. None of us seen a thing until about mid-morning. We was beginning to sweat and Mike whispered as he swung his hook, "You want something to wet your whistle?" He pointed to a jug in the broom sedge at his feet.

"What is that?" I whispered back.

"What do you think it is?" Mike said.

I edged closer to see the jug. It sparkled in the weeds.

"Don't you all stop working," Freeman called out.

Mike stooped behind a poplar bush and took a swig and then moved on. News of the jug was passed along the bank quick. I swung my hook near to it and leaned over and took a drink, holding the jug with my left hand, still swinging the hook. The whiskey burned like ether, and seethed like soda water.

One by one the men worked their way near to the poplar bush and took a drink. Some took two and got hissed at by the man closest to them. We worked and sweated in the sun, our faces red. When every man had had a drink we started working our way back again. Everybody moved slower and my arms felt so light they seemed to float. We had a party there on the steep bank. Men chuckled and joked as they worked.

"Old Sneaky Pete," Coggins said and giggled.

"No, that's white mule," Gosnell said. "You can tell by the kick."

"You all owe me fifty cents," Mike said.

"Send us a bill," Gondan said.

I think we would have got away with it. We would have drunk the blockade and sweated it out in the sun before dinner, feeling free and crazy in the work. Except that Coggins stood up too high to drink from the jug the second time. It was nearly empty and he stood straight up to get the last drops. I guess he was pretty happy by then and had lost his caution. Freeman must have seen the glint of the jug in the sun.

"Wait a minute," the guard shouted. He fired a shot into the air. "Everybody freeze!" he called. "I have five more shells in this gun and I can kill every one of you."

Freeman made Coggins bring him the jug. The guard sniffed it and said, "Having yourselves a good old time, boys? Now where did you get this?"

Nobody said a thing, and Freeman looked at each of us on the bank. But somehow he guessed it was Mike who had got the liquor. Maybe it was obvious since Sleepy Gap was so near Mike's place, and Mike was serving time for making liquor.

"Go call the warden," Freeman said to the trusty. "Tell him what has happened." There was a radio in the guard truck like a police radio. We all stood there in the bright sun. I felt a little dizzy with the liquor buzzing in my ears. I was happy to have the drink inside me, and then I felt sick that we had been caught. A day in the Outhouse was a high price to pay for a slug of liquor.

"Damn that Freeman," Coggins muttered.

"You all get back to chopping brush," Freeman shouted. "The government has not retired you yet to rocking chairs."

"It ain't Freeman you have to worry about," Gosnell said.

Mike did not seem as concerned as the rest of us. He had drunk more from the jug than we had and he was proud to be the host and benefactor to the whole gang. Also he had not been inside as long as the rest of us and had not witnessed a whipping. "I need me another drink," he said.

"Ain't you got another jug?" Gosnell said. Gosnell was in for hanging paper, and he had another year to go.

"Wish I did, boys, wish I did," Mike said. He almost sung it, he was so pleased with hisself. It was said that Mike was the song leader at the Sleepy Gap Baptist Church. I knowed he had a fine voice for he sung sometimes when he worked, and when the chaplain come to the prison and conducted services. And it was hymns Mike preferred, more even than songs from the radio.

"One drink just whetted my thirst," Filson the mother beater said. Filson had held his mother down while his wife beat her to make her sign the home place over to them.

"Boys, when you all get out you can gather at my place for a barbecue," Mike said. "And we can drink all we want."

The warden drove up in his car. It was a state car with the seal of North Carolina printed on the door. The warden set in the car a full minute before getting out. We tried to pretend we was working, but the truth is none of us could take our eyes off the car. When the warden finally got out he hitched up his pants and looked at us scattered on the bank above him. I expected him to call us down to the road to gather in front of him. But instead he motioned for Freeman to follow him and they begun to climb the bank. "Come on up here, boys," he said to us.

The warden made us line up at the top of the bank, at the edge of the woods. He made us stand back at least ten feet from the trees so Freeman could watch us all. At first I didn't see what he was doing. And then I understood that he was getting out of sight of the road below.

There was a sourwood that had been pushed over by a sleet storm. It leaned about a yard off the ground just inside the woods. The warden took two pieces of rope from his pocket and had the trusty tie Mike's wrists to the sourwood so his ear was pressed against the tree.

"You have picked the wrong man," Mike said to the warden.

"Is that so?" the warden said.

"I had a drink," Mike said. "I won't deny that."

"You certainly did," the warden said. He had the trusty cut four long switches of maple and sourwood. The warden slid the withes between his pinched fingers to strip off the leaves.

The warden turned to the line of us. "You men know I play by the rules," he said. "You learn your lessons and behave like men here and you graduate. I'm interested in only one thing: your obligations to society. But for some people extra methods is called for. They can't abide by the ordinary discipline, and they can't be educated by ordinary means." He slapped one of the hickories on his pants leg.

"Do you know where Mike got his liquor?" he said. We stood like we had not heard his question. I looked at an oak tree, and then at the white cloud above the oak tree. A jarfly broke out in whirring song. "None of you don't know nothing?" he said. "Am I right?" He turned to Mike.

"I will give you a chance to help yourself," he said to Mike. "Tell me where you got the liquor and you'll feel a lot better."

"Found it under a stump," Mike said out of the side of his mouth. There was snickering.

"The same place your mama found you," the warden said. There was more snickering.

"You all may think this is funny," the warden said. "But I don't think it's funny. It's never funny to break a man. I hate to do it. But some men has to be broke."

The warden slapped a hickory on the sourwood log beside Mike's hand. "What I'm going to do is for your own good," he said to Mike.

"Much obliged," Mike said.

"You will sing a different song in a few minutes," the warden said.

"Your mama is a slut," Mike said. It was like he had just woke up and realized the situation he was in. The surprise made him angry, and fear made him jerk at his bonds. He flung his hips around and kicked at the leaves, but he couldn't tear free.

"Mike, you have a lot of learning to do," the warden said in a gentle voice.

"Ain't you the great professor," Mike said.

The warden spit his tobacco into the brush. He had the trusty pull Mike's shirt up over his head and slide his pants down around his ankles. Mike's back and buttocks was white as an invalid's skin. Mike twisted around and farted at the warden.

"I never whip a man in anger," the warden said. "I only do it because it's my duty." He dropped three of the switches on the ground and stepped to the side of Mike. The first lick was so soft it was hardly a blow, more a flick or tickle. He switched Mike on the middle of his back, and then he switched him on his shoulders. He struck a little harder on the small of his back. My Uncle Calvin used to say you could kill a snake by switching it up and down its length. The light blows stimulated the snake's nervous system until it died of seizures. The snake writhed in frenzy and trembled in convulsions and died faster than if it had been beaten with a stick.

I could see by the set of his jaw that Mike had braced hisself for the worst pain. But the warden teased him with a dozen light flicks and stings. Then suddenly he swung with all his might and hit Mike just above his tail bone. Mike screamed with the surprise of the pain.

"Now do you want to tell me who give you the jug?" the warden said.

"To hell," Mike spat out.

The warden beat him across his legs and backside. Mike stiffened and then trembled with the cut of the licks. His skin got red, as if it had been raked by claws. The warden beat him across the back until the hickory broke, and then he took up a second switch. All the men was quiet. We couldn't take our eyes off Mike's back.

"This is a lesson for you all," the warden said. "This is advanced civics." The warden was sweating, and he wiped his forehead with the back of his wrist. As he begun hitting Mike again Mike moved first one knee and then another, like he was trying to crawl away from the bite of the switch.

"Are you ready to talk?" the warden said.

Mike only howled in reply.

The warden broke the second hickory on Mike's back and picked up the third. He begun hitting Mike on the buttocks again. He swung as though trying to put out a fire. "What did you say?" the warden shouted.

But Mike was only sobbing. He gritted his teeth to keep from crying as long as he could, but now he couldn't help hisself. His body heaved as he sobbed. His buttocks was crossed by welts big as bloodworms and night-crawlers.

"What did you say?" the warden asked.

But Mike didn't answer. He tried to choke back his sobs and swallow. Mike clenched his fists and unclenched them.

When the warden begun hitting Mike with the fourth switch we saw Mike start to foul hisself. Blood run off his back and mixed with sweat and shit on his legs. And when the warden hit him, blood and shit and sweat flung off. We stepped back to avoid the spray.

"Look at you," the warden said. "You've soiled yourself and humiliated yourself. You should be ashamed."

Mike sobbed against the sourwood log, and bark stuck to his cheek, to the tears and sweat. It was the crapping on hisself that broke him.

"What did you say, boy?" the warden said.

"I'm s-s-s-sorry," Mike hiccupped.

"What did you say?" the warden said.

"I'm s-s-s-sorry," Mike shouted.

The warden looked at us. His face was red, and his forehead was dripping with sweat. "Who give you the liquor?" he said.

"My cousin Johnny," Mike said.

"How did he get it to you?" the warden said.

"He left it by a poplar bush," Mike said. Mike sobbed against the sourwood like a baby.

"Are you going to do it again?" the warden said.

"No sir," Mike said and tried to clear his nose. "No sir, I won't never do it again."

"Are you broke?" the warden said.

"Yes sir," Mike said almost in a whisper. "I'm broke."

I glanced at the row of men. They was looking away from Mike. Some looked at the ground and some looked into the trees beyond. But none was watching Mike where he hung from the sourwood.

"That's better," the warden said. "That's much better."

I seen Mike once more, years later, after we was out of the pen. I thought he would be ashamed to see me, because of what I had witnessed done to him. But Mike acted perfectly glad to see an old acquaintance from the prison days. He wore clean overalls and held his granddaughter on his lap, sitting on a bench in the park near the courthouse on a Saturday afternoon.

"You know, I owe a lot to that warden," he said.

"I know you do," I said.

"No, I mean it," Mike said. "He changed my life. He taught me a lesson that I ain't forgot. I never went back to my old habits."

Mike chuckled and bounced his granddaughter on his knee.

"If that's the way you see it," I said.

"There ain't no other way I see it," he said, like he had convinced hisself the warden had done him a favor.

It was a late summer afternoon and I glanced up at the courthouse dome that glittered in the bright sun like a helmet. And above the dome a cloud hung in the sky white as sugar frosting. I thought how the world is always stranger than we think it is.

"There ain't no other way to see it," Mike said again.

I watched him bounce the granddaughter on his knee. Her cheeks got red with excitement and she screamed with delight. Mike grinned at her and held her hands as though they was dancing.

# WILLIAM GAY, "Where Will You Go When Your Skin Cannot Contain You?"

A native of Hohenwald, Tennessee, William Gay was born in 1941. After his seventh-grade teacher gave him a copy of Thomas Wolfe's novel *Look Homeward, Angel,* Gay resolved to become a writer himself. Following a tour of duty with the navy during the Vietnam War, he lived briefly in New York before moving to Chicago where he found a job building pinball machines. He moved back to Tennessee in the late 1970s and worked as a carpenter and housepainter while he continued to write stories at night. In 1998, at the age of fifty-seven, Gay published his first story in the *Georgia Review* and within a year signed a contract for his first novel, *The Long Home,* which won the James A. Michener Memorial Prize and was named a *New York Times* Notable Book. His second novel, *Provinces of Night,* appeared in 2000, followed by a short story collection, *I Hate to See That Evening Sun Go Down* (2003) and another novel, *Twilight* (2006). *That Evening Sun,* a film adaptation of Gay's story "I Hate to See That Evening Sun Go Down," premiered in 2009, followed by *Bloodworth,* an adaptation of *The Long Home,* in 2010. A frequent contributor to the *Oxford American* magazine, Gay was also an artist and his work graces the covers of two of his later books, *Wittgenstein's Lolita* (2006) and *Time Done Been Won't Be No More* (2010), a collection of stories, memoirs, and essays. He had completed a forthcoming novel, *The Lost Country,* and was at work on another, tentatively titled *The Wreck of the Tennessee Gravy Train,* when he died of heart failure at his home in Hohenwald in 2012.

Richard Bernstein, writing in the *New York Times,* calls William Gay's tales of rural Tennessee "earthily idiosyncratic, spookily gothic."[1] That certainly applies to Gay's masterful tale, "Where Will You Go When Your Skin Cannot Contain You?," which finds an unexpected humanity in a backwoods bogeyman, a homicidal meth dealer blinded by grief and bent on revenge.

> Violence is something I've never really been able to explain in a sensible way so that someone could see why I seem preoccupied with it. I think people are the sums of all their influences and I don't know whether you seek out those influences when you're young or whether they're the ones you're exposed to. . . . I discovered *A Good Man Is Hard to Find* by Flannery O'Connor and was just blown away by that book. . . . And the people that I grew up with . . . there were people around who were always getting into feuds and shooting somebody, and there was a lot of violence in the rural South. . . . It never rings true when I try to write about somebody whose life is in perfect shape. Most of my characters tend to be either young people or old people because to me they're more interesting—their lives are up for grabs, anything can happen.[2]

## "WHERE WILL YOU GO WHEN YOUR SKIN CANNOT CONTAIN YOU?"

The Jeepster couldn't keep still. For forty-eight hours he'd been steady on the move and no place worked for long. He'd think of somewhere to be and go there and almost immediately suck the life from it, he could feel it charring around him. He felt he was on fire and running with upraised arms into a stiff cold wind, but instead of cooling him the wind just fanned the flames. His last so-called friend had faded on him and demanded to be left by the roadside with his thumb in the air.

The Jeepster drove westward into a sun that had gone down the sky so fast it left a fiery wake like a comet. Light pooled above the horizon like blood and red light hammered off the hood of the SUV he was driving. He put on his sunglasses. In the failing day the light was falling almost horizontally and the highway glittered like some virtual highway in a fairy tale or nightmare.

His so-called friend had faded because The Jeepster was armed and dangerous. He was armed and dangerous and running on adrenaline and fury and grief and honed to such a fine edge that alcohol and drugs no longer affected him. Nothing worked on him. He had a pocket full of money and a nine-millimeter automatic shoved into the waistband of his jeans and his T-shirt pulled down over it. He had his ticket punched for the graveyard or the penitentiary and one foot on the platform and the other foot on the train. He had everything he needed to get himself killed, to push the borders back and alter the very geography of reality itself.

On the outskirts of Ackerman's Field the neon of a Texaco station bled into the dusk like a virulent stain. Night was falling like some disease he was in the act of catching. At the pumps he filled the SUV up and watched the traffic accomplish itself in a kind of wonder. Everyone should have been frozen in whatever attitude they'd held when the hammer fell on Aimee and they should hold that attitude forever. He felt like a plague set upon the world to cauterize and cleanse it.

He went through the pneumatic door. He had his Ray-Bans shoved onto the top of his shaven head and he was grinning his gap-toothed grin. Such patrons as were about regarded him warily. He looked like bad news. He looked like the letter edged in black, the telegram shoved under your door at three o'clock in the morning.

You seen that Coors man? The Jeepster asked the man at the register.

Seen what? the man asked. Somewhere behind them a cue stick tipped a ball and it went down the felt in a near-silent hush and a ball rattled into a pocket and spiraled down and then there was just silence.

The Jeepster laid money on the counter. I know all about that Coors man, he said. I know Escue was broke and he borrowed ten bucks off the Coors man for the gas to get to where Aimee was working. Where's he at?

The counterman made careful change. He don't run today, he said. Wednesday was the last day he's been here. And what if he did run, what if he was here? How could he know? He was just a guy doing Escue a favor. He didn't know.

He didn't know, he didn't know, The Jeepster said. You reckon that'll keep the dirt out of his face? I don't.

They regarded each other in silence. The Jeepster picked up his change and slid it into his pocket. He leaned toward the counterman until their faces were very close together. Could be you chipped in a few bucks yourself, he finally said.

Just so you know, the counterman said, I've got me a sawed-off here under the counter. And I got my hand right on the stock. You don't look just right to me. You look crazy. You look like you escaped from prison or the crazy house.

I didn't escape, The Jeepster said. They let me out and was glad to see me go. They said I was too far gone, they couldn't do anything for me. They said I was a bad influence.

The Jeepster in Emile's living room. Emile was thinking this must be the end-time, the end of days. The rapture with graves bursting open and folk sailing skyward like superheroes. There was no precedent for this. The Jeepster was crying. His shaven head was bowed. His fingers were knotted at the base of his skull. A letter to each finger, LOVE and HATE inscribed there by some drunk or stoned tattooist in blurred jailhouse blue. The fingers were interlocked illegibly and so spelled nothing. The Jeepster's shoulders jerked with his sobbing, there was more news to read on his left arm: HEAVEN WON'T HAVE ME AND HELL'S AFRAID I'M TAKING OVER.

Emile himself had fallen on hard times. Once the scion of a prosperous farm family, now he could only look back on long-lost days that were bathed in an amber haze of nostalgia. He'd inherited all this and for a while there were wonders. Enormous John Deere cultivators and hay balers and tractors more dear than Rolls-Royces. For a while there was coke and crack and wild parties. Friends unnumbered and naked women rampant in their willingness to be sent so high you couldn't have tracked them on radar, sports cars that did not hold up so well against trees and bridge abutments.

Little by little Emile had sold things off for pennies on the dollar and day by day the money rolled through his veins and into his lungs, and the greasy coins trickled down his throat. The cattle were sold away or wandered off. Hogs starved and the strong ate the weak. It amazed him how easily a small fortune could be pissed away. Money don't go nowhere these days, Emile said when he was down to selling off stepladders and drop cords.

Finally he was down to rolling his own, becoming an entrepreneur, slaving over his meth lab like some crazed alchemist at his test tubes and brazier on the brink of some breakthrough that would cleanse the world of sanity forever.

The appalled ghost of Emile's mother haunted these rooms, hovered fretfully in the darker corners. Wringing her spectral hands over doilies beset with beer cans and spilled ashtrays. Rats tunneling in secret trespass through the upholstery. There were man-shaped indentations in the sheetrock walls, palimpsest cavities with outflung arms where miscreants had gone in drunken rage. JESUS IS THE UNSEEN LISTENER TO EVERY CONVERSATION, an embroidered sampler warned from the wall. There were those of Emile's customers who wanted it taken down or turned to the wall. Emile left it as it was. He needs an education, Emile would say. He needs to know what it's like out here in the world. There's no secrets here.

The Jeepster looked up. He took off his Ray-Bans and shook his head as if to clear it of whatever visions beset it. Reorder everything as you might shake a kaleidoscope into a different pattern.

You got to have something, he said.

I ain't got jack shit.

Pills or something. Dilaudid.

I ain't got jack shit. I'm out on bond, and I done told you they're watchin this place. A sheriff's car parks right up there in them trees. Takin pictures. I seen some son of a bitch with a video camera. It's like bein a fuckin movie star. Man can't step outside to take a leak without windin up on videotape or asked for an autograph.

What happened?

I sent Qualls to Columbia after a bunch of medicine for my lab. He kept tryin to buy it all at the same drugstore. Like I specifically told him not to do. He'd get turned down and go on to the next drugstore. Druggists kept callin the law and callin the law. By the time they pulled him over it looked like a fuckin parade. Cops was fightin over who had priorities. He had the whole back seat and trunk full of Sudafed and shit. He rolled over on me and here they come with a search warrant. I'm out on bond.

I can't stand this.

I guess you'll have to, Emile said. Look, for what it's worth I'm sorry for you. And damn sorry for her. But I can't help you. Nobody can. You want to run time back and change the way things happened. But time won't run but one way.

I can't stand it. I keep seeing her face.

Well.

Maybe I'll go back out there to the funeral home and see her.

Maybe you ought to keep your crazy ass away from her daddy. You'll remember he's a cop.

I have to keep moving. I never felt like this. I never knew you could feel like this. I can't be still. It's like I can't stand it in my own skin.

Emile didn't say anything. He looked away. To the window where the night-mirrored glass turned back their images like sepia desperadoes in some old daguerreotype.

You still got that tow bar or did you sell it?

What?

I'm fixing to get that car. Aimee's car. Pull it off down by the river some-where.

This is not makin a whole lot of sense to me.

They wouldn't let me in out there, they won't even let me in to see her body. I went and looked at her car. Her blood's all in the seat. On the windshield. It's all there is of her left in the world I can see or touch. I aim to have it.

Get away from me, Emile said.

Aimee had turned up at his place at eight o'clock in the morning. The Jeepster still slept, it took the horn's insistent blowing to bring him in the jeans he'd slept in out onto the porch and into a day where a soft summer rain fell.

Her battered green Plymouth idled in the yard. He stood on the porch a moment studying it. In the night a spider had strung a triangular web from the porch beam and in its ornate center a single drop of water clung gleaming like a stone a jeweler had set. The Jeepster went barefoot down the doorsteps into the muddy yard.

He was studying the car. Trying to get a count on the passengers. He couldn't tell until she cranked down the glass that it was just Aimee. He stood with his hands in his pockets listening to the rhythmic swish of the windshield wipers. The dragging stutter of a faulty wiper blade.

I need a favor, she said.

It had been awhile and he just watched her face. She had always had a sly, secretive look that said, I'll bet you wish you had what I have, know what I know, could share the dreams that come for me alone when the day winds down and the light dims and it is finally quiet. She was still darkly pretty but there was something different about her. The grain of her skin, but espe-cially the eyes. Something desperate hiding there in the dark shadows and try-ing to peer out. She already looked like somebody sliding off the face of the world.

I don't have a thing. I'm trying to get off that shit.

Really?

I've had the dry heaves and the shakes. Fever. Cramps and the shits. Is that real enough for you? Oh yeah, and hallucinations. I've had them. I may be hav-ing one now. I may be back in the house with baby monkeys running up and down the window curtains.

She made a dismissive gesture, a slight curling of her upper lip. Will you do me a favor or not?

Is Escue all out of favors?

I've left him, I'm not going back. He's crazy.

No shit. Did a light just go on somewhere?

He stays on that pipe and it's fucked him up or something. His head. You can't talk to him.

I wouldn't even attempt it.

I don't understand goddamn men. Live with them and they think they own you. Want to marry you. Eat you alive. Jimmy was older and he'd been around and I thought he wouldn't be so obsessive. Sleep with him a few times and it's the same thing over again. Men.

The Jeepster looked away. Blackbirds rose from the field in a fury of wings and their pattern shifted and shifted again as if they sought some design they couldn't quite attain. He thought about Aimee and men. He knew she'd slept with at least one man for money. He knew it for a fact. The Jeepster himself had brokered the deal.

What you get for taking up with a son of a bitch old enough to be your daddy.

I see you're still the same. The hot-shit macho man. The man with the platinum balls. You'd die before you'd ask me to come back, wouldn't you?

You made your bed. Might as well spoon up and get comfortable.

Then I want to borrow a gun.

What for?

I'm afraid he'll be there tonight when I get off work. He said he was going to kill me and he will. He slapped me around some this morning. I just want him to see it. If he knows I've got it there in my purse he'll leave me alone.

I'm not loaning you a gun.

Leonard.

You'd shoot yourself. Or some old lady crossing the street. Is he following you?

He's broke, I don't think he's got the gas.

I hope he does turn up here and tries to slap me around some. I'll drop him where he stands and drag his sorry, woman-beating ass inside the house and call the law.

Loan me the pistol. You don't know how scared I am of him. You don't know what it's like.

The loop tape of some old blues song played in his head: *You don't know my, you don't know my, you don't know my mind.*

No. I'll pick you up from work. I'll be there early and check out the parking lot and if he's there I'll come in and tell you. You can call the cops. You still working at that Quik Mart?

Yes. But you won't come.

I'll be there.

Can I stay here tonight?

You come back you'll have to stay away from Escue. I won't have him on the place. Somebody will die.

I'm done with him.

The Jeepster looked across the field. Water was standing in the low places and the broken sky lay there reflected. Rain crows called from tree to tree. A woven-wire fence drowning in honeysuckle went tripping toward the horizon where it vanished in mist like the palest of smoke.

Then you can stay all the nights there are, he said.

The murmur of conversation died. Folks in the General Café looked up when The Jeepster slid into a booth but when he stared defiantly around they went back to studying their plates and shoveling up their food. There was only the click of forks and knives, the quickstep rubber-soled waitresses sliding china across Formica.

He ordered chicken-fried steak and chunky mashed potatoes and string beans and jalapeño cornbread. He sliced himself a bite of steak and began to chew. Then he didn't know what to do with it. Panic seized him. The meat grew in his mouth, a gristly, glutinous mass that forced his jaws apart, distorted his face. He'd forgotten how to eat. He sat in wonder. The bile was supposed to go somewhere but he didn't know where. What came next, forgetting to breathe? Breathing out when he should be breathing in, expelling the oxygen and hanging onto the carbon dioxide until the little lights flickered dim and dimmer and died.

He leaned and spat the mess onto his plate and rose. Beneath his T-shirt the outlined gun was plainly visible. He looked about the room. Their switchblade eyes flickered away. He stood for an awkward moment surveying them as if he might address the room. Then he put too much money on the table and crossed the enormity of the tile floor and went out the door into the trembling dusk.

So here he was again, The Jeepster back at the same old stand. On his first attempt he'd almost made it to the chapel where she lay in state before a restraining hand fell on his shoulder, but this time they were prepared. Two uniformed deputies unfolded themselves from their chairs and approached him one on either side. They turned him gently, one with an arm about his shoulders.

Leonard, he said. It's time to go outside. Go on home now. You can't come in here.

The deputy was keeping his voice down but the father had been waiting for just this visitor. The father in his khakis rose up like some sentry posted to keep the living from crossing the border into the paler world beyond. A chair fell behind him. He had to be restrained by his brothers in arms, the sorriest and saddest of spectacles. His voice was a rusty croak. Crying accusations of ruin and defilement and loss. All true. He called curses down upon The Jeepster, proclaiming his utter worthlessness, asking, no, demanding, that God's lightning burn him incandescent in his very footsteps.

As if superstitious, or at any rate cautious, the cops released him and stepped one step away. One of them opened the door and held it. Doors were always opening, doors were always closing. The Jeepster went numbly through this opening into the hot volatile night and this door fell to behind him like a thunderclap.

In these latter days The Jeepster had discovered an affinity for the night side of human nature. Places where horrific events had happened drew him with a gently perverse gravity. These desecrated places of murder and suicide had the almost-nostalgic tug of his childhood home. The faces of the perpetrators looked vaguely familiar, like long-lost kin he could but barely remember. These were places where the things that had happened were so terrible that they had imprinted themselves onto an atmosphere that still trembled faintly with the unspeakable.

The rutted road wound down and down. Other roads branched off this one and others yet, like capillaries bleeding off civilization into the wilderness, and finally he was deep in the Harrikin.

Enormous trees rampant with summer greenery reared out of the night and loomed upon the windshield and slipstreamed away. All day the air had been hot and humid and to the west a storm was forming. Soundless lightning flickered the horizon to a fierce rose, then trembled and vanished. The headlights froze a deer at the height of its arc over a strand of barbed wire like a holographic deer imaged out of The Jeepster's mind or the free-floating ectoplasm of the night.

He parked before the dark bulk of a ruined farmhouse. Such windows as remained refracted the staccato lightning. Attendant outbuildings stood like hesitant, tree-shadowed familiars.

He got out. There was the sound of water running somewhere. Off in the darkness fireflies arced like sparks thrown off by the heat. He had a liter of vodka in one hand and a quart of orange juice in the other. He drank and then sat for a time on a crumbling stone wall and studied the house. He had a momentary thought for copperheads in the rocks but he figured whatever ran in his veins was deadlier than any venom and any snake that bit him would do so at its peril. He listened to the brook muttering to itself. Night birds called from the bowered darkness of summer trees. He drank again and past the gleaming ellipse of the upraised bottle the sky bloomed with blood-red fire and after a moment thunder rumbled like voices in a dream and a wind was at the trees.

He set aside the orange juice and went back to the SUV and took a flashlight from the glove box. Its beam showed him a fallen barn, wind-writhed trees, the stone springhouse. Beneath the springhouse a stream trilled away over tumbled rocks and vanished at the edge of the flashlight's beam. You had to stoop to enter the stone door, it was a door for gnomes or little folk. The interior had the profound stillness of a cathedral, the waiting silence of a church where you'd go to pray.

This was where they'd found the farmer after he'd turned the gun on himself. Why here? What had he thought about while he'd waited for the courage to eat the barrel of the shotgun? The Jeepster turned involuntarily and spat. There was a cold metallic taste of oil in his mouth.

Light slid around the walls. Leached plaster, water beading and dripping on the concrete, the air damp and fetid. A black-spotted salamander crouched on its delicate toy feet and watched him with eyes like bits of obsidian. Its leathery orange skin looked alien to this world.

Against the far wall stood a crypt-shaped stone spring box adorned with curling moss like coarse, virid maidenhair. He trailed a hand in the icy water. In years long past, here was where they'd kept their jugged milk. Their butter. He'd have bet there was milk and butter cooling here the day it all went down. When the farmer walked in on his wife and brother in bed together. The Jeepster could see it. Overalls hung carefully on a bedpost. Worn gingham dress folded just so. Did he kill them then or watch a while? But The Jeepster knew, he was in the zone. He killed them then. And lastly himself, a story in itself.

When The Jeepster came back out, the storm was closer and the thunder constant and the leaves of the clashing trees ran like quicksilver. He drank from the vodka and climbed high steep steps to the farmhouse porch and crossed it and hesitated before the open front door. The wind stirred drifted leaves of winters past. The oblong darkness of the doorway seemed less an absence of light than a tangible object, a smooth glass rectangle so solid you could lay a hand on it. Yet he passed through it into the house. There was a floral scent of ancient funerals. The moving light showed him dangling sheaves of paper collapsed from the ceiling, wallpaper of dead, faded roses. A curled and petri-fied work shoe like a piece of proletarian sculpture.

The revenants had eased up now to show The Jeepster about. A spectral hand to the elbow, solicitously guiding him to the bedroom. Hinges grated metal on metal. A hand, pointing. There. Do you see? He nodded. The ruined bed, the hasty, tangled covers, the shot-riddled headboard. Turning him, the hand again pointing. There. Do you see? Yes, he said. The empty window opening on nothing save darkness. The Jeepster imagined the mad scramble over the sill and out the window, the naked man fleeing toward the hollow, pis-toned legs pumping, buckshot shrieking after him like angry bees, feets don't fail me now.

The Jeepster clicked out the light. He thought of the blood-stained uphol-stery strewn with pebbled glass and it did not seem enough. Nothing seemed enough. He stood for a time in the darkness, gathering strength from these lost souls for what he had to do.

He lay in the back seat of the SUV and tried to sleep. Rain pounded on the roof, wind-whipped rain rendered the glass opaque and everything beyond these windows a matter of conjecture. The vodka slept on his chest like a stuffed bear from childhood. It hadn't worked anyway, it might as well have been tap water. Things would not leave him alone, old unheeded voices plagued his ears. Brightly colored images tumbled through his mind. An enormous, stained-glass serpent had shattered inside him and was moving around blindly reassembling itself.

He'd concentrate on more pleasant times. His senior year in high school, he saw his leaping body turning in the air, the football impossibly caught as if by legerdemain, he heard the crowd calling his name. But a scant few years later he was seated alone in the empty stands with a bottle between his feet. A win-ter wind blew scraps of paper and turned paper cups against the frozen ground and the lush green playing field had turned brittle and bare. He wondered if there was a connection between these two images and, further, what that con-nection might be.

A picture of himself and Aimee the first time, try to hold on to this one. Fooling around on her bed. Her giggling against his chest. A new urgency to her lips and tongue. Leonard, quit. Quit. Oh quit. Oh. Then he was inside her and her gasp was muffled by applause from the living room and her father chuckling at the Letterman show. Other nights, other beds. The Jeepster and Aimee shared a joint history, tangled and inseparable, like two trees that have grown together, a single trunk faulted at the heart.

Drink this, smoke this, take these. Hell, take his money, you won't even remember it in the morning. You'll never see him again. Ruin, defilement, loss. One pill makes you larger, one pill makes you small, one pill puts you on the road to Clifton with a Ford truck riding your bumper.

For here's what happened, or what happened on the surface, here's what imprinted itself on the very ether and went everywhere at once, the news the summer wind whispered in The Jeepster's sleeping ear.

The truck pulled up on Aimee past Centre. Escue blew the truck horn, pounded on the steering wheel. She rolled down the glass and gave him the finger. She sped up. He sped up. She could see his twisted face in the rearview mirror. The round O of his mouth seemed to be screaming soundlessly.

When she parked on the lot before the Quik Mart he pulled in beside her. He was out of the Ford before it quit rocking on its springs. He had a .357 Magnum in his hand. As he ran around the hood of his truck she was trying to get out of her car on the passenger's side. Just as he shot out the driver's side window the passenger door on the Plymouth flew open and she half fell onto the pavement. She was on her back with her right elbow on the pavement and a hand to her forehead.

She looked as if she might be raking the hair out of her eyes. He shot her twice in the face. Somebody somewhere began to scream.

Hey. Hey goddamn it.

A man came running out of the Quik Mart with a pistol of his own. His feet went slap slap slap on the pavement. Escue turned and leveled the pistol and fired. The running man dropped to his palms and behind him the plate glass window of the Quik Mart dissolved in a shimmering waterfall.

The man was on his hands and knees feeling about for his dropped weapon when Escue put the barrel of the revolver in his own mouth with the sight hard against his palate and pulled the trigger.

Now The Jeepster opened the door of the SUV and climbed out into the rain. He raised his arms to the windy heavens. All about him turmoil and disorder. Rain came in torrents and the thunder cracked like gunfire and lightning walked among the vibratory trees. His shaven head gleamed like a rain-washed stone. He seemed to be conducting the storm with his upraised arms. He demanded the lightning take him but it would not.

Mouse-quiet and solemn, The Jeepster crossed the rich mauve carpet. Who knew what hour, the clock didn't exist that could measure times like these. This time there were no laws stationed to intercept him and he passed unimpeded into another chamber. Soft, indirect lighting fell on purple velvet curtains tied back with golden rope. He moved like an agent provocateur through the profoundest of silences.

This chamber was furnished with a steel gray casket, wherein an old man with a caved face and a great blade of a nose lay in state. Two middle-aged female mourners sat in folding chairs and watched The Jeepster's passage with fearful, tremulous eyes.

He parted another set of purple curtains. Here the room was empty save for a pale pink casket resting on a catafalque. He crossed the room and stood before it. Water dripped from his clothing onto the carpet. A fan whirred somewhere.

After a while he knew someone was standing behind him. He'd heard no footsteps but he turned to face an old man in worn, dusty black hunched in the back like a vulture, maroon tie at his throat. His thin hair was worn long on the side and combed over his bald pate. The Jeepster could smell his brilliantined hair, the talcum that paled his cheeks.

The Jeepster could tell the old man wanted to order him to leave but was afraid to. The old man didn't want to be here. He wanted to be ten thousand miles away, in some world so far away even the constellations were unknowable and the language some unintelligible gobbledygook no human ear could decipher. He wished he'd retired yesterday.

For The Jeepster looked bad. He was waterlogged and crazed and the pistol was outside his shirt now and his eyes were just the smoking black holes you'd burn in flesh with a red-hot poker.

He laid a hand on the pink metal casket. Above where the face might be. He thought he could detect a faint, humming vibration.

I can't see her, The Jeepster said.

The undertaker cleared his throat. It sounded loud after the utter silence. No, he said. She was injured severely in the face. It's a closed-casket service.

The Jeepster realized he was on the tilted edge of things, where the footing was bad and his grip tenuous at best. He felt the frayed mooring lines that held him part silently and tail away into the dark and he felt a sickening lurch in his very being. There are some places you can't come back from.

He took the pistol out of his waistband. No it's not, he said.

When the three deputies came they came down the embankment past the springhouse through the scrub brush, parting the undergrowth with their heavy, hand-cut snake sticks, and they were the very embodiment of outrage, the bereft father at their fore goading them forward. Righteous anger tricked out in khaki and boots and Sam Browne belts like fate's Gestapo set upon him.

In parodic domesticity he was going up the steps to the abandoned farmhouse with an armful of wood to build a fire for morning coffee. He'd leaned the girl against the wall, where she took her ease with her ruined face turned to the dripping trees and the dark fall of her hair drawing off the morning light. The deputies crossed the stream and quickened their pace and came on.

The leaning girl, The Jeepster, the approaching law. These scenes had the sere, charred quality of images unspooling from ancient papyrus or the broken figures crazed on shards of stone pottery.

The Jeepster rose up before them like a wild man, like a beast hounded to its lair. The father struck him in the face and a stick caught him at the base of the neck just above the shoulders and he went down the steps sprawled amid his spilled wood and struggled to his knees. A second blow drove him to his hands, and his palms seemed to be steadying the trembling of the earth itself.

He studied the ground beneath his spread hands. Ants moved among the grass stems like shadowy figures moving between the boles of trees and he saw with unimpeachable clarity that there were other worlds than this one. Worlds layered like the sections of an onion or the pages of a book. He thought he might ease into one of them and be gone, vanish like dew in a hot morning sun.

Then blood gathered on the tip of his nose and dripped and in this heightened reality he could watch the drop descend with infinitesimal slowness and when it finally struck the earth it rang like a hammer on an anvil. The ants tracked it away and abruptly he could see the connections between the worlds, strands of gossamer sheer and strong as silk.

There are events so terrible in this world their echoes roll world on distant world like ripples on water. Tug a thread and the entire tapestry alters. Pound the walls in one world and in another a portrait falls and shatters.

Goddamn, Cleave, a voice said. Hold up a minute, I believe you're about to kill him.

When the father's voice came it came from somewhere far above The Jeepster, like the voice of some Old Testament god.

I would kill him if he was worth it but he ain't. A son of a bitch like this just goes through life tearin up stuff, and somebody else has always got to sweep up the glass. He don't know what it is to hurt, he might as well be blind and deaf. He don't feel things the way the rest of us does.

# BRAD WATSON, "Kindred Spirits"

Brad Watson was born in 1955 in Meredian, Mississippi. After graduating from high school, Watson left Mississippi for Hollywood to become an actor but eventually returned home to study at Mississippi State University and the University of Alabama, where he earned a master of fine arts degree in creative writing and American literature. He then worked for a number of years as a reporter and editor for the *Montgomery Advertiser* before returning to the University of Alabama to teach writing. In 1996 Watson published his debut story collection, *Last Days of the Dog-Men,* which won the Sue Kaufman Prize for First Fiction from the American Academy of Arts and Letters. His first novel, *The Heaven of Mercury* (2002), was a finalist for the National Book Award and was awarded the Southern Book Critics Circle Award for Fiction. Watson has taught at Harvard University, the University of Alabama at Birmingham, the University of Mississippi, and the University of Wyoming. His second story collection, *Aliens in the Prime of Their Lives,* was published in 2010.

Tom De Haven calls Brad Watson's stories "weird and wise, sometimes gruesome and often brilliant."[1] All those elements are vividly present in Watson's story "Kindred Spirits," which effortlessly weaves old hunting lore into its tale of betrayal until it is hard to tell where the tall tale ends and the real story begins. Though Watson's narrator, a julep-sipping lawyer with a taste for classical music, may at first seem an unlikely source for a contemporary "Rough South" story, the story he tells—a meandering tale of murder and revenge, guns and booze, wild pigs and prehistoric-looking hunting dogs—is steeped in the old southwestern storytelling tradition.

"Kindred Spirits" got going in my head after I spent three days on a tug-boat on the Intracoastal Waterway as a reporter in the 1980s. The tug co-captain told me a story about wild pig hunting in northwest Florida, and the captain told me a story about a terrible time when his wife was seeing another man and there was nothing he could do about it. When I first tried to write what became "Kindred Spirits," it was narrated by someone like the tug captain, but that didn't work and I put it away for a while. I was living in Tuscaloosa again in the '90s, and some of my friends were either in law school or had just finished, so their experiences at that time were on my mind, and somehow (I don't really remember just how) I decided to make the narrator a lawyer who felt he had betrayed himself and his principles as much as he had been betrayed himself. It became a matter of tonal control, of the voice and the sense of loss in there leading me along.[2]

**"KINDRED SPIRITS"**

On the long green lawn that led down to the lake, Bailey's boy tumbled with their two chocolate Labs, Buddy and Junior. The seven of us sat on Bailey's veranda sipping bourbon and watching the boy and his dogs, watching partly because of what Bailey had just told us about the younger dog, Buddy's progeny, a fat brute and a bully. Bailey had chosen Buddy's mate carefully, but the union had produced a pure idiot. A little genetic imbalance, Bailey said, hard to avoid with these popular breeds.

Watching Junior you could see that this dog was aggressively stupid. A reckless, lumbering beast with no light in his eyes, floundering onto old Buddy's back, slamming into the boy and knocking him down. The boy is about ten or eleven and named Ulysses though they call him Lee (sort of a joke), thin as a tenpenny nail, with spectacles like his mama. He was eating it up, rolling in the grass and laughing like a lord-god woodpecker, Junior rooting at him like a hog.

"I hate that dog," Bailey said. "But Lee won't let me get rid of him."

The slow motions of cumulus splayed light across the lawn and lake in soft golden spars, the effect upon me narcotic. My weight pressed into the Adirondack chair as if I were paralyzed from the chest down. Bailey planned this place to be like an old-fashioned lake house, long and low with a railed porch all around. Jack McAdams, with us this day, landscaped the slope to the water, then laid St. Augustine around the dogwoods, redbuds, and a thick American beech, its smooth trunk marked with tumorous carvings. Three sycamores and a sweet gum line the shore down toward the woods. The water's surface was only slightly disturbed, like the old glass panes Bailey bought and put in his windows.

Russell took our glasses and served us frosty mint juleps from a silver tray. Silent Russell. The color and texture of Cameroon tobacco leaf, wearing his black slacks and white serving jacket. I am curious about him to the point of self-consciousness. I try not to stare, but want to gaze upon his face through a one-sided mirror. I see things in it that may or may not be there and I'm convinced of one thing, this role of the servant is merely that: Russell walks among us as the ghost of a lost civilization.

Bailey says Russell's family has been with his since the latter's post–Civil War Brazilian exile, when Bailey's great-great-grandfather fled to hack a new plantation out of the rain forest. Ten years later he returned with a new fortune and workforce, a band of wild Amazonians that jealous neighbors said he treated like kings. Only Russell's small clan lingers.

I looked at Russell and nodded to him.

"Russell," I said.

He looked at me a long moment and nodded his old gray head.

"Yah," he said, followed in his way with the barely audible "sah." After he'd handed drinks out all around, he eased back inside the house.

"Russell makes the best goddamn mint julep in the world," said Bailey, his low voice grumbly in the quiet afternoon, late summer, the first thin traces of fall in the air.

I could see two other men of Russell's exact coloring working at the barbecue pit down in the grove that led to the boathouse. Russell's boys. They'd had coals under the meat all night, Bailey said, and now we could see them stripping the seared, smoked pork into galvanized tubs. Beyond them, visible as occasional blurred slashing shadows between the trunks and limbs and leaves of small-growth hardwoods, were Bailey's penned and compromised wild pigs, deballed and meat sweetening in the lakeside air. He looked to be building up a winter meatstock, product of several hunting trips to the north Florida swamps with Skeet Bagwell and Titus Smith, who were seated next to me on Bailey's side. It seemed an unusual sport, to catch and castrate violent swine and pen them until their meat mellowed with enforced domesticity, and then to slit their throats. Russell's boys partially covered the rectangular cooking pit with sheets of roofing tin and carried the tubs of meat around back of the house to the kitchen. Along the veranda we drank our mint juleps—McAdams, Bill Burton, Hoyt Williams, Titus, Skeet, Bailey, and me—arranged in a brief curving line in Bailey's brand-new Adirondack chairs. Russell came out with more mint juleps, nodded, and slipped away.

"Here's to love," Bailey said, raising his silver cup. He smiled as if about to hurt someone. Probably himself. A malignant smile. Here we go, I said to myself, I don't want to hear it. I didn't want to hear his story any more than I wanted to take his case. He'd called the day before and invited me to the barbecue with these men, his best friends, and said he wanted me to represent him "in this business with Maryella." Bailey, I'd said, I've never handled divorces and I don't intend to change—as criminal as some of those cases may be. I suggested he call Larry Weeks, who's done very well with big divorce cases in this town. No, Bailey said, you come on out, come on. We'll talk about it. I supposed at the time it was because we've known each other since the first grade, though in the way of those who live parallel lives without ever really touching.

So here we were. There were no women around, apparently, none of these men's wives. I began to feel a familiar pain in my heart, as if it were filling with fluid, and it seemed I had to think about breathing in order to breathe. Even what little I knew about Bailey's problem at the time forced me into places I didn't want to go. So his wife has left him for his partner, I thought—so what? What else is new in the world? We all know something of that pain, to one degree or another.

Ten years ago I defended a man accused of pushing his brother off a famous outcropping in the Smoky Mountains in order to get his brother's inheritance, set for some reason at a percentage much greater than his own. It was an odd case. There'd been several other people at the lookout, where in those days a single rail kept visitors from succumbing to vertigo and tumbling down the craggy face of the cliff. My client's hand had rested in the small of his brother's back as they leaned over the railing to look down when the brother—like a fledgling tumbling from the nest, one witness said—pitched over the edge and disappeared.

It was considered an accident until my client's cousin, who had never liked or trusted him, who in fact claimed he had once dangled her by her wrists from the treehouse behind their grandmother's home until she agreed to give him her share of their cache of Bazooka bubble gum, hired a private investigator who was able to plant the seeds of doubt in the minds of enough witnesses to bring the case before a grand jury in Knoxville. Incredibly, the guy was indicted for murder one. I thought it so outrageous that when he called I immediately took over his case, even though it meant spending time traveling back and forth across the state line.

I liked the man. While he and I prepared for trial, my wife, Dorothy, and I had him out to dinner a few times and twice even took him to my family's old shanty on the Gulf Coast for the weekend. He and Dorothy hit it off well. Each was a lover of classical music (Doro had studied piano at the university until she gave up her hope of composing and switched to music history), and he was a tolerable pianist. They discussed the usual figures, Schubert and Brahms and Mozart, etc., as well as names I'd never heard of. They sat at the piano to study a particular phrase. They retired to the den to play old LPs Doro had brought to our marriage but which had gathered dust during the years I'd built my practice, never having had the energy to listen with her after dragging in at near midnight with a satchel full of work for the next morning. I often awoke at one or two in the morning, tie twisted and cinched against my throat, the dregs of a scotch and water in the glass in my lap, while the stereo needle scratched at the label of a recording long done easing strains of Sibelius from its grooves. In the bedroom I'd find Doro turned into the covers, her arms tossed over a pillow that covered her head, as was her sleeping habit, as if she were trying to smother herself.

I can look back now and see things. I pursued her when she didn't necessarily want to be pursued. The law school was just two blocks from the music school, and I would wander down the boulevard and into the resonant halls of the studios and to the room where she practiced and composed. I would stand outside the door, looking in through the narrow window no wider than half of my face, until she looked up, would have to look up, with her dark eyes as open upon mine as an animal's in the woods when it discovers you standing still and watching it, and it is watching your eyes to see if you are something alive. I did not do this every day, but only when my blood was up too high to sit at the law library desk and, thinking of the last time we had been together, I had to see her. One day when she looked up, I knew that she had not wanted to but for some reason had been unable not to, and when she did look up she knew that was it, she was mine. It was the moment when one is captured by love in spite of one's misgivings and is lost.

But light bends to greater forces, and so does fate, in time. I should not have been so stricken when she left with my client after the trial, but of course I was. An overweight man who eats bacon, drinks heavily, smokes, and never exercises should expect a heart attack, too, and does, but is nevertheless surprised when it comes and he is certainly stricken. I'd given my all to the case, I'd fought for the man. Work had become my life, after all. I'd exposed the cousin as a bankrupt, scheming bitch, read letters between the brothers that were full of fraternal endearments, and I borrowed and brought into court an expensive, full-size oil copy of Durand's famous painting, *Kindred Spirits,* depicting the painter Thomas Cole and the poet William Bryant standing on an outcropping in the Catskills, a spot less lofty than the scene of my client's alleged crime, but more beautiful in its romantic, cloistering light, and I asked them how a brother, in a setting such as this, and with witnesses less than ten feet away, could do something so *unnatural* as pitch his own flesh and blood to a bloody end. It was a stroke of brilliance. No one sees that painting without being moved to sentimental associations. Rosenbaum, the D.A., was furious I got away with it. My client also had a noble face: a straight nose, strong brow, high forehead, strong jaw and chin, clear brown eyes that declared a forthright nature. But in the end, after the hung jury and the judge's bitter words, my client and my wife moved to Tennessee, of all places, where he would set himself up in the insurance business. And here is my point, I suppose, or what makes the story worth telling.

When she began to call me three years later, in secret, explaining how he had become a cold and manipulative man, she told me he had admitted to her while drunk that he had indeed pushed his brother off the lookout, and he'd said that only I had any evidence of this, in a statement I'd taken wherein he slipped up and said the one thing that could have convicted him had the D.A. gotten his hands on it. I could hear the ghosted voices of other, garbled conversations drifting into our line. What one thing is that? I said. I don't know, she said. He wouldn't tell me. There was a pause on the line, and then she said, You could find it, Paul.

But I have never opened the file to search for the incriminating words. Moreover, although I have acquired an almost tape-recorder memory of the utterances of people in trouble, I have not bothered to prod that little pocket in my brain. I have detoured around it as easily as I swerve around a sawhorsed manhole in the street. I protected my client, as any good attorney would. I've moved on.

We walked down into the grove, past the thin smoking curtain of heat at the edge of the pit, its buckled tin, and up to the heavy-gauge wire fencing that surrounded about a half acre of wooded area bordering the cove. Here there was no grass, and the moist leaves were matted on the rich, grub- and worm-turned earth. Through the rectangular grid of the fencing we saw small pockets of ground broken up as if by the steel blades of a tiller where the pigs had rooted, and slashes and gouges in tree trunks where they'd sharpened their tusks.

I looked over at Bailey swirling the crushed ice in his cup, the righteous tendons in his jaw hardening into lumpy bands of iron. He was seething with his own maudlin story. But before he could start up, we heard a rustling followed by a low grunt, and a wild hog shot out of the undergrowth and charged. We all jumped back but Bailey as the hog skidded to a stop just short of the wire, strangely dainty feet on scraggly legs absurdly spindly beneath its massive head. Its broad shoulders tapered along its mohawkish spinal ridge to the hips of a running back and to its silly poodlish tail. The pig stood there, head lowered, small-eyed, snorting every few breaths or so, watching Bailey from beneath its thick brow. Bailey looked back at the beast, impassive, as if its appearance had eased his mind for a moment. And the boar grew even more still, staring at Bailey.

The spell was broken by the loud clanging of a bell. Russell, clanging the authentic antique triangle for our meal. The pig walked away from us then, indifferent, stiff-legged, as if mounted on little hairy stilts.

We made our way back to the porch. Russell and one of the men who'd been tending the pit came out with a broad tray of meat already sauced, and a woman (no doubt one of Russell's daughters or granddaughters) came out and set down on the table a stack of heavy plates, a pile of white bread, an iron pot full of baked beans, and we all got up to serve ourselves. When we sat back down, Bill Burton, who'd dug into his food before anybody else, made a noise like someone singing falsetto and looked up, astonished.

"By God, that's good barbecue," he said through a mouthful of meat. Burton was a plumbing contractor who'd done the plumbing for Bailey's house. He said to Skeet Bagwell, "Say you shot this pig?"

"Well," Skeet said, "let me tell you about that pig."

Like me, Skeet is a lawyer, but we aren't much alike. He rarely takes a criminal case, but goes for the money, and loves party politics and the country club and hunting trips and all that basically extended fraternity business, never makes a phone call his secretary can make for him, and needless to say he loves to tell big lies. His compadre Titus built shopping malls during the 1980s and doesn't do much of anything now.

"Titus and I *captured* that pig," Skeet said, "down in the Florida swamps. Ain't that right, Titus?"

"I wouldn't say, not exactly captured," Titus said.

"In a way, or briefly, perhaps, we captured that pig, but then we killed it. It may be a mite gamy."

"Uhn-uh," voices managed. "Not a bit!"

Skeet said, "You ain't had your blood stirred till you crossing a clearing in the swamp and hear a bunch of pigs rooting and grunting, you don't know where they are, and then you see their shapes, just these big, low, broad, hulking shadows, inside the bushes on the other side, and then they smell you and disappear, just disappear. It's eerie." Skeet took a mouthful of the barbecue, sopped up some sauce with a piece of bread, and chewed. We waited on him to swallow, sitting there on the veranda. Down on the lawn the boy, (Ulysses) Lee, ran screaming from the bounding dogs.

Skeet said it was exciting to see the pigs slip out of the woods and light out across a clearing, and the dogs' absolute joy in headlong pursuit. They were hunting these pigs with the local method, he said. You didn't shoot them. You used your dogs to capture them.

"We had this dog, part Catahoula Cur—you ever heard of them?"

"State dog of Louisiana," Hoyt said.

"Looks kind of prehistoric," Skeet said. "They breed them over in the Catahoula Swamp in Louisiana. Well, this dog was a cross between a Catahoula Cur and a pit bull, and that's the best pig dog they is. Like a compact Doberman. They can run like a deer dog and they're tough and strong as a pit bull. And they got that streak of meanness they need, because a boar is just mean as hell." Skeet said he'd seen an African boar fight a whole pack of lions' on TV one night, did we see that? Lions tore the boar to bits, but he fought the whole time. "I mean you couldn't hardly see the boar for all the lion asses stuck up in the air over him, tails swishing, ripping him up, twenty lions or more," Skeet said. They had pieces of him scattered around the savanna in seconds, but there was his old head, tusking blindly even as one of the lions licked at his heart. Skeet took another bite of barbecue and chewed, looking off down the grassy slope at the tussling boy and dogs.

"This dog Titus and I had, we bought him off a fellow down there said he was the best dog he'd ever seen for catching a hog, and he was right." Titus nodded in agreement. "We got out in the swamp with him, and *bim,* he was off on a trail, and ran us all over that swamp for about an hour, and never quit until he run down that hog.

"We come up on him out in this little clearing, and he's got this big old hog by the snout, holding his head down on the ground, hog snorting and grunting and his eyes leaking bile. I mean, that dog had him. But then we come to find out how we got this wonder dog at such a bargain."

"I had a preacher sell me a blind dog one time," Hoyt said. "Said how hot he was for a rabbit, and cheap. Sumbitch when I let loose the leash took off flying after a rabbit and run right into an oak tree, knocked hisself cold."

Everybody laughed at that.

"Preacher said, 'I never said he wasn't blind,'" Hoyt said.

"Well, this dog wasn't blind," Skeet said, "not *literally*, but you might could say he had a blind spot. He would run the hog down, like he's supposed to do, then take it by the snout and hold its old head down, so you can go up and hog-tie him and take him in. Way they do down there, like Bailey's doing here, they castrate them and pen them up, let the meat sweeten awhile before they kill 'em.

"But this dog, once you grabbed the hog by the hind legs and begun to tie him, thought his job was done, and he lets go."

Skeet paused here, looking around at us. "So there was old Titus, gentlemen, playing wheelbarrow with a wild pig that's trying to twist around and rip his nuts off with one of them tusks. I mean that son of a bitch is mean, eyes all bloodshot, foaming at the mouth. That meat ain't too tough, is it?"

Everyone mumbled in the negative.

"Ain't gamy, is it?"

Naw, uh-uh.

"So finally Titus jumped around close to a tree, lets go of the hog and hops up into it, and I'm already behind one and peeping out, and the hog jabbed his tuskers at the tree Titus was in for a minute and then shot out through the woods again, and the dog—he'd been jumping around and barking and growling and nipping at the hog—took out after him again. So Titus climbed down and we ran after them."

"Dog was good at *catching* the hog," Titus said.

"That's right," Skeet said. "Just didn't understand the seriousness of the situation, once he'd done it. Actually, the way I see it, the dog figured that once the man touched the hog, then he had taken *possession* of the hog, see, and his job—the dog's—was over.

"Anyway, you can imagine, Titus wasn't going near that hog held by that dog again, so one of these fellows we're with tries it, and the same thing happens, two more times: As soon as the man *touched the hog*, the dog let go. And it was starting to get dark. But this fellow, name was Beauregard or something—"

"Beaucarte," Titus said.

"—he comes up with a plan. And the next time the dog has the hog down, he manages with some kind of knot to hog-tie the hog without actually touching the hog, and the dog's watching his every move, you know, and looking into his eyes every now and then, thinking, Why the hell ain't he taking hold of this hog, but he holds on just fine till it's done. But then when the guy starts to drag the hog over to this pole we go'n carry him out on, the dog—since the man hasn't actually *touched* the hog at all with his hands, now—he's *still hanging on,* and pulling backwards and growling like a pup holding on to a sock. Damn hog is squawling in pain and starting to buck."

Skeet stopped here a minute to chow down on his barbecue before it got cold, and we waited on him. Bailey seemed distant, looking out over the lake, sitting still, not eating any barbecue himself.

"So the guy stops and looks back at that dog, and you could see him thinking about it. Just standing there looking at that dog. And we were tired, boy, I mean we'd been running through that damn swamp all day, and we was give out. And I could see the guy thinking about it, thinking all he had to do was reach down and touch that hog one time, and the dog would let go. And you could see the dog looking at him, still chomped down on the hog's nose, looking up at the guy as if to say, Well, you go'n touch the hog or ain't you? And that's when the guy pulls his .44 Redhawk out, cocks it, and blows the son of a bitch away."

"The hog?" says Jack McAdams, sounding hopeful.

Skeet shakes his head.

"The dog," he says.

"*Your* dog?" Hoyt says.

"That's right," Skeet said. "All in all, I guess he was doing me a favor."

Everybody stopped eating, looking at Skeet, who finished up the little bit of barbecue on his plate and sopped up the sauce and grease with a piece of white bread. He rattled the ice chips and water in the bottom of his cup and drained the sugar-whiskey water, and I saw Russell note this and slip back into the house for more drinks.

"I guess he let go then," Bailey said quietly, sunk deeply into his Adirondack. "The dog."

"No," Skeet said, "*he didn't.*

"He was a mess, head all blown way, but his jaws still clamped on that nose in a death grip. He was rigor-mortised onto that hog. You can imagine the state of mind of the hog right then, that .44 laid down the ridge of his nose and going *boom,* shooting blue flame, and that dog's head opening up, blood and brains and bone all over him, dog teeth clamping down even more on his nose. Hog went crazy. He jumped up and thrashed his head around, screaming in pain, shook the ropes almost free, and started hobbling and belly-crawling around this little clearing we were in. And he was dragging the dog around, flopping it around, and it wadn't anything now but a set of teeth attached to a carcass, just a body and jaws.

"Meanwhile old Beaucarte's feet had gotten tangled in the ropes and so there they all were, thrashing around in the near-dark, stinking swamp with a wild hog, a dead dog, and this damn cracker trying to aim his hand-cannon at the hog just to make it all stop, and finally he shot it, the hog. By then it was almost dark, and everything was still as the eye of hurricane, and the air smelled of gunpowder smoke and blood and something strange like sulfur, with the swamp rot and the gore and the sinking feeling we all had with a hunt gone wrong, and a good dog with just one flaw now dead, and everybody felt bad about it, especially this long, skinny Beaucarte.

"We dragged the hog and the dog back to the truck in the dark, tossed them in back and drove on back to the camphouse, and told these two swamp idiots on the porch, a couple of beady-eyed brothers, to take care of the hog, and then we drank some whiskey and went to bed. The next day, when we were leaving, one of the swamp idiots, name was Benny, had this old cheap pipe stuck in the corner of his mouth, brings out a big ice chest full of meat wrapped in butcher paper. And he says, 'We goin' on into town, now. Me and Fredrick put yo meat in this icebox, and Daddy'n them took some of the meat from the big'un.'"

Here Skeet stopped talking and let silence hang there a moment, and sipped from a fresh drink Russell had set down on the arm of his Adirondack. Hoyt gestured to his plate.

"So you saying this might be hog, might be dog."

"Tastes mighty sweet to be dog," Bill Burton said.

"Some of it's sweeter than the rest," Skeet allowed.

Everybody had a laugh over that, sitting there picking their teeth with minty toothpick wedges Russell had passed around from a little silver box. He freshened the drinks. The afternoon seemed to slide pleasantly, almost imperceptibly, along the equinoctial groove toward autumn.

"I tell you something," Bailey said then. "I got a story to tell, too. Skeet's story brings me to mind of it."

The immediate shift in mood was as palpable as if someone had walked up and slapped each one of us in the mouth. We sat in our Adirondacks, sunken, silent, and trying to focus on the boy on the lake bank tossing the ball to his dogs swimming the shallows. Holding our breaths this wouldn't be the old epic of Bailey's yawping grief.

"You know this fellow, my erstwhile friend and partner, Reid Covert."

"Bailey, ain't you got any dessert to go with this fine barbecue?" Skeet said.

Bailey held his hand up. "No, now, hear me out," he said, his eyes fixed somewhere out over the lake. He made a visible effort to relax. "It's a good story, it's all in fun."

All right, someone mumbled, let him tell it.

"But that's not saying it ain't *true*," Bailey said, and turns to us with such a devilish grin that we're all a little won over by it. It was a storyteller's smile. A liar's smile.

All right, everybody said, easing up, go ahead on.

"Y'all didn't know a thing about this," he said, "but I whipped that sorry sapsucker's ass three times before I finally got rid of him."

Three times! we said.

"Kicked his ass."

No! we said. We had fresh mint juleps in our hands. Russell stood to one side in his white serving jacket, looking out over the lake. Out in the yard, the boy Lee chased the chocolate Labs Buddy and Junior down to the water. He had a blue rubber-looking ball in his hand and he stopped at the bank, holding the ball up, and the dogs leaped into the air around him. Junior knocked the boy all over the place, trying to get his chops on the ball. He knocked off the boy's glasses and then grabbed the ball when the boy got down on his knees to retrieve them.

"The first time I heard about it I went into his office and confronted him," Bailey said. "He denied it. But, hell, I knew he was lying. It was after five. The nurses had gone, receptionist gone, insurance clerk gone. No patients. I told him, 'You're lying, Reid.' He just sat there then, looking stupid, and I knew I was right. I went over and slapped him. My own partner. Friend since elementary school. Went through med school together. Slapped shit out of him. 'How long has it been going on?' I said. He just sat there. I told him to get up but he wouldn't. So I slapped him again. He still just sat there. I tried to pick him up out of his chair by his shirt but he held onto the goddamn armrests, so I slapped him again. 'Stop it, Bailey,' he says then. 'Stop it, hell,' I said. I said, 'Get up, you son of a bitch.' And he says, 'Stop it, Bailey.' And so I said, 'You son of a bitch, I want you out of this office, you and I are through.' And I walked out."

We were all quiet again then. It was as bad as we'd thought it would be. Bailey hadn't worked in weeks. All his patients had to go to Birmingham. Reid Covert had taken off somewhere, and Bailey's wife, Maryella, had gone off, too.

Everybody figured they were together. And I was thinking, I guess he'll ask me to help him divide his and Reid's business, too.

"Well," Bailey went on then, "Maryella wouldn't talk to me about it, and I kept hearing they were still seeing each other. So I drove over to his house one day and pulled up as he was trying to leave. I cut off his car with mine, got out, went over, and pulled him out of his goddamn Jeep Cherokee. He didn't even get the thing into Park, it rolled over and ran into a pine tree. And I mean I pummeled him, right there in his own goddamn front yard. Berry, she came out into the yard yelling at me, went back in to call the police, and old Reid, I'm beating the shit out of him, his nose is bloody, and he's holding out his arm toward Berry and saying, No, don't call the police. I let go of him and watched him limp after her, then I got back into my car and came out here. When I got here Maryella passed me in the driveway, zooming out onto the road, dust flying. Hell, Berry must've called her instead of the cops. Hell, she left Lee out in the goddamn yard with the dogs and went to her mother's house, didn't come home for two days, and when she did I had her suitcase packed and told her to get the hell out."

All this—all the detail, anyway—was new, we had not heard it from the various sources. The boy, Lee, was throwing the blue ball into the water now and the dogs were swimming out to get it, then swimming back in, whereupon the one without it, usually the boorish Junior, would chase the one who had it, his daddy Buddy, and get it away from him. Whereupon the boy would chase down Junior, get the ball, and throw it back out into the lake.

"Look at that," Bailey said. "I tell you it was Reid's bitch Lab we mated Buddy with to get that sorry Junior? I should've drowned the goddamn dog."

A couple of us, Hoyt and me, got up for barbecue seconds. Dog or hog, it was good, and Bailey's story was eating at my stomach in a bad way. I needed something more in it.

"Y'all eat up," Bailey said. "What's left belongs to the niggers." Old Russell, standing off to one side of the barbecue table, sort of shifted his weight and blinked, still looking out over the lake. Bailey saw this and pulled his lips tight over his teeth. "Sorry, Russell," he mumbled. Russell, his eyes fixed on the lake's far shore, appeared unfazed. Bailey got up, went inside, and came back out with the bottle of Knob Creek. He poured some into his mint julep cup and drank it.

"Well, finally, I followed him one day, and I watched him meet her in the parking lot of the Yacht Club, and I followed them way out here, down to the Deer Lick landing. I'd cut my lights, and I parked up the road, and then I walked down. I had my .38 pistol with me, but I wasn't going to kill them. I had me some blanks, and I'd screwed a little sealing wax into that little depression at the end of the blanks. You ever noticed that, that little depression? When I got down there they weren't in the car. I looked around and saw a couple standing down on the beach, just shadows in that darkness, so I walked down there. They looked around when I walked up to them, and when they realized it was me it scared them pretty bad, me showing up. I stepped up to him and said, 'I told you to give it up, Reid,' and that's when he hit me, almost knocked me down. I guess he wanted to get the first lick in, for once. I went back at him, and it was a real street fight, pulling hair and wrestling and kicking and throwing a punch every now and then, and hell Maryella might have been in on it for all I know. I finally threw him down onto the sand, and his shirt ripped off in my hands. Maryella was standing with her feet in the water, with her hands over her face, and I was standing there over Reid, out of breath and worn out. And he looked up then and said, 'You're going to have to kill me to get rid of me, Bailey. I love her.' So I pulled out the pistol from my pocket and said, 'All right.' And I shot him. All five rounds."

We were all quiet as ghosts. The squeals from the boy and the playful growling of the dog Junior, and the good-natured barking of Buddy his daddy, all wafted up from the lake. The ball arced out over the water, and the dogs leapt after it with big splashes.

"Well, he hollered like he was dying," Bailey said. "I imagine it hurt, wax or not, and scared the holy shit out of him. It was loud as hell. I saw these dark blotches blossom on his skin. You know Reid always was a pale motherfucker. When he saw the blood, his head fell back onto the beach sand.

"Maryella said, 'You killed him.' By God, I thought I had, too. I thought, Jesus Christ, I am so addled I forgot to use the blanks, I have shot the son of a bitch with real bullets. I jumped down there and took a look, and in a minute I could see that I hadn't done that. The pieces of wax had pierced the skin, though, and he was bleeding from these superficial wounds. He'd fainted.

"And Maryella panicked then. She started to run away. I tackled her and dragged her back to Reid to show her he was all right, but she wouldn't quit slapping at me and screaming, 'You killed him, you killed him!' over and over again. She said she loved him, and she'd never loved me. I shoved her head under the shallow water there at the beach, but when I pulled her up again she just took a deep breath and started screaming the same thing again, 'You killed him, I hate you!' And that's when Reid jumped onto my back, and shoved me forward. I still had a hold on Maryella's neck, see, and my arms were held out stiff, like this," and he held his arms out, his hands at the end of them held in a horseshoe shape, the way they would be if they were around a neck. Bailey looked at his hands held out there, like that.

"I felt her neck crack beneath my hands," he said. "Beneath our weight, mine and Reid's." He didn't say anything for a minute. I heard his boy, Lee, calling him from down at the lake. No one answered him or looked up. We were all staring at Bailey, who wasn't looking at anything in particular. He looked tired, almost bored.

"Anyway," he said then, "I couldn't let Reid get away with causing that to happen. I found the gun and hit him over the head with it. And then I held him under until he drowned."

Bailey swirled what was left in his mint julep cup, looking down into the dregs. He turned it up and sucked at the bits of ice and mint and the soggy sugar in the bottom. Then he sat back in his chair, poured more bourbon into the cup, and said in a voice that was chilling to me, because I recognized the method of manipulation behind it, taking the shocked imagination and diverting it to the absurd: "So when I brought them back here, that's when Russell's boys skinned 'em up and put 'em over the coals."

There was silence for a long moment, and then McAdams, Bill Burton, Hoyt, Titus, and Skeet broke into a kind of forced, polite laughter.

"Shit, Bailey," McAdams said. "You just about tell it too good for me."

"So gimme some more of that human barbecue, Russell," Titus said.

"'Long pig' is the Polynesian term, I believe," Skeet said.

Their laughter came more easily now.

The boy, Lee, came running up to the porch steps.

"Daddy," he said. He was crying, his voice high and quailing. Bailey turned his darkened face to the boy as if to an executioner.

"Daddy, Junior's trying to hurt old Buddy."

We looked up. Out in the lake, Buddy swam with the ball in his mouth. Junior was trying to climb up onto Buddy's back. Both dogs looked tired, their heads barely clearing the surface. Junior mounted Buddy from behind, and as he climbed Buddy's back the older dog, his nose held straight up and the ball still in his teeth, went under.

He didn't come back up. We all of us stood up out of our chairs. Junior swam around for a minute. He swam in a circle one way, then reversed himself, and then struck out in another direction with what seemed a renewed vigor, after something. It was the blue ball, floating away. He nabbed it off the surface and swam in. He set the ball down on the bank and shook himself, then looked up toward all of us on the veranda. He started trotting up the bank toward the boy standing stricken in the yard.

Bailey had gone into the house and come out with what looked like an old Browning shotgun. He yanked it to his shoulder, sighted, and fired it just over the boy's head at the dog. The boy ducked down flat onto the grass. The dog stopped still, in a point, looking at Bailey holding the gun. He was out of effective range.

"Bailey!" Skeet shouted. "You'll hit the boy!"

Bailey's face was purplish and puffed with rage. His eyes darted all over the lawn. He saw his boy Lee lying down in the grass with an empty, terrified look in his eyes. He lowered the barrel and drew a bead on the boy. The boy, and I tell you he looked just like his mama, was looking right into his daddy's eyes. He will never be just a boy again. There was a small strangled noise down in Bailey's chest, and he swung the gun up over the grove and fired it off, *boom,* the shot racing out almost visibly over the trees. The sound caromed across the outer bank and echoed back to us, diminished. Junior took off running for the road, tail between his legs. The boy lay in the grass looking up at his father. Titus stepped up and took the shotgun away, and Bailey sat down on the pinewood floor of the veranda as if exhausted.

"Well," he said after a minute. His voice was deep and hoarse and croaky. "Well." He shook with a gentle, silent laughter. "I wonder what I ought to do." He cleared his throat. "I don't know who else to ask but you boys." He struggled up and tottered drunkenly to the barbecue table, put together a sandwich of white bread and meat, and began to devour it like a starving man. He snatched large bites and swallowed them whole, then stuck his fingers into his mouth, sucking off the grease and sauce. He gave that up and wiped his hands on his khakis, up and down, as if stropping a razor. "Russell," he said, looking around, seeming unable to focus on him, "get another round, some of that Mexican beer, maybe. We need something light to wash down this meal." He ran his fingers through his hair.

Old Russell glided up like a shadow then, taking plates, stacking them in one broad hand, smiling with his mouth but his eyes as empty and blank as the sky. "Heah, sah," he said, "let me take your plate. Let me help you with that. Let one of my boys bring your car around. Mr. Paul," he said to me, "I guess you'll be wanting to stay."

There was little more to say, after that. We formalized the transfer of deed for the old place in Brazil, along with the title to Bailey's Winnebago, to Russell. By nightfall he and his clan had eased away on their long journey to the old country, stocked with barbecue and beer and staples. The women left the kitchen agleam. Bailey and I sat by the fire in the den. They'd lain Reid Covert and Maryella on the hickory pyre that, reduced to pure embers, had eventually roasted our afternoon meal. There was nothing much left there to speak of, the coals having worked them down to fine ash in the blackened earth. I could hear a piece of music, though the sound system was hidden, nowhere to be seen. It sounded like Schubert, one of those haunting sonatas that seem made for the end of the day. In his hand Bailey held a little bundle of cloth, a tiny palm-sized knapsack that Russell had given him before he left. A little piece of the liver, sah, to keep the bad souls from haunting your dreams. A little patch of this man's forehead, who steal his own best friend's wife. This light sap from her eyes, Mr. Bailey, you hardly see it, where the witch of beauty live in her, them eyes that could not lie to you. You take it, eat, and you don't be afraid. He eased carefully out the front door and disappeared. Bailey placed the little knapsack on the glowing coals in the hearth, watched the piece of cloth begin to blacken and burn, and the bits of flesh curl and shrink into ash. He was calm now, his boy asleep fully clothed and exhausted up in his room.

In the last moments out on the porch, before we'd drifted inside in a dream of dusk, the afternoon had ticked down and shadows had deepened on the lake's far bank. The other men, dazed, had shuffled away. Russell's two younger sons had stood on the shore and tossed ropes with grappling hooks to retrieve old Buddy. Bailey's boy stood on the bank hugging himself against some chill, watching them swing the hooks back over their shoulders and sling them, the long ropes trailing out over the lake, where the hooks landed with a little splash of silver water. A momentarily delayed report reached us, softly percussive, from across the water and the lawn. Bailey stood on the steps and watched them, his hands on top of his head.

"Look at that," he whispered, the grief and regret of his life in the words. "Old Buddy."

They brought the old dog out of the water. The boy, Lee, fell to his knees. Russell's sons stood off to one side like pallbearers. Above the trees across the lake, a sky like torn orange pulp began to fade. Light seeped away as if extracted, and grainy dusk rose up from the earth. For a long while none of us moved. I listened to the dying sounds of birds out over the water and in the trees, and the faint clattering of small sharp tusks against steel fencing out in the grove, a sound that seemed to come from my own heart.

# TIM GAUTREAUX, "Sorry Blood"

Tim Gautreaux was born in 1947 in Morgan City, Louisiana. The son of a tug-boat captain, Gautreaux earned his doctorate in literature at the University of South Carolina, where he studied writing with James Dickey. At the urging of Walker Percy, Gautreaux abandoned poetry for short fiction in the 1970s and has since published stories in *Harper's, GQ, Atlantic Monthly,* and both the *O. Henry* and *Best American Short Story* annuals. His books include two story collections, *Same Place, Same Things* (1996) and *Welding with Children* (1999), which was named a *New York Times* Notable Book, and the novels *The Next Step in the Dance* (1998), *The Clearing* (2003), and *The Missing* (2009). A long-time teacher of creative writing, Gautreaux retired from Southeastern Louisiana University in 2004.

As a writing teacher, Gautreaux would devote at least one class to a trip to Wal-Mart, which he calls "a marvelous source for stories."[1] Here he serves up a prime example in "Sorry Blood," a contemporary spin on the old southern "trickster" tale that offers an intriguing take on the South's shifting sense of identity.

> The Southern writer loves where he's from, warts and all. When I think of the history of my family, I think of how hard it was for people to work and survive and how much my family members suffered living in a tough climate and tougher poverty. . . . You look back on all that history and all that misery and you almost feel like a traitor if you don't respect the people you came from and the place they made. In one way or another, you have to tell their story.[2]

### "SORRY BLOOD"

The old man walked out of Wal-Mart and stopped dead, recognizing nothing he saw in the steaming Louisiana morning. He tried to step off the curb, but his feet locked up and his chest flashed with a burst of panic. The blacktop parking lot spread away from him, glittering with the enameled tops of a thousand automobiles. One of them was his, and he struggled to form a picture but could not remember which of the family's cars he had taken out that morning. He backstepped into the shade of the store's overhang and sat on a displayed riding lawn mower. Putting his hands down on his khaki pants, he closed his eyes and fought to remember, but one by one, things began to fall away from the morning, and then the day before, and the life before. When he looked up again, all the cars seemed too small, too bright and glossy, more like fishing lures. His right arm trembled, and he regarded the spots on the back of his hand with a light-headed embarrassment. He stared down at his Red Wing brogans, the shoes of a stranger. For a half hour, he sat on the mower seat, dizziness subsiding like a summer storm.

Finally, he got up, stiff and floating, and walked off into the grid of automobiles, his white head turning from side to side under a red feed-store cap. Several angry-looking people sat in hot cars, their faces carrying the uncomprehending disappointment of boiled lobsters. He walked attentively for a long time but recognized nothing, not even his own tall image haunting panels of tinted glass.

Twice he went by a man slouched in a parked Ford sedan, an unwashed thing with a rash of rust on its lower panels. The driver, whose thin hair hung past his ears, was eating a pickled sausage out of a plastic sleeve and chewing it with his front teeth. He watched the wanderer with a slow reptilian stare each time he walked by. On the third pass, the driver of the Ford considered the still-straight back, the big shoulders. He hissed at the old man, who stopped and looked for the sound. "What's wrong with you, gramps?"

He went to the window and stared into the car at the man whose stomach enveloped the lower curve of the steering wheel. An empty quart beer bottle lay on the front seat. "Do you know me?" the old man asked in a voice that was soft and lost.

The driver looked at him a long time, his eyes moving down his body as though he were a column of figures. "Yeah, Dad," he said at last. "Don't you remember me?" He put an unfiltered cigarette in his mouth and lit it with a kitchen match. "I'm your son."

The old man's hand went to his chin. "My son," he said, like a fact.

"Come on." The man in the Ford smiled only with his mouth. "You're just having a little trouble remembering."

The old man got in and placed a hand on the chalky dash. "What have I been doing?"

"Shopping for me is all. Now give me back my wallet, the one you took in the store with you." The driver held out a meaty hand.

The other man pulled a wallet from a hip pocket and handed it over.

In a minute, they were leaving the parking lot, riding a trash-strewn highway out of town into the sandy pine barrens of Tangipahoa Parish. The old man watched the littered roadside for clues. "I can't remember my own name," he said, looking down at his plaid shirt.

"It's Ted," the driver told him, giving him a quick look. "Ted Williams." He checked his side-view mirrors.

"I don't even remember your name, son. I must be sick." The old man wanted to feel his head for fever, but he was afraid he would touch a stranger.

"My name is Andy," the driver said, fixing a veined eye on him for a long moment. After a few miles, he turned off the main highway onto an unpaved road. The old man listened to the knock and ping of rock striking the driveshaft of the car. Then the gravel became patchy and thin, the road blotched with a naked, carroty earth like the hide of a sick dog. Bony cattle heaved their heads between strands of barbed wire, scavenging for roadside weeds. The Ford bumped past mildewed trailers sinking into rain-eaten plots. Farther on, the land was too soggy for trailers, too poor even for the lane's desperate cattle. After two miles of this, they pulled up to a redbrick house squatting in a swampy two-acre lot. Limbs were down everywhere, and catbriers and poison oak covered the rusty fence that sagged between the yard and cutover woods running in every direction.

"This is home," Andy said, pulling him from the car. "You remember now?" He held the old man's arm and felt it for muscle.

Ted looked around for more clues but said nothing. He watched Andy walk around the rear of the house and return with a shovel and a pair of boots. "Follow me, Dad." They walked to a swale full of coppery standing water that ran along the side of the property, ten feet from the fence. "This has to be dug out, two deep scoops side by side, all the way down to the ditch at the rear of the property. One hundred yards." He held the shovel out at arm's length.

"I don't feel very strong," he said, bending slowly to unlace his shoes. He stepped backward out of them and slipped into the oversized Red Ball boots.

"You're a big man. Maybe your mind ain't so hot, but you can work for a while yet." And when Ted rocked up the first shovelful of sumpy mud, Andy smiled, showing a pair of yellow incisors.

He worked for an hour, carefully, watching the straightness of the ditch, listening to his heart strum in his ears, studying the awful lawn, which was draining like a boil into the trough he opened for it. The whole lot was flat and low, made of a sterile clay that never dried out between thunderstorms rolling up from the Gulf. After four or five yards, he had to sit down and let the pine and pecan trees swim around him as though they were laboring to stay upright in a great wind. Andy came out of the house carrying a lawn chair and a pitcher of cloudy liquid.

"Can I have some?" the old man asked.

Andy showed his teeth. "Nah. These are margaritas. You'll fall out for sure if you drink one." As an afterthought, he added, "There's water in the hose."

All morning, Andy drank from the pitcher, and the old man looked back over his shoulder, trying to place him. The shovel turned up a sopping red clay tainted with runoff from a septic tank, and Ted tried to remember such poor soil. The day was still, no traffic bumped down the dirt lane, and the tinkling of the ice cubes and the click of a cigarette lighter were the only sounds the old man heard. About one-thirty he put down his shovel for the twentieth time and breathed deeply, like a man coming up from underwater. He had used a shovel before—his body told him that—but he couldn't remember where or when. Andy drew up his lawn chair, abandoning the empty pitcher in pigweed growing against the fence. The old man could smell his breath when he came close, something like cleaning fluid, and a memory tried to fire up in his brain, but when Andy asked a question, the image broke apart like a dropped ember.

"You ever been beat up by a woman?" Andy asked.

The old man was too tired to look at him. Sweat weighed him down.

Andy scratched his belly through his yellow knit shirt. "Remember? She told me she'd beat me again and then divorce my ass if I didn't fix this yard up." He spoke with one eye closed, as though he was too drunk to see with both of them at the same time. "She's big," he said. "Makes a lot of money but hits hard. Gave me over a hundred stitches once." He held up a flaccid arm. "Broke this one in two places." The old man looked at him then, studying the slouching shoulders, the patchy skin in his scalp. He saw that he was desperate, and the old man moved back a step. "She's coming back soon, the bitch is. I told her I couldn't do it. That's why I went to the discount parking lot to hire one of those bums that work for food." He tried to rattle an ice cube in his empty tumbler, but the last one had long since melted. "Those guys won't work," he told him, pulling his head back and looking down his lumpy nose at nothing. "They just hold those cardboard signs saying they'll work so they can get a handout, the lazy bastards."

Pinheads of light were exploding in the old man's peripheral vision. "Can I have something to eat?" he asked, looking toward the house and frowning.

Andy led him into the kitchen, which smelled of garbage. The tile floor was cloudy with dirt, and a hill of melamine dishes lay capsized in the murky sink water. Andy unplugged the phone and left the room with it. Returning empty-handed, he fell into a kitchen chair and lit up a cigarette. The old man guessed where the food was and opened a can of Vienna sausages, twisting them out one at a time with a fork. "Maybe I should go to a doctor?" he said, chewing slowly, as if trying to place the taste.

"Ted. Dad. The best job I ever had was in a nursing home remember?" He watched the old man's eyes. "I dealt with people like you all day. I know what to do with you."

Ted examined the kitchen the way he might regard things during a visit to a museum. He looked and looked.

The afternoon passed like a slow, humid dream, and he completed fifty yards of ditch. By sundown, he was trembling and wet. Had his memory come back, he would have known he was too old for this work. He leaned on the polished wood of the shovel handle and looked at his straight line, almost remembering something, dimly aware that where he was, he had not been before. His memory was like a long novel left open and ruffled by a breeze to a different chapter further along. Andy had disappeared into the house to sleep off the tequila, and the old man came in to find himself something to eat. The pantry showed a good stock of chili, but not one pot was clean, so he scrubbed the least foul for ten minutes and put the food on to heat.

Later, Andy appeared in the kitchen doorway, wavering like the drunk he was. He led Ted to a room that contained only a stripped bed. The old man put two fingers to his chin. "Where are my clothes?"

"You don't remember anything," Andy said quickly, turning to walk down the hall. "I have some overalls that'll fit if you want to clean up and change."

Ted lay down on the splotched mattress as though claiming it. This bed, it's mine, he thought. Turning onto his stomach, he willed himself to remember the musty smell. Yes, he thought. My name is Ted. I am where I am.

In the middle of the night, his bladder woke him, and on the way back to bed, he saw Andy seated in the boxlike living room watching a pornographic movie in which a hooded man was whipping a naked woman with a rope. He walked up behind him, watching not the television but Andy's head, the shape of it. A quart beer bottle lay sweating in his lap. The old man rolled his shoulders back. "Only white trash would watch that," he said.

Andy turned around, slow and stiff, like an old man himself. "Hey, Dad. Pull up a chair and get off on this." He looked back to the set.

Ted hit him from behind. It was a roundhouse open-palm swat on the ear that knocked him out of the chair and sent the spewing beer bottle pinwheeling across the floor. Andy hit the tile on his stomach, and it was some time before he could turn up on one elbow to give the big man a disbelieving, angry look. "You old shit. Just wait till I get up."

"White trash," the old man thundered. "No kid of mine is going to be like that." He came closer. Andy rolled against the TV cart and held up a hand. The old man raised his right foot as though he would plant it on his neck.

"Hold on, Dad."

"Turn the thing off," he said.

"What?"

"Turn the thing off!" the old man shouted, and Andy pressed the power button with a knuckle just as a big calloused heel came down next to his head.

"Okay. Okay." He blinked and pressed his back against the television, inching away from the old man, who seemed even larger in the small room.

And then a long, bony face fringed with white hair drifted down above his own, examining him closely, looking at his features, the shape of his nose. The old man put out a finger and traced Andy's right ear as if evaluating its quality. "Maybe you've got from me some sorry blood," he said, and his voice shook from saying it, that such a soft and stinking man could come out of him. He pulled back and closed his eyes as though he couldn't stand sight itself. "Let the good blood come out, and it'll tell you what to do," he said, his back bent with soreness, his hands turning to the rear. "You can't let your sorry blood run you."

Andy struggled to his feet in a pool of beer and swayed against the television, watching the old man disappear into the hall. His face burned where he'd been hit, and his right ear rang like struck brass. He moved into the kitchen, where he watched a photograph taped to the refrigerator, an image of his wife standing next to a deer hanging in a tree, her right hand balled around a long knife. He sat down, perhaps forgetting Ted, the spilled beer, even his wife's hard fists, and he fell asleep on his arms at the kitchen table.

The next morning, the old man woke up and looked around the bare bedroom, remembering it from the day before, and almost recalling something else, maybe a person. He concentrated, but the image he saw was something far away, seen without his eyeglasses. He rubbed his thumbs over his fingertips, and the feel of someone was there.

In the kitchen, he found Andy and put on water for coffee, watching his son until the kettle whistled. He loaded a French drip pot and found bread, scraped the mold off and toasted four slices. He retrieved eggs and a lardy bacon from the refrigerator. When Andy picked up his shaggy head, a dark stink of armpit stirred alive, and the old man told him to go wash himself.

In a half hour, Andy came back into the kitchen, his face nicked and bleeding from a month-old blade, a different T-shirt forming a second skin. He sat and ate without a word, but drank no coffee. After a few bites, he rummaged in a refrigerator drawer, retrieving a can of beer. The old man looked at the early sun caught in the dew on the lawn and then glanced back at the beer. "Remind me of where you work," he said.

Andy took a long pull on the can. "I'm too sick to work. You know that." He melted into a slouch and looked through the screen door toward a broken lawn mower dismantled in his carport. "It's all I can do to keep up her place. Every damn thing's broke, and I got to do it all by hand."

"Why can't I remember?" He sat down with his own breakfast and began eating, thinking, This is an egg. What am I?

Andy watched the old man's expression and perhaps felt a little neon trickle of alcohol brightening his bloodstream, kindling a single Btu of kindness, and he leaned over. "I seen it happen before. In a few days, your mind'll come back." He drained the beer and let out a rattling belch. "Right now, get back on that ditch."

The old man put a hand on a shoulder. "I'm stiff." He left the hand there.

"Come on." He fished three beer cans from the refrigerator.

"You might be a little achy, but my back can't take the shovel business at all. You've got to finish that ditch today." He looked into the old man's eyes as though he'd lost something in them. "Quick as you can."

"I don't know."

Andy scratched his ear and, finding it sore, gave the old man a dark look. "Get up and find that shovel, damn you."

Andy drove to a crossroads store, and Ted wandered the yard looking at the bug-infested trees. The other man returned to sit in the shade of a worm-nibbled pecan, where he opened a beer and began to read a paper he had bought. Ted picked up the shovel and cut the soft earth, turning up neat, sopping crescents. In the police reports column was a brief account of an Etienne LeBlanc, a retired farmer from St. Mary Parish who had been staying with his son in Pine

Oil when he disappeared. The son stated that his father had moved in with him a year ago, had begun to have spells of forgetfulness, and that he wandered. These spells had started the previous year on the day the old man's wife had died while they were shopping at the discount center. Andy looked over at Ted and snickered. He went to the house for another beer and looked again at the photograph on the refrigerator. His wife's stomach reached out farther than her breasts, and her angry red hair shrouded a face tainted by tattooed luminescent-green eye shadow. Her lips were ignited with a permanent chemical pigment that left them bloodred even in the mornings, when he was sometimes startled to wake and find the dyed parts of her shining next to him. She was a dredge-boat cook and was on her regular two-week shift at the mouth of the Mississippi. She had told him that if a drainage ditch was not dug through the side yard by the time she got back, she would come after him with a piece of firewood.

He had tried. The afternoon she left, he had bought a shovel on the way back from the liquor store at the crossroads, but on the second spadeful, he had struck a root and despaired, his heart bumping up in rhythm, his breath drawing short. That night, he couldn't sleep; he left the shovel stuck upright in the side yard, like his headstone. Over the next ten days, the sleeplessness got worse and finally affected his kidneys, causing him to get up six times in one night to use the bathroom, until by dawn he was as dry as a cracker. He drove out to buy quarts of beer, winding up in the Wal-Mart parking lot, staring out the window of his old car, as if by concentration alone he could conjure someone to take on his burden. And then he had seen the old man pass by his hood, aimless as a string of smoke.

Two hours later, the heat rose up inside Ted, and he looked enviously at a cool can resting on Andy's catfish belly. He tried to remember what beer tasted like and could sense a buzzing tingle on the tip of his tongue, a blue-ice feel in the middle of his mouth. Ted looked hard at his son and again could not place him. Water was building in his little ditch and he put his foot once more on the shovel, pushing it in but not pulling back on the handle. "I need something to drink."

Andy did not open his eyes. "Well, go in the house and get it. But I want you back out here in a minute."

He went into the kitchen and stood by the sink, taking a glass tumblerful of tap water and drinking it down slowly. He rinsed the glass and opened the cabinet to replace it, when his eye caught sight of an inexpensive stack of dishes showing a blue willow design; a little white spark fired off in the darkness of his brain, almost lighting up a memory. Opening another cabinet, he looked for signs of the woman, for this was some woman's kitchen, and he felt he must know her, but everywhere he looked was cluttered and smelled of insecticide and seemed like no place a woman should have. The photograph on the refrigerator of a big female holding a knife meant nothing to him. He ran a thick finger along the shelf where the coffee was stored, looking for something that was not there. It was bare wood, and a splinter poked him lightly in a finger joint. He turned and walked to Andy's room, looking into a closet, touching jeans, coveralls, pullovers that could have been for a man or a woman, and then five dull dresses shoved against the closet wall. He tried to remember the cloth, until from outside came a slurred shout, and he turned for the bedroom door, running a thumb under an overalls strap that bit into his shoulders.

The sun rose high and the old man suffered, his borrowed khaki shirt growing dark on his straining flesh. Every time he completed ten feet of ditch, Andy would move his chair along beside him like a guard. They broke for lunch, and at one-thirty, when they went back into the yard, a thunderstorm fired up ten miles away, and the clouds and breeze saved them from the sun. Andy looked at pictures in magazines, drank, and drew hard on many cigarettes. At three o'clock, the old man looked behind him and saw he was thirty feet from the big parish ditch at the rear of the lot. The thought came to him that there might be another job after this one. The roof, he noticed, needed mending, and he imagined himself straddling a gable in the heat. He sat down on the grass, wondering what would happen to him when he finished. Sometimes he thought that he might not be able to finish, that he was digging his own grave.

The little splinter began to bother him and he looked down at the hurt, remembering the raspy edge of the wooden shelf. He blinked twice. Andy had fallen asleep, a colorful magazine fluttering in his lap. Paper, the old man thought. Shelf paper. His wife would have never put anything in a cabinet without first putting down fresh paper over the wood, and then something came back like images on an out-of-focus movie screen when the audience claps and whistles and roars and the projectionist wakes up and gives his machine a twist, and life, movement, and color unite in a razory picture, and at once he remembered his wife and his children and the venerable 1969 Oldsmobile he had driven to the discount store. Etienne LeBlanc gave a little cry, stood up, and looked around at the alien yard and the squat house with the curling roof shingles, remembering everything that ever happened to him in a shoveled-apart sequence, even the time he had come back to the world standing in a cornfield in Texas, or on a Ferris wheel in Baton Rouge, or in the cabin of a shrimp boat off Point au Fer in the Gulf.

He glanced at the sleeping man and was afraid. Remembering his blood pressure pills, he went into the house to find them in his familiar clothes. He looked around the mildew-haunted house, which was unlike the airy cypress home place he still owned down in St. Mary Parish, a big-windowed farmhouse hung with rafts of family photographs. He examined a barren hallway. This place was a closed-up closet of empty walls and wilted drapes, and he wondered what kind of people owned no images of their kin. Andy and his wife were like visitors from another planet, marooned, childless beings enduring their solitude. In the kitchen, he put his hand where the phone used to be, recalling his son's number. He looked out through the screen door to where a fat, bald man slouched asleep in a litter of shiny cans and curling magazines, a wreck of a man, who'd built neither mind nor body, nor soul. He saw the swampy yard, the broken lawn mower, the muddy, splintered rakes and tools scattered in the carport, more ruined than the hundred-year-old implements in his abandoned barn down in the cane fields. He saw ninety yards of shallow ditch. He pushed the screen door out. Something in his blood drew him into the yard.

His shadow fell over the sleeping man as he studied his yellow skin and pasty skull, the thin-haired, overflowing softness of him as he sat off to one side in the aluminum chair, a naked woman frowning in fear in his lap. Etienne LeBlanc held the shovel horizontally with both hands, thinking that he could hit him once in the head for punishment and leave him stunned on the grass and rolling in his rabid magazines while he walked somewhere to call the police, that Andy might learn something at last from a bang on the head. And who would blame an old man for doing such a thing? Here was a criminal, though not an able or very smart one, and such people generally took the heaviest blows of life. His spotted hands tightened on the hickory handle.

Then he again scanned the house and yard, which would never be worth looking at from the road, would never change for the better because the very earth under it all was totally worthless, a boot-sucking, iron-fouled claypan good only for ruining the play clothes of children. He thought of the black soil of his farm, his wife in the field, the wife who had died on his arm a year before as they were buying tomato plants. Looking toward the road, he thought how far away he was from anyone who knew him. Returning to the end of the little ditch, he sank the shovel deep, put up his hands, and pulled sharply, the blade answering with a loud suck of mud that raised one of Andy's eyelids.

"Get on it, Ted," he said, stirring in the chair, unfocused and dizzy and sick. The old man had done two feet before Andy looked up at him and straightened his back at what he saw in his eyes. "What you looking at, you old shit?"

Etienne LeBlanc sank the blade behind a four-inch collar of mud. "Nothing, son. Not a thing."

"You got to finish this evening. Sometimes she comes back early, maybe even tomorrow afternoon." He sat up with the difficulty of an invalid in a nursing home, looking around the base of his chair for something to drink, a magazine falling off his lap into the seedy grass. "Speed up if you know what's good for you."

For the next two hours, the old man paced himself, throwing the dirt into a straight, watery mound on the right side of the hole, looking behind him to gauge the time. Andy got another six-pack from the house and once more drank himself to sleep. Around suppertime, the old man walked over and nudged the folding chair.

"Wake up." He put his hand on a pasty arm.

"What?" The eyes opened like a sick hound's.

"I'm fixing to make the last cut." Etienne motioned toward the ditch. "Thought you might want to see that." They walked to the rear of the lot, where the old man inserted the shovel sideways to the channel and pulled up a big wedge, the water cutting through and widening out the last foot of ditch, dumping down two feet into the bigger run.

Andy looked back to the middle of his yard. "Maybe this will help the damned bug problem," he said, putting his face close to the old man's. "Mosquitoes drive her nuts."

Etienne LeBlanc saw the strange nose, which had been broken before birth, and looked away with a jerk of the head.

The next morning, it was not yet first light when the old man woke to a noise in his room. Someone kicked the mattress lightly. "Come on," a voice said. "We're going for a ride."

He did not like the sound of the statement, but he got up and put on the clothes he had worn at the discount store and followed out to the driveway. He could barely hear the ditch tickle the dark and was afraid. Andy stood close and asked him what he could remember.

"What?"

"You heard me. I've got to know what you remember." The old man made his mind work carefully. "I remember the ditch," he said.

"And what else?"

The old man averted his eyes. "I remember my name."

Andy whistled a single note. "And what is it?"

"Ted Williams." There was a little bit of gray light out on the lawn, and the old man watched Andy try to think.

"Okay," he said at last. "Get in the car. You lay down in the backseat." The old man did as he was told and felt the car start and turn for the road, then turn again, and he hoped that all the turning in his head would not lead him back to a world of meaningless faces and things, hoped that he would not forget to recall, for he knew that the only thing he was was memory.

They had not driven a hundred feet down the lane when a set of bright lights came toward them and Andy began crying out an elaborate string of curses. The old man looked over the seat and saw a pickup truck in the middle of the road. "It's her," Andy said, his voice trembling and high. "Don't talk to her. Let me handle it." It was not quite light enough to see his face, so the old man read his voice and found it vibrating with dread.

The pickup stopped, and in the illumination from the headlights, Etienne saw a woman get out, a big woman whose tight coveralls fit her the way a tarpaulin binds a machine. Her hair was red like armature wire and braided in coppery ropes that fell down over her heavy breasts. Coming to the driver's window, she bent down. She had a big mouth and wide lips. "What's going on, you slimy worm?" Her voice was a cracked cymbal.

Andy tried a smile. "Honey. Hey there. I just decided to get an early—"

She reached in and put a big thumb on his Adam's apple. "You never get up before ten."

"Honest," he whined, the words squirting past his pinched vocal chords.

Her neck stiffened when she saw the old man. "Shut up. Who's this?"

Andy opened his mouth and closed it, opened it again and said with a yodel, "Just an old drinking buddy. I was bringing him home."

She squinted at the old man. "Why you in the backseat?"

Etienne looked into the fat slits of her eyes and remembered a sow that had almost torn off his foot a half century before.

"He told me to sit back here."

She straightened up and backed away from the car. "All right, get out. Some kind of bullshit is going on here." The old man did as she asked, and in the gray light she looked him over, sniffing derisively. "Who the hell are you?"

He tried to think of something to say, wondering what would cause the least damage. He thought down into his veins for an answer, but his mind began to capsize like an overburdened skiff. "I'm his father," he said at last. "I live with him."

Her big head rolled sideways like a dog's. "Who told you that?"

"I'm his father," he said again.

She put a paw on his shoulder and drew him in. He could smell beer on her sour breath. "Let me guess. Your memory ain't so hot, right? He found you a couple blocks from a nursing home, hey? You know, he tried this stuff before." The glance she threw her husband was horrible to see. "Here, let me look at you." She pulled him into the glare of the headlights and noticed his pants. "How'd you get this mud on you, pops?" She showed her big square teeth when she asked the question.

"I was digging a ditch," he said. Her broad face tightened, the meat on her skull turning to veiny marble. At once, she walked back to her truck and pulled from the bed a shorthandled square-point shovel. When Andy saw what she had, he struggled from behind the steering wheel, got out, and tried to run, but she was on him in a second. The old man winced as he heard the dull ring of the shovel blade and saw Andy go down in a skitter of gravel at the rear of the car. She hit him again with a halfhearted swing. Andy cried out, "Ahhhhh don't, don't," but his wife screamed back and gave him the corner of the shovel right on a rib.

"You gummy little turd with eyes," she said, giving him another dig with the shovel. "I asked you to do one thing for me on your own, one numbskull job," she said, emphasizing the word *job* with a slap of the shovel back on his belly, "and you kidnap some old bastard who doesn't know who he is and get him to do it for you."

"Please," Andy cried, raising up a hand on which one finger angled off crazily.

"Look at him, you moron," she shrieked. "He's a hundred son-of-a-bitching years old. If he had died, we'd a gone to jail for good." She dropped the shovel and picked him up by the armpits, slamming him down on the car's trunk, giving him open-handed slaps like a gangster in a cheap movie.

The old man looked down the gravel road to where it brightened in the distance. He tried not to hear the ugly noises behind him. He tried to think of town and his family, but when Andy's cries began to fracture like an animal's caught in a steel-jawed trap, he walked around the back of the car and pulled hard on the woman's wrist. "You're going to kill him," he scolded, shaking her arm. "What's wrong with you?"

She straightened up slowly and put both hands on his shirt. "Nothing is wrong with me," she raged, pushing him away. She seemed ready to come after him, but when she reached out again, a blade of metal gonged down on her head, her eye sockets flashed white, and she collapsed in a spray of gravel. Andy lowered the shovel and leaned on the handle. Then he spat blood and fell down on one knee.

"Aw, God," he wheezed.

The old man backed away from the two figures panting in the dust, the sound of the iron ringing against the woman's head already forming a white scar in his brain. He looked down the lane and saw her idling pickup. In a minute, he was in the truck, backing away in a cloud of rock dust to a wide spot in the road, where he swung around for town, glancing in the rearview mirror at a limping figure waving wide a garden tool. He drove fast out of the sorry countryside, gained the blacktop, and sped up. At a paintless crossroads store, he stopped, and his mind floated over points of the compass. His hands moved left before his brain told them to, and memory turned the truck. In fifteen minutes, he saw, at the edge of town, the cinder-block plinth of the discount center. Soon, the gray side of the building loomed above him, and he slid out of the woman's truck, walking around to the front of the store without knowing why, just that it was proper to complete some type of circle. The bottom of the sun cleared the horizon-making parking lot, and he saw two cars, his old wine-colored Oldsmobile and, next to it, like an embryonic version of the same vehicle, an anonymous modern sedan. Etienne LeBlanc shuffled across the asphalt lake, breathing hard, and there he saw a young man asleep behind the steering wheel in the smaller car. He leaned over him and studied his face, saw the LeBlanc nose, reached in at last and traced the round-topped ears of his wife. He knew him, and his mind closed like a fist on this grandson and everything else, even his wife fading in his arms, even the stunned scowl of the copper-haired woman as she was hammered into the gravel. As if memory could be a decision, he accepted it all, knowing now that the only thing worse than reliving nightmares until the day he died was enduring a life full of strangers. He closed his eyes and called on the old farm in his head to stay where it was, remembered its cypress house, its flat and misty lake of sugarcane keeping the impressions of a morning wind.

# DANIEL WOODRELL, *Winter's Bone*

A native of the Missouri Ozarks, Daniel Woodrell was born in 1953 and grew up near St. Louis and Kansas City. After dropping out of high school to join the marines, Woodrell hitchhiked around America, working at various odd jobs before studying at the University of Kansas and later at the Iowa Writers' Workshop, where he received his master of fine arts degree. Since his first book, *Under the Bright Lights,* appeared in 1986, he has published several more novels, including *Give Us a Kiss: A Country Noir* (1996), *Tomato Red* (1998), *The Death of Sweet Mister* (2001), and *Woe to Live On* (1987), which was made into the film *Ride with the Devil* in 1999. His novel *Winter's Bone* (2006) was nominated for the *Los Angeles Times* Book Prize for Fiction and made into an Oscar-nominated film in 2009. His first story collection, *The Outlaw Album,* was published in 2011. A self-described "full-tilt freelancer," Woodrell lives in the small Ozark town of West Plains, Missouri, with his wife, the novelist Katie Estill.[1]

"Woodrell's Ozarks," writes Bill Brashler, "are cut as clearly as Flannery O'Connor's Georgia and packed with characters just as volatile and proud and unpredictable."[2] In this chapter from *Winter's Bone,* sixteen-year-old Ree Dolly seeks out her outlaw kin as she searches the hills and hollows for her missing father.

> There's a whole vein of American fiction that never got the above-board recognition but that you just can't kill with a stick. It keeps coming back and back. Guys like Horace McCoy (*They Shoot Horses, Don't They?*) and Edward Anderson (*Thieves Like Us*), guys I feel a real kinship with. You can call it social realism, or you can call it noir, or something else altogether that I haven't thought of.[3]

FROM *WINTER'S BONE*

She'd start with Uncle Teardrop, though Uncle Teardrop scared her. He lived three miles down the creek but she walked on the railroad tracks. Snow covered the tracks and made humps over the rails and the twin humps guided her. She broke her own trail through the snow and booted the miles from her path. The morning sky was gray and crouching, the wind had snap and drew water to her eyes. She wore a green hooded sweatshirt and Mamaw's black coat. Ree nearly always wore a dress or skirt, but with combat boots, and the skirt this day was a bluish plaid. Her knees kicked free of the plaid when she threw her long legs forward and stomped the snow.

The world seemed huddled and hushed and her crunching steps cracked loud as ax whacks. As she crunched past houses built on yon slopes yard dogs barked faintly from under porches but none came into the cold to make a run at her and flash teeth. Smoke poured from every chimney and was promptly flattened east by the wind. There was deer sign trod below trestles that stood over the creek and thin ice clung around rocks in the shallows. Where the creek forked she left the tracks and walked uphill through deeper snow beside an old pioneer fencerow made of piled stones.

Uncle Teardrop's place sat beyond one daunting ridge and up a narrow draw. The house had been built small but extra bedrooms and box windows and other ideas had been added on by different residents who'd had hammers and leftover wood. There always seemed to be walls covered by black tarpaper standing alone for months and months waiting for more walls and a roof to come along and complete a room. Stovepipes angled from the house on every which side.

Three dogs that were a mess of hunting breeds lived under the big screened deck. Ree had known them since they were pups and called out as she reached the yard and they came to sniff her nethers and wag welcome. They barked, jumped, and slapped tongues at her until Victoria opened the main door.

She said, "Somebody dead?"

"Not that I heard."

"You walked over in this nasty crud just for a visit, dear? You must be purty awful lonely."

"I'm lookin' for Dad. I got to run him down, and quick."

That certain women who did not seem desperate or crazy could be so deeply attracted to Uncle Teardrop confused and frightened Ree. He was a nightmare to look at but he'd torn through a fistful of appealing wives. Victoria had once been number three and was now number five. She was a tall blunt-boned woman made lush in her sections with long auburn hair she usually wore rolled up into a heavy wobbly bun. She had a closet that held no jeans or slacks but was stuffed with dresses old and new and most of Ree's things had first been worn by her. In winter Victoria was given to reading gardening books and seed catalogues and at spring planting she disdained the commonplace Big Boy or Early Girl tomatoes in favor of exotic international strains she got by mail and doted on and always tasted like a mouthful of far pretty lands.

"Well, then, come on in, kiddo. Shake off the chill. Jessup ain't here, but coffee's hot." Victoria held the door for Ree. Victoria smelled wonderful up close, like she always did, some scent she had that when smelled went into the blood like dope and left you near woozy. She looked good and smelled good and Ree favored her over any other Dolly woman but Mom. "Teardrop mightn't be up yet, so let's keep it down 'til he is."

They sat at the eating table. A skylight had been cut into the ceiling and leaked rainwater from the low corners sometimes but helped a lot to brighten the room. Ree could see through the house to the front door and over to the rear door and noted that a long gun stood ready beside both. A silver pistol and clip rested in a nut bowl on the lazy Susan centered upon the table. Beside the pistol there was a big bag of pot and a pretty big bag of crank.

Victoria said, "Ree, I forget—you take it black, or with cream?"

"With cream when there is any."

"Ain't that the truth."

They hunched over the table and sipped. A cuckoo clock chirped nine times. Record albums lined along the floor went nearly the complete length of a wall. There was a fancy-looking sound system on a bookshelf, plus a four-foot rack of CDs. The furniture was mostly wooden, country-type stuff. One piece was a big round cushioned chair on a sapling frame that you sat in the exact middle of like you were squatted inside a bloomed flower. Swirly-patterned lavender cloth from Arabia was tacked to a wall as decoration.

"The law came by. That Baskin one. He said if Dad don't show for his court day next week we got to move out of the house. Dad signed it over to go his bond. They'll take the place from us. And the timber acres, too. Victoria, I *really, really* got to run Dad to ground and get him to show."

Uncle Teardrop stood stretching in the bedroom doorway and said, "You ought not do that." He wore a white T-shirt and plum sweatpants stuffed into untied boots. He was a nudge over six feet tall but had fidgeted his weight way down and become all muscle wires and bone knobs with a sunken belly. "Don't go runnin' after Jessup." Teardrop sat at the table. "Coffee." He rapped his fingers to the tabletop and made a hoofbeat rhythm. "What's this shit all about, anyhow?"

"I got to find Dad'n make sure he shows in court."

"That's a man's personal choice, little girl. That's not somethin' you oughta be buttin' your smarty nose into. Show or don't show, that choice is up to the one that's goin' to jail to make. Not you."

Uncle Teardrop was Jessup's elder and had been a crank chef longer but he'd had a lab go wrong and it had eaten the left ear off his head and burned a savage melted scar down his neck to the middle of his back. There wasn't enough ear nub remaining to hang sunglasses on. The hair around the ear was gone, too, and the scar on his neck showed above his collar. Three blue teardrops done in jailhouse ink fell in a row from the corner of the eye on his scarred side. Folks said the teardrops meant he'd three times done grisly prison deeds that needed doing but didn't need to be gabbed about. They said the teardrops told you everything you had to know about the man and the lost ear just repeated it. He generally tried to sit with his melted side to the wall.

Ree said, "Come on, you know where he's at, don't you?"

"And where a man's at ain't necessarily for you to know, neither."

"But, do you—"

"Ain't seen him."

Teardrop stared at Ree with a flat expression of finality and Victoria jumped in between them, asking, "How's your mom?"

Ree tried to hold Teardrop's gaze but blinked uncontrollably. It was like staring at something fanged and coiled from too close without a stick in hand.

"Not better."

"And the boys?"

Ree broke and looked down, scared and slumping.

"A little pindlin' but not pukey sick," she said. She looked to her lap and her clenched hands and drove her fingernails into her palms, gouging fiercely, raising pink crescents on her milk skin, then turned toward Uncle Teardrop and leaned desperately his way. "Could he be runnin' with Little Arthur and them again? You think? That bunch from Hawkfall? Should I look for him around there?"

Teardrop raised his hand and drew it back to smack her and let fly but diverted the smacking hand inches from Ree's face to the nut bowl. His fingers dove rattling into the nuts, beneath the silver pistol, and lifted it from the lazy Susan. He bounced the weapon on his flat palm as though judging the weight with his hand for a scale, sighed, then ran a finger gently along the barrel to brush away grains of salt.

"Don't you, nor nobody else, neither, *ever* go down around Hawkfall askin' them people shit about stuff they ain't *offerin'* to talk about. That's a real good way to end up et by hogs, or wishin' you was. You ain't no silly-assed town girl. You know better'n that foolishness."

"But we're all related, ain't we?"

"Our relations get watered kinda thin between this valley here and Hawkfall. It's better'n bein' a foreigner or town people, but it ain't nowhere near the same as bein' *from* Hawkfall."

Victoria said, "You know all those people down there, Teardrop. You could ask."

"Shut up."

"I just mean, none of them's goin' to be in a great big hurry to tangle with you, neither. If Jessup's over there, Ree needs to see him. *Bad.*"

"I said shut up once already, with my mouth."

Ree felt bogged and forlorn, doomed to a spreading swamp of hateful obligations. There would be no ready fix or answer or help. She felt like crying but wouldn't. She could be beat with a garden rake and never cry and had proved that twice before Mamaw saw an unsmiling angel pointing from the treetops at dusk and quit the bottle. She would never cry where her tears might be seen and counted against her. "Jesus-fuckin'-Christ, Dad's your *only* little brother!"

"You think I forgot that?" He grabbed the clip and slammed it into the pistol, then ejected it and tossed pistol and clip back into the nut bowl. He made a fist with his right hand and rubbed it with his left. "Jessup'n me run together for nigh on forty years—but I *don't know* where he's at, and I ain't goin' to go around askin' after him, neither."

Ree knew better than to say another word, but was going to anyhow, when Victoria grabbed her hand and held it, squeezed, then said, "Now, *when is it* you was tellin' me you'll be old enough to join the army?"

"Next birthday."

"Then you'll be off from here?"

"I hope."

"Good for you. Good deal. But, what'll the boys and—"

Teardrop lurched from his chair and snatched Ree by the hair and pulled her head hard his way and yanked back so her throat was bared and her face pointed up. He ran his eyes into her like a serpent down a hole, made her feel his slither in her heart and guts, made her tremble. He jerked her head one way and another, then pressed a hand around her windpipe and held her still. He leaned his face to hers from above and nuzzled his melt against her cheek, nuzzled up and down, then slid his lips to her forehead, kissed her once and let go.

He picked up the crank bag from the lazy Susan. He held it toward the skylight and shook the bag while looking closely at the shifting powder. He carried the bag toward the bedroom and Victoria motioned Ree to sit still, then slowly followed him. She pulled the door shut and whispered something. A talk with two voices started low and calm but soon one voice raised alone and spoke several tart muffled sentences. Ree could not follow any words through the wall. There was a lull of silence more uncomfortable than the tart sentences had been. Victoria came back, head lowered, blowing her nose into a pale blue tissue.

"Teardrop says you best keep your ass real close to the willows, dear." She dropped fifty dollars in tens on the tabletop and fanned the bills. "He hopes this helps. Want me to roll a doobie for your walk?"

# RON RASH, "Speckled Trout"

Born in 1954, Appalachian native Ron Rash grew up in Boiling Springs, North Carolina. After graduating from Gardner-Webb College and Clemson University, Rash taught English for several years before publishing his first story collection, *The Night the New Jesus Fell to Earth and Other Stories from Cliffside, North Carolina,* in 1994. Over the next decade he published two books of poetry, *Eureka Mill* (1998) and *Among the Believers* (2000), and another story collection, *Casualties* (2000). In 2002 Rash published his third poetry collection, *Raising the Dead,* and his first novel, *One Foot in Eden,* which was awarded the Novello Literary Award and the Appalachian Book of the Year Award. Since then, Rash has published four more novels, *Saints at the River* (2004), *The World Made Straight* (2006), *Serena* (2008), and *The Cove* (2012), as well as the story collections *Chemistry and Other Stories* (2007) and *Burning Bright,* which won the Frank O'Connor Short Story Award in 2010. Rash is currently the Parris Distinguished Professor in Appalachian Cultural Studies at Western Carolina University.

Like his fellow Appalachian Robert Morgan, Ron Rash is an accomplished poet, though in recent years he has made a name for himself as writer of fiction. In "Speckled Trout," which won an O. Henry Prize in 2005, Rash follows the fortunes of a sixteen-year-old boy who stumbles upon a neighbor's secret and decides to go into business for himself.

> In a sense, as a southern writer you are almost always fighting certain stereotypes. There are certain expectations of a southern novel. There's going to be a crazy aunt in the attic and probably a couple of bodies in the basement, and you always have these kind of bizarre characters. But at the same time,

a lot of that's true. . . . One thing I am pretty much convinced of is that we are all kind of crazy in the world—some groups hide it better than others, maybe. Southerners seem to revel in their oddness at times.[1]

### "SPECKLED TROUT"

Lanny came upon the marijuana plants while fishing Caney Creek. It was a Saturday, and after helping his father sucker tobacco all morning, he'd had the truck and the rest of the afternoon and evening for himself. He'd changed into his fishing clothes and driven the three miles of dirt road to the French Broad. He drove fast, the rod and reel clattering side to side in the truck bed and clouds of red dust rising in his wake. He had the windows down and if the radio worked he'd have had it blasting. The driver's license in his billfold was six months old but only in the last month had his daddy let him drive the truck by himself.

He parked by the bridge and walked upriver toward where Caney Creek entered. Afternoon sunlight slanted over Brushy Mountain and tinged the water the deep gold of cured tobacco. A big fish leaped in the shallows, but Lanny's spinning rod was broken down and even if it hadn't been he would not have bothered to make a cast. There was nothing in the river he could sell, only stocked rainbows and browns, knottyheads, and catfish. The men who fished the river were mostly old men who stayed in one place for hours, motionless as the stumps and rocks they sat on. Lanny liked to keep moving, and he fished where even the younger fishermen wouldn't go.

In forty minutes he was half a mile up Caney Creek, the spinning rod still broken down. The gorge narrowed to a thirty-foot wall of water and rock, below it the deepest pool on the creek. This was the place where everyone else turned back. Lanny waded through waist-high water to reach the left side of the waterfall. Then he began climbing, using juts and fissures in the rock for leverage and resting places. When he got to the top he put the rod together and tied a gold Panther Martin on the line.

The only fish this far up were what fishing magazines called brook trout, though Lanny had never heard Old Man Jenkins or anyone else call them anything other than speckled trout. Jenkins swore they tasted better than any brown or rainbow and paid Lanny fifty cents apiece no matter how small they were. Old Man Jenkins ate them head and all, like sardines.

Mountain laurel slapped Lanny's face and arms, and he scraped his hands and elbows climbing straight up rocks there was no other way around. The only path was water now. He thought of his daddy back at the farmhouse and smiled to himself. The old man had told him never to fish a place like this alone, because a broken leg or a rattlesnake bite could get you stone dead before anyone found you. That was near about the only kind of talk he got anymore from the old man, Lanny thought to himself as he tested his knot, always being lectured about something—how fast he drove, who he hung out with—like he was eight years old instead of sixteen, like the old man himself hadn't raised all sorts of hell when he was young.

The only places with enough water to hold fish were the pools, some no bigger than a wash bucket. Lanny flicked the spinner into these pools and in every third or fourth one a small, orange-finned trout came flopping out onto the bank, the spinner's treble hook snagged in its mouth. Lanny would slap the speckled's head against a rock and feel the fish shudder in his hand and die. If he missed a strike, he cast again into the same pool. Unlike browns and rainbows, the speckleds would hit twice, occasionally even three times. Old Man Jenkins had told Lanny when he was a boy most every stream in the county was thick with speckleds, but they'd been too easy caught and soon enough fished out, which was why now you had to go to the back of beyond to find them.

Lanny already had eight fish in his creel when he passed the No Trespassing sign nailed in an oak tree. The sign was scabbed with rust like the ten-year-old car tag on his granddaddy's barn, and he paid no more attention to the sign than when he'd first seen it a month ago. He knew he was on Toomey land, and he knew the stories. How Linwood Toomey once used his thumb to gouge a man's eye out in a bar fight and another time opened a man's face from ear to mouth with a broken beer bottle. Stories about events Lanny's daddy had witnessed before, as his daddy put it, he'd got straight with the Lord. But Lanny had heard other things. About how Linwood Toomey and his son were too lazy and hard drinking to hold steady jobs. Too lazy and drunk to walk the quarter mile from their farmhouse to look for trespassers, Lanny figured.

He waded on upstream, going farther than he'd ever been. He caught more speckleds, and soon ten dollars' worth bulged in his creel. Enough money for gas, maybe even a couple of bootleg beers, he told himself, and though it wasn't near the money he'd been making at the Pay-Lo bagging groceries, at least he could do this alone and not have to deal with some old bitch of a store manager with nothing better to do than watch his every move, then fire him just because he was late a few times.

He came to where the creek forked and that was where he saw a sudden high greening a few yards above him on the left. He left the water and climbed the bank to make sure it was what he thought it was. The plants were staked like tomatoes and set in rows the same way as tobacco or corn. He knew they were worth money, a lot of money, because Lanny knew how much his friend Shank paid for an ounce of pot and this wasn't just ounces but maybe pounds.

He heard something behind him and turned, ready to drop the rod and reel and make a run for it. On the other side of the creek, a gray squirrel scrambled up a blackjack oak. Lanny told himself that there was no reason to get all jumpy, that nobody would have seen him coming up the creek.

He let his eyes scan what lay beyond the plants. He didn't see anything moving, not even a cow or chicken. Nothing but some open ground and then a stand of trees. He rubbed a pot leaf between his finger and thumb, and it felt like money to him, more money than he'd make at the Pay-Lo. He looked around one more time before he took the knife from its sheath and cut down five plants. The stalks had a twiny toughness like rope.

That was the easy part. Dragging the stalks a mile down the creek was a lot harder, especially while trying to keep the leaves and buds from being stripped off. When he got to the river he hid the plants in the underbrush and walked the trail to make sure no one was fishing. Then he carried the plants to the road edge, stashed them in the ditch, and got the truck. He emptied the creel into the ditch, the trout stiff and glaze-eyed. He wouldn't be delivering Old Man Jenkins any speckleds this evening.

Lanny drove back home with the plants hidden under willow branches and potato sacks. He planned to stay only long enough to get a shower and put on some clean clothes, but as he walked through the front room his father looked up from the TV.

"We ain't ate yet."

"I'll get something in town," Lanny said.

"No, your momma's fixing supper right now, and she's set the table for three."

"I ain't got time. Shank is expecting me."

"You can make time, boy. Or I might take a notion to go somewhere in that truck myself this evening."

It was seven-thirty before Lanny drove into the Hardee's parking lot and parked beside Shank's battered Camaro. He got out of the truck and walked over to Shank's window.

"You ain't going to believe what I got in back of the truck."

Shank grinned.

"It ain't that old prune-faced bitch that fired you, is it?"

"No, this is worth something."

Shank got out of the Camaro and walked around to the truck bed with Lanny. Lanny looked to see if anyone was watching, then lifted a sack so Shank could see one of the stalks.

"I got five of 'em."

"Shit fire, boy. Where'd that come from?"

"Found it when I was fishing."

Shank pulled the sack back farther.

"I need to start doing my fishing with you. It's clear I been going to the wrong places."

A car drove up to the drive-through and Shank pulled the sack back over the plants.

"What you planning to do with it?"

"Make some money, if I can figure out who'll buy it."

"Leonard will, I bet."

"He don't know me, though. I ain't one of his potheads."

"Well, I am," Shank said. "Let me lock my car and we'll go pay him a visit."

"How about we go over to Dink's first and get some beer."

"Leonard's got beer. His is cheaper and it ain't piss-warm like what we got at Dink's last time."

They drove out of Marshall, following 221 toward Mars Hill. The carburetor knocked and popped as the pickup struggled up Jenkins Mountain. Soon enough Lanny figured he'd have money for a kit, maybe even enough to buy a whole new carburetor.

"You in for a treat, meeting Leonard," Shank said. "They ain't another like him, leastways in this county."

"I heard tell he was a lawyer once."

"Naw, he just went to law school a few months. They kicked his ass out because he was stoned all the time."

After a mile they turned off the blacktop and onto a dirt road. On both sides what had once been pasture was now thick with blackjack oak and briars. They passed a deserted farmhouse and turned onto another road no better than a logging trail.

The woods opened into a small meadow, at the center a battered green and white trailer, its windows painted black. On one side of the trailer a satellite dish sprouted like an enormous mushroom, on the other side a Jeep Cherokee, its back fender crumpled. Two Dobermans scrambled out from under the trailer, barking as they raced toward the truck. They leaped at Lanny's window, their claws raking the door as he quickly rolled up the window.

The trailer door opened and a man with a gray ponytail and wearing only a pair of khaki shorts stepped onto the cinder-block steps. He yelled at the dogs and when that did no good he came out to the truck and kicked at them until they slunk back from where they had emerged.

Lanny looked at a man who wasn't any taller than himself and looked to outweigh him only because of a stomach that sagged over the front of his shorts like a half-deflated balloon.

"That's Leonard?"

"Yeah. The one and only."

Leonard walked over to Shank's window.

"I got nothing but beer and a few nickel bags. Supplies are going to be low until people start to harvest."

"Well, we likely come at a good time then." Shank turned to Lanny. "Let's show Leonard what you brought him."

Lanny got out and pulled back the branches and potato sacks.

"Where'd you get that from?" Leonard asked.

"Found it," Lanny said.

"Found it, did you. And you figured finders keepers."

"Yeah," said Lanny.

Leonard let his fingers brush some of the leaves.

"Looks like you dragged it through every briar patch and laurel slick between here and the county line."

"There's plenty of buds left on it," Shank said.

"What you give me for it?" Lanny asked.

Leonard lifted each stalk, looking at it the same way Lanny had seen buyers look at tobacco.

"Fifty dollars."

"You trying to cheat me," Lanny said. "I'll find somebody else to buy it."

As soon as he spoke Lanny wished he hadn't, because he'd heard from more than one person that Leonard Hamby was a man you didn't want to get on the wrong side of. He was about to say that he reckoned fifty dollars would be fine but Leonard spoke first.

"You may have an exalted view of your entrepreneurial abilities," Leonard said.

Lanny didn't understand all the words but he understood the tone. It was smart-ass but it wasn't angry.

"I'll give you sixty dollars, and I'll double that if you bring me some that doesn't look like it's been run through a hay baler. Plus I got some cold beers inside. My treat."

"Okay," Lanny said, surprised at Leonard but more surprised at himself, how tough he'd sounded. He tried not to smile as he thought how when he got back to Marshall he'd be able to tell his friends he'd called Leonard Hamby a cheater to his face and Leonard hadn't done a damn thing about it but offer more money and free beer.

Leonard took a money clip from his front pocket and peeled off three twenties and handed them to Lanny. Leonard nodded toward the meadow's far corner.

"Put them over there next to my tomatoes. Then come inside if you got a notion to."

Lanny and Shank carried the plants through the knee-high grass and laid them next to the tomatoes. As they approached the trailer, Lanny watched where the Dobermans had vanished under it. He didn't lift his eyes until he reached the steps.

Inside, Lanny's vision took a few moments to adjust because the only light came from a TV screen. Strings of unlit Christmas lights ran across the walls and over door eaves like bad wiring. A dusty couch slouched against the back wall. In the corner Leonard sat in a fake-leather recliner patched with black electrician's tape. Except for a stereo system, the rest of the room was shelves filled with books and CDs. Music was playing, music that didn't have any guitars or words.

"Have a seat," Leonard said and nodded at the couch.

A woman stood in the foyer between the living room and kitchen. She was a tall, bony woman, and the cutoff jeans and halter top she wore had little flesh to hold them up. She'd gotten a bad sunburn and there were pink patches on her skin where she'd peeled. To Lanny she mostly looked wormy and mangy, like some stray dog around a garbage dump. Except for her eyes. They were a deep blue, like a jaybird's feathers. If you could just keep looking into her eyes, she'd be a pretty woman, Lanny told himself.

"How about getting these boys a couple of beers, Wendy," Leonard said.

"Get them your ownself," the woman said and disappeared into the back of the trailer.

Leonard shook his head but said nothing as he got up. He brought back two longneck Budweisers and a sandwich bag filled with pot and some rolling papers.

He handed the beers to Shank and Lanny and sat down. Lanny was thirsty, and he drank quickly as he watched Leonard carefully shake some pot out of the Baggie and onto the paper. Leonard licked the paper and twisted both ends, then lit it.

The orange tip brightened as Leonard drew the smoke in. He handed the joint to Shank, who drew on it as well and handed it back.

"What about your buddy?"

"He don't smoke pot. Scared his daddy would find out and beat the tar out of him."

"That ain't so," Lanny said. "I just like a beer buzz better."

Lanny lifted the bottle to his lips and drank until the bottle was empty.

"I'd like me another one."

"Quite the drinker, aren't you," Leonard said. "Just make sure you don't overdo it. I don't want you passed out and pissing on my couch."

"I ain't gonna piss on your couch."

Leonard took another drag off the joint and passed it back to Shank.

"They're in the refrigerator," Leonard said. "You can get one easy as I can."

Lanny stood up and for a moment felt off plumb, maybe because he'd drunk the beer so fast. When the world steadied he got the beer and sat back down on the couch. He looked at the TV, some kind of western but without the sound on he couldn't tell what was happening. He drank the second beer quick as the first while Shank and Leonard finished smoking the pot.

Shank had his eyes closed.

"Man, I'm feeling good," he said.

Lanny studied Leonard who sat in the recliner, trying to figure out what it was that made Leonard Hamby a man you didn't want to mess with. Leonard looked soft, Lanny thought, white and soft like bread dough. Just because a man had a couple of mean dogs didn't make him such a badass, he told himself. He thought about his own daddy and Linwood Toomey, big men you could look at and tell right away you'd not want to cross them. Lanny wondered if anyone would ever call him a badass and wished again that he didn't take after his mother, who was short and thin-boned.

"What's this shit you're listening to, Leonard?" Lanny said.

"It's called *Appalachian Spring*. It's by Copland."

"Ain't never heard of them."

Leonard looked amused.

"Are you sure? They used to be the warm-up act for Lynyrd Skynyrd."

"I don't believe that."

"No matter. Copland is an acquired taste, and I don't anticipate your listening to a classical music station any time in the future."

Lanny knew Leonard was putting him down, talking over him like he was stupid, and it made him think of his teachers at the high school, teachers who used smart-ass words against him when he gave them trouble because they were too old and scared to try anything else. He got up and made his way to the refrigerator, damned if he was going to ask permission. He got the beer out and opened the top but didn't go back to the couch. He went down the hallway to find the bathroom.

The bedroom door was open, and he could see the woman sitting on the bed reading a magazine. He pissed and then walked into the bedroom and stood next to her.

The woman laid down the magazine.

"What do you want?"

Lanny grinned.

"What you offering?"

Even buzzed up with beer, he knew it was a stupid thing to say. It seemed to him that ever since he'd got to Leonard's his mouth had been a faucet he couldn't shut off.

The woman's blue eyes stared at him like he was nothing more than a sack of shit.

"I ain't offering you anything," she said. "Even if I was, a little peckerhead like you wouldn't know what to do with it."

The woman looked toward the door.

"Leonard," she shouted.

Leonard appeared at the doorway.

"It's past time to get your Cub Scout meeting over."

Leonard nodded at Lanny.

"I believe you boys have overstayed your welcome."

"I was getting ready to leave anyhow," Lanny said. He turned toward the door and the beer slipped from his hand and spilled on the bed.

"Nothing but a little peckerhead," the woman said.

In a few moments he and Shank were outside. The evening sun glowed in the treetop like a snagged orange balloon. The first lightning bugs rode over the grass as though carried on an invisible current.

"You get more plants, come again," Leonard said and closed the trailer door.

Lanny went back the next Saturday, two burlap sacks stuffed into his belt. After he'd been fired from the Pay-Lo, he'd about given up hope on earning enough money for his own truck, but now things had changed. Now he had what was pretty damn near a money tree and all he had to do was get its leaves and buds to Leonard Hamby. He climbed up the waterfall, the trip easier without a creel and rod. Once he passed the No Trespassing sign, he moved slower, quieter. I bet Linwood Toomey didn't even plant it, Lanny told himself. I bet

it was somebody who figured the Toomeys were too sorry to notice pot growing on their land.

When he came close to where the plants were, he crawled up the bank,
slowly raising his head like a soldier in a trench. He scanned the tree line across
the field and saw no one. He told himself even if someone hid in the trees, they
could never get across the field to catch him before he was long gone down the
creek.

Lanny cut the stalks just below the last leaves. Six plants filled the sacks. He
thought about cutting more, taking what he had to the truck and coming back
to get the rest, but he figured that was too risky. He made his way back down
the creek. He didn't see anyone on the river trail, but if he had he'd have said it
was poke shoots in the sacks if they'd asked.

When he drove up to the trailer, Leonard was watering the tomatoes with
a hose. Leonard cut off the water and herded the Dobermans away from the
truck. Lanny got out and walked around to the truck bed.

"How come you grow your own tomatoes but not your own pot?"

"Because I'm a low-risk kind of guy. Since they've started using the planes
and helicopters, it's gotten too chancy unless you have a place way back in some
hollow."

One of the Dobermans growled from beneath the trailer but did not show
its face.

"Where's your partner?"

"I don't need no partner," Lanny said. He lifted the sacks from the truck
bed and emptied them onto the ground between him and Leonard.

"That's one hundred and twenty dollars' worth," Lanny said.

Leonard stepped closer and studied the plants.

"Fair is fair," he said and pulled the money clip from his pocket. He handed
Lanny five twenty-dollar bills and four fives.

Lanny crumpled the bills in his fist and stuffed them into his pocket, but
he did not get back in the truck.

"What?" Leonard finally said.

"I figured you to ask me in for a beer."

"I don't think so. I don't much want to play host this afternoon."

"You don't think I'm good enough to set foot in that roachy old trailer of
yours."

Leonard looked at Lanny and smiled.

"Boy, you remind me of a banty rooster, strutting around not afraid of anything, puffing your feathers out anytime anyone looks at you wrong. You think
you're a genuine, hard-core badass, don't you?"

"I ain't afraid of you, if that's what you're getting at. If your own woman ain't scared of you, why should I be?"

Leonard looked at the money clip. He tilted it in his hand until the sun caught the metal and a bright flash hit Lanny in the face. Lanny jerked his head away from the glare.

Leonard laughed and put the money clip back in his pocket.

"After the world has its way with you a few years, it'll knock some of the strut out of you. If you live that long."

"I ain't wanting your advice," Lanny said. "I just want some beer."

Leonard went into the trailer and brought out a six-pack.

"Here," he said. "A farewell present. Don't bother to come around here anymore."

"What if I get you some more plants?"

"I don't think you better try to do that. Whoever's pot that is will be harvesting in the next few days. You best not be anywhere near when they're doing it either."

"What if I do get more?"

"Same price, but if you want any beer you best be willing to pay bootleg price like your buddies."

The next day, soon as Sunday lunch was finished, Lanny put on jeans and a T-shirt and tennis shoes and headed toward the French Broad. The day was hot and humid, and the only people on the river were a man and two boys swimming near the far bank. By the time he reached the creek his T-shirt was soaked and sweat stung his eyes.

Upstream the trees blocked out most of the sun and the cold water he waded through cooled him. At the waterfall, an otter slid into the pool. Lanny watched its body surge through the water, straight and sleek as a torpedo, before disappearing under the far bank. He wondered how much an otter pelt was worth and figured come winter it might be worth finding out. He kneeled and cupped his hand, the pool's water so cold it hurt his teeth.

He climbed the left side of the falls, then made his way upstream until he got to the No Trespassing sign. If someone waited for him, Lanny believed that by now the person would have figured out he'd come up the creek, so he stepped up on the right bank and climbed the ridge into the woods. He followed the sound of water until he figured he'd gone far enough and came down the slope slow and quiet, stopping every few yards to listen. When he got to the creek, he looked upstream and down before crossing.

The plants were still there. He pulled the sacks from his belt and walked toward the first plant, his eyes on the trees across the field.

The ground gave slightly beneath his right foot. He did not hear the spring click. What he heard was metal striking against bone. Pain flamed up Lanny's leg to consume his whole body.

When he came to, he was on the ground, his face inches from a pot plant. This ain't nothing but a bad dream, he told himself, thinking that if he believed it hard enough it might become true. He used his forearm to lift his head enough to look at the leg and the leg twisted slightly and the pain hit him like a fist. The world turned deep blue and he thought he was going to pass out again, but in a few moments the pain eased a little.

He looked at his foot and immediately wished he hadn't. The trap's jaws clenched around his leg just above the ankle. Blood soaked the tennis shoe red and he could see bone. Bile surged up from his stomach. Don't look at it any more until you have to, he told himself and lay his head back on the ground.

His face turned toward the sun now, and he guessed it was still early afternoon. Maybe it ain't that bad, he told himself. Maybe if I just lay here awhile it'll ease up some and I can get the trap off. He lay still as possible, breathing long, shallow breaths, trying to think about something else. He remembered what Old Man Jenkins had said about how one man could pretty much fish out a stream of speckled trout by himself if he took a notion to. Lanny wondered how many speckled trout he'd be able to catch out of Caney Creek before they were all gone. He wondered if after he did he'd be able to find another way-back trickle of water that held them.

He must have passed out again, because when he opened his eyes the sun hovered just above the tree line. When he tested the leg, it caught fire every bit as fierce as before. He wondered how late it would be tonight before his parents got worried and how long it would take after that before someone found his truck and people started searching. Tomorrow at the earliest, he told himself, and even then they'd search the river before looking anywhere else.

He lifted his head a few inches and shouted toward the woods. No one called back, and he imagined Linwood Toomey and his son passed-out drunk in their farmhouse. Being so close to the ground muffled his voice, so he used a forearm to raise himself a little higher and called again.

I'm going to have to sit up, he told himself, and just the thought of doing so made the bile rise again in his throat. He took deep breaths and used both arms to lift himself into a sitting position. The pain smashed against his body but just as quickly eased. The world began draining itself of color until everything around him seemed shaded with gray. He leaned back on the ground, sweat popping out on his face and arms like blisters. Everything seemed farther away, the sky and trees and plants, as though he were being lowered into a well. He shivered and wondered why he hadn't brought a sweatshirt with him.

Two men came out of the woods. They walked toward him with no more hurry than men come to check their tobacco for cutworms. Lanny knew the big man in front was Linwood Toomey and the man trailing him his son. He could not remember the son's name but had seen him in town a few times. What he remembered was that the son had been away from the county for nearly a decade and that some said he'd been in the marines and others said prison. The younger man wore a dirty white T-shirt and jeans, the older blue coveralls with no shirt underneath. Grease coated their hands and arms.

They stood above him but did not speak. Linwood Toomey took a rag from his back pocket and rubbed his hands and wrists. Lanny wondered if they weren't there at all, were nothing but some imagining the hurting caused.

"My leg's broke," Lanny said, figuring if they replied they must be real.

"It may well be," Linwood Toomey said. "I reckon it's near about cut clear off."

The younger man spoke.

"What we going to do?"

Linwood Toomey did not answer the question but eased himself onto the ground. They were almost eye level now.

"Who's your people?"

"My daddy's James Burgess. My momma was Ruthie Candler before she got married."

Linwood Toomey smiled.

"I know your daddy. Me and him used to drink some together, but that was back when he was sowing his wild oats. I'm still sowing mine, but I switched from oats. Found something that pays more."

Linwood Toomey stuffed the rag in his back pocket.

"You found it too."

"I reckon I need me a doctor," Lanny said. He was feeling better now, knowing Linwood Toomey was there beside him. His leg didn't hurt nearly as much now as it had before, and he told himself he could probably walk on it if he had to once Linwood Toomey got the trap off.

"What we going to do?" the son said again.

The older man looked up.

"We're going to do what needs to be done."

Linwood Toomey looked back at Lanny. He spoke slowly and his voice was soft.

"Coming back up here a second time took some guts, son. Even if I'd have figured out you was the one done it I'd have let it go, just for the feistiness of your doing such a thing. But coming a third time was downright foolish, and greedy. You're old enough to know better."

"I'm sorry," Lanny said.

Linwood Toomey reached out his hand and gently brushed some of the dirt off Lanny's face.

"I know you are, son."

Lanny liked the way Linwood Toomey spoke. The words were soothing, like rain on a tin roof. He was forgetting something, something important he needed to tell Linwood Toomey. Then he remembered.

"I reckon we best get on to the doctor, Mr. Toomey."

"There's no rush, son," Linwood Toomey said. "The doctor won't do nothing but finish cutting that lower leg off. We got to harvest these plants first. What if we was to take you down to the hospital and the law started wondering why we'd set a bear trap. They might figure there's something up here we wanted to keep folks from poking around and finding."

Linwood Toomey's words had started to blur and swirl in Lanny's mind. They were hard to hold in place long enough to make sense. But what he did understand was Linwood Toomey's words weren't said in a smart-ass way like Leonard Hamby's or Lanny's teachers' or spoken like he was still a child the way his parents' were. Lanny wanted to explain to Linwood Toomey how much he appreciated that, but to do so would mean having several sentences of words to pull apart from one another, and right now that was just too many. He tried to think of a small string of words he might untangle.

Linwood Toomey took a flat glass bottle from his back pocket and uncapped it.

"Here, son," he said, holding the bottle to Lanny's lips.

Lanny gagged slightly but kept most of the whiskey down. He tried to remember what had brought him this far up the creek. Linwood Toomey pressed the bottle to his lips again.

"Take another big swallow," he said. "It'll cut the pain while you're waiting."

Lanny did as he was told and felt the whiskey spread down into his belly. It was warm and soothing, like an extra quilt on a cold night. Lanny thought of something he could say in just a few words.

"You reckon you could get that trap off my foot?"

"Sure," Linwood Toomey said. He slid over a few feet to reach the trap, then looked up at his son.

"Step on that lever, Hubert, and I'll get his leg out."

The pain rose up Lanny's leg again but it seemed less a part of him now. It seemed to him Linwood Toomey's words had soothed the bad hurting away.

"That's got it," Linwood Toomey said.

"Now what?" the son said.

"Go call Edgar and tell him we'll be bringing plants sooner than we thought. Bring back them machetes and we'll get this done."

The younger man walked toward the house.

"The whiskey help that leg some?" Linwood Toomey asked.

"Yes sir," Lanny mumbled, his eyes now closed. Even though Linwood Toomey was beside him, the man seemed to be drifting away along with the pain.

Linwood Toomey said something else but each word was like a balloon slipped free from Lanny's grasp. Then there was silence except for the gurgle of the creek, and Lanny remembered it was the speckled trout that had brought him here. He thought of how you could not see the orange fins and red flank spots but only the dark backs in the rippling water, and how it was only when they lay gasping on the green bank moss that you realized how bright and pretty they were.

# WILL ALLISON, "Atlas Towing"

Born and raised in Columbia, South Carolina, Will Allison attended Case Western Reserve University and later earned his master of fine arts degree from Ohio State University. In addition to working a number of odd jobs (busboy, waiter, landscaper, clerical temp, baseball-card dealer), Allison has taught creative writing at Ohio State and Butler Universities and worked as an editor at *Story, Zoetrope: All Story,* and *Novel & Short Story Writer's Market.* His stories have appeared in a number of journals, including *American Short Fiction, Shenandoah, One Story,* and the *Kenyon Review.* Allison's first novel, *What You Have Left,* was a Book Sense pick and a Barnes & Noble Discover Great New Writers selection in 2007. His second novel, *Long Drive Home,* was published in 2011. He lives in South Orange, New Jersey, with his wife and daughter.

"A story of fast cars and colliding emotions," *What You Have Left* "runs quicker than a dirt-track car on a Saturday night," says Mark Childress. "The characters are heartbreaking, and absolutely real—good people spinning out of control."[1] In this tense, psychologically probing chapter from Allison's first novel, a tow-truck driver discovers the perils of fatherhood when a racetrack rival accidentally kills his own son.

> My father was a big NASCAR fan. He was high-school pals with Cale Yarborough, and he volunteered as a track steward at the now-defunct Columbia Speedway in the 1960s. (I still have his track steward arm band; it's pretty cool.) In the 1970s, he used to take my brother and me to races all over the South, mostly at dirt tracks. We'd usually park in the infield, and he'd watch the race and drink beer while my brother and I, not caring about the races, tried to find some trouble to get into.[2]

"ATLAS TOWING" FROM

*WHAT YOU HAVE LEFT*

Around the time Wylie Greer's daughter was born, he had the bad luck to get mixed up with a man he knew—a brand-new father like himself—who got drunk one night and accidentally killed his infant son. The man's name was Lester Hardin, and on Thursday nights he raced his old Ford in the hobby division out at Columbia Speedway, same as Maddy used to. Lester kept to himself in the pit area and never had two words for Maddy and Wylie, but there was nothing in particular about him to make you think he'd hurt his own son. He was just another gearhead who hated racing against a woman and no doubt wished Maddy good riddance when she got pregnant and quit.

It wasn't until Lester heard Maddy was selling the Fairlane that he tried getting friendly with them. One night in the summer of 1971, he buddied up to Wylie in the infield to inquire about the car. This was a few months after Wylie and Maddy had moved into a clapboard cottage on her father's dairy farm, trying to save for the baby. At the time Wylie was working as a mechanic at the Ford dealership, but on Thursday nights he'd been moonlighting at the track, picking up a few extra bucks clearing wrecks for an outfit called Atlas Towing. Mostly the job was an excuse to watch the races now that Maddy wasn't driving anymore—that and a chance to talk up the Fairlane to the other drivers. After all the blood and sweat he'd poured into that car, after all the races he and Maddy had won, he hated the thought of selling it, but they needed the cash.

Wylie didn't resent Maddy or the baby or even the prospect of fatherhood in general, though it was true, here in the homestretch, that he'd started second-guessing himself. Every time Maddy grabbed his hand and held it to her stomach (and she did this constantly) he was more convinced that he didn't have what it took, that he lacked the enthusiasm or patience for kids—in short, that he'd make a half-assed father, no better than his own, the kind of man who ends up ruining his family or leaving it.

When Lester ambled over, Maddy was holed up inside the wrecker reading Dr. Spock while Wylie watched the late models take practice laps. Lester offered him a beer from the six-pack dangling on his finger, then tapped his can against Wylie's.

"To fatherhood," he said. "To babies that sleep all night and look like their daddies."

Lester's wife, Gladys, was pregnant, too, eight months to Maddy's six, but Wylie didn't feel like talking babies with a guy who acted as though they were just another notch on his belt. In fact, he didn't much feel like talking babies at all. When Lester started telling him about the fancy cigars he'd bought for the big day, Wylie tuned him out and found himself staring at the wrecker's door, the hand-painted silhouette of Atlas straining under the weight of the globe.

By the time Lester finally got around to asking about the car, Gladys had started back from the concession stand with a milkshake, picking her way through the muddy infield. She had the glazed-over look in her eyes that Maddy was starting to get—like she was so deep in her own private babyland that any minute she might wander off or float away—but the second the mothers-to-be recognized each other, they both clicked into focus. Maddy hauled herself out of the truck, the two of them suddenly carrying on like long-lost sisters, though before that night they'd been nothing more than casual friends. After a minute or so, Lester horned in, trying to make nice with Maddy. He pointed at her stomach and asked her did she have a little Richard Petty in there.

"It's a girl," Maddy said, an idea she'd been clinging to since the day she learned she was pregnant.

"Ah." Lester crushed his beer can and tossed it in the grass. "Future race queen."

Maddy stood there with her arms crossed, staring Lester down until he understood he'd put his foot in his mouth.

"Louise Smith, then!" he said. "Ethel Flock!" These were old-time lady drivers, a couple of Maddy's heroes. She let him off the hook with a thin smile and turned back to Gladys, leaving Wylie and Lester to talk money.

Lester wanted the Fairlane at half the asking price. Wylie almost told him where to stick it, but no one else was interested and Maddy's due date was coming up fast; half was better than nothing at all. At the end of the night, worn down by Lester's haggling, Wylie finally caved. They shook on it, Lester said he'd call as soon as he got the cash together, and that was the last Wylie heard from him.

Over the next few weeks, though, their wives were on the phone almost every day, and before long it wasn't just the details of Maddy's pregnancy that crowded out all other topics of conversation between her and Wylie—now he had to make room in his head for Gladys's pregnancy, too. Maddy had gained *x* pounds so far; Gladys was up to *y*. Maddy had terrible leg cramps. Gladys had terrible gas. Neither of them believed in pacifiers. Both of them were going to breast-feed. Early on, Wylie had been willing—even eager—to listen, but the more he'd learned about babies, the more he realized he'd never know all that was required, and after a while, he'd simply given up.

When Nat was born, Maddy visited Gladys in the hospital, and afterward she kept Gladys company and helped out with the baby over at the Hardins' place. Wylie got regular reports on Nat—what thick brown hair he had, what a bruiser he was, how much he drooled. Occasionally Wylie also got word through his wife that Lester was having trouble coming up with the money for the Fairlane, that Gladys was on his case for even thinking about buying it, but now that she and Gladys were so close, Maddy didn't want to get involved.

Then one night, when Nat was about two months old, Gladys came home from work to discover him facedown in his crib. The deputy coroner ruled it an accidental suffocation. Wylie heard about Nat before Maddy did, from a guy in parts who'd stopped by the car wash that Lester managed over on Rosewood Drive. Wylie left the dealership early, drove straight home in a steady rain. Maddy was already two days overdue, gingerly pacing the house, and he wanted to give her the news himself, rather than have her hear it from a hysterical Gladys. When he told her, she dropped the ladle she'd been stirring the chili with and walked out of the kitchen. He found her in the bathroom on the edge of the tub, poking at her stomach, and when she looked up at him, her look said, *Promise it'll be okay*, but also, *You can't make it okay, and if it's not, I'll always blame you.*

"She's been kicking all day," she said. "Now she won't move."

Wylie put his arm around his wife and told her that what had happened to Lester and Gladys wasn't going to happen to them. He told her, as they sat there listening to the rain and waiting for the baby to kick, that Lester and Gladys's loss tilted the odds in their favor.

Five days later, Wylie was standing in a recovery room at Richland Memorial with his mother and father-in-law, holding his daughter for the first time. "We are so lucky," Maddy said. "Do you have any idea how lucky we are?" She was propped up in bed, bleary-eyed and red-faced from thirteen hours of labor, but happy—crying with happiness and relief, and gazing at her husband and daughter as if the world started and ended right there. She'd never seemed to doubt that Wylie was cut out for kids, and so he'd been living off her faith in him as if it were his own, although he was sure that faith had less to do with him than with how badly she wanted a baby. Now, as she sat there beaming, he clucked his tongue at Holly and waited to feel something besides scared. He had hoped for what Maddy was feeling—love at first sight, love washing over him like a wave. But here he was, just holding a baby. It could have been anybody's baby. His mother and Cal kept saying she was the prettiest little thing, and she did have pretty lips, but her hands looked too big for her body, and she seemed so feeble, so raw. He took a seat on the bed and played This Little Piggy with her toes, telling himself to give it some time.

Later, after the parents left and the nurse had taken Holly away, Wylie went down to the cafeteria. On his way back, he stopped at the nursery. Looking through the window at the row of babies, he doubted he'd be able to tell which one was Holly, but there she was, staring off into space like a little insomniac, as if she already had a head full of worries. He tapped on the glass and waved, trying to get her attention.

When he got back to the room, Maddy was still awake, sitting up in bed and looking out the door. "I think that's the room Gladys had," she said. "Right across the hall." She leaned back, moved her dinner tray so Wylie would have a place to sit. "Do you think I'm a terrible friend?"

It had been five days since Nat died, and Maddy still hadn't spoken to Gladys. This was during the time when everyone still believed Nat's death had been a natural one, before Lester confessed. Out at the track, the hobby drivers had held a charity race to help pay for the funeral, but Maddy had stayed home. She'd skipped the funeral, too. She'd even stopped answering the phone, afraid it might be Gladys.

Wylie kissed Maddy's neck. She tasted salty, like she used to after a race. "You haven't heard from her, either."

"But I should have been at the funeral. I didn't even send flowers."

"Then call her," he said. "She'll understand."

Maddy sighed. "The thing is, I don't want to."

Maddy had wanted Wylie to take a week off work when the baby was born, but without the money from the Fairlane, all he could manage was a couple of days. His mother and Cal were eager to help out with Holly, but Maddy wanted to feel like she was in control before she let the grandparents swoop in, and from the looks of it, that wasn't about to happen anytime soon. It was amazing, really, how quickly things went to hell. Holly cried and cried and wouldn't stop. Crying wasn't even the word for it. Screaming, shrieking, wailing, she worked herself into a frenzy. The only thing that shut her up was Maddy's breast, and she wanted it constantly—every two hours, every hour. Wylie and Maddy never slept. She accused him of sulking; he accused her of spoiling the baby. In no time, they were on the brink of hating each other, and Wylie felt the weight of it bearing down on him, despair like nothing he'd ever known.

On the third morning, before work, Wylie slipped out of the house during one of Holly's meltdowns, telling Maddy he needed to give the Fairlane a tune-up. She followed him to the door with the crying baby.

"That's it," she said. "Just run off and hide. Like father, like son."

Wylie stopped halfway across the yard, made himself breathe. "Fine, honey. You do the car, I'll watch the baby."

"You wouldn't know where to start," Maddy said, letting the screen door slam shut.

Wylie had finally gotten around to running an ad in the paper once he realized Lester couldn't afford the car, but in the whirlwind leading up to Holly's arrival, he'd let the ad lapse, and the car had been parked at the end of the lane ever since, a FOR SALE sign fading in the windshield. He swapped out the spark plugs and was almost done changing the oil when he looked up to see Maddy coming down the gravel lane, stone-faced and barefoot, Holly asleep in her arms. She patted the car's fender. "I've come to say my good-byes," she said.

For three years, that car had been their life, and during the early months of Maddy's pregnancy, it stung Wylie to think of the summers they'd spent in the hobby division, how their climb up the NASCAR ladder was finished before they'd reached the second rung. But eventually he bought into the idea that a baby could be better than racing, that a baby could bring him and Maddy closer together.

He asked Maddy if she wanted to take the car for a spin, and she said no, she just wanted to sit in it for a while. As soon as she settled in behind the wheel, Holly woke, hungry again. The baby was so frantic she had trouble latching on to Maddy's nipple. Normally Wylie would have helped, parting Holly's lips the way the nurse had done, but his hands were slick with motor oil, so he waited until Maddy had things under control, then lowered the hood and gave her a thumbs-up, just like he used to do before each race. Maddy was focused on the baby, though, and with the morning dew still streaking the windshield, she didn't even seem to see him.

In between fitful meals, Holly continued to wail, so after Wylie got off work they took her to the doctor. The doctor told them she was fine. Maddy despised him for saying so—"Nat's doctor said he was fine, too"—and Wylie despised her for despising him. The night before, she'd ventured that maybe Holly's crying was God's way of punishing her for abandoning Gladys. This from a woman who hadn't set foot in a church since she was confirmed. Wylie didn't think God had anything to do with it; the problem had to be that Holly wasn't getting enough to eat. Something was wrong with Maddy's milk, or there just wasn't enough of it. Otherwise, why was Holly always hungry? But the doctor told them her weight was right on target. "If you're still worried," he said, "you can always try formula." Maddy sneered at this, too. If God wanted babies to drink formula, she told Wylie, she'd have tin cans for tits.

That night, after Holly's midnight meal, Wylie drifted off into a hazy twilight between waking and sleeping and then rolled over to find himself alone in bed. A light was on in the kitchen. Maddy stood at the counter in her nightshirt, paging through a cookbook and marshaling ingredients: eggs, flour, a bottle of vanilla extract.

"What are you doing?"

"Making Gladys a pound cake," she said.

"It's one in the morning."

She cracked an egg and dropped the shell into the garbage. "Then go back to bed." She wouldn't even look at him.

Twenty minutes later, Holly started crying. He got up and changed her diaper—the only one of her problems he knew how to fix. When he was done, he brought her to Maddy.

"I think she's hungry again."

"The kitchen is closed," Maddy said. "I just fed her an hour ago." She was sitting at the table, looking like she'd had about all she could take. There was flour everywhere.

"If we got some formula," Wylie said, rocking Holly against his shoulder, "I could give her a bottle while you slept."

Maddy sighed, as if the very sight of him wore her out. "How many times do I have to tell you? There's a *reason* milk is coming out of me." She got up from the table and took a few bills from the coffee can on top of the refrigerator. She told Wylie to go to the bakery in the morning, buy a pound cake, and deliver it to Gladys. "Try to get one that looks homemade." She rummaged under the counter. "Put it in this."

Wylie stared at the Tupperware container she was holding. "You're kidding, right?" Going to see Lester and Gladys was the last thing he wanted to do. He was sorry Maddy felt bad, but he was tired, and they weren't his friends, and frankly he didn't want to face them any more than she did. The whole business with the Fairlane just made things that much worse. Though he didn't appreciate Lester stringing him along, wasting his time, he didn't want to show up on the guy's doorstep and make him feel like he had to apologize—not at a time like this.

"Go ahead and get a card, too," Maddy said. "Sign my name. But don't be gone long. I can't do everything here."

Wylie took the container and held it up for Holly to touch. He was determined not to raise his voice. "Honey," he said, "if you want to give Gladys a cake, take it over there yourself."

Lester and Gladys lived in a neighborhood of small brick duplexes in West Columbia, about a mile from the track. Wylie found their place easily enough, but he didn't know what he was going to say to them, so he kept driving, aimless, hoping their rusty Dart would be gone by the time he came back. He ended up out by the track and turned off into the rutted meadow that doubled as a parking lot. It was Thursday, and he was due back there that night; he'd called in sick at the dealership, but he hadn't been able to find anyone at Atlas to cover his shift at the track. He wished he could curl up in his car and sleep until then. The gate on the front stretch was wide open, and inside he could see the owner, Sid Gooden, slowly working his way around the banked oval atop his state-surplus motor grader, pushing the clay and sand back toward the bottom of the track.

The summer before, Maddy had been leading a qualifying heat when she fishtailed and hit the guardrail, which wasn't much of a rail at all, just sheets of plywood nailed to a fence. As she sat there crosswise on the track, stalled out and waiting for the red flag, the rest of the pack came sliding through the turn. You could hear the whole infield suck in its breath, bracing for a crash. Wylie always told himself that Maddy was invincible out there—he couldn't afford to think about it any other way—but seeing her come so close to getting T-boned rattled him. When she got back to the pit area, he asked her to sit out the feature race so he could look over the car. He didn't think she'd go for it—she'd been in wrecks before, had shrugged them off and hopped back in the saddle—but that night, after she finished cursing her luck and loose dirt, she allowed that maybe it wasn't a bad idea.

The following Sunday, he took her over to Darlington and dropped half a paycheck on good seats for the Southern 500, the race Maddy dreamed of running. He was thinking it'd be just the thing to help them shake off the cobwebs, but Maddy spent most of the race staring at the pregnant girl next to them—was so busy staring, in fact, that she missed Buddy Baker's Dodge crossing the finish line. Wylie was lowering his binoculars when she hooked an arm around his waist and shouted into his ear. "Let's! Have! A baby!"

At first he thought she was joking, making fun of the pregnant girl for the way she'd been rubbing her stomach all afternoon. Anyhow, the plan had always been that they'd try for a baby after they quit racing, a day Wylie figured was a long ways off. But Maddy was in his ear again, ahead of him as usual, telling him she was afraid she might not be around to *have* a baby if she kept racing.

Now, as he watched Sid take another turn on his grader, smoothing out the grooves, Wylie thought of the two hobby titles Maddy had won, how good he'd felt knowing she couldn't do it without him and that he'd never let her down. That's how he felt that afternoon at Darlington when he said yes to having a baby. It was the last time he'd felt that way.

Gladys answered the door. It was almost lunchtime, but she was still in her bathrobe, squinting at Wylie through the torn screen as if she hadn't seen sunlight in days, a road map of red in her eyes. When she noticed the cake, she invited him in like she didn't have a choice.

"Lester," she called, "friend of yours."

The curtains were drawn in the narrow living room, and except for the traffic out on 321, the house was quiet. Wylie hadn't expected Lester to be home. He hadn't even meant to come in. He'd hoped to hand off the cake at the front door and be gone. Now he tried for a sympathetic smile and told Gladys how sorry Maddy was that she couldn't come herself. "She had the baby on Sunday," he said.

"Please tell her I've been meaning to stop by," Gladys said, but it didn't sound like she meant it. It sounded like she just wanted to be left alone. She stood there cinching her robe until Lester came out of the kitchen. When he shook Wylie's hand, he clasped it with both of his, the way a preacher does. Wylie told them he and Maddy had been praying for them ever since they heard about Nat. "We're deeply sorry for your loss," he said. This was something he'd rehearsed in the truck, and to his ears, that's how it sounded.

"You're a good guy to come all the way out here," Lester said. "I just put on some coffee. Let's sit down and have some of that—what do you got there?"

"Maddy's pound cake."

"Gladys loves pound cake, don't you, hon?" He put an arm around his wife, but she shrugged him off.

"I'm not hungry," she said, and then she went into the bedroom and shut the door. Lester looked embarrassed. He rubbed a hand back and forth across his crew cut. Wylie was about to say he should be getting home when Lester cleared his throat.

"I keep telling her we can try again," he said, shaking his head. "She don't want to hear it." He glanced at the bedroom door, then held up the cake as if to say, *But there's this.* Wylie followed him into the kitchen and sat at the dinette while Lester cut two slices. "You know, it could have been a lot worse," Lester said, lowering his voice. "I mean, Christ, the kid was only eight weeks old. It's not like we had much time to get attached to him." He set a cup of coffee in front of Wylie. "Right? You must know what I mean."

Wylie supposed he did. If something terrible was going to happen to your baby, better sooner than later, before she started trusting you to make everything okay. Still, as soon as he nodded, it felt like a betrayal. Pretty soon he'd be telling Lester he wasn't sure why he'd wanted a baby in the first place. "Me and Maddy," he said, "we just feel so lucky—"

Lester cut him off. "Goes without saying." His smile was tight. He took a bite of cake and Wylie got to work on his, too, promising himself he'd get out of there as soon as he was done. He was almost finished when Lester lit a cigarette and warmed up to him again, apologizing about the Fairlane. Wylie told him it was no big deal, but Lester went on and on, saying he'd never meant to leave Wylie in the lurch. Things had gotten so busy with the baby, he said, and money was tight. He still wanted to buy the car, though, assuming Wylie hadn't already sold it.

"Not yet," Wylie said.

Lester slid the pack of smokes across the table, said that originally the car was going to be a present for himself, to celebrate the baby, but now he wanted it as a surprise for Gladys. He said that since she started hanging around Maddy more, she'd been talking about entering a powderpuff derby—not *racing* racing, just girls versus girls—and although he'd been against it at first, now he thought it might do her some good. Wylie shook a cigarette from the pack and nodded along. He didn't believe Lester would end up buying the car any more than he believed Gladys would want it, but he decided to give Lester the benefit of the doubt and told him he'd hold off renewing the ad, give them time to work something out.

"In that case," Lester said, "why don't I come get the car today?" He said he could swing by the bank, bring Wylie a deposit that afternoon, and pay him the rest next week. Wylie tapped the end of his cigarette on the table. This wasn't at all what he'd had in mind, but he was in too deep to back out now, and he was too tired to argue. He hadn't slept in four days, his wife would sooner growl at him than smile, and he was starting to think he'd rather sit there smoking with Lester than go home and face his own kid's howling. He took one last gulp of coffee and stood to leave.

"Deal."

On the way home, Wylie fell asleep at the wheel and drifted off the road, his tires biting into the grassy shoulder. A row of scrub pines floated before him. He jerked upright and wrestled the car onto the blacktop, cursing Maddy for sending him to see Gladys, cursing himself for giving in to Lester again. Shaken, he stopped at a convenience store for another cup of coffee and—debating whether to buy it even as he approached the register—a can of formula. Just in case Maddy changes her mind, he told himself. When he got home, she was asleep in bed with Holly. The baby stirred as he looked in on them, and before he had time to think twice, he whisked her out of the room. He knew you were supposed to heat the formula, but he was afraid Maddy would wake up, so he told Holly she'd have to drink it cold. He sat at the dining room table with her in the crook of his arm like a football, brushing the nipple against her cheek the way he'd seen Maddy do, dribbling formula onto her lips. She turned her head from side to side, trying to get away from it. "Come on, cupcake," he said. "Let's be reasonable." She began to fuss, and when he persisted, sweating and shaking, she started to cry in earnest. He had to remind himself that she wasn't doing it on purpose; she was only a baby. She needed to eat, whether she wanted to or not, and he didn't know when he'd get another chance. Finally, he worked the nipple between her lips, and when she tried to spit it out, he held firm, determined that she'd at least have a taste, no matter how much she fought and flailed her little arms. It wasn't until she began to choke that he finally eased up. As he pulled the bottle away, she coughed formula onto his arm and shrieked, a sound as terrible as a loose fan belt. "Now, now," he said, "there, there," but she went on and on, screaming bloody murder. It was all he could do not to shove the bottle back into her mouth, just to shut her up.

Somehow Maddy slept through the whole thing, and Wylie spent the next hour trying to make it up to Holly, carrying her around the house and singing nursery rhymes while he waited for Lester. Once she stopped crying, she didn't seem to hold a grudge. It was as if Sid had come along with his grader, smoothing out all the ruts between them.

Lester never showed up with the money, and he wasn't at the races that night, either. Same old, same old, Wylie thought. He'd been a half hour late getting to the track himself and, despite three large Cokes, nodded off in the wrecker. A track steward had to tap on the window to wake him when one of the drivers blew a tire.

Back home, it was business as usual—distraught wife, crying baby. This time Wylie suggested they get out for a walk. The night was warm and breezy, and they followed the dirt lane past the soybean field, past the farmhouse where

Cal had been cooling his heels until Maddy lifted her restraining order. Holly was asleep on Wylie's shoulder within minutes.

"Look at you," Maddy said. "You're a natural." For the first time all day, she seemed relaxed. She slipped her hand in his, swung her arm as they walked. Wylie stroked Holly's head and glanced up at the stars. *This* was how he'd always imagined life with a baby, he and Maddy exhausted but not defeated, pulling together.

They were nearing the end of the lane when they heard the crash. At first Wylie thought somebody had hit a deer, but then there was another crash, and another. As they got closer to the highway, he could see in the moonlight a figure standing on the hood of the Fairlane, stomping the windshield. He wanted it to be some local kid, Bluff Road riffraff but he recognized the Dart idling on the roadside. After one last stomp, Lester hopped down and grabbed what looked to be a crowbar from his backseat. Wylie tried to pass the baby to Maddy, but she held on to his arm.

"Don't," she whispered. "He's drunk off his ass."

And then Lester began to whale on the Fairlane's fender. The first blow woke Holly, but Lester didn't hear her crying until he'd taken three or four more swings. Turning, he peered through the darkness, the crowbar cocked in his hand. Wylie took a step toward him.

"All right, Lester," he called. "Better get on home now."

For a moment Lester stood and stared, his shoulders heaving with each breath. Holly continued to howl. In the distance, headlights appeared, the rumble of a tractor trailer. Finally Lester reared back and flung the crowbar into the underbrush across the road. The Dart sprayed a rooster tail of gravel as he pulled away.

When his taillights faded, Wylie and Maddy walked over for a look at the Fairlane, saw what a number he'd done—all four tires knifed, the driver's seat shredded down to foam and springs, the windshield intact but caved in. Wylie picked up the FOR SALE sign, brushed it off, tossed it onto the seat. Once upon a time, he'd poured his heart and soul into that car. Now all he cared about, really, was how he'd get Lester to pay for the damage.

"Guess he changed his mind about the car," Wylie said.

Maddy just shook her head like she'd been expecting this all along. Wylie thought she'd be more upset, but he saw then that she'd let go, too, that whatever happened to the Fairlane now didn't much matter to her.

The next morning, when Wylie called the police, the dispatcher asked him to repeat Lester's name, said wait a minute, then came back on the line and informed him that Lester Hardin was already in custody. She asked Wylie to come down to the station to file his report. When he got there, he was greeted by a detective, an older man with puffy eyes and a dark suit that looked slept in. They knew each other from the dealership: the detective brought in his '68 Fastback GT for an oil change every two thousand miles on the nose. His office was as tidy as his car, a small, bright room with photos of his wife and daughter arranged on the windowsill. He pulled up a seat for Wylie. When Wylie asked what Lester was doing in jail, the detective took off his glasses, rubbed his eyes, and told him.

Shortly after he'd finished with Maddy's car, Lester had walked into the Richland County sheriff's office and confessed to the first officer he saw, a young deputy at the front desk. Lester told him about the night he'd been home alone with Nat while Gladys was waiting tables at the Waffle House. They'd been having their usual fight before she left, and he was sick of hearing her complain about money, about his job at the car wash, about having to leave her baby four nights a week just so they could make ends meet. Lester spent the evening in front of the TV with a bottle of whiskey, listening to the baby cry and trying to decide what to do about his life. When he'd had enough of the noise, he went into the nursery and held Nat, muffling the baby's cries against his chest. All he was trying to do, he told the deputy, was shut Nat up, get him to go to sleep. But the harder the baby cried, the harder Lester held him, and by the time he let go, Nat wasn't breathing. Lester then placed him facedown in the crib, and that's how Gladys found her baby when she got home. When he was done talking, Lester begged the deputy to shoot him.

At first, Wylie couldn't quite get his head around what he was hearing. It was so horrible, he thought Lester must have made it up. What was worse, every time he tried to make it real, every time he tried to picture Lester smothering his baby, what he saw instead was himself cramming that bottle into Holly's mouth. The two events ran together like water in his mind. For a moment *he* had an impulse to confess, if for no other reason than to hear the detective tell him he'd done nothing wrong. He sat quietly while the detective finished the story. He was saying that Lester finally confessed to Gladys last night, had actually gotten down on his knees and pleaded for forgiveness, at which point she'd told him she wished he were dead.

"Then she gave him a choice," the detective said. "Turn himself in, or she'd do it for him."

Wylie sat up straight, heard himself asking if Lester meant to kill the baby. The detective shrugged. "He says he didn't. Says it was an accident. We're just trying to find out what we can, which is why I wanted to hear about last night." He pulled out a notepad and began asking questions about what happened with Lester and the Fairlane. Wylie had trouble concentrating. He had to force himself to make eye contact with the detective. Starting with the night Lester approached him at the track, he told everything he could remember, hoping he'd say something that would be of use. The anger he was feeling toward Lester went beyond what he'd done to the Fairlane, beyond Nat's death even. A half hour later, as Wylie walked out of the station and into the morning glare, he wished the policeman had honored Lester's request and shot him on the spot.

Wylie had been planning to swing by Atlas and borrow a flatbed, then haul the Fairlane out to a buddy's junkyard in Irmo and sell it for parts, take whatever they'd give him. Now that seemed like more than he could manage. He stopped for a six-pack and pointed his car home, gunning the engine past the juke joints and matchbox houses along Bluff Road, slowing down only to look at the ruined shell of the Fairlane as he turned off the highway. Halfway between the farmhouse and the cottage, he pulled over and switched off the ignition, sat there drinking and staring across the field at the cows. One beer, two beers, three. He told himself he was working up the courage to tell Maddy about Lester, but mostly he was thinking about his father: his brooding, his shouting, the whistle of his belt. It occurred to Wylie that maybe his father had done him a favor, that maybe he'd left to keep from doing more harm.

After the fourth beer, Wylie slid the bottles under his seat and drove the rest of the way home. Maddy was out front with Holly and a fistful of Kleenex, sitting on the porch swing where she and Wylie used to spend evenings watching the sun set behind Cal's silos. She looked like she was done for. At first Wylie thought she'd already heard about Lester, but it wasn't that—just another morning of trying and failing to please Holly. He was barely out of the truck when Maddy thrust the baby into his arms.

"You take her," she said. She blew her nose and began telling him about Holly's latest fit, how she'd tried feeding her on one side and then the other, but nothing was good enough. "She's not even a week old and she already hates me." Maddy was so worked up, she didn't ask Wylie about his visit to the police station until they were inside. When he told her about Lester, she covered her mouth, shook her head as if it weren't true. "Poor Nat!" she said. "Poor Nat! Poor little baby!" That got Holly going again, and if it hadn't been for the four beers cushioning him from all the crying and misery, Wylie thought he might have started bawling himself.

Later, though, when Maddy had gotten past the shock of it, she told him she was actually relieved. "When it was a baby dying in his sleep, that was even worse," she said. "That could happen to anyone."

They were sitting on the floor with Holly between them on a blanket. Wylie lifted her up and blew a raspberry on her stomach but stopped when he noticed Maddy watching him. He thought she was about to accuse him of smelling like beer. "You know, if it weren't for you," she said, "he might never have confessed. Seeing you must have done it, made him realize what he'd done. Otherwise, why would he bust up our car on his way to the police?"

Wylie stood and carried Holly to the window. He thought about the Fairlane, imagined Lester plunging a knife into its tires, stomping the windshield. He had to admit, he liked the idea of being the one who'd pushed him over the edge. He liked the idea of Lester wishing he were in his shoes. But for all he knew, the only things separating him from Lester were circumstance and a little luck, and he was surprised Maddy didn't see it this way, too.

Maddy got up and went into the bathroom, asked Wylie from behind the door to check Holly's diaper. The toilet flushed, and then she said, "What I don't get is, how could Gladys not have known? She lived with the guy. She was married to him." Wylie unpinned Holly's diaper, saw that it was clean, and refastened it. When Maddy turned on the faucet, he picked up a small blue pillow from the rocking chair. Holly was kicking as he held it above her face. He tried to imagine lowering the pillow, pressing down, but he couldn't do it, not even for a second—as if that proved anything. But who was to say? Maybe Maddy was right. Maybe she saw something in Wylie he couldn't yet see in himself. He pulled the pillow away and whispered, "Peekaboo," trying to make a game of it. He figured Holly would start crying then, but she just lay there, blinking. That was what really got him: she didn't even have the sense to be afraid.

"Not that I blame Gladys," Maddy was saying. "Besides, she really needs me now. I was thinking I'd go see her tomorrow, if you'd drive me over." She shut off the water. "Are you listening?"

Wylie leaned over and kissed Holly on the tip of her nose. When he stood up, the room spun a little. He had time to set the pillow aside as Maddy came out of the bathroom, but he kept on holding it, and then he felt her behind him in the doorway, probably leaning there with her arms crossed, wondering why he was standing over their baby with a pillow. "I'm listening," he said.

# ANN PANCAKE, "Redneck Boys"

Ann Pancake was raised in West Virginia, first in Summersville, in the coal-mining region, then near her family's farm in Romney. After graduating from West Virginia University, Pancake taught English in Japan, American Samoa, and Thailand and later earned a master's degree in English from the University of North Carolina at Chapel Hill and a doctorate in English from the University of Washington. A winner of the Whiting Writers Award and a National Endowment for the Arts Creative Writing Fellowship Grant, Pancake has published stories in the *Georgia Review, Shenandoah,* the *Virginia Quarterly Review,* and *New Stories from the South.* Her story collection, *Given Ground,* received the 2000 Bread Loaf Bakeless Fiction Prize, and her novel, *Strange as This Weather Has Been,* was named one of *Kirkus Review*'s Top Ten Fiction Books of 2007. A passionate opponent of strip mining, Pancake currently lives in Seattle and teaches creative writing in the low-residency master of fine arts program at Pacific Lutheran University.

In awarding Pancake's story collection the Bakeless Fiction Prize, David Bradley praised her "astoundingly rich rendering of the Appalachian Mountain country—one of America's most often caricatured and most poorly understood heartlands."[1] In "Redneck Boys" a young mother reconsiders her past and the woman she has become after an old friend stops by for a surprise late-night visit.

I started writing this story almost twenty years ago, and I didn't figure out how to finish it until almost ten years after that. But despite the distance now between "Redneck Boys" and me, I can reread the first paragraph and right away feel the original telling of it in my throat and on my tongue.

People ask me often why I continue to write about marginalized people in Appalachia, and while there are a lot of reasons, that feel of voice in my mouth is a big one. I realize that for me the quickest way to voice is through the visceral, and the quickest way to the visceral is through land, language, and people back home. In other words, it's only in the rough my writing can get any traction. I can't get started without a little grit on the tongue.[2]

### "REDNECK BOYS"

Richard has gone on and died, she thinks when she hears the knuckle on the door. Took two weeks after the accident, he was strong. The other three dead at the scene. She glances at the digital clock on top of Richard's New Testament, then she covers her face with her hands. The yellow stink of the hospital still hangs in her hair. It's 3:07 A.M., and Richard has gone on and died.

She pulls on yesterday's jeans and feels her way through the hall, not ready yet for a light in her eyes. Cusses when she hits barefoot the matchbox cars her son's left lying around. She's so certain it's her brother, who was made messenger back towards the beginning of this mess, she doesn't even pull back the curtain to see. She stops behind the door to steady her breath, which is coming quick and thin even though she's expected the news for days. But when she unbolts the door, it is a boy, a man, she hasn't seen in a few years.

He blows steam in the porchlight, straddling the floor frame Richard never had time to finish. Coatless, his arms pork-colored in the cold. He has forced himself into corduroy pants he's outgrown and wears a pair of workboots so mudcaked they've doubled in size. He grins. She knew him some time ago. And he grins at her, his face gone swollen, then loose under the chin, the way boys get around here.

"Cam," is what he says.

She draws back to let Splint pass. He unlaces the muddy boots and leaves them on the ground under the porch frame. The surprise she might have felt if he'd shown up before Richard's wreck—and she's not sure she would have felt surprise then—has been wrung out of her by the two-week vigil. Splint walks to the sofa where he wraps himself in an afghan and chafes his upper arms with his palms. He swipes at the runny nose with his shoulder. Cam remembers what she's wearing—just a long-john shirt of Richard's over the jeans, no bra—and for a moment, her face heats with self-consciousness. Then the heat leaves her face for other places in her body. Angry at herself, Cam wills the heat away.

"Where's your boy?" Splint asks. Then, "I heard about Richard."

"Down to Mom's," Cam answers.

"You're up on this mountain without even a dog at night?"

Splint squats in front of the woodstove, still shawled in the afghan that doesn't quite fall to his waist. Cam watches the soft lobs between the waistband of the corduroys and the hem of the hiked-up T-shirt. Burrs snagged in his pantscuffs. Cam wonders what he's done now to end up coatless in the middle of a freezing night. Then she doesn't wonder. She crouches on the edge of the sofa behind him, her chest clenched, and she waits for what he'll do next.

What he does is open the stove door and huddle up to it closer, giving Cam a better look at his soft back. Hound-built he was as a boy, a little bowlegged and warped along the spine, the new muscles riding long and taut and rangy right under the skin. Freckle-ticked shoulders. She recalls trailing him one August afternoon up a creekbed where he'd stashed a six-pack of Old Milwaukee in sycamore roots. He'd outgrown that shirt, too, a tank top, and she had watched it ride up, watched the tight small of his back. The muscles coming so soon, too early, on those boys.

"Why don't you poke up the fire for me?" Splint startles her. She starts to move, then pauses, asks herself who she's answering to and why. But she's been raised to obedience. She leans forward and picks up a split chunk on the hearth. Its raw insides tear the skin on her palm, even though it is a hard hand that has handled many stovelogs. She shoves the log in the embers, kneels, and blows until the coals flare up. Then, as she reaches to shut the door, Splint's own hand snakes out of the afghan and grabs her arm. Cam goes icy in the roots of her hair. She yanks away, harder than she needs to. The stove door stays open, the pipe drawing hard and loud. A sizzle and whupping in the flue.

"It's too bad about Richard," Splint says. "He was always a good boy."

Cam can't tell if he's mocking her.

"And a hard worker, huh?"

This is funeral talk, and Cam doesn't answer.

"You never were a big talker," Splint says. "Guess you don't got any cigarettes around here?"

He pulls a big splinter from the stove to light the Virginia Slim she gives him. Cam knows he knows Richard is just like the others. Went down off the mountain at five A.M. to meet his ride, traveled two hours to build northern Virginia condominiums all day, traveled the hundred miles back to a six-room house he was putting together on weekends and didn't finish before the wreck. Celotex walls and the floors unsanded. Yeah, Richard was a hard worker, just like all the other boys. Only Splint wouldn't work hard, and Splint ended up in jail.

"I still think about you," he says. He'd been staring into the stove, but now he cocks his head sidewise to look at Cam, kneeling a little behind him. She has her bare feet drawn up under her, and not just for warmth. To be all of a piece like that, pulled together, makes her feel safe from herself. Her eyes drift to his hands in the firelight there, them hanging loose in his lap. It occurs to her she has never seen them so clean although the heat draws an odor from his body, the odor of ground in the woods. But the hands—no grease in the knuckle creases or in the prints, the nails clear and unbroken. Back when she knew him, the hands were all the time dirty. He spent half his time with his head in an engine, the other half under the chassis. Frittered his cash away on parts and auto wrecker junk, and when it still wouldn't run, he'd steal. What've you been into now, buddy? Cam thinks. Splint pulls up the tail of his shirt to stob his running nose.

The last time she and Splint ran, they were seniors in high school. Splint told her to meet him a ways down her road so her parents wouldn't see, and he showed up in a brand-new Camaro, she recognized the car. Sixteenth birthday present to some lawyer's kid at school, but Splint was playing his own music. Lynyrd Skynyrd. Cam got drunk before they hit the paved road, grain alcohol and orange pop, the music thrushing through her stomach and legs, while Splint cussed the car for handling like a piece of shit. She cranked down her window, stuck her head in the wind. Wind, leaves, hills, but no sky. Sky too far overhead to see from a car. Just ground, pounding by on either side. It was spring, and by that time, they knew about the college, the scholarship.

They eventually reached Frawl's Flat, the second straightest piece of road in the county, and they started seeing how fast the Camaro would go. Stupid-drunk like they were, the state police snuck up on them easy. Splint squealed off down the highway, and even though the car was a piece of shit, they might have outrun the cops, or, more likely, could have ditched the car and both run off in the woods. But Splint did something else.

He swerved back a narrow, heavy-wooded road, braked, and screamed at Cam to get out, shoving at her shoulder as he yelled. And Cam did. She tumbled out, the car down to maybe fifteen miles an hour by then, landed on her hip in the ditch, then scrambled up the shale bank into the scrub oak and sumac. The staties were so close they caught Splint where she could watch. Crouched in the brush, cold sober, she saw the three of them moving in and out the headlights and taillights. He'd just turned eighteen, and they put him in jail for a while that time. They didn't know to look for Cam.

"Oh, you were bright," Splint is saying, and she winces at how the gravel has come in his craw. Tobacco voice. "Bright. All that running around you did and they still gave you a scholarship."

Cam doesn't answer back. Splint knows there was one person in their class as bright as Cam, and that was Splint. She knows Splint knows she got a boy instead of a college degree. She realizes she's unnumbed enough to need a drink, and she heads to the kitchen to fetch one. Aware of what Splint will want, she starts to open the refrigerator, then stops. On the door, her boy's drawings, motorcycles and eighteen-wheelers. Instead, she pulls a bottle of Jim Beam and two jelly glasses from the crates they are using until they have money for cabinets. The whiskey she and Richard shared, but the beer in the refrigerator belongs to just Richard.

She even called Splint once or twice during the year she spent at the university in gray Morgantown. Then she left the state and saw a little of the world, ha. Waited tables in Daytona for eight months before she met a boy named Eric, and they went west, that was for six. What she remembers best—or worst—at any rate, what she remembers clearest—is the way this Eric talked. In six months, she never could get used to it. Hardened every consonant, choked up every vowel. Such an awkward, a cramped way to work your words out your mouth. It got to where she couldn't stand to hear him say her name, how he'd clip it off, one syllable. Cam. Like he had no idea about the all of her. Back home, they speak it full. They say it Ca-yum. Back here.

Splint drains his glass, shivers his head and shoulders, stretches. The afghan drops to the floor. He swaggers over to Richard's gun cabinet, and Cam sees how he carries himself like a middle-aged man. Still small in his hips, he is, but big across the belly, and him no more than thirty. Although her eyes stay on Splint, her mind sees her own body at the same time. She knows she's gone in the other direction, a rare way to go around here. Cam knows she's worn rutted and flat. Splint strokes the rifle stocks along their grains, draws one out and pretends to sight it down the hall. It is Richard's, and Cam feels an urge to lift it from Splint's hands. Between his third and fourth fingers, the cigarette smolders, there under the finger playing the trigger. "Pow," Splint says.

She'd known she'd never stay with Eric, but Richard was just something that happened when she came home for Christmas. Fifteen minutes in Richard's dad's pickup behind the Moose, the windows fogged, and then Richard sat up with his jeans around his ankles and printed their names in the steam. Like a twelve-year-old girl, Cam thought at the time. Some little twelve-year-old girl. No, she never felt for Richard. What she felt for Splint. She was so fresh back home she was still homesick and she just wanted to hear them talk,

talk to her, it could have been any boy who talked that way. She ran into Richard that night. But Richard was a good boy and a hard worker, everybody said so. She could have done way worse; her mom made sure to remind her of this often. After a while, she wrote Eric in Phoenix. (Seventy-five, eighty miles an hour across that flat Oklahoma, Texas, New Mexico. Highways like grooves, and the land. She fixed that land, she remade it every night. She dreamed it green where it was brown, rumpled it where flat.) He wrote back once. Told her he always knew she'd end up with some redneck boy.

The second time she and Splint ran, they were thirteen. They met at the end of her road right around dawn, the hills smoking fog twists and a damp raw in the air. They flagged the Greyhound when it came, the Greyhound would pick you up anywhere back then, but although they'd had their sights set on North Carolina, the money Splint thieved off his older sister got them no farther than middle-of-nowhere Gormania. When the driver realized they'd ridden past how far they could pay, he threw them off at a mountaintop truck stop and told the cook to call the sheriff.

The deputy who showed up had only one ear. He phoned their parents with the receiver flat against the earhole. It was Cam gave him the numbers, and Splint wouldn't speak to her for four weeks after. She remembers Splint all tough over his black coffee in that drafty restaurant, pretending Cam wasn't there. The waitress locking up the cigarette machine. The deputy told her how his ear got shot off stalking deer poachers, but after he left, the cook said his wife did it with sewing scissors. When Splint's dad appeared, three hours later, he, too, pretended Cam wasn't there. He jerked Splint to his feet and dragged him out behind the building while Cam slunk along the wall to watch. Splint slouched between the Stroehmann bread racks and raw kitchen slop. The scraggly garbage birds in a panic. But his father just looked at him and shook his head, then cussed him without imagination. The same two words, over and over, his voice flat as an idling motor. In the constant wind across the mountaintop, his father's coveralls flapped against his legs, making them look skinnier than they were. Finally he threw a milk crate at Splint. Splint caught it.

"I still think about you," Splint is saying again. He has put away the rifle and settles on the sofa, leaving her room which she doesn't take. He's trying to start something, but this time, she tells herself, she won't follow.

Richard always called it love. Ten years of late suppers and, even on weekends, him asleep in front of the TV by eight P.M. Two hours later, he'd wake and they'd shift to the bed, the brief bucking there. Afterwards, he'd sleep again, as sudden and as deep as if he'd been cold-cocked. Richard was a good boy and a hard worker. And now he's waited for two weeks, in his patient, plodding way, to be killed in a car wreck. That week's driver asleep at the wheel ten miles short of home after a day of drywalling.

Cam feels as tired as if she'd been awake for all her thirty years.

The first time she and Splint had run, they were twelve years old, at 4-H camp. The camp lay five miles back a dirt road where they hauled kids in schoolbuses until the mountains opened into a sudden clearing along the river. Like a secret place. The county had turned 1950s chicken coops into bunk-houses and jammed them mattress to mattress with castoff iron beds, and Cam slept uneasy there under the screenless windows, the barnboard flaps propped open for the little air. She had seen Splint at school, but this was the first time she noticed. And as she watched from a distance, she heard what was live in him like a dog might hear it. What was live in him, she heard a high-pitched whine. The beds in the coop were packed so close together she could feel on her cheeks the nightbreath of the girls on either side. And the whine a hot line from her almost-breasts to her navel.

On the last evening, they had a Sadie Hawkins shotgun wedding, where the girls were supposed to catch the boys. The counselors lined them up, the boys with a fifty-foot headstart, then blew a whistle and turned them loose. Cam aimed at Splint. Splint knew she was after him, and he headed towards the river, where they were forbidden to go. All around Cam, big girls seized little squealy boys, older boys faked half-hearted escapes. Splint fled, but at twelve, Cam was his size, and as fast, and as strong. She saw him disappear in the tree-line along the river, then she was dodging through trees herself, and she caught up with him on the rock bar there. Panting, but not yet spent, she reached out to grab him, but she scared, then just touched at him like playing tag. Splint was trotting backwards, bent in at the waist, dodging and laughing. They heard others following them to the river, heard them hollering through the trees. "Pretend you ain't caught me yet," Splint said.

He wheeled and sloshed into the river, high stepping until the water hit his hips, then he dropped on his stomach and struck out swimming. Cam, just as strong, as swift, right behind.

The far side had no shore to it, just an eroded mud bank. They hauled themselves up the exposed maple roots, and then they were in woods, they were hidden, alone. Cam was twelve years old, she thought she knew what to do. Splint grappled her back, too much teeth in the kiss, his hands in unlikely places. They rubbed at each other through their soaked clothes, serious and quick, and the threat of the others swimming the river pushed them faster.

Cam was finding her way, so absorbed it was like being asleep, when she realized Splint wasn't doing anything back. He rolled away from her into the weeds and sat up with his face between his knees, his thin back to her. Too naive to feel hurt, Cam crawled closer. She heard a strange little animal noise that made her want to pet. Finally, she understood Splint was crying.

Something taps her feet folded under her. Splint has rolled his jelly glass across the floor.

"Girl, if you don't talk to me, I'm going to do something drastic."

Cam looks at him. "What are you doing up here in the middle of the night without a coat?"

Splint laughs, soft. "Got into it with a girl driving home. She threw me out of her car." He rises off the sofa, leans down to open the stove door, and strips away his T-shirt. He stands fat in front of the fire, soaking heat in his skin.

Cam's all the time finding her own boy sketching pickup trucks and stock cars on notebook paper, oh, he is careful, detailed and neat. Until the very end. Then something breaks in him, unstops, and he turns violent and free. He gouges deep black lines behind the vehicles to show how fast they can go. When he was littler, and they still lived in Richard's parents' basement, he'd ride the back of the couch like a motorcycle, forcing air through his lips for the throttle. That he is not Richard's, she is almost sure, but he seems not Eric's either. Seems mothered and fathered by her and the place. She stands next to Splint now, following his stare in the fire. Without looking at her, Splint lifts her hand and presses it against his naked side.

"I'm not having sex with you," Cam says.

"That's not how come I'm here," says Splint.

He drops her hand and walks to the closet behind the front door. He pulls out a quilted flannel shirt of Richard's and buttons it on. Shoving aside the blaze-orange hunting jacket and coats that belong to Cam, he finally reaches the end of the rack and mutters.

"He's got his good one back in the bedroom," Cam says.

She finds the big Sunday coat. Splint takes it. Cam doesn't think about offering him a ride until after he's gone.

He got mad about the crying, screwed his fists in his eyes and muddied his face. Cam mumbled it didn't matter. By that time, counselors were yelling at them from across the water, how much trouble they were in if they didn't come right back. Cam stood up and Splint followed. They crept out of the trees and climbed down the bank without looking at the grownups. They waded out to thigh-deep and started paddling.

They pulled that water slow, kicked sloppy. They were putting off their punishment. Cam remembers the water still springtime cold a foot under the surface, this was June. The eyeball green of the river, and how you could see

current only in the little bubble clusters gliding down its top. She swam a little behind Splint, her head about parallel with his stomach, and when she
remembers back, she understands how young he was. Twelve, same as her, yes,
but a boy-twelve, and she thinks of her own son and feels sad and shameful for
how she did Splint.

Because she was so close to him as they swam, and because she couldn't help
but look at him, and because the way they glided along cut the water clean—
no foam to speak of, no wave—Cam saw clearly what happened next.

She saw Splint break his stroke to reach out and toss aside a floating stick.
His legs frogged behind him. This was about the solstice, it was still very light,
she could see. He reached out, not looking too closely, not paying attention.
He was just moving a thing in his way. But when Splint grabbed hold the
branch, Cam saw it liven in his fist and change shapes. She saw it spill water,
jerk curvey in his hand. She saw it uncurl itself upright over Splint's head.

And was it a snake before he grabbed hold, or after he did? Cam used to
wonder before she grew up. Now she only wonders why neither of them
screamed.

# ALEX TAYLOR, "The Coal Thief"

A native of Rosine, Kentucky, Alex Taylor started out writing ghost stories as a boy but switched to subjects closer to home after reading Faulkner's *The Sound and the Fury* in high school. Along the way he worked a variety of odd jobs (sorghum peddler, car detailer, day laborer on tobacco farms) while earning his bachelor's degree at Western Kentucky University and a master of fine arts degree in creative writing at the University of Mississippi, where he studied with Barry Hannah. Taylor's stories have appeared in numerous journals, including *American Short Fiction, Carolina Quarterly,* and the *Oxford American.* His debut collection, *The Name of the Nearest River,* was published in 2010. Taylor teaches creative writing at McNeese State University in Louisiana.

Fellow Kentuckian Chris Offutt has praised Taylor's stories for their precisely observed characters, "real people enduring real dilemmas: resourceful, hopeful, and compassionate."[1] In "The Coal Thief," a boy and his uncle find themselves in a desperate situation after a scheme to help them survive the winter goes awry.

> I grew up in a tiny town called Rosine, over in the Western Coal Fields of Kentucky. The population is around fifty folks. I tell people this and they don't believe me. Sometimes, I get the feeling most people don't believe the Rough South exists. It's a myth, a foggy tale told in lantern light. While this belief can be frustrating, I find a certain joy in telling the Truth that everyone believes is a lie.[2]

Under the oak trees there was the smell of tobacco smoke and damp bark and dirt. The early winter light sifting through the branches showed a world stiff and still, the bank of gravel ballast just beyond the trees and then the train rails shining in the cold. Still miles distant, the morning freight blew its whistle. Soon it would breast the curve and roll past the tangle of briars where Luke hid with his uncle Ransom, but for now the train was still covered by the trees and its wail fled away through the thin misting of snow, lost and gone.

Luke watched the rails glinting blue against the pale ground, and wished for it to be night again, the fields honed with frost and he and Auncie beside the coal stove while the wind crawled through the grass beyond the door. But it would be hours before the gray light rolled away again. Now, the creosote shone on the crossties and the snow thickened in the wind, glinting like powdered glass. The train blew, closer, and Luke pushed his hands under his arms to warm them.

"Watch you don't slip when you catch it. The rungs will have ice on them," said Ransom.

Crouched beside Luke in the dead leaves and pine needles, he drew on a cigarette. The smoke pooled around his face and then blew away.

"How much do we need?" Luke asked.

"As much as you can kick off the cars." Ransom took the cigarette from his mouth, studied the wet gray end of it, and then pushed it back between his lips. "Make sure you jump before it gets to the top of the hill. It'll be carrying the mail on the down slope and you'll never make it if you wait 'til then."

He pulled an empty feedsack from his coat and held it out to Luke.

"Here. I figured you'd forget so I brought an extra."

Luke tucked the sack into his coat pocket, ashamed he had forgotten, that he was only a boy and that Ransom was right about him.

He heard the drivers churning now, the train bawling down the track like something scalded, the black smoke looming above the trees. He tried to remember everything Ransom had told him about catching trains. *The ways to get by in this world—ease into it, don't grab too fast, but let it pick you up. Don't think.* He sifted through these old lessons like a primer, but when the engine appeared down the track, dark and heavy as a rain cloud, he was afraid again.

Far down in his chest, his ribs shivered from the bucking of the rails, and snow scuttled across his neck. The sound of the train drew into him, slow and deep. Blowing on his hands, he stood to meet it.

*Don't resist. Don't think about your daddy.*

Luke wiped the snow from his eyelashes and followed Ransom out of the briars.

*Don't think.*

But he did.

He thought of other times, of years wilting into the ground cover of memory. This winter, he was only twelve, but his life felt halved already, portioned by the years before and after his father had been killed falling from a coal car. There hadn't been much left, only enough to fill a box of poplar wood too small for any man to lie down in. Any whole man.

Now he watched the train booming down the rails. Wind drew snow off the coal piled high in the cars and the engine wheezed, slowing as it came up the grade. His toes felt numb at the end of his boots and he kicked the ground to herd the blood back into his legs. There in the cold, he felt empty, as if he were no more than his ragged coat and shirt, no more than clothes draped over a cross of sticks to spook crows from a cornfield.

He felt like he might blow away.

He dug through his pockets and found the stale biscuit Auncie had given him that morning. She'd said he would get hungry and made him take it. He ate it now, the crumbs falling over his chin, and he tried to remember the lie he'd told her about where he was going, but his mind was cold and empty. All he recalled was the black dust at the bottom of the coal bucket and Auncie's blue hands reaching for him, her telling him how he didn't have to go, how she could make fire from anything, damp kindling and dress fabric, anything.

But he had gone. Because Auncie couldn't make fire from anything. She was aged, her body bent from long years of trouble, and she could tend to no fire. Nights in the house, she let the stove go cold and had to wake Luke to light it again. She was withery in these frigid months. Her mind slowed and left her dull and wandering, unable at times to even have sense enough to put socks on.

Following Ransom through the dim morning, Luke had looked back at the house settled between the persimmon trees with not a sliver of smoke rising from its chimney, and he was glad to be out in the world where the cold was no surprise. Stealing the coal was nothing. Bringing it home in a feedsack was nothing. But Auncie's hands on his coat and hearing himself lie to her while she sat in the icy kitchen—that was the hard part. Even now, Luke thought, she's got no idea. She's got no idea how cold it's going to get tonight.

The biscuit was hard and stale but good. It made him angry to taste it; to think of Auncie always good and always alone in the house made him angry as well. He was only a boy, but that thought didn't help. Coal buckets went empty and houses turned cold for boys just as they did for men and old women. There weren't any favors. There were no favors, so why shouldn't he lie to Auncie and go out in the white morning to steal coal and laugh at the thought of warm fire, of closed rooms where steamy things cooked, of the cold shut away behind a door?

He reached down and took a handful of snow from the ground, eating it slowly to wash the biscuit down. Ransom put a hand on his shoulder and pointed to the train.

"Pick up your legs when you run for it," he said. "Just reach out. She'll pick you up like a mailsack if you let her."

The train moaned again and then was flowing past them, stretching out through the trees like a shed skin. The air rushing from it was hot enough to chap Luke's cheeks, and the smell of burnt coal rose pungent and sour. Luke's heart cowered in his chest, the noise of the train pushing it deep inside him, but when Ransom began to run he followed, his boots slipping in the loose gravel. The crossties jerked under the rails and the track spikes rang out, but he was there, reaching for the icy car ladder.

And then the train took him up.

Below him, the wheels gnawed over the rails, but he held on, climbing until he reached the top of the car. Snow whirled over the coal, streaking the sky and hiding the trees behind a gauzy veil. The wind pricked his face. If he squinted, he could make out Ransom working several cars ahead, kicking the coal from the train, but the snow shifted and everything blurred.

He was very cold now. His hands ached, the knuckles showing like knots of blue rope. He sat to work in order to warm himself. He pushed his hands through the stoker coal, pushing it over the edge of the car, his hands black from the soot as the heat of the work began to draw up into his arms.

But now the train was gathering speed. The wind slapped Luke's ears and he looked over the coal cars barreling on through the snow. He knew he'd stayed on too long and was afraid. The engine had already crested the hilltop, drawing the rest of the train after it like the trail of a black robe.

The speed shook him. He hadn't paid attention and now the time for a safe jump was past. He looked for Ransom, but the cars ahead were empty.

*He's done got off,* he thought. *He's done left me.*

The pale ground was only a blur below him and when the train wailed, he stumbled, falling backward into the coal. The bricks scraped his neck and the sky above him was slate gray. Briefly, he thought of riding the train out, but he knew he couldn't do that.

He would have to jump.

It was witch-cold on top of the freight car, and the train was taking him on through white fields and winter-darkened trees, its engine burning, and he would have to jump.

Luke pulled himself up from the coal and went to the ladder. He climbed down. The ice on the rungs melted under his fingers. Below, the ground was a white river, rapid and flowing. All around, the wind swelled and the snow and coal cinders nicked his cheeks. All that was left for him to do was let go and he did. He let go and pushed himself away from the train, sprawling down into the hard gravel of the road bank, his body shuddering when it hit the ground. There was a thunder of wheels, and wind struck the oaks just below him, the air splashing everywhere. One of his legs throbbed. Blood was in his mouth. But he heard the trees clattering and the train bleeding away through the country and he stood up because he could.

He thought suddenly of the tightrope walkers he'd seen at the circus, people that ran across wires without falling. It was something he wanted to learn. Alone in his bed the night of his father's funeral he tried to cry, but his mind wandered again to the circus, the thing he wanted to join. The moon was a cupped white hand in the window ready to scoop up his tears, but they wouldn't come. He recalled his father's breath soured with bourbon and the jingling of brass fasteners on his overalls, his whiskers scratching Luke's cheeks when he kissed him goodnight, but none of that seemed enough to cry over and he thought of the circus again, the smell of manure and sawdust, the strange, bearded men in bright clothes that never lost their balance above the crowd of faces. He thought of what it would be like to die from falling. He wondered if it would feel like moonlight spilling on a cold wooden floor while winter lay adrift in the world.

Now his head filled with a dim pulsing. His lips were wet and he touched them, and his fingers came away bloody, but he was there, all in one piece. He almost laughed at what he'd done.

"Before you do anything, you better cry for your daddy some first." That's what Auncie had told him when he said he wanted to be an acrobat. But he couldn't cry. Not when there were men in the world unafraid of high drafty heights.

Ransom came walking up through the snow. His feedsack was full of coal already and he lurched from the weight of it.

"Thought maybe you'd decided to ride that cannonball out of the county," he said.

"I jumped," said Luke, smiling. "I waited too long, but I jumped anyway."

Ransom nodded, his face grave and wearied from staring through the snow. Flecks of coal dust clung to his lips. He took a freshly rolled cigarette from his pocket and ducked away from the wind to light it. When it was going good, he passed it to Luke.

"Next time you'll keep your eyes peeled," he said.

Luke only held the cigarette, its end glowing like a jewel. There was no need to smoke. Holding it and smelling the sour reek of the tobacco was enough.

"Come on," said Ransom.

They went back down the tracks to where the coal lay spilled on the ground. Snow fell down the collar of Luke's coat, but his leg hurt and the cigarette fumed in his hand and all of that pain and smoke seemed to warm him. Far away, the train squalled again and even that noise, distant and hidden by the trees, was full of heat and burning things.

Luke began filling his sack. He worked until he was panting, a glaze of sweat on his lip, his nose running.

"Ain't this a heap?" he said. His voice was beaming, but there was no answer. Luke turned and saw Ransom staring down the tracks, his face shaken and sad, his smudged gray lips drawn in against his dark teeth.

"Luke," he whispered.

A man was walking up the tracks toward them. He wore a long wool coat and a two-piece suit of tweed under that, and the light shivered against his polished boots. There was no hat on his head and the snow dotted the sleek hair greased back over his scalp in a dark frozen wave, and he seemed unbelievable, a trick of the flakes and frigid shadows.

"Who is it?" asked Luke.

"Hush," said Ransom. "He'll tell us who he is."

The man stopped a few yards from them. He stood in the middle of the tracks and his mustache was damp with snow under his nose. He was very tall and had a face like carved soap. He kept his hands in his pockets.

"Morning, boys," he said, nodding.

Ransom shifted the bag of coal to his right hand. "Morning."

The man took his hands from his pockets and Luke saw he wore a pair of leather gloves, the fresh grain shining in the snowy wet air.

"Looks to me like y'all been at some hard work." The man pointed to the bags of coal.

"We ain't broke a sweat just yet," said Ransom.

"No. Too chilly for that today, I reckon."

A strong silence crawled out of the trees. Snow whispered over the ground, but there was no other sound. In that quiet, Luke studied the tall man standing between the tracks, and thought it strange there were men like this in the world who dressed everyday in tailored suits and fresh slacks. This man was tall and the wool jacket lay clumped over his shoulders and there was a strong smell of bathwater on him.

"Do you know who I am?" the man asked.

Ransom shook his head. "Never seen you before in my life," he said.

The man grinned. "No," he said. "And you may never see me again after today. But I bet you can guess where it is I came from."

Ransom spat and wiped his mouth with the back of his hand. "I'd be guessing," he said. "But I'd say you got a badge and a gun on you somewheres."

The man drew the wool coat back. Under his arm, the handle of a revolver poked out of a holster. There was an embossed piece of metal pinned to his chest. When the man saw they had both gotten a look, he let the coat fall to place again.

"The Paducah line is my boss," he said. Then he nodded at Luke.

"Who's the boy?"

"Nobody," said Ransom. "He ain't nothing. Just a boy."

"He's not yours?"

"No. I don't know him."

"Well. You don't know many people now do you?"

Ransom didn't say anything. He wouldn't look at Luke, but stared off through the trees where the snow had spilled. His face wasn't flushed from the cold anymore, but worn and colorless, and it made Luke afraid to see the power the man in the wool coat had over his uncle, as if stitched sleeves and raggedy jackets were no match for ironed-smooth trousers.

"Hey, son," said the man, smiling at Luke. "Where'd you come from?"

Luke felt his hands begin to shake. He hid them in his pockets and tried to speak, but his voice was feathery dust in his throat.

"Nowhere," he sputtered. "I ain't nobody."

The man put his hands on his hips and stared at him. "Nobody," he said. "Nobody from nowhere. Sure. I know you. Well, let me tell you. There's a law for folk that don't have no name same for ones that do. Kicking coal off a train ain't legal for nobody."

The man reached in his coat and took out two pairs of handcuffs.

The metal clicked and glinted and looked very cold.

"Once you get these on, maybe you'll remember who you are," said the man.

He stepped forward, but Ransom dropped his bag of coal and the man stopped, his eyes peering bluntly through the snow at the two figures before him.

"Just put them on me," said Ransom. "You ain't got to cuff him. He's only a boy."

The man paused, holding the cuffs out. His mouth was open and Luke saw the pale tongue moving between his teeth.

"He was big enough to steal that coal so I reckon he's big enough to wear these cuffs," the man said.

"No. He ain't that big. Look at him," said Ransom.

Luke felt the man watching him. His neck was fevered and sweat crawled down his ribs and he had to look away through the trees rising on the hill where the snow curled in the wind like the feathers of a burst bird. Somehow, he thought of Auncie, alone in the cold house. He saw her hands scattering over the coal stove, her fingers pressed to its belly as if she could midwife some ghost of heat from it, but when he tried he could squeeze those thoughts out of his mind and see only the snow clotting over the tracks, and his heart rushed through his chest, a thickness that made his mouth dry.

"What could he do to you?" said Ransom.

"It ain't what he could do. It's what the both of you could do together."

"You put those cuffs on him and you'll never live it down."

"What's that mean?"

"Means I was in the war and did plenty of things I'm not proud of. But I never once chained up a boy. I was never that scared the whole time I was over there."

The man's lips tightened. He threw a pair of cuffs into the snow then put the others in his coat.

"Pick those up then and put them on yourself," he said to Ransom.

Ransom squatted and clicked the cuffs over his wrists. His hands had turned a vivid red in the cold and they shivered, but his face was still with flakes of snow lingering on his cheeks. When he stood up again, the man went to him and clamped the cuffs tighter until the skin shone bloodless around the metal.

"How those feel to you?" the man asked.

"Well, if they fit any better I just don't think I could stand it," said Ransom.

"I don't reckon they'll help you remember your name, will they?"

"No sir, tight metal and broken wrists usually don't serve my memory."

The man wiped the snow from his mustache and spat, but the wind rose and blew the phlegm against his coat and he raked it away, wiping the glove against his trousers when he was finished.

"Well," he said. "We'll find out who the both of you are once we get to county lockup." He pointed to Luke. "You get to tote the coal since you ain't wearing no cuffs. The Paducah company will be wanting it back."

Luke picked up the sacks of coal. They were heavy and his arms ached, but he hurried anyway, lurching and struggling as if it were the weight of water from a deep well he carried.

"Y'all walk in front of me here," said the man. He pointed to the tracks, but neither Luke or Ransom moved. "Come on," said the man. "It's cold enough to freeze your balls off out here."

"Where you'd park your car?" Ransom asked.

The man grunted and buttoned the front of his coat. "That don't really matter. We'll get there."

"Could get there faster if we cut through the woods," said Ransom. "I bet you're parked on the Percyville Trace. I know a real quick way through the trees that'll get us over there."

The man looked through the snow at the levee of black trees, the flakes thickening as they fell through the empty branches to cover the ground, blotting out all traces of travel. His breath crawled in and out of him and his face was blank.

"If you know a quicker way then show me," he said, finally. "I hate being cold worse than anything."

Ransom grinned and looked at the man. "If I show you this shortcut, what is it that you're going to do for me?"

The man raked the snow from his coat sleeves. He stared at Ransom. His eyes were blank and cold. "I don't make deals with trash," he said.

"Then I guess we're just going to have to get back to the car the long way."

"I guess so."

"We're going to have to take our time and get real cold in the going there." Ransom chuckled. "What's the coldest you ever been, Mister?"

The man said nothing. Snow had crept into the creases of his coat and slid into his collar. His face pulsed redly under the thick dark mustache he wore, the phlegm running from his nose beginning to crust on the whiskers. He pulled a silver watch from the fob pocket of his vest, checked the time, then snapped the hasp lid and grunted.

"If you can show me a shortcut," he said, "I'll see to it they go light on you and nothing won't happen to the boy. That's the best I can deal. You understand?"

Ransom nodded. "I understand real well," he said. "I know how bad it is to be cold in a strange place you ain't never been before."

Then they all straggled down the gravel bank, Ransom going first with Luke and the man in the wool jacket following him into the forest.

The ground rose steadily under them, building into a hill, and they walked in silence, their breath gathering in thick clouds. In the trees there was no wind, but they could hear it drawing through the open spaces they had left, the loose air gasping through fields and over the tracks, but where they were the snow and gray light fell listless and faint as hair. The woods were smothered in cold.

Luke could hear the man walking just behind him, his boots scratching through the frost, but he stared at Ransom's shoulders bulging against his tight black coat and did not look back. The feedsacks rubbed blisters on his hands, but he went on. The pain was easy, hidden by the cold he felt, and these woods were something he knew. His father had hunted squirrels here with him and he knew the way the trees grew, white oaks on the eastern hillsides and loblolly pine on the west. In the fall, he could find ginseng sprouting among the moss of the northern slope. In the cool places where the shade was heavy. He could find lots of things. When he looked now, he saw them all again, the ginseng and goldenseal and mayapple shooting up through the black soil, the earth surrendering its hidden life, all of it waiting to bloom again once the cold was gone. There was no need to be afraid. The coal was not heavy and the blisters on his hands didn't hurt.

They came to the top of the hill and Ransom called for them to stop. Luke dropped the sacks of coal and they slumped against his legs. He pushed his hands in his pockets, wriggling his fingers to warm them.

"I think I took a wrong turn somewhere," said Ransom. "You can't get to the Percyville Trace this way."

Ransom breathed slow and the man in the tweed suit paced on ahead, his face turning back and forth as he looked among the trees. When he turned to them again, he didn't say anything, but his eyes were full of a hardness that hadn't been there before.

"I thought you said you knew a quicker way," he said.

Ransom shrugged. "Thought that I did," he said. "But it's hard to tell rightly where you are in these trees sometimes. You can get lost real simply."

The man in the wool coat wiped at his running nose and grunted. The brass cuffbuttons at the ends of his sleeves flickered like candlefire.

"Let's head up this way," he said bluntly.

Ransom and Luke followed him down the slope, the powdered snow wetting their pant legs and their breath heaving loose inside them. After a time, the man stopped, put his hands on his hips, and stood looking about as if searching for something dropped or lost.

"Can't get to the Percyville Trace going this way neither," said Ransom, smiling. "I knew it from the start."

The man pulled at his mustache. "If you knew you should've said something before now," he said.

"Well, I seen you was bound and determined to get yourself lost so I didn't speak up. Myself, I only been lost in the woods once before today and didn't want to give advice to a feller that was clearly an expert on that kind of business."

The man's eyes flared. "Tell me where to go," he said.

"Well, I would. But it's kindly hard for me to point with my hands cuffed like this."

The man spat and shook his head. He turned away from them and looked off through the trees again. Luke could hear him whispering to himself, a sound quiet and frigid as the snow falling through the oak boughs, and it made him glad to think of the man lost in the trees he had always known.

"Listen here," said the man, turning to face them again. "You're gonna tell me how to get back to the Percyville Trace."

"Well," said Ransom. "Way you talk might make us think you didn't enjoy our company. What's the hurry?"

"I ain't standing out here in the cold all day with you two."

"Looks to me like you ain't got much say in that no more," said Ransom.

The man grunted. He paced off through the trees, squinting at the snow and light, and then stopped.

"Now these woods are an odd thing for somebody ain't never been in them before now." Ransom began to talk slowly. "You go in them thinking you can tell your way around, but the trees got a way of making you lost. You could be close enough to spit on whatever it is you're looking for and never know it's in here."

Ransom squatted in the snow. He looked up through the trees, then brought his hands to his face and breathed through his fingers. Then he looked at Luke hunched inside his jacket and he nodded at the sacks of coal lying at the boy's feet.

"My daddy brought me in here when I wasn't eight years old," Ransom continued. "Walked me through the trees and then left me. This was in the summertime. I didn't have no water with me and by the time I finally found my way out I guess I'd drunk the sweat out of somebody's boots I was so thirsty. Don't you know I looked a sight, too. Covered in ticks and briar scrapes."

Ransom stared at Luke while he talked. Every little bit he nodded at the sacks of coal and Luke couldn't think what that might mean, what he wanted him to do, but he felt the cold leaking out of him and heat rolled in his belly.

"Course my daddy weren't mean for doing that. It's an odd business raising a boy. That's all. You got to give them a chance at standing by theirself in the world. And there ain't no shame in making it hard on them neither. I think about that day when I was lost out here and it was so hot the birds had stopped talking and the woods were so empty it was like I was the only thing living in the world. Day like that will teach a boy some things."

The man in the wool jacket came back through the snow. Ransom stood up and they glared at each other, the man's face shivering and blotched. Ransom's eyes calm and still.

"Think I've heard enough," said the man. "Now show me how to get back to the Percyville Trace."

Ransom shook his head. "I ain't showing you a damn thing," he said.

The man pulled the revolver from his coat and pointed it at Ransom.

"You going to shoot us, Mister?" Luke asked.

The man did not look away from Ransom. "I'm gonna take y'all out these woods is what I'm gonna do." He jerked the barrel toward the trees. "Lead us on," he said to Ransom.

Ransom didn't move. He stared at the blue gun barrel, the breath trickling over his lips. His face was still calm as if what he watched was no more than the dawn breaking loosely and dim over the fields and trees, the man with the gun only a piece of quivering shadow the light would soon take.

"Get to walking," said the man.

Ransom jerked his head once, then again.

*He ain't going to do it,* Luke thought. *He's going to get us killed.*

The man's breath was faster now, whistling through the spaces in his teeth, and the blood had come to his face, the blotches melding together so his cheeks glowed the color of hot iron.

Luke knew he was going to shoot them both. Out here in the snow, in these forest depths, no one would hear. The sound would be muffled by the thinly trickling snow, and the thought made Luke very hot inside his jacket. He felt the wind frisking his clothes, sliding down his collar.

"You going to shoot us?" he asked again.

The man kept his eyes and the revolver pointed at Ransom. His hand was shaking now but he didn't try to hide it.

"You're gonna take me out of this place," he said.

"No," said Ransom. "I ain't neither."

The man's face went blank. The color fled from his cheeks. He stepped forward and swung the pistol, bringing the butt down hard on Ransom's neck, the sound dull and thick. Ransom crumpled to the ground, his eyes shut tight. The man stood over him, his back turned to Luke. He was raising the pistol again, but would use the business end of it this time. Then Ransom rolled onto his back, his face a fierce tear, his eyes jagged streaks as he looked at Luke.

"The coal!" Ransom shouted. "Get him with the coal!"

Luke was startled by his voice, so full of fear and blunt pain. But the man in the wool coat was turning to him now, slowly, the edge of his pale face glinting like a shard of moonlight, and Luke did not have time to be afraid anymore. He jerked up a sack of coal and swung it hard. It hit the man in the chest and he sprawled backward into the snow, his mouth open as if this were all a mild surprise. Luke hit him again with the coal, in the belly this time, and the sack burst, spilling coal chunks over the snow.

The man grunted and rolled onto his stomach. He was trying to stand up, but Ransom tackled him from behind, and they twisted together, throwing snow into the air, their faces slurring while they fought.

*The gun,* thought Luke. *He's still got the gun and he ain't dropped it.*

Watching them struggle, he was afraid again. The fear had come surging back through him after the coal sack burst, and now he stood rigid, looking on the pair of men fighting in the snow as if it were something eventual that couldn't be helped. He was cold all over and when the shot came, it was a sound as dull and forceless as an ax striking ice. There was no echo. There was only the grunt of the gun, thick and clumsy. The two men were both lying still now, piled together, but Luke saw the blood sprayed over the snow, its heat melting holes in the frost.

Slowly, he moved forward. His head felt stiff and his eyes watered from the cold, but he went to them.

*This is me walking a high wire,* he thought. *This is the thing you see before you die from falling.*

Ransom was dead. His ruined face was wet with blood, the eyes wide just below the bullet hole. The man in the wool jacket rolled from underneath his body. He pointed the revolver at him, but Luke kept coming. He was cold and afraid and he stood over Ransom's body, the slack mouth and pale lips like the face of a man waiting for a long drink.

"You both tried to kill me," gasped the man in the wool jacket. He staggered up from the snow and kept his gun on Luke. He was breathing heavy now and the front of his suit was slick with blood.

Luke squatted beside his uncle Ransom. Far off, the moan of another train drifted to him through the trees. The wind came crouching up through the brambles and thorns, slinking over the snow. Luke looked at the sky twisted and caught in the oak branches. He thought of Auncie stirring some cold pan of beans, shuffling from the empty coal stove to the window to watch for him, waiting for him to come and warm the home, to make things well with fire.

"You goddamn hillbillies," said the man. His lip was bleeding and he spat redness onto the snowy ground. He wiped his face with his gloves. Then he picked up a handful of snow and held it to his lip, the water dribbling off his chin. "You both tried to kill me," he said again.

Luke stood up fully. Ransom was dead now. Ransom was dead and his father was dead and Auncie was waiting lonely and freezing in the tiny house and he was here in the snow, his fingers going numb with cold.

"Mister," he said. "Do they got some nice warm beds at that jail in town?"

The man shook his head, the swoop of shining black hair blowing frayed over his brow. The blood on his coat and trousers looked like woodstain and he kept touching it, wiping its wetness with his gloved fingers.

"We got to get out of these goddamn woods," he said. "I can't hardly feel my toes anymore."

The man's face had turned a bleak cindery gray. His lips looked as if they'd been painted with billiard chalk and his hands shook as he pointed off through the trees.

"C'mon. Show me," he said. "Show me where to go."

Luke looked at Ransom's body where it lay in the frost like strewn water. "I can't take us out of here," he said. "I don't know the way to go."

The man in the coat flew at him, grabbing his collar and yanking him close so that his breath clawed at Luke's eyeballs, cold and barbarous. "You little shit," he said. "You little goddamn shit. You know the way and you're going to tell me." The man held the revolver under Luke's chin. The barrel felt sharp and icy against his skin. Slowly, the man raised his free hand and pointed at Ransom. "You don't show me the way out of here and I'll blow you're head off same as I did to him."

Luke felt the blood rushing through him, molten and thick.

*He will do it,* Luke thought. *He will kill me out here same as stomping a mouse.*

"Okay," he said. "Let me go. I think I know the way back to the tracks. Let me go and I'll see if I can get us there."

The man's grip slackened and his hands fell away from Luke's collar. He straightened the front of his jacket for him and a grin grew under his mustache, his spacey white teeth coming out of the dark whiskers like stars.

"That's a good boy," he said. He waved the pistol at the trees. "Lead me on."

Luke nodded. He went to the one unbroken sack of coal and picked it up, hefting it over his shoulder.

"What the hell are you doing with that?" the man asked.

"Taking it with me," said Luke. "You said the Paducah Line wanted it back."

The man grunted. "You goddamn crazy hillbillies," he said. "I don't see why they don't put the whole damn bunch of y'all in a cage somewhere. You'd eat each other alive and then nobody would have to worry with you no more."

"Sure," said Luke, nodding. "Okay. Sure. Let's get going then. On over this way. That's the right way to go."

He hobbled off through the thickest part of the trees. The man followed, his boots whispering through the fine morning-fallen snow. Luke went on and he did not look back at Ransom lying dead in the frost, his blood cooling in the snow. He did not look back because he did not have to. All he needed was right in front of him. It was the closed frozen woods, the trees rearing black against the white sky like cracks in porcelain, the snow so thick now that it had hidden their footprints, the swelling hills and deep hollows where things could be lost so simply that no one would ever even think to look for them again. It was the coal riding his back. That was all anyone could need. And he could go on for just a little while longer through the cold, leading the man in the wool coat over the snow-covered lands that were strange to men of his kind, men who wore gloves of grainy leather and smelled of sudsy baths. Luke could go with him in the pale blanched world, both of them getting cold, cold, cold until the man would stop, his slow breath crawling out between the blue lips, the breath slow and slowly crawling until it was all still and nothing but quiet remained. Then Luke could go on home to Auncie and make big fires in the stove with the coal and warm himself under blankets and be not afraid.

He could do this because it was all there was left for him to do. Walking in the snow with the man trailing behind him, Luke remembered the acrobats again. Those were men unafraid. Odd fellows borne aloft on high wires like the angels Auncie sang hymns about. And the main part of walking a wire was waiting. Waiting for the exact perfect moment when all was balanced and you could put your foot down and go on again.

"We're going the right way," Luke said over his shoulder. "We're not far now."

He heard the man grunt, but there was no other sound. The snow had stopped and all was quiet.

Luke went on through it. His hands were cold and bare, but he was going to the place where he was needed, and a great surge of joy sprang in him so that he stepped up onto a fallen oak log and walked along it, treading softly, one arm out for balance.

"Goddamn crazy hillbillies," he heard the man say.

But Luke did not turn to look and he did not fall. Already he knew the man's breath was slowing, the cold making him stone. Soon the man would lie down in the snow and his heart would grow quiet. Luke knew he could wait for it to happen. Walking along the oak log, he knew he could wait for a long time. A long cold time.

# Notes

**PREFACE**

1. Nancy Pearl, "Grit Lit," in *Book Lust: Recommended Reading for Every Mood, Moment, and Reason* (Seattle, Wash.: Sasquatch Books, 2003), 106.

2. Tony Earley, "Mephisto Tennessee Waltz," review of *The Long Home,* by William Gay, *New York Times,* November 21, 1999, http://www.nytimes.com/books/99/11/21/reviews/991121.21earleyt.html.

**INTRODUCTION**

1. The line comes from Cummings's poem "Buffalo Bill's." Brown actually lists the legend differently, but David Aronson gets it right in the introduction to his interview with Crews, "Writing Is an Act of Discovery: Harry Crews," in *Getting Naked with Harry Crews: Interviews,* ed. Erik Bledsoe (Gainesville: University Press of Florida, 1999), 268.

2. Joann Biondi, "Still Macho after All These Years," in *Getting Naked with Harry Crews,* 264.

3. Ibid, 263.

4. Harry Crews, "A Day at the Dogfights," in *Florida Frenzy* (Gainesville: University Press of Florida, 1983), 59; Crews, "Going Down in Valdeez," in *Blood and Grits* (New York: Harper Perennial, 1979, 1988), 72; Crews, "A Night at a Waterfall," in *Blood and Grits,* 42.

5. For a good example, see Ruth Ellen Rasche's 1992 profile, "Blue-Eyed Boy," in *Getting Naked with Harry Crews,* in which Crews describes designing his Mohawk haircut "with malice and forethought." Says Crews's mother, "He says he wants to give people something to look at, something to talk about. I guess he has." Rasche, "Blue-Eyed Boy," in *Getting Naked with Harry Crews,* 294.

6. See George Terll, "Remembrances of Tim McLaurin: A Document in Oral History," ed. Jerry Leath Mills, *Pembroke Magazine,* no. 36 (2004): 70.

7. "Author Tim McLaurin illustrated the concept of conflict in storytelling by brandishing a yard-long viper before his astonished audience and explaining, 'If there's no conflict, there's no story.'" Novello Festival website, http://novellofestival.net/about.asp (accessed September 16, 2005).

8. Hal Crowther, quoted in Joe Mandel, ed., "A Tribute to Tim McLaurin," *Pembroke Magazine,* no. 36 (2004): 127.

9. Harry Crews, "Television's Junkyard Dog," in *Blood and Grits,* 145.

10. Dorothy Allison, "Deciding to Live: Preface to the First Edition," in *Trash* (New York: Plume, 1988, 2002), 7.

11. Cormac McCarthy's absence from this anthology is not due to editorial oversight but to the author's own "blanket policy" of not allowing his work to be excerpted. McCarthy's work, especially his early Tennessee novels, should be required reading for any serious student of Grit Lit and the Rough South.

12. Lewis Nordan, foreword to *Tobacco Road,* by Erskine Caldwell (Athens: University of Georgia Press, 1932, 1995), vi.

13. Flannery O'Connor, "Some Aspects of the Grotesque in Southern Fiction," in *Mystery and Manners: Occasional Prose,* ed. Sally and Robert Fitzgerald (New York: Farrar, Straus & Giroux, 1962, 1977), 38; see also John Seelye, "Georgia Boys: The Redclay Satyrs of Erskine Caldwell and Harry Crews," *Virginia Quarterly Review* 56 (Autumn 1980): 612–26.

14. William Faulkner, introduction to *Sanctuary* (1931; New York: Modern Library, 1932), vi.

15. William Byrd II, "The Dividing Line Expedition," in *The Literary South,* ed. Louis D. Rubin Jr. (Baton Rouge: Louisiana State University Press, 1986), 33.

16. Faulkner, introduction to *Sanctuary,* v; Faulkner, *The Town* (New York: Random House, 1961), 40.

17. See Bill Crider, "Sons of *Tobacco Road:* 'Backwoods' Novels," *Journal of Popular Culture* 16, no. 3 (1982): 47–59.

18. O'Connor, "The Crop," in *The Complete Stories of Flannery O'Connor* (New York: Farrar, Straus & Giroux, 1971, 1988), 34–36; O'Connor, "On Her Own Work," in *Mystery and Manners,* 118.

19. Flannery O'Connor, "The Fiction Writer & His Country," in *Mystery and Manners,* 34.

20. Crews, *Blood and Grits,* 145.

21. Allison, "Introduction: Stubborn Girls and Mean Stories," in *Trash,* xv–xvi, xii, ix.

22. Harry Crews, *A Childhood,* reprinted in *Classic Crews* (New York: Poseidon Press, 1993), 158.

23. Duane Carr, "Harry Crews: The Dispossessed as Poor White Trash," in *A Question of Class: The Redneck Stereotype in Southern Fiction* (Bowling Green, Ohio: Bowling Green State University Popular Press, 1996), 136; James H. Watkins, "'The Use of *I,* Lovely and Terrifying Word': Autobiographical Authority and the Representation of 'Redneck' Masculinity in *A Childhood,*" in *Perspectives on Harry Crews,* ed. Erik Bledsoe (Jackson: University Press of Mississippi, 2001), 18, 20.

24. Allison, *Trash,* vii, xii, vii, xvi.

25. Robert Gingher, "Grit Lit," in *The Companion to Southern Literature: Themes, Genres, Places, People, Movements, and Motifs,* ed. Joseph M. Flora and Lucinda H. Mackethan (Baton Rouge: Louisiana State University Press, 2002), 319.

26. Allen Tate, "Memoirs and Opinions," in *Memories and Essays, Old and New, 1926–1974* (Manchester, U.K.: Carcanet Press, 1976), 5–8; Joseph Blotner, *Faulkner: A Biography* (1974; repr., one-vol. ed., New York: Vintage, 1991), 684–85.

27. Hal Crowther, "The Last Autochthon: Listening to the Land," in *Gather at the River: Notes from the Post-Millennial South* (Baton Rouge: Louisiana State University Press), 82.

28. See Clay Risen, "Out of Nowhere: After Decades of Laboring in Complete Obscurity, Middle Tennessee Author William Gay Has Finally Found Literary Acclaim," *Nashville Scene,* January 16, 2003, http://www.nashvillescene.com/nashville/out-of-nowhere/Content?oid=1188010.

29. For another version of the "Wild Larry" story, see Gary Hawkins's profile "Just One More: Larry Brown (1951–2004)," *Oxford American,* Spring 2005, 138; for Barry Hannah's last word on the infamous pistol incident, see his interview with Lacey Galbraith, "Barry Hannah, the Art of Fiction No. 184," *Paris Review* 172 (Winter 2004), 62–63.

30. See photo in David Molpus, "Flea Markets and Rural Life Fodder for South Carolina Writer," *Morning Edition,* National Public Radio, August 16, 2001, http://www.npr.org/programs/morning/features/2001/aug/southern/010816.southern.singleton.html.

31. "Watson's muscular prose stands shoulder to shoulder with the best cracker realists, from Faulkner to Larry Brown.—*Kirkus Reviews*" (blurb inside the 1997 Delta paperback edition of Watson's *Last Days of the Dog-Men*); "When *Fay* was released in 2000, *Booklist* . . . called it an 'awful, beautiful work from the King of White Trash.'" (Bob Minzesheimer, "Remembering Larry Brown," *USA Today,* November 29, 2004, http://www.usatoday.com/life/books/news/2004-11-29-larry-brown-appreciation_x.htm).

32. Keith Perry, "Fireman-Writer, Bad Boy Novelist, King of Grit Lit: 'Building' Larry Brown(s) at Algonquin Books of Chapel Hill," in *Larry Brown and the Blue-Collar South,* ed. Jean W. Cash and Keith Perry (Jackson: University Press of Mississippi, 2008), 146, 139, 151.

33. Robert Gingher, "Grit Lit," in *The Companion to Southern Literature,* 319; Scott Romine, *The Real South: Southern Narrative in the Age of Cultural Reproduction* (Baton Rouge: Louisiana State University Press, 2008), 61.

34. Robert Rebein, *Hicks, Tribes, and Dirty Realists: American Fiction after Postmodernism* (Lexington: University Press of Kentucky, 2001), 68, 73.

35. Romine, *The Real South,* 61; Barry Hannah, *Ray* (New York: Knopf, 1980), 100.

36. Crews, *A Childhood,* in *Classic Crews,* 28, 45.

37. Fred Hobson, "The Savage South: An Inquiry into the Origins, Endurance, and Presumed Demise of an Image," in *The Silencing of Emily Mullen and Other Essays* (Baton Rouge: Louisiana State University Press, 2005), 130.

38. Chris Offutt, "Melungeons," in *Out of the Woods* (New York: Scribner, 1999), 51; Tim McLaurin, quoted in "An Interview with Tim McLaurin," by Joe Mandel, *Pembroke Magazine,* no. 36 (2004): 133.

39. Crews, *A Childhood,* in *Classic Crews,* 23; Crews, "Television's Junkyard Dog," in *Blood and Grits,* 141.

40. Tim McLaurin, quoted in "An Interview," *Pembroke Magazine,* 133.

41. Harry Crews, "The Violence That Finds Us," in *2 by Crews* (Northridge, Calif.: Lord John Press, 1984), 16.

42. Barry Hannah, quoted in "Writer Barry Hannah," interviewed by Terry Gross, *Fresh Air,* National Public Radio, July 31, 2001, http://www.npr.org/templates/story/story.php?storyId=1126675.

43. Harry Crews, quoted in "Harry Crews," by William Walsh, in *Getting Naked with Harry Crews,* 242.

44. Crews, "The Violence That Finds Us," in *2 by Crews,* 17.

45. Cormac McCarthy, quoted in Richard B. Woodward, "Cormac McCarthy's Venomous Fiction," *New York Times,* April 19, 1992, http://www.nytimes.com/books/98/05/17/specials/mccarthy-venom.html?_r=1&oref=slogin; Woodward, "Cormac Country," *Vanity Fair,* August 2005, 103; McCarthy, quoted in Woodward, "Cormac Country," *Vanity Fair,* 103–4.

46. Crews, *2 by Crews,* 3.

47. Lewis Nordan, *The Sharpshooter Blues* (Chapel Hill, N.C.: Algonquin Books, 1995), 62.

48. Crews, "Tuesday Night with Cody, Jimbo, and a Fish of Some Proportion," in *Florida Frenzy,* 66.

49. O'Connor, appendix to *Mystery and Manners,* 234.

50. Crews, "A Day at the Dogfights," in *Florida Frenzy,* 57.

51. Tim McLaurin, *Keeper of the Moon: A Southern Boyhood* (New York: Anchor Books, 1991, 1992), 35.

52. Tom Franklin, "Poachers," in *Poachers* (New York: William Morrow, 1999), 189.

53. Larry Brown, "92 Days," in *Big Bad Love* (Chapel Hill, N.C.: Algonquin, 1990), 143.

54. J. Wayne Flynt, *Dixie's Forgotten People: The South's Poor Whites,* new ed. (Bloomington: Indiana University Press, 2004), 1–2. See also Gerald R. Johnson's 1935 essay, "The Horrible South," in which he lambasts Erskine Caldwell and the "horror-mongers" of the "Raw-Head-and-Bloody-Bones" school of southern fiction for "[tilling] a field that is both narrow and barren." Though he commended him for "[grappling] courageously and vigorously with the problems of the modern South," Johnson complained that Caldwell was "wasting a fine talent" by writing about "half-wits" and those in the "Southern social depths," and that his "artistic effectiveness" was being used for little more than to "spread an iridescent shimmer over the slime." Johnson, *South-Watching: Selected Essays,* ed. Fred Hobson (Chapel Hill: University of North Carolina Press, 1983), 37, 40, 42.

55. Wray, Matt. *Not Quite White: White Trash and the Boundaries of Whiteness* (Durham, N.C.: Duke University Press, 2006), 1.

56. Flynt, *Dixie's Forgotten People,* xviii; Brown, dedication to his novel *Fay* (Chapel Hill, N.C.: Algonquin Books, 2000).

57. See Martin Luther King Jr.'s 1965 speech "Our God Is Marching On!," in which he describes how "the southern aristocracy took the world and gave the poor white man Jim Crow," a "psychological bird that told him that no matter how bad off he was, at least he was a white man, better than the black man." Martin Luther King Jr., "'Our God Is Marching On!' Montgomery, Alabama, Speech (1965)," in *A Testament of Hope: The Essential Writings and Speeches of Martin Luther King, Jr.* (New York: HarperOne, 1990), 227–30.

58. James C. Cobb, *Away Down South: A History of Southern Identity* (Oxford: Oxford University Press, 2005), 222, 227; for a photo of that "Redneck Power" T-shirt, see José Blanco F., "Becoming Billy Carter: Clothes Make the Man (and His Many Characters)," *Southern Cultures* 16 (Summer 2010): 21.

59. Dorothy Allison, e-mail message to the author, March 18, 2011.

60. For an early reference to "Grit Lit," see Mary Voboril, "Harry Goes Cruising for a Bruising," *Miami Herald,* June 28, 1987; reprinted in *Getting Naked with Harry Crews,* 228.

61. Gary Hawkins, quoted in "Afterword: On *The Rough South of Larry Brown:* An Interview with Filmmaker Gary Hawkins," by Katherine Powell, in *Larry Brown and the Blue-Collar South,* ed. Jean W. Cash and Keith Perry (Jackson: University Press of Mississippi, 2008), 170.

62. Dorothy Allison, quoted in Aaron Collier and Casey Tuggle, "Character Sketches from the Conference on Southern Literature," *Chatterati,* April 7, 2009, http://chattarati.com/metro/economy/2009/4/7/character-sketches-the-conference-southern-literat/.

63. Noel Polk, "Upon Being Southernovelized: My Town, My Department, My Friends, and Me in a Carpetbagger Novel," in *Outside the Southern Myth* (Jackson: University Press of Mississippi, 1997), 13.

64. Walker Percy, quoted in Jan Nordby Gretlund, "Laying the Ghost of Marcus Aurelius?," in *Conversations with Walker Percy,* ed. Lewis A. Lawson and Victor A. Kramer (Jackson: University Press of Mississippi, 1985), 214.

65. Erik Bledsoe, "The Rise of Southern Redneck and White Trash Writers," *Southern Cultures* 6 (Spring 2000): 78.

66. Rick Bragg, *All Over but the Shoutin'* (New York: Pantheon, 1997), 61, xvii, 66.

67. John N. Duvall, *Race and White Identity in Southern Fiction: From Faulkner to Morrison* (New York: Palgrave Macmillan, 2008), xviii; Allison, *Bastard Out of Carolina* (New York: Plume, 1993), 102.

68. Candler Hunt, quoted on George Singleton's website, www.georgesingleton.com (accessed July 7, 2011).

69. Jill McCorkle, *Ferris Beach* (Chapel Hill, N.C.: Algonquin, 1990), 46.

70. Crews, *A Childhood,* in *Classic Crews,* 101.

71. Lee Smith, "Preface: Driving Miss Daisy Crazy; or, Losing the Mind of the South," in *New Stories from the South: The Year's Best, 2001* (Chapel Hill, N.C.: Algonquin Books, 2001), xiii.

72. Lee Smith, e-mail message to the author, March 23, 2011.

73. Ann Pancake, e-mail message to the author, March 20, 2011.

74. Dorothy Allison, e-mail message to the author, March 18, 2011.

75. James Wood, "Red Planet: The Sanguinary Sublime of Cormac McCarthy," review of *No Country for Old Men,* by Cormac McCarthy, *New Yorker,* July 25, 2005, 88.

76. Dorothy Allison, quoted on back cover, *Winter's Bone,* by Daniel Woodrell (New York: Little, Brown and Co., 2006).

77. Tim Gautreaux, "Preface: Warts and All," in *New Stories from the South: The Year's Best, 2004* (Chapel Hill, N.C.: Algonquin Books, 2004), ix.

78. Erskine Caldwell, "Saturday Afternoon," in *The Pocket Book of Erskine Caldwell Stories* (New York: Pocket Books, 1947), 256.

79. Tim Gautreaux, "Warts," *New Stories,* ix, vii.

80. William Gay, quoted in "An Interview with William Gay," by Georgia Afton, *Water-Stone Review* 7 (2004): 11.

81. Dorothy Allison, "River of Names" in *Trash,* 12; Brad Watson, "Kindred Spirits," in *Last Days of the Dog-Men* (New York: W. W. Norton, 1996), 128.

82. Pinckney Benedict, e-mail message to the author, March 28, 2011.

83. Larry Brown, *Dirty Work* (Chapel Hill, N.C.: Algonquin Books, 1989), 128–29; Brown, "A Roadside Resurrection," in *The Christ-Haunted South: Faith and Doubt in Southern Fiction,* ed. Susan Ketchin (Jackson: University Press of Mississippi, 1994), 123.

84. William Gay, *The Long Home* (Denver, Colo.: MacMurray & Beck, 1999), 91–98; Gay, *Provinces of Night* (New York: Doubleday, 2000), 46–53.

85. Mark Richard, "Strays," in *The Ice at the Bottom of the World* (New York: Knopf, 1989), 9.

86. Harry Crews, *A Feast of Snakes* (New York: Atheneum, 1976), 23.

87. Lewis Nordan, *The Sharpshooter Blues* (Chapel Hill, N.C.: Algonquin Books, 1995), 58.

88. Ed Park, "Like Cormac McCarthy, but Funny," *Believer,* March 2003, http://www.believermag.com/issues/200303/?read=article_park; Cormac McCarthy, *Suttree* (New York: Random House, 1979), 48, 33; McCarthy, *Child of God* (New York: Random House, 1974), 120, 77, 79.

89. Roy Blount Jr., introduction to *Roy Blount's Book of Southern Humor* (New York: W. W. Norton & Co., 1994), 31.

90. Lewis M. Killian, *White Southerners,* rev. ed. (Amherst: University of Massachusetts Press, 1985), 5.

91. Rick Bragg, *All Over but the Shoutin',* 56.

### HARRY CREWS, *A CHILDHOOD:*
### *THE BIOGRAPHY OF A PLACE*

1. Richard Sherrill, "A Son of the Hungry South," review of *A Childhood,* by Harry Crews, *New York Times,* December 24, 1978, 17.

2. Harry Crews, *A Childhood,* reprinted in *Classic Crews* (New York: Poseidon Press, 1993), 23.

### DOROTHY ALLISON, "DECIDING TO LIVE"

1. Dorothy Allison, quoted in "Dorothy Allison: Author of *Bastard Out of Carolina* Talks with Robert Birnbaum," by Robert Birnbaum *identitytheory.com* October 21, 2002, http://www.identitytheory.com/people/birnbaum67.html; Allison, *Trash,* 1, 7.

2. Allison, quoted in "Dorothy Allison Talks about Working-Class Guilt, the Film Version of 'Bastard Out of Carolina' and Coming Out—as a Science Fiction Fan," by Laura Miller, *Salon.com* March 31, 1998, http://www.salon.com/books/int/1998/03/cov_si_31intb.html.

### LARRY BROWN, *ON FIRE: A PERSONAL ACCOUNT*
### *OF LIFE AND DEATH AND CHOICES*

1. Larry Brown, quoted in "Interview with Larry Brown: Bread Loaf 1992," by Dorie LaRue, in *Conversations with Larry Brown,* ed. Jay Watson (Jackson: University Press of Mississippi, 2007), 49; Brown, quoted in "Telling Stories: An Interview with Larry Brown," by Michael Manley, in *Conversations,* 72.

2. Brown, quoted in "An Interview with Larry Brown," by Kay Bonetti, *Conversations with American Novelists: The Best Interviews from the Missouri Review and the American Audio Prose Library,* ed. Kay Bonetti et al. (Columbia: University of Missouri Press, 1997), 248.

### TIM MCLAURIN, *KEEPER OF THE MOON:*
### *A SOUTHERN BOYHOOD*

1. Roy Blount Jr., quoted on back cover, *Keeper of the Moon,* by Tim McLaurin.

2. Tim McLaurin, *The River Less Run* (Asheboro, N.C.: Down Home Press, 2000), 128.

### RICK BRAGG, *AVA'S MAN* AND
### *ALL OVER BUT THE SHOUTIN'*

1. Rick Bragg, "In His Own Words," Random House website, http://www.randomhouse.com/acmart/catalog/display.pperl?isbn=9780679774020&view=printrg (accessed July 13, 2011).

2. Anthony Walton, "The Hard Road from Dixie," review of *All Over but the Shoutin',* by Rick Bragg, *New York Times,* September 14, 1997, http://www.nytimes.com/books/97/09/14/reviews/970914.14waltont.html?_r=1&scp=1&sq=anthony%20walton%20rick%20bragg%20hard%20road&st=cse.

3. Rick Bragg, e-mail message to the author, March 28, 2011.

### LEWIS NORDAN, "A BODY IN THE RIVER"

1. Lewis Nordan, *Boy with Loaded Gun: A Memoir* (Chapel Hill, N.C.: Algonquin Books 2000), 82.

2. Nordan, quoted in "Get Back to Where You Once Belonged: Down in Delta Land with Lewis Nordan," by James L. Dickerson, *Book Page,* February 2000, http://www.bookpage .com/0002bp/lewis_nordan.html.

### HARRY CREWS, *A FEAST OF SNAKES*

1. Harry Crews, quoted in "The Freedom to Act: An Interview with Harry Crews," by Rodney Elrod, in *Getting Naked with Harry Crews: Interviews,* ed. Erik Bledsoe (Gainesville: University Press of Florida, 1999), 182.

### BARRY HANNAH, "RIDE, FLY, PENETRATE, LOITER"

1. Brad Watson, quoted in "Barry Hannah, Brad Watson, and Larry Brown: The Radio Session," by Jay Watson, in *Conversations with Larry Brown,* ed. Jay Watson (Jackson: University Press of Mississippi, 2007), 138.

2. Barry Hannah, quoted in "Writer Barry Hannah," by Terry Gross, *Fresh Air,* National Public Radio, July 31, 2001, http://www.npr.org/templates/story/story.php?storyId=1126675.

### BREECE D'J PANCAKE, "THE SCRAPPER"

1. Andre Dubus III, "A New Afterword," in *The Stories of Breece D'J Pancake* (New York: Back Bay Books, 2002), 185.

2. Dominic Luxford, "Breece Is Back," *Austin Chronicle,* July 26, 2002, 2011, http://www .austinchronicle.com/gyrobase/Issue/story?oid=oid%3A98255.

### LARRY BROWN, "SAMARITANS"

1. Larry Brown, quoted in "Larry Brown: Proceeding out from Calamity," by Susan Ketchin, in *Conversations with Larry Brown,* ed. Jay Watson (Jackson: University Press of Mississippi, 2007), 29.

2. Brown, quoted in "The Rough South of Larry Brown," by Gary Hawkins, *Conversations with Larry Brown,* 160.

### TIM MCLAURIN, *THE ACORN PLAN*

1. Tim McLaurin, *The Acorn Plan* (New York: Norton, 1988), 1.

2. McLaurin, quoted in "An Interview with Tim McLaurin," by Joe Mandel, *Pembroke Magazine,* no. 36 (2004): 133.

### DOROTHY ALLISON, "RIVER OF NAMES"

1. Dorothy Allison, "Lecture I: Mean Stories and Stubborn Girls," *The Tanner Lectures on Human Values,* delivered at Stanford University May 14 and 15, 2001, 306, 310–11, http:// www.tannerlectures.utah.edu/lectures/documents/Allison_02.pdf (accessed January 11, 2012).

### PINCKNEY BENEDICT, "PIT"

1. Mary Morris, quoted on back cover, *Town Smokes,* by Pinckney Benedict (Princeton, N.J.: Ontario Review Books, 2002).

2. Pinckney Benedict, e-mail message to the author, March 28, 2011.

### LEWIS NORDAN, *THE SHARPSHOOTER BLUES*

1. Unsigned review of *Music of the Swamp,* by Lewis Nordan, *Publishers Weekly,* July 29, 1991, http://www.publishersweekly.com/978-0-945575-76-4.

2. Lewis Nordan, quoted in "An Interview with Lewis Nordan," by Blake Maher, *Southern Quarterly* 34, no. 1 (1995): 118.

### JIM GRIMSLEY, "YOUR DADDY IN TIME"

1. Lynna Williams, quoted in Richard Hermes, "The Ability to Imagine," *Emory Magazine* 75 (Autumn 1999), http://www.emory.edu/EMORY_MAGAZINE/fall99/grimsley.html.

2. Jim Grimsley, quoted in Lisa Howorth, "Jim Grimsley: Tales of Southern Courage," *Publishers Weekly,* November 15, 1999, http://www.publishersweekly.com/pw/print/19991115/27959-jim-grimsley-tales-of-southern-courage-.html.

### CHRIS OFFUTT, "MELUNGEONS"

1. Mark Lucas, "Review: *Out of the Woods: Stories,*" *Carolina Quarterly* 52 (Spring 2000): 88–89.

2. Chris Offutt, *The Same River Twice* (New York: Simon & Schuster, 1993), 19–20.

### GEORGE SINGLETON, "JACKSONVILLE"

1. Tony Earley, quoted on back cover, *The Half-Mammals of Dixie,* by George Singleton (Chapel Hill, N.C.: Algonquin Books, 2002).

2. George Singleton, e-mail message to the author, April 6, 2011.

### DALE RAY PHILLIPS, "WHAT IT COST TRAVELERS"

1. Dale Ray Phillips, quoted in "Old Times on the Haw: An Interview with Dale Ray Phillips," by George Hovis and Timothy Williams, *Carolina Quarterly* 55 (Summer 2003): 67.

2. Dale Ray Phillips, *My People's Waltz* (New York: Norton, 1999), 88, 106, 113.

3. Phillips, e-mail message to the author, June 27, 2011.

### LEE SMITH, *SAVING GRACE*

1. Unsigned review of *Oral History,* by Lee Smith, *Village Voice,* August 2, 1983.

2. Smith, e-mail message to the author, March 23, 2011.

### ROBERT MORGAN, "SLEEPY GAP"

1. Dwight Garner, "This Old House," review of *Gap Creek,* by Robert Morgan, *New York Times,* October 10, 1999, http://www.nytimes.com/books/99/10/10/reviews/991010.10garnert.html.

2. Robert Morgan, quoted in "Interview: Robert Morgan," by Ron Hogan, *Beatrice.com* (2000), http://www.beatrice.com/interviews/morgan/ (accessed July 6, 2011).

## WILLIAM GAY, "WHERE WILL YOU GO WHEN YOUR SKIN CANNOT CONTAIN YOU?"

1. Richard Bernstein, "Voodoo and Baby Bones among Other Oddities," review of *Provinces of Night,* by William Gay, *New York Times,* January 1, 2001, http://www.nytimes.com/2001/01/01/books/books-of-the-times-voodoo-and-baby-bones-among-other-oddities.html.

2. William Gay, quoted in "Interview: William Gay," by Kenny Torella, April 13, 2008, Middle Tennessee State University Tennessee Literary Project website, http://www.mtsu.edu/tnlitproj/TLP_William_Gay_Interview.pdf (accessed July 6, 2011).

## BRAD WATSON, "KINDRED SPIRITS"

1. Tom De Haven, "Barking up the Wrong Trees," review of *Last Days of the Dog-Men,* by Brad Watson, *New York Times Book Review,* June 9, 1996. Accessed through Newspaper Source Plus (accession number 29807235).

2. Brad Watson, e-mail message to the author, January 28, 2011.

## TIM GAUTREAUX, "SORRY BLOOD"

1. Tim Gautreaux, quoted in "Tim Gautreaux: Grace in Ordinary Places," by Amy Wellborn, no date, http://www.amywelborn.com/gautreaux/article.html (accessed July 6, 2011).

2. Gautreaux, quoted in "Tim Gautreaux," by Christopher Scanlan, *Creative Loafing Atlanta,* June 17, 2004, http://clatl.com/atlanta/tim-gautreaux/Content?oid=1248256.

## DANIEL WOODRELL, *WINTER'S BONE*

1. Daniel Woodrell, quoted in "*Winter's Bone:* Superlative Teen Angst," by Scott Simon, *Weekend Edition,* National Public Radio, Saturday, August 5, 2006, http://www.wbur.org/npr/5615980/winters-bone-superlative-teen-angst.

2. Bill Brashler, "A Journey to the Volatile, 'Country Noir' Ozarks," *Chicago Tribune,* March 31, 1996, http://articles.chicagotribune.com/1996–03–31/entertainment/9603310026_1_doyle-redmond-daniel-woodrell-big-annie.

3. Daniel Woodrell, quoted in "Seeing Red: The Writer's Life and Life in Venus Holler, Courtesy of Daniel Woodrell," by Leonard Gill, *Memphis Flyer,* September 10, 1998, Books section, http://www.memphisflyer.com/backissues/issue499/book499.htm.

## RON RASH, "SPECKLED TROUT"

1. Ron Rash, quoted in "Ron Rash," by Robert Birnbaum, *Morning News,* November 7, 2005, http://www.themorningnews.org/archives/birnbaum_v/ron_rash.php.

## WILL ALLISON, "ATLAS TOWING"

1. Mark Childress, quoted on back cover, *What You Have Left,* by Will Allison (New York: Free Press, 2007).

2. Will Allison, e-mail message to the author, June 2, 2007.

## ANN PANCAKE, "REDNECK BOYS"

1. David Bradley, quoted on back cover, *Given Ground,* by Ann Pancake (Lebanon, N.H.: Middlebury College Press, 2001).

2. Ann Pancake, e-mail message to the author, March 25, 2011.

**ALEX TAYLOR, "THE COAL THIEF"**

1. Chris Offutt, quoted on back cover, *The Name of the Nearest River,* by Alex Taylor (Louisville, Ky.: Sarabande Books, 2010).

2. Alex Taylor, e-mail message to the author, June 22, 2011.

# References and Supplemental Materials

CRITICAL STUDIES

Baker, Barbara A., ed. *Lewis Nordan: Humor, Heartbreak, and Hope.* Auburn, Ala.: Pebble Hill Books, 2012.

Baker, Larry. "'If I Do My Job Right': Harry Crews and His Readers." *Georgia Review* 61 (Winter 2007): 684–700.

Bauer, Margaret Donovan. *Understanding Tim Gautreaux.* Columbia: University of South Carolina Press, 2010.

Bledsoe, Erik, ed. *Getting Naked with Harry Crews: Interviews.* Gainesville: University Press of Florida, 1999.

———, ed. *Perspectives on Harry Crews.* Jackson: University Press of Mississippi, 2001.

———. "The Rise of Southern Redneck and White Trash Writers." *Southern Cultures* 6 (Spring 2000): 68–90.

Bonetti, Kay. "An Interview with Larry Brown." In *Conversations with American Novelists: The Best Interviews from the Missouri Review and the American Audio Prose Library.* Edited by Kay Bonetti, Greg Michalson, Speer Morgan, and Sam Stowers, 234–54. Columbia: University of Missouri Press, 1997.

Bouson, J. Brooks. "'You Nothing but Trash': White Trash Shame in Dorothy Allison's *Bastard Out of Carolina.*" *Southern Literary Journal* 34. (Fall 2001): 101–23.

Brown, Fred. "Cormac McCarthy: On the Trail of a Legend." *Knoxville News Sentinel,* December 16, 2007, http://www.knoxnews.com/news/2007/dec/16/1216cormac/.

Brown, Larry. "Harry Crews: Mentor and Friend." In *Billy Ray's Farm: Essays from a Place Called Tula,* 17–28. Chapel Hill, N.C.: Algonquin, 2001.

Carr, Duane. "Harry Crews: The Dispossessed as Poor White Trash." In *A Question of Class: The Redneck Stereotype in Southern Fiction,* 135–37. Bowling Green, Ohio: Bowling Green State University Popular Press, 1996.

Cash, Jean W. *Larry Brown: A Writer's Life.* Jackson: University Press of Mississippi, 2011.

Cash, Jean W., and Keith Perry, eds. *Larry Brown and the Blue-Collar South.* Jackson: University Press of Mississippi, 2008.

Chappell, Fred. "David Bottoms and the Evolution of the GOB Aesthetic." *Sewanee Review* 117 (Fall 2009): 592–610.

Cobb, James C. *Away Down South: A History of Southern Identity.* Oxford: Oxford University Press, 2005.

———. "'We Ain't No White Trash No More': Southern Whites and the Reconstruction of White Identity." In *The Southern State of Mind,* edited by Jan Nordby Gretlund, 135–46. Columbia: University of South Carolina Press, 1999.

Cook, Sylvia Jenkins. *From Tobacco Road to Route 66: The Southern Poor White in Fiction.* Chapel Hill: University of North Carolina Press, 1976.

Crider, Bill. "Sons of *Tobacco Road:* 'Backwoods' Novels." *Journal of Popular Culture* 16 (Winter 1982): 47–59.

Crowther, Hal. "The Last Autochthon: Listening to the Land." In *Gather at the River: Notes from the Post-Millennial South,* 79–83. Baton Rouge: Louisiana State University Press, 2005.

Docka, Danielle. "The Cultural Mythology of White Trash." *Catch* 34 (Spring 2002): 24–28.

Duvall, John N. *Race and White Identity in Southern Fiction: From Faulkner to Morrison.* New York: Palgrave Macmillan, 2008.

Earley, Tony. "Mephisto Tennessee Waltz." Review of *The Long Home,* by William Gay. *New York Times,* November 21, 1999, http://www.nytimes.com/books/99/11/21/reviews/991121 .21earleyt.html.

Flynt, J. Wayne. *Dixie's Forgotten People: The South's Poor Whites.* New ed. Bloomington: Indiana University Press, 2004.

Frye, Steven. *Understanding Cormac McCarthy.* Columbia: University of South Carolina Press, 2009.

Galbraith, Lacey. "Barry Hannah, the Art of Fiction No. 184." *Paris Review* 172 (Winter 2004), http://www.theparisreview.org/interviews/5438/the-art-of-fiction-no-184-barry-hannah.

Gautreaux, Tim. "Preface: Warts and All." In *New Stories from the South: The Year's Best, 2004.* Edited by Shannon Ravenel, vii–x. Chapel Hill, N.C.: Algonquin Books, 2004.

Gingher, Robert. "Grit Lit." In *The Companion to Southern Literature: Themes, Genres, Places, People, Movements, and Motifs,* edited by Joseph M. Flora and Lucinda H. Mackethan, 319–20. Baton Rouge: Louisiana State University Press, 2002.

Goad, Jim. *The Redneck Manifesto: How Hillbillies, Hicks, and White Trash Became America's Scapegoats.* New York: Simon & Schuster, 1997.

Gray, Richard. "Recorded and Unrecorded Histories: Recent Southern Writing and Social Change." In *The Southern State of Mind,* edited by Jan Nordby Gretlund, 67–79. Columbia: University of South Carolina Press, 1999.

Guinn, Matthew. *After Southern Modernism: Fiction of the Contemporary South.* Jackson: University Press of Mississippi, 2000.

Hawkins, Gary. "Just One More: Larry Brown (1951–2004)." *Oxford American,* Spring 2005, 138–43.

Hobson, Fred. "The Savage South: An Inquiry into the Origins, Endurance, and Presumed Demise of an Image." In *The Silencing of Emily Mullen and Other Essays,* 113–31. Baton Rouge: Louisiana State University Press, 2005.

Huber, Patrick. "A Short History of Redneck: The Fashioning of a Southern White Masculine Identity." In *Southern Cultures: The Fifteenth Anniversary Reader,* edited by Harry L. Watson and Larry Griffin, 303–27. Chapel Hill: University of North Carolina Press, 2008.

Jeffrey, David K., ed. *A Grit's Triumph: Essays on the Works of Harry Crews.* Port Washington, N.Y.: Associated Faculty Press, 1983.

Johnson, Gerald W. "The Horrible South." In *South-Watching: Selected Essays,* 29–42. Edited by Fred Hobson. Chapel Hill: University of North Carolina Press, 1983.

Jones, Suzanne. "Refighting Old Wars and Masculine Conventions in Fiction by Larry Brown and Madison Smartt Bell." In *The Southern State of Mind,* edited by Jan Nordby Gretlund, 107–20. Columbia: University of South Carolina Press, 1999.

Killian, Lewis M. *White Southerners.* Rev. ed. Amherst: University of Massachusetts Press, 1985.

Kirby, Jack Temple. *Media-Made Dixie: The South in the American Imagination.* Baton Rouge: Louisiana State University Press, 1978.

Mandel, Joe, ed. "A Tribute to Tim McLaurin." *Pembroke Magazine,* no. 36 (2004): 60–138.

McDonald, Kathlene. "Talking Trash, Talking Back: Resistance to Stereotypes in Dorothy Allison's *Bastard Out of Carolina.*" *Women's Studies Quarterly* 26 (Spring–Summer 1998): 15–25.

Morrison, Toni. *Playing in the Dark: Whiteness and the Literary Imagination.* New York: Random House, 1993.

Nordan, Lewis. Foreword to *Tobacco Road,* by Erskine Caldwell, v–ix. Athens: University of Georgia Press, 1995.

Pearl, Nancy. "Grit Lit." In *Book Lust: Recommended Reading for Every Mood, Moment, and Reason,* 106. Seattle, Wash.: Sasquatch Books, 2003.

Polk, Noel. *Outside the Southern Myth.* Jackson: University Press of Mississippi, 1997.

Rebein, Robert. *Hicks, Tribes, and Dirty Realists: American Fiction after Postmodernism.* Lexington: University Press of Kentucky, 2001.

Reed, John Shelton. *Southern Folk, Plain & Fancy: Native White Social Types.* Athens: University of Georgia Press, 1986.

Risen, Clay. "Out of Nowhere: After Decades of Laboring in Complete Obscurity, Middle Tennessee Author William Gay Has Finally Found Literary Acclaim." *Nashville Scene,* January 16, 2003, http://www.nashvillescene.com/nashville/out-ofnowhere/Content?oid=1188010.

Romine, Scott. *The Real South: Southern Narrative in the Age of Cultural Reproduction.* Baton Rouge: Louisiana State University Press, 2008.

Smith, Lee. "Preface: Driving Miss Daisy Crazy; or, Losing the Mind of the South." In *New Stories from the South: The Year's Best, 2001,* edited by Shannon Ravenel, vii–xvi. Chapel Hill, N.C.: Algonquin Books, 2001.

Watson, Jay, ed. *Conversations with Larry Brown.* Jackson: University Press of Mississippi, 2007.

Wood, James. "Red Planet: The Sanguinary Sublime of Cormac McCarthy." *New Yorker,* July 25, 2005, http://www.newyorker.com/archive/2005/07/25/050725crbo_books.

Woodward, Richard B. "Cormac Country." *Vanity Fair,* August 2005, 98–104.

———. "Cormac McCarthy's Venomous Fiction." *New York Times,* April 19, 1992, http://www.nytimes.com/books/98/05/17/specials/mccarthy-venom.html?_r=1&oref=slogin.

Wray, Matt. *Not Quite White: White Trash and the Boundaries of Whiteness.* Durham, N.C.: Duke University Press, 2006.

Wray, Matt, and Annalee Newitz, eds. *White Trash: Race and Class in America.* New York: Routledge, 1997.

**RECOMMENDED READING/VIEWING/LISTENING**

A list of contemporary Grit Lit, Rough South, and other related writers with selected titles (assuming you've already read classic Grit Lit writers Erskine Caldwell, William Faulkner, and Flannery O'Connor).

*Recommended Reading*

Andrews, Raymond. *Appalachee Red.* New York: Dial Press, 1978.

———. *Baby Sweet's.* New York: Dial Press, 1983.

———. *Rosiebelle Lee Wildcat Tennessee.* New York: Dial Press, 1980.

Atkins, Ace. *Dark End of the Street.* New York: William Morrow, 2002.

———. *Wicked City.* New York: Putnam, 2008.

Barton, Marlin. *Dancing by the River.* Savannah, Ga.: Frederick C. Beil, 2005.

———. *The Dry Well.* Savannah, Ga.: Frederick C. Beil, 2001.

Bass, Rick. *In the Loyal Mountains.* New York: Mariner, 1997.

———. *The Watch.* New York: Norton, 1989.

Betts, Doris. *The Astronomer and Other Stories.* New York: Harper & Row, 1965. See especially "The Dead Mule."

———. *Beasts of the Southern Wild and Other Stories.* New York: Harper & Row, 1973.

Boggs, Belle. *Mattaponi Queen.* Minneapolis, Minn.: Graywolf Press, 2010.

Bottoms, David. *Armored Hearts: Selected and New Poems.* Port Townsend, Wash.: Copper Canyon Press, 2000.

———. *Shooting Rats at the Bibb County Dump.* New York: William Morrow, 1980.

Bottoms, Greg. *Sentimental, Heartbroken Rednecks.* New York: Context Books, 2001.

Boyd, Blanche McCrary. *The Redneck Way of Knowledge.* New York: Knopf, 1982.

Brandon, John. *Arkansas.* San Francisco, Calif.: McSweeney's Books, 2008.

———. *Citrus County.* San Francisco, Calif.: McSweeney's Books, 2010.

Burke, James Lee. *The Convict and Other Stories.* Baton Rouge: Louisiana State University Press, 1985.

———. *Jesus Out to Sea.* New York: Simon & Schuster, 2007.

Butler, Jack. *Jujitsu for Christ.* Atlanta, Ga.: August House, 1986.

———. *Living in Little Rock with Miss Little Rock.* New York: Knopf, 1993.

Chappell, Fred. *Ancestors and Others.* New York: St. Martin's Press, 2009.

———. *Farewell, I'm Bound to Leave You.* New York: Picador, 1996.

Childress, Mark. *Crazy in Alabama.* New York: Putnam, 1993.

———. *A World Made of Fire.* New York: Knopf, 1984.

Chitwood, Michael. *Finishing Touches.* Chapel Hill, N.C.: Tryon Publishing, 2006.

———. *From Whence.* Baton Rouge: Louisiana State University Press, 2007. See especially "Telling It."

Clark, Martin. *The Many Aspects of Mobile Home Living.* New York: Knopf, 2000.

———. *Plain Heathen Mischief.* New York: Knopf, 2004.

Crone, Moira. *What Gets into Us.* Jackson: University Press of Mississippi, 2006.

———. *Winnebago Mysteries & Other Stories.* New York: Fiction Collective, 1984.

Currey, Richard. *The Wars of Heaven.* New York: Houghton Mifflin, 1990.

Cushman, Steve. *Portisville.* Charlotte, N.C.: Novello Festival Press, 2004.

Dexter, Pete. *Paris Trout.* New York: Random House, 1988.

Dickey, James. *Deliverance.* New York: Houghton Mifflin, 1970.

Earle, Steve. *Doghouse Roses.* New York: Houghton Mifflin, 2001.

———. *I'll Never Get Out of This World Alive.* New York: Houghton Mifflin Harcourt, 2011.

Earley, Tony. *Here We Are in Paradise.* New York: Little, Brown & Company, 1985.

———. *Jim the Boy.* New York: Little, Brown & Company, 2000.

Edgerton, Clyde. *The Bible Salesman.* New York: Little, Brown, 2008.

———. *Killer Diller.* Chapel Hill, N.C.: Algonquin Books, 1991.

———. *Walking across Egypt.* Chapel Hill, N.C.: Algonquin Books, 1987.

———. *Where Trouble Sleeps.* Chapel Hill, N.C.: Algonquin Books, 1997.

Ford, Richard. *A Piece of My Heart.* New York: Harper & Row, 1976.

Fowler, Connie May. *Before Women Had Wings.* New York: G. P. Putnam's Sons, 1996.

Frazier, Charles. *Cold Mountain.* New York: Atlantic Monthly Press, 1997.

———. *Nightwoods.* New York: Random House, 2011.

Gaines, Ernest. *Bloodline: Five Stories.* New York: Dial Press, 1968.

———. *A Gathering of Old Men.* New York: Knopf, 1983.

———. *A Lesson before Dying.* New York: Knopf, 1993.

Giardina, Denise. *Storming Heaven.* New York: Norton & Company, 1987.

———. *The Unquiet Earth.* New York: Norton, 1992.

Gibbons, Kaye. *Ellen Foster.* Chapel Hill, N.C.: Algonquin Books, 1987.

Greene, Amy. *Bloodroot.* New York: Knopf, 2010.

Grisham, John. *Ford County.* New York: Doubleday, 2009.

Harris, Jimmy Carl. *Walking Wounded.* Oak Ridge, Tenn.: Iris Press, 2006.

Haynes, Melinda. *Chalktown.* New York: Hyperion, 2001.

———. *Mother of Pearl.* New York: Hyperion, 1999.

Hays, Donald. *Dying Light.* San Francisco, Calif.: MacAdam/Cage, 2005.

Hoar, Jere. *Body Parts.* Jackson: University Press of Mississippi, 1997.

———. *The Hit.* New York: Context, 2002.

Holbrook, Chris. *Hell and Ohio: Stories of Southern Appalachia.* Frankfort, Ky.: Gnomon Press, 1995.

———. *Upheaval.* Lexington: University Press of Kentucky, 2009.

Hollon, Frank Turner. *The Wait.* San Francisco, Calif.: MacAdam/Cage, 2008.

House, Silas. *Clay's Quilt.* Chapel Hill, N.C.: Algonquin Books, 2001.

———. *The Coal Tattoo.* Chapel Hill, N.C.: Algonquin Books, 2004.

———. *A Parchment of Leaves.* Chapel Hill, N.C.: Algonquin Books, 2002.

Hudgens, Dallas. *Drive Like Hell.* New York: Scribner, 2004.

Johnson, Barb. *More of This World or Maybe Another.* New York: Harper Perennial, 2009.

Jones, Edward P. *The Known World.* New York: Amistad, 2003.

Jones, Holly Goddard. *Girl Trouble.* New York: Harper Perennial, 2009.

Kenan, Randall. *Let the Dead Bury Their Dead.* New York: Grove Press, 1989.

———. *A Visitation of Spirits.* New York: Harcourt Brace Jovanovich, 1992.

Key, Watt. *Alabama Moon.* New York: Farrar, Straus and Giroux, 2006.

———. *Dirt Road Home.* New York: Farrar, Straus and Giroux, 2010.

Malone, Michael. *Red Clay, Blue Cadillac: Stories of Twelve Southern Women.* Naperville, Ill.: Sourcebooks, 2002.

Marion, Stephen. *Hollow Ground.* Chapel Hill, N.C.: Algonquin Books, 2002.

Mason, Bobbie Ann. *In Country.* New York: Harper & Row, 1985.

———. *Shiloh and Other Stories.* New York: Harper & Row, 1982.

McCarthy, Cormac. *Child of God.* New York: Random House, 1974.

———. *The Orchard Keeper.* New York: Random House, 1965.

———. *Outer Dark.* New York: Random, 1968.

———. *Suttree.* New York: Random House, 1979.

McClanahan, Scott. *Stories I.* Pittsburgh, Pa.: Six Gallery Press, 2008.

———. *Stories II.* Pittsburgh, Pa.: Six Gallery Press, 2009.

McCorkle, Jill. *Ferris Beach.* Chapel Hill, N.C.: Algonquin Books, 1990.

McManus, John. *Born on a Train.* New York: Picador, 2003.

———. *Stop Breaking Down.* New York: Picador 2000.

Morgan, C. E. *All the Living*. New York: Farrar, Straus and Giroux, 2009.

Nieman, Valerie. *Fidelities*. Morgantown: West Virginia University Press, 2004.

Parrish, Tim. *Redstick Men*. Jackson: University Press of Mississippi, 2000.

Phillips, Jayne Anne. *Black Tickets*. New York: Delacorte Press, 1979.

———. *Fast Lanes*. New York: Dutton, 1987.

———. *Shelter*. New York: Houghton Mifflin, 1994.

Portis, Charles. *Norwood*. New York: Simon & Schuster, 1966.

———. *True Grit*. New York: Simon & Schuster, 1968.

Powell, Mark. *Prodigals*. Knoxville: University of Tennessee Press, 2002.

Ray, Janisse. *Ecology of a Cracker Childhood*. Minneapolis, Minn.: Milkweed Editions, 1999.

Richard, Mark. *House of Prayer No. 2*. New York: Nan A. Talese, 2011.

———. *The Ice at the Bottom of the World*. New York: Knopf, 1989. See especially "Strays."

Secreast, Donald. *The Rat Becomes Light*. New York: HarperCollins, 1990.

———. *White Trash, Red Velvet*. New York: HarperCollins, 1993.

Sparks, Minton. *Desperate Ransom*. Nashville, Tenn.: Thomas Nelson, 2007.

———. *White Lightning*. Nashville, Tenn.: Thomas Nelson, 2008.

Taylor, M. Glenn. *The Ballad of Trenchmouth Taggart*. Morgantown, W.Va.: Vandalia Press, 2008.

———. *The Marrowbone Marble Company*. New York: Harpercollins, 2010.

Thompson, Sidney. *Sideshow*. Montgomery, Ala.: River City Publishing, 2006.

Tusa, Chris. *Dirty Little Angels*. Livingston, Ala.: Livingston Press, 2009.

Walker, Alice. *The Color Purple*. New York: Harcourt, 1982.

Walls, Jeannette. *The Glass Castle*. New York: Scribner, 2005.

———. *Half-Broke Horses*. New York: Scribner, 2009.

Weil, Josh. *The New Valley: Novellas*. New York: Grove, 2009.

White, Charles Dodd. *Lambs of Men*. Sacramento, Calif.: Casperian Books, 2010.

Whorton, James, Jr. *Approximately Heaven*. New York: Free Press, 2003.

Wilcox, James. *Modern Baptists*. New York: Dial Press, 1983.

Wilkinson, Crystal. *Blackberries, Blackberries*. New Milford, Conn.: Toby Press, 2000.

———. *Water Street*. New Milford, Conn.: Toby Press, 2002.

Willeford, Charles. *Cockfighter*. New York: Crown, 1972.

Yarborough, Steve. *The Oxygen Man*. Denver, Colo.: MacMurray & Beck, 1999.

———. *Visible Spirits*. New York: Knopf, 2001.

*Grit Lit beyond the South*

Counting Cousins

Bill, Frank. *Crimes in Southern Indiana*. New York: Farrar, Straus & Giroux, 2011. (Indiana)

Campbell, Bonnie Jo. *American Salvage*. Detroit, Mich.: Wayne State University Press, 2009.

———. *Once upon a River*. New York: Norton, 2011.

———. *Q Road*. New York: Scribner, 2002. (Michigan)

Coake, Christopher. *We're in Trouble*. New York: Harcourt, 2005. (Midwest)

Davidson, Craig. *Rust and Bone*. New York: Norton, 2005. (Ontario)

Dexter, Peter. *Deadwood*. New York: Random House, 1986. (South Dakota)

Dubus, Andre, III. *The Cage Keeper and Other Stories*. New York: Dutton, 1989.

———. *Townie*. New York: Norton, 2011. (Massachusetts and beyond)

Ford, Richard. *Rock Springs*. New York: Atlantic Monthly Press, 1986.

———. *The Ultimate Good Luck*. New York: Houghton Mifflin, 1981. (Montana, Mexico, and beyond)

Hague, Richard. *Alive in Hard Country*. Huron, Ohio: Bottom Dog Press, 2003.

———. *Milltown Natural: Essays and Stories from a Life*. Huron, Ohio: Bottom Dog Press, 1997. (Ohio)

Heathcock, Alan. *Volt*. Minneapolis, Minn.: Graywolf Press, 2011. (Midwest)

McCarthy, Cormac. *Blood Meridian*. New York: Random House, 1985.

———. *The Border Trilogy*. New York: Everyman's Library, 1999.

———. *No Country for Old Men*. New York: Knopf, 2005. (Texas, Mexico, and beyond)

McGuane, Thomas. *Ninety-Two in the Shade*. New York: Farrar, Straus & Giroux, 1973.

———. *Nobody's Angel*. New York: Random House, 1982. (Montana and beyond)

Nichols, Jim. *Slow Monkeys and Other Stories*. Pittsburgh, Pa.: Carnegie Mellon Press, 2002. (Maine)

Percy, Benjamin. *Refresh, Refresh*. Minneapolis, Minn.: Graywolf Press, 2007.

———. *The Wilding*. Minneapolis, Minn.: Graywolf Press, 2010. (Oregon)

Pollock, Donald Ray. *The Devil All the Time*. New York: Doubleday, 2011.

———. *Knockemstiff*. New York: Doubleday, 2008. (Ohio and beyond)

Schwipps, Greg. *What This River Keeps*. Denver, Colo.: Ghost Road Press, 2009. (Indiana)

Shepard, Sam. *Cruising Paradise*. New York: Knopf, 1996.

———. *Day Out of Days*. New York: Knopf, 2010.

———. *Great Dream of Heaven*. New York: Knopf, 2002. (West and beyond)

Willeford, Charles. *I Was Looking for a Street*. Woodstock, Vt.: Countryman Press, 1988. (Los Angeles and beyond)

City Cousins

Jones, Thom. *Cold Snap*. Little, Brown, 1995.

———. *The Pugilist at Rest*. New York: Little, Brown, 1993. (Washington state)

Lange, Richard. *Dead Boys*. New York: Little, Brown, 2007. (Los Angeles)

Lehane, Dennis. *Coronado*. New York: William Morrow, 2006. (Boston and beyond)

Meyer, Philipp. *American Rust*. New York: Spiegel & Grau, 2009. (Baltimore, Midwest, etc.)

Toole, F. X. *Rope Burns: Stories from the Corner*. New York: Ecco, 2000. (California)

*Recommended Viewing*

Documentaries

*Dancing Outlaw*. DVD. Directed by Jacob Young, 1991. Morgantown, W.Va.: Moviefish, WNPB-TV, 2005.

*Harry Crews: Blood and Words*. Video. Directed by Wayne Schowalter. Wayne Schowalter Productions, 1983.

*Harry Crews: Guilty as Charged*. Video. Directed by Tom Thurman & Chris Iovenko. Danville, Ky.: Fly by Noir Films, 1993.

*Harry Crews: Survival Is Triumph Enough*. DVD. Directed by Tyler Turkle. Tallahassee, Fla.: Winterstone Productions, 2007.

*The Rough South of Harry Crews*. Video. Directed by Gary Hawkins. Research Triangle Park: University of North Carolina Center for Public Television, 1992.

*The Rough South of Larry Brown.* DVD. Directed by Gary Hawkins. Durham, N.C.: Center for Documentary Studies at Duke University, 2008.

*The Rough South of Tim McLaurin.* Video. Directed by Gary Hawkins. Research Triangle Park: University of North Carolina Center for Public Television, 1993.

*Searching for the Wrong-Eyed Jesus.* DVD. Directed by Andrew Douglas, 2003. Chicago, Ill.: Home Vision, 2006.

*2 or 3 Things but Nothing for Sure* [Dorothy Allison]. Short film. Directed by Tina D. Feliciantonio and Jane C. Wagner. New York: Naked Eye Productions, 1997.

*The Wild and Wonderful Whites of West Virginia.* DVD. Directed by Julien Nitzberg, 2009. New York: Tribeca Film, 2010.

Feature Films

*Bastard Out of Carolina* [Dorothy Allison]. DVD. Directed by Angelica Huston, 1996; New York: Fox Lobert, Wellspring, 2000.

*Big Bad Love.* DVD. Directed by Arliss Howard, 2001; Santa Monica, Calif.: MGM/UA Home Video, 2002.

*Bloodworth* [based on William Gay's *Provinces of Night*]. DVD. Directed by Shane Dax Taylor, 2010. Culver City, Calif.: Sony Pictures Entertainment, 2011.

*The Hawk Is Dying* [Harry Crews]. DVD. Directed by Julian Goldberger, 2006. Culver City, Calif.: Strand Releasing, 2007.

*Matewan.* DVD. Directed by John Sayles, 1987. Santa Monica, Calif.: Artisan, 2001.

*Shotgun Stories.* DVD. Directed by Jeff Nichols, 2007. Los Angeles, Calif.: Liberation Entertainment, 2008.

*Sling Blade.* DVD. Directed by Billy Bob Thornton, 1996. Santa Monica, Calif.: Miramax Lionsgate, 2011.

*That Evening Sun* [William Gay]. DVD. Directed by Scott Teems, 2009. Chatsworth, Calif.: Image Entertainment, 2010.

*Winter's Bone* [Daniel Woodrell]. DVD. Directed by Debra Granik, 2010. Santa Monica, Calif.: Lionsgate, 2010.

Short Film

*A Death in the Woods* [William Gay]. Short Film. Directed by Scott Teems. Orlando, Fla.: BigDiesel Films, 2007.

*Recommended Listening*

Sparks, Minton. *Middlin Sisters.* CD. Nashville, Tenn.: Dualtone Records, 2001. [Spoken word with music.]

———. *Sin Sick.* CD. Nashville, Tenn.: Rural Records, 2005.

———. *This Dress.* CD. Nashville, Tenn.: Rural Records, 2002.

Various Artists. *Just One More: A Musical Tribute to Larry Brown.* CD. Chicago, Ill.: Bloodshot Records, 2007. Includes original songs and recordings by Larry Brown and Clyde Edgerton.

Various Artists. *Thacker Mountain Radio: An Anthology of Words and Music.* CD. Oxford, Miss.: Thacker Mountain Records, 2002. Includes readings by Larry Brown, William Gay, and Chris Offutt.

# Index

**LIBRARY OF CONGRESS CATALOGING-IN-PUBLICATION DATA**

Grit lit : a rough South reader / edited by Brian Carpenter and Tom Franklin.
    p. cm.
Includes bibliographical references and index.
ISBN 978-1-61117-082-5 (cloth : alk. paper)—ISBN 978-1-61117-083-2 (pbk : alk. paper)
  1. Short stories, American—Southern States.  2. Southern States—Social life and
customs—
Fiction.  I. Carpenter, Brian R. II.
Franklin, Tom.
PA551.G75 2012
813'.0108975—DC23                               2012011627